THE FIRST BOOK OF INVESTING

The Absolute Beginner's Guide to Building Wealth Safely

SAMUEL CASE

Prima Publishing
P.O. Box 1260BK
Rocklin, CA 95677
(916) 632-4400

Prima Publishing
Rocklin, CA

Library of Congress Cataloging-in-Publication Data

Case, Samuel.
   First book of investing : the absolute beginner's guide to building wealth safely / Samuel Case.
     p. cm.
  Includes index.
  ISBN 1-55958-292-8
  ISBN 0-7615-0008-1 (pbk.)
  1. Investments—United States. 2. Investment analysis.
I. Title.
HG4910.C355 1994
332.6'78—dc20   92-42949
                                                         CIP

96 97 AA 10 9 8 7 6 5 4 3
Printed in the United States of America

How to Order:

Single copies may be ordered from Prima Publishing, P.O. Box 1260BK, Rocklin, CA 95677; telephone (916) 632-4400. Quantity discounts are also available. On your letterhead, include information concerning the intended use of the books and the number of books you wish to purchase.

To all my family and friends

CONTENTS

Acknowledgments   vii

Introduction   1

Part 1: An Overview for Beginners   7

1   The World of Investment   9
2   Dealing with Money Consciously   15
3   Personal Finance   33
4   The Stock Market   41
5   Buying and Selling Stocks   53
6   Mutual Funds   61
7   Fixed-Income Investments   78
8   Finding and Interpreting Financial Information   91
9   Financial Advisers   108
10   Real Estate: Owning a Home   116
11   Real Estate as an Investment   125

Part 2: Intermediate Investing   137

12   Socially Responsible Investing   139
13   International Investing   147
14   The Model Portfolio   158

15   Building a Successful Portfolio   167

16   Individual Portfolios   174

17   Retirement   191

18   Going Further with Stocks   201

19   Buying Methods   215

20   Bad Times   227

21   Bonds   239

22   Using Your Computer   254

Part 3: High-Risk Investing   **259**

23   Investing in Yourself: Starting Your Own Business
        by John Case   261

24   Caveat Emptor: Let the Buyer Beware   271

25   Precious Metals, Rare Coins, and Other Collectibles   283

26   Futures   296

27   Options   305

28   Starting to Invest   316

     Appendix A   The Model Portfolio: An Example   326

     Appendix B   Socially Responsible Funds   328

     Appendix C   Fractions into Decimals   330

     Appendix D   Fifty Years of Returns   331

     Appendix E   Compound Interest   332

     Index   335

ACKNOWLEDGMENTS

Although there are many people who contribute to the making of a book, there are even more who contribute to the making of a writer. Some people have given me general help and encouragement, others have given help specific to this book. A few have done both, and I would like to acknowledge and thank them all.

First of all, both my mother and father, Josephine and Everett, always supported my writing. And the fact that both are published writers gave me models to work with from an early age.

My sister Josephine and brother Jim have not only given encouragement but have, on occasion, lent houses to write in. The interest and enthusiasm of my brother John for the early drafts of this book were crucial to an author starting out. John, who has written several books on business and economics, also contributed the chapter on starting your own business, and gave much valuable advice.

One of the earliest fans of my writing and storytelling was my daughter, Syrena. She has continued her interest and support as I shifted from children's stories to investing.

And finally, the one who has lived with me through the various trials and vicissitudes of the last few years: my wonderful wife, Judy Aizuss. Judy not only gave much support, she also did all the initial editing on the manuscript. If the reader finds that the strange ways of the World of Investment are explained in an understandable fashion, he or she owes much to Judy's editing.

Over the years, I have always been supported in my writing by my friends. In particular, I want to thank Dan Drasin, Judith Edmonds, and Betty and Don Stone for all their interest and encouragement.

I'm grateful to Dan Geiger and Susanna Moore at the Vanguard Foundation for their insights and information about socially responsible investing.

My thanks to Joanne Handfield of Conscious Times for her initial formatting and design. Although I eventually decided not to publish the book myself, Joanne's work was a very important step in the progression of the manuscript to book form.

My heartfelt thanks go to Michael Le Page for all his invaluable counseling. Jennifer Basye, my editor at Prima Publishing, has provided ongoing support and information about the publishing process. Jennifer Boynton and Melanie Field at Bookman Productions, and copy editor Anne Montague have worked hard with me on the final manuscript. And Gary Morgan gave of his time and talent very generously in preparing the fine illustrations that adorn the pages of this book.

So many people! It reminds me of the story of Leo Durocher, who, upon being congratulated for managing the New York Giants to another pennant, declared grandly: "I couldna done it without the team!" Like Leo, I couldna done it either without a wonderful team of helpers, supporters, and cheerleaders behind me. Thanks are not enough. I only hope that I can be as supportive of their endeavors as they have been of mine.

Sam Case
Fairfax, California

INTRODUCTION

The purpose of this book is to help you make money. It will tell you the first things you need to know about investing in the various financial markets. This book is meant to be read before you do anything else.

If you have already tried to read some investment books, you may be aware that most of the authors expect you to know certain basic things. This book makes no such assumptions. If you *do* know a few basic things, you're that much ahead; you can still learn from this material. If you need to start from scratch, then this is truly your book. This is the book I wish I had had when I started learning about investing. I hope it will save you as much time and money as it could have saved me.

The traditional way of learning about investing has been the trial-and-error method. Most new investors try various markets, lose money, and finally acquire some knowledge through bitter experience. This is roughly analogous to learning how to drive by having a series of accidents. Others try to avoid such painful lessons by immediately giving their assets to a financial manager, before they have learned how to choose a good one. This can be another prescription for disaster.

Experience can indeed be useful, but there is no reason you can't start out a winner. With a little care and the knowledge you will gain from this book, you can set up a program that will preserve and increase your money while you continue to learn about investing.

Many people have had bad experiences not just with math, but with anything to do with math—and that includes investments. This can lead to a negative state of mind and a firm belief that you are incapable of really grasping any concept involving numbers. If this has been a problem for you, you should know that this book was written with you in mind. The small amount of arithmetic employed is only the simplest, most basic kind and is clarified with true-to-life examples. I have tried out various chapters on people with extremely high math-anxiety quotients, and have made revisions in response to their suggestions.

My hope is not only that you will easily understand everything in this book, but that this understanding will give you a new, positive feeling about yourself in relation to such things as math and investments—in short, that you will feel empowered. For those to whom math is a snap, I hope you will feel empowered just by learning about a fascinating new field.

When you undertake a foreign language, it's easy to get overwhelmed by the sheer amount of things to learn. The authors of the language texts are aware of this problem, however, and present a step-by-step approach, starting with the most basic, most important things first.

For new investors trying to learn the language of the marketplace, however, there has been no such comforting text to turn to. You are presented not only with a bewildering array of books, newsletters, and advertisements, but also with a large number of individuals who purport to have the kind of information you can't live without. Some of this material may be useful, but you have to be aware that the people giving it out are salespeople who stand to benefit from your investment with them. Before dealing with the marketplaces and the people working in them, the new investor needs to know a few basic things, as well as the best places to look for more detailed information.

One of the purposes of this book is to help you decide which areas of investment you want to pursue, or simply learn more about. These kinds of decisions need to include more than just financial considerations. For example, some people enjoy owning rental property and dealing with tenants; others are temperamentally unsuited to this task. In this book, we ask you to consider more than just the bottom line in choosing where to place your money and your energy.

You will find more sections on the stock market than on any other topic, because this has been the preferred market for the majority of investors, particularly new investors. This historical preference should not keep you from pursuing other areas, however. What's most important is what feels right to you.

To help you pursue the areas that interest you, you will find at the end of many chapters a list of sources for further information on the chapter topic. These books, newsletters, tapes, and courses of instruction were chosen not just for their authors' knowledge of their fields, but also for their ability to communicate in a clear, interesting manner—a skill sometimes lacking in the World of Investment.

The problem in this field is not in finding information, but in finding *quality* information. I have included only a few recommendations for further research, but they are the best. By keeping down the sheer volume of material I hope to prevent the dangerous I-don't-want-to-hear-another-word-about-30-year-zero-coupon-bonds-EVER! syndrome.

It may be that after reading this book and a few others, you'll decide that you're not really interested in the difference between T-bills and zero-coupon bonds, and that what you really want is an expert to do it for you. That's fine. Some people find investing an absorbing occupation or an interesting sideline; others treat it more like a business. But there are always some who view it simply as an unpleasant task.

It's important to have some knowledge of investments, however, so you can choose a good investment manager and keep tabs on your portfolio ("portfolio" means simply your combined investments of various kinds). Later in the book, we will talk about the ways to choose the best investment advisers and managers.

I am reminded, in this regard, of Richard Bach, the author of *Jonathan Livingston Seagull*, who took the considerable royalties from this best seller and gave them to a friend, who happened to be an investment manager. As he recounts in a subsequent book, Bach then went off to fly his airplanes and date beautiful women, depending on his friend to send him a check whenever he needed it. After a few years of this, he got a call saying that the money was gone—all of it. And the Internal Revenue Service was demanding a million dollars in back taxes by the next week.

So you can see, perhaps, that some knowledge and interest in your money is a good thing, whether or not you plan to manage it yourself.

HOW THIS BOOK IS ARRANGED

This book is meant not just as an introduction to the World of Investment, but as a manual to get you started. Part I—the first 11 chapters—covers the first things a new investor needs to know about this world.

In Part II, we will begin to apply what we've learned and discuss more advanced methods of investing. Part III includes the high-risk investments—what to watch out for as well as what might look interesting as you become more experienced.

This book is arranged so that you, as a new investor, will know what is most important to consider *first*. The amount of material in this field has been overwhelming to many people, leading them to throw up their hands and go back to the trial-and-error method. Too many investment books add to this confusion by simply presenting an entire mass of information without emphasizing which are the primary, most basic things you need to know first.

It may surprise you to see how quickly you will learn your way around once you know these basics. The World of Investment has its own language, but otherwise it is much like the rest of the world—governed partly by rational thinking, partly by emotions. As you learn what to expect, you will be able to set up your own investments so that they— and you—will be able to handle the ups and downs of the markets.

PART 1

AN OVERVIEW FOR BEGINNERS

CHAPTER 1

THE WORLD OF INVESTMENT

So ... what do you want from investing? High adventure in strange and exotic places, roller-coaster rides, thrills and chills? Or perhaps a steadier trip on a comfortable train or a sedate cruise ship?

If you prefer the first, you may be a trader or a speculator rather than an investor. Traders concentrate on *price*, buying and selling over a short period, often on the same day. Investors concentrate on long-term *value*, ignoring day-to-day price fluctuations.

For example, a trader might buy shares of IBM because he or she believes the price of the stock is about to go up sharply. If it does go up, the trader will sell and take a profit. An investor would buy IBM because the company looks good over the next few years. The investor is looking for long-term appreciation or a steady income, or both.

It's important for the new investor to realize that many advertisements for "investments" are actually ads for risky speculations. The information and sources presented in this book, on the other hand, are for *investors:* those people who

If You Can't Stand the Heat, Stay Out of the Kitchen . . .

At the beginning of each section dealing with a specific kind of investment, you will find risk-reward thermometers.

Small Company Stocks, for example, have thermometers that look like this. The chance of a large gain—or reward—is high, but the chance of losing money—the risk—is also high.

Government Bonds, on the other hand, have risk-reward thermometers that look like this. You won't hit any jackpots, but your risk is extremely low.

Risk and reward are almost always on opposite ends of a teeter-totter. As one goes up, the other goes down. The story of speculation is the story of trying to find exceptions to this rule. Investors, on the other hand, accept it as a given rule and work with it.

are interested in a safe and reasonable appreciation of their capital over a period of years.

But even as an investor, you will still have to choose between different degrees of risk. It's your job to decide how adventurous you want to be. It's our job in this book to prepare you to choose intelligently.

The first thing that any new investor needs to know is that there are no sure things in the World of Investment. It is a place of shifting sands. A method of investing that has worked wonderfully in the past may suddenly fail without warning due to a whole new set of circumstances.

Some investment advisers speak with such authority that they seem to have all the answers. But it never ceases to astonish me how three different advisers presented with the

same set of statistics will come up with three different predictions on the direction of any given market or company.
And these are not just differences in emphasis—these are
radical disagreements.

In the colorful parlance of the marketplace, an adviser
who believes a market is on the rise is called a *bull*, whereas
one who believes that another 1929-type crash is just around
the corner is a *bear*. The Financial News Network features
a daily "Guru Review" that lists the ratio of bullish to bearish
advisers. This is supposed to be an indication of where the
stock market is heading. In reality, it is of little help, because
often the "gurus" are evenly divided between bulls and
bears.

Some advisers are better than others, particularly when
it comes to individual stocks. In this book, we will direct you
to a few and tell you how to find others. But it is important
that you give up any search for certainty before you set out.
A market may proceed in an orderly and seemingly pre-
dictable fashion for a time and then suddenly stand on its
head, leaving the investor in a not-too-pleasant Wonderland
that bears some similarities to Alice's.

Do you remember the Latin inscription on the archway
or main building of your school? "Knowledge Is Power,"
it said, or perhaps "The Truth Shall Set You Free." Over

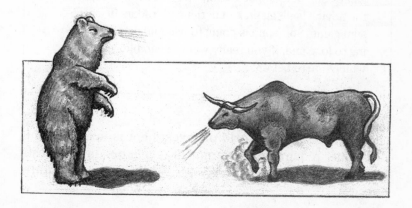

Three Ways of Dealing with Money

There are essentially three ways of dealing with money (besides spending it all, or hiding it in a mattress). You can invest it, speculate with it, or gamble. There are important differences among the three.

Investors have expectations that the place they put their money is reasonably safe and that they will realize a fair—if conservative—return. Investors are usually willing to leave their money in the same place for a number of years.

Speculators are open to more risk. They are generally people who are knowledgeable about a certain market and hope to use this knowledge to realize profits, usually over a short period of time—days, weeks, or months.

Gamblers essentially throw themselves at the mercy of the fates. We are all acquainted with casino gambling, but investing in a risky market with little knowledge of that market is also gambling.

What would be speculation to a knowledgeable person is gambling to the novice—and with odds worse than those offered by the casinos.

The reason the odds are worse is that unlike most games of chance, speculation involves *some* skill, and the novice is up against experienced traders in a zero-sum game. Someone is going to win and someone is going to lose and, if you really want to gamble, you know which one to bet on. . . .

the entrance to the World of Investment is inscribed the disclaimer required by government regulators on all investment advice: "Past Performance Is No Guarantee of Future Success."

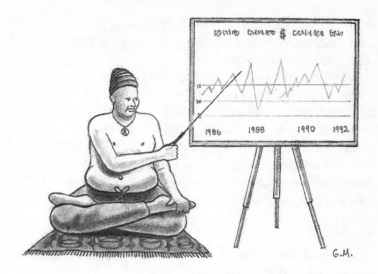

But if certainty is a scarce commodity, there are certainly ways of minimizing your risk. The goal is to get a good return on your money and still sleep soundly at night. We're going to show you how to do that. Onward!

Even at this early stage, it's not too soon to start thinking about what kind of investor you will be. Conservative? Very conservative? Or are you drawn more to small Australian gold-mining operations? (Let me tell you about this amazing outfit that my cousin Jack is a part owner of. . . .) What kind of investing will you be happy and comfortable with?

And it's never too early to start thinking about what you want to focus on with your investments. Retirement? College education? Achieving financial independence? Or simply getting a good, safe return on your money?

Most of us are used to employing our skills to make money. Investing, however, involves using money to make money—and doing this almost always requires a different set of skills than the ones we have developed at our jobs. Don't fall into the trap of thinking that because you are very successful at your work, you will just naturally be successful at investing. You built-up your professional skills over time with much training and diligence; learning to invest will also take some time and effort.

Investing money for the greatest possible return can be a most interesting and exciting endeavor. Before getting into it, though, you may need to deal with some emotions connected with how you got the money. Waiting a few months, giving yourself time to work things out and get used to your new situation, learning all you can about investing before risking any money—all this will leave you in a much better position to be a successful investor.

Resources

American Association of Individual Investors, 625 N. Michigan Avenue, Chicago, IL 60611. (312) 280-0170. Membership: $49/year. Includes subscription to the *AAII Journal*, published monthly except June and December.

This organization can be a very useful source for the new investor. A membership gives you an automatic subscription to its monthly journal. The articles deal mostly with stocks and bonds; you won't find much about real estate or other forms of investments.

In joining the association, you open yourself up to a whole range of information and activities. It sells an Investment Home Study Course and an investment seminar on videotape. I found the study course to be somewhat dry and full of complex math, but the video is entertaining and easy to watch—especially good for people who learn more easily from watching and listening than from reading.

Once you're a member, you can subscribe to another newsletter for $30 that deals with computerized investing—an excellent resource for computer users.

The association will also put you in touch with their local chapters. If you're interested, you can go to meetings, seminars, or join an investment club. All in all, a good resource for a new investor—especially if you want contact with other investors.

CHAPTER 2

DEALING WITH
MONEY CONSCIOUSLY

Investors are, more often than not, treated as a single entity. The emphasis is placed on where you want to go with your investments. Where you might be coming *from*, however, is just as important, because it can strongly affect your attitude toward money.

This is an issue for us in this book because how you invest your money should be determined as much as possible by your immediate and long-term financial needs. If your personal history strongly colors your feelings about money, what you do with it may reflect your subconscious emotional needs more than the practical considerations.

The manner in which you come into money can also affect how you feel about it. So, in this chapter, we're going to talk about inheriting and winning lotteries, in addition to family background and personal psychology.

FAMILIES

Whether you are from a wealthy, middle-income, or low-income background, you have probably absorbed certain ideas about money and about yourself in relation to money. It can be extremely useful to look at these ideas—and to realize that you are not alone in having them.

Money has been a very guarded subject in our society. I have heard people from all backgrounds complain that their family neither talked about it nor gave them any help in learning how to deal with it. Schools teach an enormous amount about the economy, but very little about personal economics.

Wealthy people are often embarrassed about having more than others. People on the low end of the scale are embarrassed and often angry about not having as much as most people. But, until recently, very few people talked about these feelings. Now, at last, along with other taboo topics, such as sex, money is beginning to be discussed more openly. Whatever your background may be, I encourage you to look closely at your own feelings and attitudes.

MEN

Men are born knowing how to invest. They have an innate feel for the markets and can jump into a situation they know almost nothing about and make a killing. The most successful men are those who aren't afraid to risk a lot of money on a chancy venture.

If you believe all this, then maybe I can interest you in my cousin Jack's latest venture, which is developing a line of chickens with teeth. . . .

It would be funny, except that a lot of men do take these ideas as gospel and feel they have failed if they don't match up to such fantasies. Overconfidence seems to occur in men as often as underconfidence does in women. Add to this a tendency to use money as a way of competing with other men and you have a situation to watch out for.

This is another area where you are much more likely to hear the success stories than the failures. Would *you* volunteer that you'd lost $50,000 on a Caribbean treasure-hunting venture? On the other hand, if a guy had actually found the treasure ship, you can bet that everyone within earshot would know about it.

This is the kind of skewed information process that leads men to think that others are making it big without much trouble, so why shouldn't they? The trouble is that they're hearing only about the ones who make a big splash; the ones who jump in to find there's no water in the pool don't get reported.

They are also not hearing about the amount of time and energy that goes into successful ventures. In war, it is said that battles are won before they actually occur. The same is true of investments: The real successes almost always result from careful planning.

WOMEN

We seem to have raised numbers of men in this country who have an inflated idea of their abilities. And this, sadly, seems to be matched by the number of women with low opinions of their powers. It's ironic, then, that a number of recent surveys have shown that in almost every professional field they have entered, women's performance has been either equal to or better than that of their male counterparts.

In a recent poll, 58% of the people questioned said they didn't know how to invest. This figure went up to 71% of the women questioned; only 9% of women said they were confident about investing. In this field, too, however, these figures are misleading. Another survey, taken by the National

Association of Investors Corporation, showed that all-female investor clubs do better than all-male or mixed clubs.

Louis Rukeyser, the star of *Wall Street Week*, television's first investment talk show, believes the reason for this better performance is that "women tend to go into the market with clearer objectives and to see money for what it is—a tool."

As in many other areas in this society, women operate at a disadvantage in the World of Investment. For starters, it is often assumed that men will manage the investments. Too often, in families and in schools, girls are not encouraged to learn money management, beyond running a household. And, for whatever reason, more girls than boys seem to get turned off to arithmetic at an early age.

There are other issues, too, that can make dealing with money more difficult for women. Some men feel threatened and resentful if their wives earn more money than they do—or simply *have* more, such as an inheritance. That a woman could be successful managing investments may also be threatening to some men.

Attitudes are changing in this area, as in so many others, but slowly. Many women still believe they are unable to learn about investing, and simply give up control of their money to their husbands or investment managers.

Women, Money, and Power

At this point, I want to make a clear distinction between a passive giving up of control and a conscious, considered decision to let someone else manage your money.

Many people—both women and men—discover that they have little interest in day-to-day financial dealings. For these people, a spouse who is willing and competent to manage investments can be a real blessing. Or an informed choice of an investment manager may be the route to go.

The ones who are taken advantage of, however (and too often these are women) are those who give up their power by default, because they don't feel qualified to handle their own money. Underconfidence can be just as damaging as overconfidence. But underconfidence, though it may sometimes be indicative of a deeper lack of self-esteem, can often be corrected simply by learning about a field and beginning to feel competent in it.

I would urge the women reading this book to give investing a try. At the end of this chapter, you will find listed some organizations whose specific purpose is to encourage and instruct women who want to handle their own investments. I encourage you to pursue this kind of learning—and for more than just practical reasons. Money is a kind of power, and learning to manage your own money is a way of claiming your own power.

Then, even if you later decide to hire a financial manager, the decision will be a confident, informed one, not a passive giving up of power. More than likely, the adviser will find that he or she has a client who is curious, assertive, and sure of what she wants—someone who wants to work *with* the adviser.

INHERITING

The issues raised by inheriting money are, of course, not just emotional and philosophical. Later on, we will talk about the best ways to invest. Before we get to the actual investing, however, there are a few things you can do to make life a whole lot easier for yourself.

If you have just inherited, you are probably getting lots of advice—and this advice may come from people who are experienced in investing. These may be family and friends— people who have your best interests at heart, so their advice may be hard to resist.

Difficult as it may seem, the best thing you can do with your assets at this time is nothing. If you have inherited cash, put it in an insured savings account at your bank and just leave it alone for a while.

There are good reasons for this. If you have inherited money or received a life insurance settlement from somebody dear to you, you are probably grieving. Grieving takes its own time—it should not be rushed. While you need to do what's necessary to keep your life going, it's not the best moment to embark on ambitious new ventures like investing. You can learn about investing, but it's a good idea to put off important decisions until you can give them your full attention.

Make a will, or alter your will to include your new assets. Different states have different laws about where your money will go if you have no will. There's a very good chance that you will disagree with these laws, but your heirs will have no recourse without a will.

Nothing can eat up money faster than a long hospital stay or some other disaster. You need to make sure that you have enough health insurance and liability insurance on your auto and home.

When you feel ready, start discussing what to do with your inheritance with your spouse—or with whoever else may be involved in your life and finances. Getting straight with those close to you about goals and the means of achieving them can be a tremendous boost toward financial success.

Now is the time to get straight with yourself. If you feel conflicted about the money, or simply need to sort things out, don't hesitate to seek out a good counselor or therapist. The small amount of time and money you spend may be the best investment you will make.

Finally, if you are tempted to go out and buy expensive things—the things you've dreamed of having—it's a good time to remember why so many of the rich stay rich, and even increase what they have. The way they do this is to spend only income while holding onto capital (capital is the total amount you have to invest).

How Much Is Enough?

Many inheritors fall into the false belief that they have
inherited a "fortune" and their troubles are over. An
amount like $400,000, for example, can look like a lot of
money if you've been earning only a fraction of that sum
each year.

If you want to invest safely, however, *and* make the
amount grow, you should figure on a maximum income
of about $25,000 to $30,000 a year (6% to 7.5% a year). If
you invest all of it for income, you could safely get
$35,000 to $40,000 (9% to 10% a year), but you would be
sacrificing any chance for future growth. Without
growth, inflation will eat away steadily at your yearly income. (At present rates of inflation, your purchasing
power will effectively be cut in two in 15 years.)

The above percentages and the income they yield
may change from year to year, but they should give you a
general idea of how much income you can expect to get.

If you're willing to forgo the income for a while and
invest the money for growth, it will increase pretty
quickly. Depending on how aggressively you invest it,
and on the performance of the markets, you should be
able to double the amount in five to ten years.

So you have three choices: income only, income *and*
growth, or growth only. You do have a fourth choice, of
course, which is to spend it all, like the prodigal son in
the Bible. Perhaps if he had heard of mutual funds, he
wouldn't have been such a trial to his father. . . .

If you immediately buy a boat with part of your inheritance, there will be that much less capital to invest for
growth or income. If, on the other hand, you wait for a year,
you may earn enough from your investments to buy the boat

while retaining all your capital. Next year, you could buy another boat, or perhaps redo the kitchen.

The trick is to hold onto your capital. This is the goose that lays the golden egg. Spend the capital and you kill the goose.

These days, you can get some excellent support in dealing with all the issues raised by inheriting. At the end of this chapter, you will find listings for a number of remarkable foundations.

Assistance for Inheritors

Over the next 30 years, there's going to be a lot of money changing hands. The combined personal net worth of Americans over 50 is approximately $8 trillion.

This may sound like a lot, but the amounts that most people will inherit are generally not enough to support a lifestyle of the rich and famous. Families in the upper third of the economic scale generally have anywhere from $70,000 to $225,000 to bequeath (though some, of course, will leave much more). This kind of money will buy only a *small* yacht. . . .

Investing wisely, then, so that the principal amount grows over the years can be very important. It is so important, in fact, that it's probably not something you want to jump into as soon as you get the money. First, you need to deal with the emotional issues that may be raised by receiving your inheritance.

The estate lawyers who send out the checks or ownership papers to inheritors should have a rubber stamp reading: WARNING! HIGHLY CHARGED MATERIAL! Because talking about issues surrounding money has been taboo, only recently has it become clear that many people have trouble dealing with their inheritance. We discuss this subject here because too often inheritors resolve their conflicts by losing the money, either by spending it or by investing unwisely. Others put it away in a bank and try to ignore it.

Let's look at some of the emotionally charged issues that come up for inheritors.

One of the deepest sources of internal conflict can come from receiving money as a result of the death of a loved one. This can be a real mindbender: your good fortune comes because this person has died! Many people find it difficult to deal with the money under these circumstances.

Those who handle this particular conflict best tend to look on their inheritance as the last gift from their loved one—a gift that person wanted them to enjoy and benefit from.

Inheritors who resolve *this* conflict, however, often find themselves concerned that their friends or coworkers are not sharing in their good fortune. After years of working and sometimes struggling side by side, suddenly *you* are the one who gets a break.

As if this weren't enough, many inheritors also find themselves in a philosophical bind. If you are proud of always having worked for your money, receiving this "free" money may challenge your image of yourself as a strong, self-reliant person.

Those who inherit large amounts may have to resolve yet another philosophical dilemma: their wealth compared to the poverty of so many millions in this country and the rest of the world. Some feel guilty about this disparity, and this guilt can prevent them from handling the money wisely.

Though each person has to resolve these conflicts and emotions individually, there seem to be a few general concepts that can help. The first is to realize that you are not alone in having these feelings. Knowing that others have successfully worked through similar conflicts can give you a boost.

Another realization that can be helpful is that *money is power*. Resistance to dealing with money can be resistance to accepting new personal power. Whether your inheritance is large or small, it gives you new power to change your life for the better. If you have come into a large amount, you have more power to change aspects of the society we live in. At the end of the chapter you will find a listing for the Funding Exchange. This is the hub of a network of remarkable foundations located in cities around the country. Among other things, they are an invaluable resource for anyone who has inherited.

These foundations provide a range of programs, including seminars on different kinds of investments, assistance in finding a good financial adviser (especially those advisers specializing in socially responsible investments), and conferences and workshops for those with inherited wealth. What this last means is that you can, if you wish, be with other people who have inherited and discuss the personal and practical issues that may concern you.

Isolation is often a common feeling among inheritors. Those who attend these workshops and social gatherings tell of their great relief at finally being able to talk about their concerns with others. Many people who have recently come into an inheritance find that they can learn from those who have already dealt with many of the problems they face.

Among their other resources, many of the foundations publish books and pamphlets for new investors. You will find various investment guides, especially for socially responsible investing; books on philanthropy; and books for women investors, among others.

If you become a donor, you are encouraged to involve yourself in the planning and organization of the foundations' various programs. This includes not only the programs mentioned above, but also community work and educational programs. This kind of hands-on philanthropy is optional— you can become involved to any degree you want—but they do encourage personal participation. They don't just want your money—they want your input and involvement, too.

LOTTERY WINNERS

When Curtis "Mack" Sharp won $5.6 million in the New York lottery in 1982, he arrived at the lottery headquarters with his girlfriend on one arm and his ex-wife on the other. He set up a million-dollar trust fund for his former wife, while his girlfriend received a $10,000 engagement ring and a $13,000 wedding dress. He bought a large house, a large Cadillac, and paid for a $100,000 wedding.

Later, when he settled down a bit, Sharp handed over the management of his assets to a bank. He then proved that his generosity was not limited to himself and his family by helping to establish the largest homeless shelter in New Jersey. He also became a fund-raiser for African relief groups.

Coming into a lot of money via the lottery or other sudden ways can be a wonderful thing. It can give you more freedom to do what you want, set aside money for education or retirement, and be generous, like Mack Sharp. You should be aware, nevertheless, that winning can have some pitfalls. These do not need to be serious; all you have to do is to watch for them and gain from the experience of past winners.

For starters, people who win large amounts of money sometimes report that they begin to lose their friends. Friends sometimes assume that winners are going to move up in the world and leave them behind. There can be resentment or, occasionally, an assumption that their newly rich friend will lend them money on a long-term basis (such loans put a great strain on friendships, according to winners who have made them).

Some winners quit their jobs and later regret it. Others wisely stay on the job, at least until they get accustomed to the change in their life. This period of getting used to your new situation needs to be taken seriously. Real change in people tends to happen over periods of months and years, not days and weeks. You owe it to yourself to park the main part of the money in a bank and just let it sit, while you begin to get comfortable with the idea of having it.

For the first few months after receiving your winnings, you should hold off on following all the advice you're bound to get. This is the time to sort things out in your mind and talk it over with your spouse or whoever else is involved with the money. It's a good time to think about what's important to you, what you'd like to do, and the directions you want your life to go in.

It's also a good time to start learning about investing. You can do this on your own or with the help of a professional. A personal financial adviser can help you look at all the different aspects of your finances—something that can be extremely helpful for someone dealing with a whole new financial life.

Like people who inherit, some lottery winners feel guilty about having more than others. Some try to deal with this guilt by being overgenerous—or by actually losing the money through bad investments or overspending. If you feel you don't deserve to make more money—or even keep what you have—then there is a very good chance you will handle it unwisely. The message your conscious mind gets from your subconscious is, "Lose it!"

If you experience a great deal of guilt or anxiety, it can be to your advantage to see a counselor or therapist. There are, sadly, big winners out there who have lost it all—and others who feel that the money has ruined their lives. This shouldn't happen to you, and it won't if you're aware of what to watch for.

About 40% of the people in this country play the lotteries. That's a lot of people, a lot of money, and quite a few winners, large and small. Remember that even if you've won only $5,000 or $10,000 or $20,000, investing all or part of it and leaving it alone will turn you into a big winner in 10 to 20 years (see the compound-interest chart in Appendix E).

Those who win millions usually have the built-in safety factor of receiving the money in installments. Even so, however, it's important not to commit too much of it in advance. If you can put away a healthy portion of it each year, you'll still be a winner when your yearly payments end.

For example, if you are a $2 million winner, your money may come to you over 20 years at the rate of $100,000 a year. If you take $17,500 of that each year and invest it at the rate of 10%, by the end of the 20 years you will have over $1 million. This should allow you to continue to get $100,000 a year for the rest of your life ($1,000,000 × 0.10 a year = $100,000).

There is a fantasylike quality to inheriting or winning a lottery. This can make the money seem unreal—and cause people to deal with it in unrealistic ways. All that is required to bring it out of the fantasy realm, however, is to realize the money is the result of somebody's—or a lot of somebodies'—life energy. The money didn't just grow, it was worked for. Understanding this creates a certain respect for what you have, and this respect will help you to use and invest it sensibly.

ENJOYING SUDDEN RICHES WISELY

Money has such stature in our society that it's easy to believe just having a lot of it will make you happy. This can seem especially true to those who have been struggling just to get by. And, indeed, for a while, simply buying and enjoying the things you have never had can be a wonderful experience.

Those who seem to do the best over time among those who come into money, however, are the ones who use it to help them do some productive work they enjoy. That and having the chance to be with family and friends seems to be what really makes people happy. Some know this without being told, while others arrive at it the hard way.

If you have been on the low end of the economic scale and have come into some money, you might consider investing in yourself. Perhaps you never had the time or the resources to go to college or even to finish high school. These days, it's pretty easy to take a high school equivalency test and start taking some classes in a community college.

No matter what your age or background, you will not be out of place in a community college. One of my favorite things about the community college I attended for a year was that the students *were* of all different ages and backgrounds.

It's become a cliché, but it really *is* never too late to go after your dreams. I recently read about an 85-year-old man who graduated from college with the great support and affection of his fellow students. Others—young and old—start new businesses or creative endeavors.

To some, like Mack Sharp, giving away part of what they have is a source of great satisfaction. It's not necessary to be as flamboyant as Mr. Sharp, though, to do a substantial amount of good. Many charitable organizations would welcome not only your money but your volunteer time.

Counseling and Therapy

Once you've learned the basics about personal finance and investing, any further problems in dealing with money can often be traced to emotional sources. If after learning the basics, you find that you are still treating money in an irrational manner—spending beyond your budget, especially with credit cards, investing in very risky ventures, feeling continual anxiety around finances—some internal issues are driving you and need to be resolved.

Many people think that seeing a counselor or therapist indicates a serious emotional condition, requiring years of treatment. In actuality, however, individuals or couples often see a counselor for just a few sessions to work out specific problems.

Here's an example. Sally was mortified because Jeff always paid the household bills late—often so late that they would get calls from the phone company or the department stores. Sally was the type who always paid the bills the moment they arrived.

Being unable to resolve their dispute, they went to see a couples counselor. After only a few sessions, it became clear that Jeff was delaying paying the bills as a way of asserting himself. He was having a difficult time at work with a demanding boss but, in addition, he had always had a tendency to feel put upon and pressured. Now he was resisting this pressure by taking his own sweet time to respond to creditors.

Sally, on the other hand, had used performance as a way of getting love in her family. Paying the bills immediately was her way of being a "good girl." Being "good" had become extremely important because she associated it with getting love.

Once the two of them saw clearly what was driving them, they were better able to understand each other—and modify their behavior.

Money is the single greatest source of disputes among couples. These disputes are not *always* as easy to resolve as those of Sally and Jeff, but often they are. If a couple has real motivation to work out a problem, it's amazing how quickly they can do so.

Occasionally, however, what starts out as a single problem can lead into deeper issues that need a longer time to resolve. If money to pay for extended therapy is a problem, you can usually find counseling clinics with lower fees or sliding scales. From a purely financial viewpoint, however, I know of no investment that can give you greater return with a lower risk. Working through long-standing emotional blocks can lead to the kind of freer, happier life that transcends any financial considerations.

Just a note to those who have never seen a therapist: You should feel comfortable with and have confidence in this person. Try to choose someone who comes highly recommended, but even then use your intuition. He or she might be an excellent counselor, but not the right one for you. It's an important decision, because you're dealing with very important issues.

PLAYING THE GAME CONSCIOUSLY

In this chapter, we've talked about the different places you might be coming from as an investor. Your family background, your personal history, and the way you came into your money can all strongly influence your feelings about having it. Becoming aware of how these influences may affect you can be just as important as learning the best ways to invest.

In his book *The Trick to Money Is Having Some!*, Stuart Wilde makes the point that although dealing with money seems to be a game you play with forces outside yourself, it is actually more a game you play *with* yourself. Making this game more conscious can help put the odds in your favor.

Resources

The Trick to Money Is Having Some! by Stuart Wilde. White Dove International, 1989. $10.95 (paperback).

This book falls into the general category of "prosperity consciousness"—how to gain wealth by rearranging how you think about money. But whereas many such books and seminars have a rah-rah, missionary zeal to them, Wilde treats the whole subject with refreshing lightness and humor. You may not agree with all he says, but it's a good bet that his ideas will make you take a look at your attitudes toward money and prosperity. An exciting, challenging, and fun book.

Funding Exchange. 666 Broadway, Suite 500, New York, NY 10012. (212) 529-5300.

The member foundations of the Funding Exchange are listed below. These organizations are an excellent resource for inheritors, those interested in social investing and social change, or simply new investors looking for a little help (they will recommend honest, competent advisers, among other things).

Appalachian Community Fund
517 Union Ave., #206
Knoxville, TN 37902
(615) 523-5783
Funding region: West Virginia
and the Appalachian counties
of Virginia, Kentucky, and
Tennessee

Bread and Roses Community
Fund
924 Cherry St.
Philadelphia, PA 19107
(215) 928-1880
Funding region: Five-county
region of greater Philadelphia
and Camden, NJ

Chinook Fund
212 W. 32nd Ave.
Denver, CO 80211
(303) 455-6905
Funding region: Colorado

Crossroads Fund
3411 W. Diversey, #20
Chicago, IL 60647
(312) 227-7676
Funding region: Chicago
metropolitan area

Fund for Southern Communities
552 Hill St. S.E.
Atlanta, GA 30312
(404) 577-3178
Funding region: Georgia, North and
South Carolina

Haymarket People's Fund
42 Seaverns Ave.
Boston, MA 02130
(617) 522-7676
Funding region: New England

Headwaters Fund
122 W. Franklin Ave.
Minneapolis, MN 55404
(612) 879-0602
Funding region: Minneapolis/
St. Paul

Liberty Hill Foundation
1320 C Santa Monica Mall
Santa Monica, CA 90401
(213) 458-1450
Funding region: Los Angeles
County and San Diego

Live Oak Fund
P.O. Box 4601
Austin, TX 78765
(512) 476-5714
Funding region: Texas

The People's Fund
1325 Nuuanu Ave.
Honolulu, HI 96814
(808) 526-2441
Funding region: Hawaii

McKenzie River Gathering
Foundation
3558 S.E. Hawthorne
Portland, OR 97214
(503) 233-0271
Funding region: Oregon

Vanguard Public Foundation
14 Precita Ave.
San Francisco, CA 94110
(415) 285-2005
Funding region: San Francisco Bay
Area and Northern California

North Star Fund
666 Broadway, Suite 500
New York, NY 10012
(212) 460-5511
Funding region: New York City

Wisconsin Community Fund
122 State St., #305
Madison, WI 53703
(608) 251-6834
Funding region: Wisconsin

National Network of Women's Funds. 1821 University Ave., Suite 409N, St. Paul, MN 55104. (612) 641-0742.

The NNWF is a national association of more than 60 women's funds in different cities across the country. These funds, with the help of thousands of donors of time and money, support programs to develop women's leadership and overcome various kinds of inequalities and discrimination against women.

As part of their goal to empower women, some of the member funds have programs to aid women investors. If you feel the need for such a program, or if you simply want to be a member of a fund, you can ask the NNWF for the name of the organization nearest you. An excellent resource for women.

CHAPTER 3

PERSONAL FINANCE

I saw Bill Donaghue on the Financial News Network the other day talking about a surefire, absolutely foolproof way of getting 15% to 20% on your money. Donaghue is a well-known investment adviser and the author of several investment books, so the audience listened attentively. There was a general groan, however, when (after a dramatic pause) he suggested that they invest in paying off their credit cards.

Groans notwithstanding, Donaghue was illustrating a very important point: You cannot separate your personal financial decisions from your investments. They are inextricably bound together. Suppose you worked hard at picking a particular mutual fund and were rewarded for your efforts by a $1,500 increase for the year. On the $10,000 you invested, this amounts to a 15% return ($10,000 × 0.15 = $1,500). Not bad . . .

While you're congratulating yourself, however, the year-end tax statements for your credit cards arrive, indicating that over the year you have paid the banks $1,850 in interest payments on your outstanding balances. (If you owe an average of $10,000 at 18.5%, you're paying $1,850 a year in interest.) Suddenly your 15% profit with the fund doesn't look so good. You would have done better—$350 better—by investing $10,000 in paying off your credit cards, thereby "earning" 18.5%.

Similarly, what would be the use of a retired couple's careful management of their investment capital if they neglected to carry enough health insurance? Their entire portfolio could be wiped out by one major operation and hospital stay.

MONEY AND EMOTIONS

Some people seem to be naturally good at managing money: they have a feel for how much they can spend and still stay within a sensible budget. They consider things like insurance, wills, and setting aside enough for Tommy's orthodontal bills. The other 90% of us, though, often have a little trouble. But skills like these can be learned. And they are very similar to the skills you will need to become a successful investor.

The first thing to do is not to steel yourself and vow to stop spending so much—you've tried that and it probably hasn't worked. You need, instead, to sit down and look at your spending and planning habits. Money is very closely tied to emotions: if you begin to change the way you manage money, you can expect to run up against internal resistances. These resistances need to be looked at and considered, not fought and overcome—the fighting is what you've been doing for years.

This process of trying to change and dealing with your emotions can lead you into unforeseen areas. Many people, for example, overspend because they feel discontented with aspects of their lives: the spending lets them do something nice for themselves. To stop overspending may allow the feelings of discontent to emerge more strongly and these feelings may demand a real change in their lives. This is just one of many ways our emotions can affect our finances.

I strongly recommend Joe Dominguez's seminar, which is listed in the Resources, as a way of starting to look at your relationship with money. It's enough of a challenge to manage finances and invest successfully without doing battle with yourself at the same time. This seminar on audiotape will help to get all of you on the same side.

WHAT TO LOOK AT

To be a successful investor, you need to take care of all your finances. Otherwise, you run the risk of having the rug pulled out from under you by some unforeseen event, and watching your hard-won profits go down the drain. Here are the main areas you need to look at:

- Money management: Do you keep your checkbook balanced, or could you take a world tour on the amount of returned-check fees each year? Do you have a budget? Do you stay at least within a few thousand dollars of your budget each month? (Just kidding . . . I hope.)

- Personal financial statement: It's a very good idea to know just what your assets are—and your liabilities. This is the first step toward control of your finances. Financial statement forms are available at most stationery stores. Your bank will also be happy to give you one.

- Insurance: health, automobile, disability, homeowner's or renter's. You need them all, and you need to be sure that the amount you will be paid will be enough. If you have a family or other people who depend on you, life insurance must be seriously considered.

- Goals: What are your financial goals? And, if you are married, are they similar to your spouse's goals?

- Taxes: Are you paying Uncle Sam only what you need to, or could you benefit from a tax adviser? I recommend getting a good one if you don't have one already. They are not expensive, but could save you a great deal.

- Debt: Are you paying so much in interest on your credit cards or other loans that a missed paycheck or two could cause you major difficulty? Keeping the amount of debt and the interest payments under control can help your financial picture immensely.

- Retirement: You say you're too young to start thinking about it? Think again. The sooner you start, the less you'll need to put away each month and the longer it can grow. (See the compound-interest table in Appendix E.)

You will do yourself a big favor if you get some help in considering these things. At the very least, consult the financial planning book listed in the Resources. This is the best I've found on the subject: clear, easy to read, everything that books like this should be (but often are not). You'll be amazed at the things you didn't even *know* you needed to know.

If you feel you could use professional help, you can discuss your finances with a financial planner.

TAXES

Your success as an investor depends partly on how you deal with your tax situation. For example, you need to know the best way to calculate your gains and losses, what deductions you're allowed, how to deal with capital gains and passive losses, the tax benefits of retirement plans . . . need I go on?

The whole subject of taxes requires a more detailed treatment than the format of this book permits. Our job here is simply to impress upon you the importance of either learning as much as you can or hiring a top-notch tax adviser.

If you are going to manage your own investments, the tax book recommended in Resources is very good at presenting clearly an often complex subject. Even if you plan to hire an adviser, you would benefit by reading this book. As with other professional advisers, the more you know, the more you will benefit from the advice.

WILLS

Somewhere in the reams and reams of legal codes in your state there are specific rules about what happens to your money if you don't leave a will. You may think that it will all automatically go to your spouse, but this is not necessarily true. Not leaving a will is a great way of enriching lawyers and delighting the kind of bureaucrats who love long, drawn-out, complex proceedings.

Leaving a will that is unclear or legally questionable will also delight the same people. Handwritten, unwitnessed wills are not even accepted in some states; other states require not two witnesses, but three.

See a lawyer and have it done right. It can cost as little as a few hundred dollars, depending on the lawyer and the complexity of the will. The welfare of your loved ones is what is at stake. Parents of young children need to consider who they would want to be the children's guardians in the event of the parents' death. This kind of thing must be laid out properly in the will.

For those who wish to leave money to charity, it is imperative to specify which organizations and how much. Many organizations will help you set up trusts that can benefit not only them, but save taxes for you and your heirs.

Our purpose here is not to make a comprehensive list of all the things to consider, but to emphasize the importance of doing something soon. The financial planning book recommended in Resources has a good section on wills and estate planning. That book and a good lawyer will tell you what you need to know.

What If Something Happens to You?

You've made a will, you say. Great! But suppose you're the one who handles all the investments. What happens to them if something happens to you?

An older friend of mine recently went to help out upon the death of his brother-in-law. The man's widow had no idea what to do or how much she had to live on. All she knew was that while her husband had supported her, there never seemed to be enough money. She was resigned to surviving on Social Security for the rest of her days.

My friend was soon enmeshed in one of the most disordered offices he had ever seen. It took him a couple of weeks to sort through it all, but when he had finished, he was astounded to find that his brother-in-law had accumulated some $300,000 in assets. There were old bank books lying around, shares of various securities stuffed into desk drawers along with worthless papers—my friend likened it to mining for gold in a trash heap.

This story had a happy ending. More often, disorder can lead people to believe that there is *more* there than actually exists. A couple of lessons can be learned from this tale.

First, it's a good idea to get your spouse involved in your investments, at least to the extent that he or she knows what's going on.

Second, putting your papers into some order will make it much easier for whoever has to deal with things. Stationery stores sell books with titles like "Personal Financial Organizer," with pages all set up to record your various investments. That, coupled with written instructions on what to do, will be a tremendous help to whoever has to handle your portfolio.

Lastly, do make sure that whoever needs to knows where your will is. It might be a good idea to write that small, but crucial, bit of information in the same book that lists your portfolio.

Resources

Transforming Your Relationship with Money and Achieving Financial Independence. Joe Dominguez. New Road Map Foundation, P.O. Box 15981, Seattle, WA 98115. (206) 527-0437. Six-hour seminar on audiotape with workbook. $60.

This seminar goes deeper than most financial seminars. Dominguez asks you to do no less than a complete reevaluation of your relationship to money and finance. This is a consciousness-raising experience; all your attitudes toward money that you take for granted are challenged. If you are in conflict and emotional distress around your finances, it can also be a healing experience.

The seminar includes how-to instruction on early retirement, but the information is the kind that anyone who wants to live cheaply and well can use.

All this sounds heavy, but it's not. Dominguez is an entertaining speaker—occasionally a stand-up comic—so the information goes down easily.

The Price Waterhouse Book of Personal Financial Planning by Stanley H. Breitbard and Donna Sammons Carpenter. Henry Holt, 1988, revised 1990. $14.95 (paperback).

This book covers in detail the topics mentioned in this chapter. It's well laid out and easy to read. If you're doubtful about whether you really need it, leaf through it in your bookstore or library. I guarantee that in 10 minutes, you will find at least three things you didn't know—and need to know.

The Price Waterhouse Investors' Tax Adviser by Price Waterhouse and Donna S. Carpenter. Pocket Books. $5.50 (paperback).

No, I do not have any deal with Price Waterhouse to recommend their books. Donna Carpenter just happens to be one of the better writers about financial matters. Watch for the latest edition of this manual, because Congress and the IRS enjoy changing the tax laws every year or so. If your investments are substantial—or if you just want to know what's going on—you need this book. Like the financial planning book cited above, this one contains information you didn't even know you needed to know.

How to Get Out of Debt, Stay Out of Debt and Live Prosperously by Jerrold Mundis. Bantam Books, 1988. $4.95 (paperback).

Many people think they're ready to invest, when what they really need to do first is pay off excessive debt and rethink their financial lives. This book is for people who have dug themselves into a financial hole and can't see how to climb out. Mundis describes himself as a recovered debtor, and much of the book is based on the techniques of the national Debtors Anonymous program, which helped him to get control of his financial life. Some compulsive spenders may need the support such a group can lend; others may be able to help themselves with this book alone. The program for getting control is all laid out, step by step. All you have to do is follow it.

CHAPTER 4

THE STOCK MARKET

S uppose you decide to form a company. At some point, you'll need to buy equipment and raw materials, and to hire workers. To do this, you're going to need capital. There are several ways of getting this capital: You can invest your own money, you can borrow, or you can sell part of the company to investors.

If your credit is good, you may borrow from a bank, or you may choose to borrow from individuals. The way you borrow from individuals is to issue *bonds*. Bonds are fancy IOUs: your company promises to pay back the lenders in a given number of years. In the meantime, the lenders receive interest payments from the company.

The alternative to borrowing is to sell part of the company. The way you do this is to issue *shares* of the company—shares of your stock, or inventory. ("Shares of stock" has come to be shortened to simply "stocks.") Investors who believe your company's future looks good will buy the stocks and thereby become part owners. Their money is the capital you can use to start or expand your business.

By issuing stock, you have transformed your company from a *privately owned* firm to a *publicly held* corporation. There are still many large privately owned companies, but there are many more firms whose stock is available for investors.

In case you have ever wondered what investment bankers do, this is it. Their job is to arrange financing for new companies or new financing for existing firms. If you wanted to issue stocks or bonds for your company, or arrange for a loan, you would go to an investment banker.

A LITTLE HISTORY

Issuing certificates as proof of a loan or of part ownership goes back to the late Middle Ages, when trade and commerce were beginning to pick up. By the late 17th century, it had become common for individuals to invest in companies. These shareholders were usually wealthy men who took an active interest in the affairs of the company. They would trade shares in the companies directly from each other.

As more people became investors, however, a need developed for intermediaries—*brokers* who could buy and sell shares of different companies for their clients. In cities like London, Paris, and Amsterdam, these brokers began to meet in coffeehouses and parks to trade shares. The New York Stock Exchange had its origins in a regular meeting of 24 merchants and auctioneers under a buttonwood tree in 1792 near what is now Wall Street.

As time went on, these meetings gradually became larger and more formalized until, by the mid–19th century, most exchanges had moved into their own buildings. Today, despite the exponential growth in the number of companies and shareholders, the concept of an exchange is still the same: brokers trading stocks for clients. See the "How Are

How Are Your Stocks Traded?

The traditional method of trading stocks in the parks and coffeehouses was that of an auction: stocks were sold to the highest bidder, and purchased from the lowest offerer. This method persists today; computerized trading notwithstanding, the price is still determined by what the highest bidder will pay and how low the seller will go.

The trading on the stock exchanges still bears traces of its origins in parks and coffeehouses. The New York Stock Exchange has a trading area in an auditorium-size room called the trading floor. Brokerages from around the country contact their broker "on the floor" of the exchange to place orders for their clients (these days, the orders are placed by computer hookups). The floor broker then contacts a broker—also on the floor—who specializes in the stock being traded (a "specialist"), and arranges the trade.

For years, this was the way all stocks were traded; before the days of computers, brokers would phone or wire the orders. Nowadays, only large orders are handled in this manner. Orders to buy or sell less than 1,200 shares of a stock go directly to the specialist's computer and are executed automatically at the current price.

Your Stocks Traded?" box for a description of how this is accomplished.

Today, there are 142 stock exchanges in major cities around the world, trading hundreds of millions of shares each day. Over 47 million Americans own stocks directly; millions more own stocks through their interest in company or union pension funds, or by owning mutual funds.

The pension funds, universities, foundations, churches, and banks that manage trust accounts, called *institutional investors*, are responsible for about 40% of stock ownership. Foreign investors and foreign governments also own large quantities of U.S. stocks. (During the Cold War years, the communist ideology of the Soviet Union didn't prevent the Soviet government from buying millions of dollars' worth of stocks on the New York Stock Exchange.)

There are 2,200 stocks listed on the New York Stock Exchange, about 1,000 on the American Exchange, and hundreds more on regional exchanges around the country. There are also thousands of smaller companies whose stock is not traded on any exchange; they are instead bought and sold in what is termed the *over-the-counter* market (OTC).

The National Association of Securities Dealers Automated Quotation system, or NASDAQ, lists 3,000 of the more heavily traded over-the-counter stocks. NASDAQ pioneered the computer network method of trading. There is, therefore, no central exchange for NASDAQ; instead, dealers specializing in various NASDAQ stocks are located all over the country. If you wish to buy or sell one of these stocks, your broker will put in an order to a NASDAQ dealer and the trade will be executed entirely by computer.

Finally, there are some 11,000 smaller companies whose stocks are listed in the so-called *pink sheets*. Whereas NASDAQ stocks are listed in the newspapers, only brokers have access to the daily price lists called pink sheets.

All these facts and figures are presented simply to give you some familiarity with the markets you may be buying in to. There is no difference in the procedure for buying and selling in the various markets—you just call up your broker and place the order. There *is* some difference in the companies whose stock you are buying, however. For example, most of the companies listed on the New York Exchange are large, well-established corporations; those listed on NASDAQ tend to be smaller, newer companies.

Pre-Owned Stock

When you buy shares of stock in a corporation, you are buying "secondhand" stock—or, as the dealers of expensive cars like to put it, "pre-owned." When you buy and sell these pre-owned shares, you are dealing in the *secondary market* for stocks.

Occasionally a company will put out a *new issue* of stock (also called a new offering), adding to the number of its shares already being traded on the markets. *This is the only time the company gets new investment capital*—it makes no profit if the shares already on the market rise in value, because it no longer owns these shares.

Except for the new issues, then, the stock you buy through your broker is being sold to you by another investor, not the corporation that originally issued it. The company will give you a brand-new stock certificate with your name on it, but this is similar to taking an old dollar bill into a bank and getting a new one. No new money—or stock—has been created, just new paper.

These markets for stocks are explained more fully in Chapter 8. For now, let's turn to the different kinds of companies whose stocks are traded in these markets.

DIFFERENT STOCKS FOR DIFFERENT FOLKS

The companies with stock available to investors range from the giant, international corporations to the tiny electronics firms with 50 employees. In later chapters, we will suggest how the new investor might include these different categories in a portfolio.

Blue chip stocks are in the largest and strongest companies—General Motors, General Electric, IBM, AT&T, etc. Their stock is considered safer than most, because of the enormous resources backing it up. "Safe," in this case, means that these corporations are very unlikely to fail, and that they are likely to continue to pay dividends to their shareholders even in difficult times. In addition, though their stock prices may go down in bad times, they are likely to rebound in better times.

Secondary issues come from firms a bit smaller and not so well known, but which are, nonetheless, large, well-established corporations. Both blue chip and secondary-issue companies often diversify into many fields, which makes them less vulnerable to a downturn in a single area of the economy.

Income stocks are in companies that have a record of paying good dividends to their shareholders. Utilities—your telephone and gas and electric companies—are at the top of this list.

Growth stocks are those from newer and smaller firms—for instance, many high-tech companies. Growth companies may be part of a new industry or simply companies making a product with a new twist in an already established industry. If you buy their stock, you are generally hoping for appreciation in the stock price as the company grows. The dividends are usually less than those of the blue chips or the secondary issues, and the risk is greater.

Penny stocks come from the very small companies. They are the long shots of the stock market—high risk, but with a chance at great appreciation should the company succeed.

You are also likely to be confronted with terms like "cyclical stocks" and "defensive stocks." *Cyclical stocks* tend to rise and fall with the business cycles of the economy. Stocks of the auto companies and the steel companies that supply them are examples of cyclical stocks. People are less likely to buy cars in depressed times, so corporate profits are more likely to fall—and the stock prices will follow suit.

Regardless of the business cycles, however, people always need to eat and have heat and light in their homes. The income of the food companies and the utilities will, therefore, tend to remain more stable in a recession—and so will the value of their stocks. For this reason, they are called *defensive stocks*.

DIVIDENDS

As part owner of a company, you are entitled to part of the yearly profit, should your company make one. The profits are disbursed (usually) quarterly, and the monies are called dividends. Your 100 shares of General Electric, for example, will bring you about $50 a quarter, or $200 a year, at the current rate.

Dividends need to be distinguished from *earnings*. The earnings per share of a company are the total amount of after-tax profits divided by the number of shares of common stock ("common" stock is what you normally buy; there is another kind called "preferred" stock, which is discussed in Chapter 18). Out of these earnings have to come various expenses—payments on debts, investment in new equipment, the new yacht for the top brass, and so on. Only after these things have been taken care of are the shareholders given their due.

Dividends are generally offered by older, well-established companies. The new kids on the block are too busy making ends meet and investing in expansion to worry about paying their shareholders. People buy their stock because they believe there will be good earnings down the line and this will drive their prices up. You can find a company's dividend in the listings in the financial pages (this is explained in Chapter 8).

The large corporations—the so-called blue chip companies—generally give dividends of 2% to 5% of the value of your stock. For example, if you bought 100 shares of GE stock for $7,000, your $200-a-year dividend will mean a return of a little less than 3% on your investment of $7,000 ($200 divided by $7,000 = .0285 = 2.85%). Utility companies usually give substantially higher dividends than most other corporations. These stocks with high dividends are termed *high-yield* stocks.

Investors looking for good income and stability love the telephone, gas, and electric companies. Even in bad times, people usually pay their utility bills, so the dividends of those companies tend to be more secure than those of other industry groups. This stable income means the price of their stock generally fluctuates less than that of other groups.

Occasionally, you will be surprised when you open your quarterly envelope—sometimes pleasantly, sometimes not. You may get an extra payment or your company may raise its dividend. Conversely, in a bad year, you may get less money or, sad to say, none at all. Occasionally, you may get a payment in the form of more stock, instead of cash.

If you like, you can instruct the company to automatically reinvest your dividends in more stock, if the company has such a plan. Over a number of years, this can make for a nice addition to your holdings—and with no brokers' commissions! Do remember, however, that even if the dividends are reinvested, Uncle Sam will want his yearly cut—dividends are always counted as income.

CHOOSING THE BEST STOCK

So . . . now you know more about stocks. But which stocks are the best ones to buy? How do you choose the companies that are on the way up? Simply on the basis of the increasing number of publications about this subject, companies producing paper would seem like a good investment.

You will soon find, if you invest in the stock market, that the amount of advice available can be overwhelming, not to mention contradictory. One adviser might recommend selling GE stock because of the downturn in defense orders, while another might urge buying it on the basis of its new orders from NASA.

So what to do? Well, there are two ways to go about selecting a stock to buy. One is to do all the research yourself: study the financial strength of a company that interests you, its prospects in its industry group, its sales growth, profit margins, and other pertinent pieces of information. There is more on this kind of analysis in Chapter 18.

This kind of research is the basis of the recommendations you hear for buying and selling (at least it should be!). Some will find this kind of research fascinating, while others will not want to spend the time required to really learn about a company.

The second way to choose is to engage an adviser. Investment managers and stockbrokers are two possibilities. But there is another way to engage advisers: Subscribe to one or more investment newsletters.

Newsletters

There are professional financial advisers out there who spend their entire day poring over the financial statements of various companies, following the economic life of the nation and world and gazing into crystal balls. (Well, maybe not crystal balls, but there *are* several who use astrology.) Some of these advisers are top-notch, others are not—and I know what your next question is, even without my crystal ball. The answer is that you look at their record. Past performance may not guarantee future success, but it's still the best way to choose an adviser.

And yes, there is a good way to learn the records of the advisers who publish newsletters. It's called the *Hulbert Financial Digest*, and it is the first newsletter to which you should subscribe if you're serious about picking the best stocks. *Hulbert's* tracks about 140 newsletters, and catalogs the success or failure of their recommendations over the last 10 years. It is easy to choose the top newsletters: their formats are clear and straightforward.

Several excellent newsletters are recommended in this book (including some smaller ones not covered by *Hulbert's*) that will be especially useful to new investors. Ask for a sample copy of the publication—you can usually get a back issue for free. Some newsletters let you order a trial subscription, usually good for two or three months. (Most newsletters are published either monthly or twice monthly.) You can thus see whether its style of investing matches your own before you order a year's subscription.

If you want to look at others, you can subscribe to *Hulbert's* and pick out the ones with the best records in your field of interest. It's a good idea to subscribe to a few and get the benefit of the different perspectives, though more than five can lead to our common enemy: information overload.

Besides giving advice on specific stocks and the condition of the markets, these newsletters often include essays on world politics, historical references, and anecdotes from the publishers' years of investing. While I don't recommend buying individual stocks until you become more knowledgeable, one way of gaining that knowledge is to read the good newsletters. In a few months, you may find that you've absorbed a great deal about investing simply by osmosis.

A word of caution, though: These guys are good, but they're not infallible. Remember that in the search for certainty, the financial markets are the worst place to look. The best method of picking stocks is usually a combination of listening to the experts and using your own research and intuition.

Sometimes the savviest advisers will pick companies with top-flight balance sheets and excellent prospects, only to see the stock decline because of other factors. Especially in the short run, the investing public's perception of a company's prospects is extremely important. In addition, the economic climate in both the nation and the world can have a major effect on whole markets or on industry groups.

Resources

Newsletters for the New Investor

Hulbert Financial Digest, 316 Commerce St., Alexandria, VA 22314. Monthly. $135/year; $37.50/five-issue trial subscription.

Useful as it is, *Hulbert's* should be taken as just another tool, not gospel. Be aware that various people have taken issue with Mark Hulbert's method of rating newsletters' performance.

Also remember that the '80s—where most of the statistics come from—were go-go years when most stocks rose dramatically. You will see some very impressive statistics, especially from the growth-oriented newsletters. It's hard to predict, but the '90s may be a time when more conservatively oriented newsletters will be the most successful.

You need to beware of ads that refer to *Hulbert's* ratings. You will often see the phrase "top rated by *Hulbert's*." The key question here is, "For how long?" Try to choose the letters that have performed well over a number of years, not the one that had a couple of lucky picks during the last quarter and showed a 70% increase.

Profitable Investing, Philips Publishing Inc., 7811 Montrose Road, Potomac, MD 20854. Monthly. $149/year.

Richard Band is your basic conservative investor, an expert on utility stocks, bonds, and high-yield money market funds. He is also generous with general investment advice.

Books

The Money Masters by John Train. Harper & Row, 1989. $12.00 (paperback).

This book tells the stories of nine famous investors. Though they each emphasized different things, certain qualities were common to all nine: a firm discipline that nevertheless allows for flexibility, creativity, and patience. An excellent and entertaining book from which the new investor can learn some basics about successful investing—and even about evaluating stocks.

CHAPTER 5

BUYING AND SELLING STOCKS

The basics of buying and selling stocks are not difficult to understand. The more complex aspects, like how to pick the best stocks or when to buy and sell, will be dealt with in later chapters.

Stock certificates represent ownership in a company. Perhaps some of the excitement of stocks comes from the fact that, especially in America, people dream of owning a business or at least part of a business. If you were to buy 100 shares of International Business Machines stock, you would be an owner of one of the great corporations of the world (along with a few million other investors, who together own 302,361,000 shares).

As an owner, your fortunes will be tied to those of the company. If its sales of home computers increase, your quarterly dividend payment and the value of your stock may go up. If the smaller computer companies cut sharply into IBM's sales, the stock may go down.

As in any market, an increase in the number of people wanting to buy a stock will drive the price up, an increase in the number of sellers will drive it down. This is the law of supply and demand.

Of course, the reasons that people buy or sell are not always related to the actual value of the company. If rumors abound about an amazing new kind of computer chip, the stock analysts will start worrying about the companies that produce computers with the old chips. The public listens to their worries and begins to sell its computer company stock, including IBM.

Meanwhile, however, IBM is working on a new chip of its own, which they feel is equally as amazing as the other chip. But its stock goes down because the investing public is not aware of the significance of IBM's new chip. They *believe* that losses are coming, so they sell their IBM stock. (This, of course, creates a buying opportunity for those who know the whole story.)

So . . . suppose you're one of the few who realize that IBM is a good buy at this new lower price. How do you go about actually buying some shares of IBM stock? What you do is find a stockbroker.

BROKERS

"Broker" is just another word for dealer or agent. Their business is to act as go-betweens in the buying and selling of stocks and bonds, and their income is in the form of fees—called *commissions*—for these services.

Most stockbrokers are members of brokerage companies. These companies deal directly with individuals on the various stock exchanges and computer networks who actually do the buying and selling of securities. (The term *securities* includes stock certificates and bonds; *equities* refers specifically to stocks.)

First you need to know that there are two kinds of brokerage houses: full-commission brokers—also called full-service brokers—and discount brokers.

Until the 1970s, there were only full-commission brokers. They recommended stocks to their clients, answered questions, and were always there for advice and consultation. They all charged pretty much the same commissions, which followed the "minimum fixed commission rates" set by the New York Stock Exchange.

In 1975, however, the Securities and Exchange Commission (the federal government body charged with regulating the securities industry) decided that these "minimum rates" amounted to price-fixing. The New York Exchange was ordered to abolish them, and the field was cleared for price competition between the brokerages.

The so-called discount brokerages were started on the hunch that many people didn't really want all the advice given by brokers, and would be willing to forgo it in return for lower commissions. They were right: Substantially lower commissions drew customers. There are now numerous discount brokerages, some of which have grown very large very quickly.

Commissions

How much commission can you expect to pay when you buy 100 shares of IBM? Suppose IBM is selling for $90 a share; you give the broker the $9,000 for the 100 shares, plus about a $120 commission at a full-commission broker. When you sell the stock, you pay another $120 commission. At a discount broker, you would pay about a $60 commission, which is a 50% savings.

Brokers have complicated systems for calculating commissions; some are based on the number of shares traded, some on the dollar amount of the transaction. All brokers have a commission minimum, however. A minimum of $50

About Brokers

So . . . what are the best ways to choose a broker?

After you have finished this book, you will have a good idea of the various ways to get investment advice. Then, as you read more, talk with friends, and generally learn more about the markets, what kind of investing you want to do will become clearer. At that point, what kind of broker would be best for you should also become clear. Today, thanks to the free market, you have quite a few choices.

The larger full-service brokers, such as Dean Witter Reynolds, PaineWebber, Merrill Lynch, E.F. Hutton, Prudential-Bache, and Shearson Lehmann Brothers, offer a whole range of services to their customers. In addition to the advice you get from your personal broker, you have access to financial planning, tax consulting, free seminars, research material, and free reports on promising companies. Your higher commissions pay for these.

Incidentally, the various brokerages call their brokers by different names: "financial consultants," "account executives," "institutional salesmen." Regardless of what they are called, their main job is to advise you and trade securities for you.

If you like the idea of a smaller, local firm, you will find quite a few in any city. They may not provide as many services, but will do just as good a job at trading securities. Whether their advice is as good as the larger firms' depends more on the firm and individual broker. The most important thing is to find a broker you feel is competent and has your best interests at heart.

Large discount brokers such as Charles Schwab, Fidelity, and Quick & Reilly will not give you advice, but they will provide various services. You can have a check-

ing account, a Visa card, set up a trust or an individual
retirement account, and place buy and sell orders 24
hours a day. The brokers you talk to are usually accustomed to new investors and happy to answer any questions about the mechanics of buying and selling.
Commissions are roughly one-half to two-thirds those of
the full-commission brokers.

A growing number of brokerages "discount the discounters." If you eventually begin to trade securities
fairly often and/or in large quantities, the fees can be
quite small: sometimes as much as half the cost of the
larger discounters and a quarter to a third the cost of the
full-commission brokers! These companies don't usually
provide as many services as their big brothers, though as
they become better established, more services are beginning to appear.

The super discounters are not hard to find—just
open any financial newspaper and zero in on the largest
ads. You can send for their brochures and compare their
commission schedules and services.

Many banks also buy and sell securities for you, and
many financial advisers and managers are licensed to
trade securities. If you decide to hire an adviser, this may
be the simplest way for you to buy and sell.

would translate to a commission of 5% on a trade of $1,000
of stock ($1,000 × .05 = $50). On larger transactions, the
commission will be a much smaller percentage of the dollar
amount. For example, at a discount brokerage, you might
only pay a $125 commission on a trade that involves $20,000
worth of stock.

What you are paying for with a full-commission broker
is a personal investment adviser, specializing in stocks and

bonds. It's important to remember, however, that you are also getting a salesperson whose income depends on commissions.

Many new investors assume that because they are inexperienced, they should engage a broker as an adviser. This is not necessarily true. Many brokers are less well trained in the art of analyzing securities than they are in the art of selling. To earn greater commissions, some engage in questionable practices, such as urging clients to buy or sell stock simply to earn commissions for themselves. These practices are discussed more fully in Chapter 9.

Before you choose a full-service broker, I hope you will study this chapter—and the rest of the book. There are good brokers out there, just as there are other good financial advisers. To separate them from the turkeys, however, you need to know what to look for.

How to Buy and Sell

Later chapters will discuss in more detail the different types of brokerage accounts, the various ways of buying and selling stock, and how to read the stock tables in the newspaper. For now, here is a brief explanation just to dispel some of the aura of mystery that many new investors perceive around the trading of stocks.

Once you have decided on a broker, you will open an account—in this case, a "regular account" or "cash account" (also called "special cash account"). You will deposit money to purchase stocks in your brokerage account, money that will earn interest just as it would in a money market account at your bank.

Now, suppose you have decided to buy stock in IBM. All you do is call the broker and say, "I'd like to buy a hundred shares of IBM." The broker will say, "IBM is currently trading at ninety and three-quarters" (meaning $90.75 a share). "Shall I execute the order?" You say, "Yes, go ahead," and that's it! (Selling is exactly the same procedure; all you do is substitute the word "sell" for "buy.")

Your account is debited \$9,075 (100 shares × \$90.75 = \$9,075) plus commission, and you have bought into the world of high technology. If you don't have enough in your brokerage account to cover the cost of the purchase, the broker will send you a bill, which you must pay in five business days.

You will receive a fancy certificate saying that you own 100 shares of International Business Machines Corporation. You can hold on to this certificate yourself if you want, preferably in a bank safe-deposit box, or you can ask your broker to safeguard it for you. This is called holding the securities "in street name" (meaning the name of the brokerage company).

Holding stocks and bonds in street name is generally the preferred method, since it relieves you of the responsibility of safeguarding the documents. It also means you don't need to deliver the certificates to the broker each time you sell some stock. The broker then sends you monthly statements that list the shares you own in each company and their current value.

CHANGES IN OUTLOOK

Once you have invested in a company, you may discover some changes in your outlook. Your fortunes now depend not only on the company's performance in the marketplace, but on the national and world economy as well. If the economy takes a nosedive, so will the stock market, your stock included. The reverse is also true: good times will be good for the market.

Why is this? Because in times of recession, most companies don't make as much money. Earnings tend to be smaller, which means that payments to shareholders (dividends) are also smaller. Investors know this—and they also know that a great many other people are going to be selling, which will drive prices down. So they often get rid of many of their stocks and put the money in whatever seems safe, like bank savings accounts or government bonds.

The reverse is true when the economy starts to pick up. Investors take their money out of banks and start buying stocks in anticipation of higher corporate earnings—and because they know that stock prices go up as other investors start buying. Because there are so many people who want to buy, those who hold the stocks demand higher prices for them. As a result, the overall value of the stock market starts to rise.

Of course, you don't have to sell your stocks just because the market is down. Later, we'll discuss the pros and cons of holding investments through good times and bad. You need to be prepared for the ups and downs of the business cycles, though, and for the probability that your stock's value will go down in bad times, even if the corporation that issued it is doing well.

You may have done your best to invest in a company you believe will do well over the long term. But, as with any investment, your fortunes now depend partly on events beyond your control. You may find yourself reading with new interest not just the financial pages, but the national and world news. Welcome to the World of Investment!

Chapter 6

Mutual Funds

hen some new investors see the complexities and risks involved in choosing a portfolio of individual stocks, they often throw up their hands and start looking for a good investment adviser. They would like to manage their own accounts, but it all seems like too much to add to their already busy lives.

There is, however, a third way. It's possible to buy a portfolio of hundreds of stocks and hire a whole group of professional managers to look after them for you. This is what you do when you buy mutual funds.

Most companies produce goods or services. You invest because you believe a company will show a profit selling these goods or services. Mutual funds are also companies —investment companies—but *their* way of making profits is to invest in the stocks and bonds of the firms that produce goods and services. You invest in a mutual fund because you believe the managers of that fund are skilled at choosing which companies will be the most profitable. If they make the right choices and the stocks of these firms go up, the shares of the mutual fund also rise in value.

When you buy shares in a mutual fund, you are combining your money with that of thousands of other investors. The managers of the fund use this pool to invest in the securities of many different companies. They diversify so that should one or two companies do poorly, their poor performance will be balanced by the good performance of the others.

Quite a few individuals have decided that mutual funds are the right place for them: 25 million investors own more than $200 billion worth of mutual fund shares. There are currently more than 3,000 different mutual funds, and their number continues to increase.

Mutual funds come in all sizes. Some have total assets of less than $1 million, whereas others manage investments in the billions. The largest, the Fidelity Magellan Fund, has assets of over $15 *billion*. The number of different companies in which a fund may own stocks and bonds also varies greatly—from 20 to 200 is common, though some of the larger funds own stock in 300 or 400 companies.

Almost anywhere you look in the World of Investment, you will find a mutual fund. There are funds that specialize in growth stocks, bonds, international securities, even real estate. For the speculator, there are funds that own gold mines, silver mines, or stock options. If you are a socially conscious investor, you can buy funds that own only the securities of socially responsible companies.

Mutual funds are an easy way to invest in a specific area. For example, suppose you think the price of oil is on the way up. Instead of making a risky speculation on an oil futures contract, you can put your money in a mutual fund that specializes in energy companies. If you want to invest in gold, you don't have to go to the trouble of buying gold coins or bullion—or even shares in Cousin Jack's Australian gold mine: You can invest in a fund specializing in gold-mining companies. As you might guess, the stock prices of these companies follow the price of gold very closely.

You're going to hear a lot about mutual funds in this book, because they're perfect for the new investor. Why?

- Professional managers have records that can be checked in much less time than it takes to research an individual company.
- There is safety in diversity: each fund's portfolio represents a number of companies.
- A good balance in your own portfolio is easy to achieve by buying several different kinds of mutual funds. You'll see how to do this in the chapters on portfolios.

A further advantage is that you can start investing in a mutual fund for as little as $500 to $1,000. This makes them perfect for small investors. Once you have started with your initial investment, you can then continue to add money as you wish. Many people invest a set amount each month—there is usually a minimum of $25 to $50 for these additions.

How to Buy

Shares in mutual funds are bought and sold somewhat differently from stocks. Instead of ordering a certain number of shares, you place fund orders using round dollar figures. You will say to your broker, "I want to buy two thousand dollars' worth of Twentieth Century Growth Fund." The broker will then make the purchase and charge you a commission for the service.

Unlike most investments, you can also buy mutual funds *without the aid of a broker*. You can call up the fund office directly; for example, you could call the 20th Century office, ask them to send you an application, and return it

To Broker or Not to Broker
(That Is the Question)

In setting up your portfolio, the question inevitably arises: Do you want to buy through a broker or directly from the individual funds? The answer is that dealing through a brokerage account is usually easier, but more costly.

Discount brokers commonly charge a minimum commission of about $30 each time you buy or sell a mutual fund. Fees generally run at the rate of 0.6% on the first $15,000; 0.2% on the remaining $15,000 to $100,000 (this may vary among the different discounters). Note that the figure is *0.6%*, not 6%; 0.6% = .006.

A $10,000 purchase would cost $60 in commissions ($10,000 × .006 = $60). A $50,000 purchase would be 0.6% on the first $15,000 = $90, plus 0.2% on the remaining $35,000 = $70, for a total of $160.

As you can see, discount brokerage commissions are not very high for middle-range and large buyers of mutual funds, particularly when looked at as a percentage of the purchase. A purchase of $5,000, for example, would cost the minimum $30 fee—which is only 0.6% of the total. And the buyer or seller of $50,000 worth of a fund would pay only a 0.32% commission on the purchase ($160 = 0.32% of $50,000).

What this means is that large and middle-range investors have a real choice. Dealing with a broker involves some extra cost, but it also offers the convenience of buying and selling with one phone number and having all your funds in one place. The brokerage will send out a monthly statement listing all your funds and showing their present values. This can make things much easier, particularly for those who are setting up a portfolio of investments for the first time.

A couple of notes: We are talking about *discount* brokers here—the full-commission brokerages will charge more. And remember that there is a commission when you sell a fund as well as when you buy it.

Smaller investors, on the other hand, will do much better investing directly with the no-load funds. Someone trying to create a portfolio by investing $300 a month would pay the minimum fee of $30 to a broker for each purchase. This equals 10% of the $300—and that equals *too much*.

Another disadvantage of buying through a broker is that the broker may not carry the mutual fund you want. The large discount brokerages carry anywhere from 400 to 600 of the larger funds; if you are looking for one of the smaller ones, there's a good chance you will have to buy directly from the fund office.

with the $2,000 for their Growth Fund. (The toll-free numbers of the various fund offices can be found in the books listed at the end of this chapter.) In this particular case, you would not be charged any commission by the fund.

Many mutual funds charge a kind of initiation fee, which they call a *sales load*, or simply a *load*. The 20th Century Growth Fund happens to be a *no-load* fund, so there is no fee to buy in to it. Other funds, however, may charge 2% or 3% of the amount of your purchase—or more. To buy in to United Science and Energy Fund, you will pay a 9.3% load. If you were to buy $10,000 worth of this fund, this would mean a payment of $930 in fees (9.3% = .093; 0.93 × $10,000 = $930). A 10% rise in the fund during the first year would amount to a $1,000 profit on paper—but your actual return would be only $70 after you subtract the $930 load.

Some funds charge a fee when you *sell* your shares in the fund. This fee is called a *back-end load*, as opposed to the more common *front-end load* when you buy in. It is also called a *redemption fee* or a *deferred sales charge*.

Logically, you might assume that the funds which charge high loads do better than the no-load funds—that the managers must be doing *something* to earn the extra money. This, however, has been statistically proved *not* to be the case. Overall, there is virtually no difference in the performance of load and no-load mutual funds. Some individual funds may do better than others, but this is true of the no-loads as well as the load funds. So why pay these fees, when you can buy a fund that is just as good with no fees? Why, indeed?

You need to be aware that some of the larger brokerages and investment management companies have their own mutual funds—and these funds usually have loads attached to them. You may be directed to these funds by your broker, but you can ask to be directed away from them—to high-performing no-load funds.

All the funds charge management fees of 0.5% to 1% a year. These you should expect—after all, the managers have to get paid somehow. You won't see these fees on the statement of your account; they are deducted from the fund's assets before the total value is calculated—"off the top," as it were.

Some funds, both load and no-load, have what are called *12b-1 plans*. These plans allow the fund managers to use the assets of the fund to pay for such expenses as advertising, brokers' commissions, and sending out informational material. The 12b-1 charges can range from 0.10% to 1.25% per year and, like the management fees, are deducted directly from the fund's assets.

These fees are essentially "hidden loads." For example, if you have owned a fund for five years, a 12b-1 fee of 1% a year would be the approximate equivalent of a 5% front-end load.

Be sure to watch for the various loads and fees when you check out the particulars of a fund (the recommended books will list all the fees). There are many excellent funds with no loads and minimal or nonexistent 12b-1 fees. Except in rare cases, there is no reason you should pay more than the yearly management fees when you own a mutual fund.

OPEN-END FUNDS AND CLOSED-END FUNDS

The mutual funds we are discussing in this chapter are called *open-end funds.* All this means is that, unlike most companies, the fund has no limit to the number of shares it issues. When you buy in to a fund, they will simply print up new shares for you. (You can ask that the share certificates be sent to you, though most people opt to have them kept at the fund office.)

Open-end mutual funds are not traded on the stock exchanges (you will find them listed in a separate section of the financial pages). This is because you buy and sell shares only from the fund itself, not from other investors on the open market.

Closed-end funds are similar to the open-end ones in that they own securities of many different companies. Closed-end funds, however, like most publicly owned companies, issue a *limited* number of shares, and these shares are traded on the stock exchanges. As with other stocks, you buy shares from other investors through a stockbroker, not from the fund office. Closed-end funds are discussed in detail in Chapter 13.

READING THE MUTUAL FUND TABLES

Each day, the total value of all the securities and cash in an open-end fund is added up. This total is divided by the number of shares the fund has issued, and the resulting figure is called the *net asset value* (NAV). This is the price of one share of the fund, and it is the figure you will see in the mutual funds section of the financial pages.

If the NAV figure is followed by "NL," this means the fund is a no-load fund. If, on the other hand, another, larger number follows the net asset value, the fund has a front-end load attached. The second number is the offer price—the amount it will cost you to buy a share of the fund.

FIDELITY INVESTMENT

Fund	NAV	Offer Price	NAV Change
Balanced	11.93	NL	+0.06
Blue Chip Growth	17.60	18.14	+0.09

The Fidelity Balanced Fund is a no-load (NL) fund. You can buy one share at the net asset value price of $11.93. The change in the NAV from the day before is +0.06; that is, yesterday the price was $11.87.

The Fidelity Blue Chip Growth Fund is a load fund. The $18.14 is the cost per share—$0.54 higher than the net asset value. This reflects a load charge of about 3%. If you buy in to the fund, you will pay $18.14 per share, but should you turn around and try to *sell* the same shares back to the fund, you would get only $17.60 for each. For you to show any profit, the net asset value will have to increase past $18.14.

As we mentioned above, mutual funds are usually purchased in round dollar figures. If you order $1,000 of the Fidelity Balanced Fund at $11.93 per share, they will send you a notice saying that you bought 83.8222 shares ($1,000 ÷ $11.93 per share = 83.8222 shares). You should be prepared for such decimalized figures when you buy mutual funds.

If, over the next few weeks or months, the companies owned by the Balanced Fund do well and the net asset value goes up to, say, $13.25, you would multiply this new figure

How Prices Are Set

Because open-end mutual funds issue new shares to new buyers, the law of supply and demand does not affect the price of these shares. Stock prices rise and fall according to the demand by investors for the *limited* supply of shares issued by a company. Sellers can demand a higher price if the stock is popular. In the case of mutual funds, however, the only seller is the fund office. Instead of demanding a higher price from new investors, the fund simply issues them new shares at the going price.

The price, or net asset value, of shares in an open-end mutual fund is determined solely by the total value of the assets held by the fund. This is one of the few instances in the World of Investment where supply and demand is not at work in setting a price.

by the number of your shares to arrive at the value of the shares ($13.25 × 83.8222 = $1,110.64). You will be ahead by $110.64.

FUND FAMILIES

A mutual fund is usually part of a "family" of funds—a group of funds owned by one management company. In order to encourage people to invest all their money with them, management companies create funds with different investment purposes. The Fidelity Group of Funds, for example, offered 115 different funds at last count, each of which had a different focus for its investments. This is unusually large—most fund families consist of anywhere from 5 to 30 funds. Some of the other large companies are Scudder, Dreyfus, T. Rowe Price, and Vanguard.

Do certain families of funds perform better than others? Yes, but the individual investor should concentrate more on individual funds—their performance over time, the loads and fees, and the prospects for the type of investments owned by the fund. Occasionally, it's useful to know about the parent companies: for example, all Scudder funds are no-load, and the Vanguard funds generally have low management fees.

DIVIDENDS AND DISTRIBUTIONS

Because the stocks and/or bonds owned by a mutual fund produce interest and dividends, the fund will accumulate income over the course of a year. In addition, the securities may increase in value; if the fund managers sell these at a profit, this sale will also produce income in the form of capital gains.

This income is passed on to shareholders in the form of *distributions* during the year. You can receive checks monthly or quarterly if you need the income. If, on the other hand, you are investing only for the growth of your capital, you can ask the fund to automatically *reinvest* all your income in additional shares of the fund.

These reinvested amounts may not seem very large at first, but when compounded over the years, they can make for a substantial increase in your holdings. *The new investor should know that the performance figures for mutual funds almost always assume all income is reinvested.* (You should also know that the performance figures do not subtract taxes from the income generated by the fund.)

The amount of dividends and distributions from a mutual fund will depend on the kind of investments it owns.

Funds investing in high-rated corporate bonds may give returns of 7% to 10% based on the income from the bonds. A fund investing in small-growth companies, on the other hand, might have little or no income from dividends. Any profit you make from this fund will be the result of appreciation in the market value of the stocks owned by the fund.

Whether you receive the distributions in cash or have them reinvested, Uncle Sam will want his cut. At the end of the year, the mutual fund office will send you a form listing the dividends, interest, and capital gains for the year—all the information you need for your taxes.

Investors are sometimes confused by the tax rules surrounding mutual funds. Believe it or not, the Internal Revenue Service has a very helpful booklet explaining these rules, complete with examples of how the rules work in different situations. Ask for Publication 564 at an IRS office.

A FUND FOR EVERY PURPOSE

No matter what part of the World of Investment you're interested in, you can almost always find a mutual fund that covers it. There are five general categories of funds and then a very large number of specific categories.

In addition, you can find all different levels of the risk-reward thermometer among the many funds. In spite of the safety inherent in owning many different companies, some funds are quite risky because they invest in things like junk bonds or stock options. Other funds are extremely conservative, investing only in top-rated bonds and blue chip stocks.

General Categories

Aggressive Growth Funds. You would invest in an aggressive growth fund to maximize the chances of increasing your investment capital in a short period of time (i.e., get rich quick). Because the companies held by the fund are often in the process of growing, their stock dividends are commonly small or nonexistent. Distributions will, therefore, tend to be minimal. Aggressive growth funds, as a group, are the most volatile—they tend to lose the most value in bear markets and gain the most in bull markets.

Growth Funds.   Growth funds—also called conservative growth funds—are interested in a long-term appreciation of capital. They are likely to invest in blue chip companies that pay dividends, but are still oriented toward growth. Income will be higher and risk lower than with the aggressive funds, but these funds can also lose a good deal of value in a bear market. Because of the high quality of the stocks, however, recovery is usually excellent when the market improves.

Growth and Income.   Growth and income funds (also known as income or equity-income funds) attempt to provide a substantial income, while still encouraging growth of capital. They tend to invest in convertible bonds (see Chapter 7) and utility stocks. These securities usually fluctuate less than those of the growth-oriented companies, so these funds tend to be more stable.

Balanced Funds.   Moving on down the risk-reward scale, the first purpose of the balanced funds is preservation of capital. The portfolios of these funds are "balanced" between stocks and bonds; traditionally they will hold 60% of assets in stocks, 40% in bonds. Like the growth and income funds, the balanced funds provide high income, but will be even less volatile in response to market fluctuations.

Bond Funds.   Investors put their money in bonds and bond funds because they yield a high cash income and provide balance in a portfolio of stock funds. The interest payments from top-rated bonds will continue even in a depressed stock market. Although there are funds that hold high-risk bonds called "junk bonds," most bond funds are purchased for their stability and high income yield.

Specialized Funds

Here are a few of the more popular types of specialized mutual funds.

International Funds. International funds have provided excellent returns for their investors over the last 20 years. These funds invest in the stocks and bonds of foreign companies, thereby providing welcome diversity to an all-American portfolio. Some international funds invest all over the world, while others cover a specific area, like the Pacific Basin or Europe. You can find international funds in all of the five general categories listed above: aggressive growth, growth, growth and income, balanced, and bond.

Socially Responsible Funds. Relatively new on the scene, the socially responsible funds invest only in companies that exhibit a social conscience. Companies that take care of the environment and are aware of the rights and needs of their workers are "in"; firms that produce pollution, weapons of war, cigarettes, or alcohol are "out." Most socially responsible funds have performed very well over the last five years. See Chapter 12 for more about these funds.

Precious-Metals Funds. For risk-tolerant investors only! Precious-metals funds invest in gold and silver mines, bullion, other rare metals like platinum, and, occasionally, metals futures contracts. These funds are not for the

weak-hearted, the funds nevertheless provide an easier way
of investing in metals than actually buying coins or bullion.

Some of the other specialized funds invest in the securities of companies in these categories: real estate (companies that hold income property and real estate sales
companies); small companies; utilities; technology; health
care; energy; and biotechnology. There are also specialized
bond funds, such as those holding only tax-free municipal
bonds or government bonds.

In recent years, funds called *index funds* have become
more popular. In Chapter 8, we will discuss the various stock
indexes used to measure the performance of the stock market, such as the Dow Jones averages and the Standard &
Poors 500 (S&P 500). Right now, all you need to know is that
the S&P 500 Index tracks the ups and downs of the stocks
of 500 corporations on the New York and American Exchanges and the over-the-counter market. It is an excellent
indicator of the direction of the stock market as a whole.

Index funds buy stock in all the companies of an index.
For example, the Vanguard Index Trust 500 Fund invests in
the stock of all 500 companies in the S&P 500. Investing in an
index fund like this one is as close as you can come to investing in the entire stock market. What's the advantage?
One advantage is that the managers of such funds don't have
much to do in the way of buying and selling, so brokerage
commissions are very low and management fees are small.

Index funds did very well during the 1980s because the
stock market as a whole increased sharply in value. Whether
the 1990s will see a repeat of this performance depends
entirely on whether the stock market is run by the bulls or
the bears.

CHOOSING THE BEST FUNDS

Information on mutual funds is not difficult to find. The
American Association of Individual Investors (AAII) issues

an excellent yearly guide to no-load funds. This is listed at the end of this chapter, along with a few other guides. Your broker will have a booklet listing the funds traded by the brokerage. *Barron's* (the weekly financial newspaper) puts out a comprehensive guide to the funds each quarter; you receive this as part of your subscription.

These guides will list the investment category of the fund, the loads and fees, and the dividend yield during the last year. They will also show the "performance" of the fund during the last few months and over several years— that is, how much you would have gained (or lost) had you invested a given amount in the fund. Some of the recommended books will give more detailed information, such as the investment objective of a given fund and its performance compared to other funds in the same category. All the guides will list the address and 800 number of the fund office.

If you are thinking of buying a fund, you can call the fund's 800 number and ask them to send you a *prospectus*. This short booklet will tell you the investment policy of the fund, its performance since its inception, and the companies in its portfolio.

A word of caution: The past-performance figures for mutual funds can be misleading, particularly for the funds specializing in a narrow market group. For example, a fund specializing in energy stocks may have had a fantastic record for the past year, but its performance this year may be terrible if the economic climate is difficult for the energy companies. Try to find the funds with a good record over several years *and* good prospects for the future.

The advisers who write the newsletters I mention in this book often recommend mutual funds in addition to individual securities. These newsletters are an excellent source for top-performing funds.

Until you gain experience and a feel for the markets, I recommend that you avoid buying individual stocks and bonds. Mutual funds are an excellent place for the new investor to start.

Pax World Fund

Let's look at an example of a mutual fund. Pax World Fund was started in 1970. It is a no-load, "balanced" fund: roughly 60% of its portfolio is in stocks and 40% in bonds. Shareholders number 65,000; assets are close to $500 million.

Pax has recently been investing primarily in health-care, food, and utilities. It presently owns 29 different stocks. Here are its largest stock holdings:

Stock	Shares	Value	% of Net Assets
Quaker Oats	375,000	$27,000,000	5.5%
Merck and Co.	700,000	25,200,000	5.3
H. J. Heinz	675,000	24,300,000	5.2
Campbell	600,000	23,625,000	4.7
Peoples' Energy	683,000	22,197,000	4.3

All bonds owned by Pax are top-rated government bonds.

Following are the rates of return each year:

1983	1984	1985	1986	1987	1988	1989	1990	1991	1992
24.17%	7.39	25.79	8.45	2.49	11.70	24.81	10.53	20.8	.63

To figure the increase for an investment in any year, multiply by the percentage shown. In 1988, for example, there was an increase of 11.70%. If you had invested $1,000 at the first of the year, you would have had $1,170 at the end. Notice how the rates of return vary widely from year to year. You should expect this from any mutual fund which invests in stocks.

For more information on Pax World Fund, turn to Appendix B.

In Chapter 14, we'll discuss not only which categories of funds have performed the best in the past, but which ones show the most promise for the future. And in Chapters 15 and 16, we'll look at how to choose the funds most appropriate to your situation. Finally, in Appendix A, you will find a short list of the best-performing funds to choose from.

Resources

The Individual Investor's Guide to No-Load Mutual Funds.
The Resources section of Chapter 1 explains how to join the American Association of Individual Investors (AAII). The yearly edition of this manual comes free with membership. If you don't want to join the AAII, the guide is available in bookstores, but the price is $24.95! (It's more cost-effective to join AAII.)

Either way, this book can be extremely helpful to new investors. The performance of about 500 no-load funds is reviewed over the past five years. The first few chapters present useful information about funds in general, and interpretations of the performance figures. An excellent place to start.

Morningstar Mutual Funds, Morningstar Inc., 53 W. Jackson Blvd., Chicago, IL 60604. (312) 427-1985. $395/year; $55/three-month trial.

This is the service to sign up for as you become more experienced. Professional advisers use services such as Morningstar to procure more detailed information on the funds they recommend to their clients. Your subscription gets you a great big three-ring binder with the particulars on 1,200 different funds. Every two weeks, you receive an update on 127 funds, which you add to the folder. The information on each fund is updated every 20 weeks.

Morningstar provides you with much more detailed information than most fund guides—and more of it. Despite the amount of information, however, the presentation is clear and straightforward. There is a guide that explains in plain English the reasons for all the different facts and figures. This is for the investor who wants to be really thorough in managing his or her portfolio.

CHAPTER 7

FIXED-INCOME INVESTMENTS

CDs

When you open a savings account at your local bank or credit union, you are lending your money to the bank. They will pay you interest for the use of your money because they can then lend it to others at a higher rate.

With a regular savings account, you can withdraw all your money at any time. The banks, however, would like you to leave your money with them for a longer period of time, so they will know how much they have to lend out. For this reason, they created *certificates of deposit*, or *CDs*. You commit a certain amount of money for a certain length of time, and they will pay you a higher interest rate than that of regular savings accounts.

You can buy certificates of deposit for periods ranging from three months to five years. The most common CDs have terms of six months to two years, and the minimum deposits range from around $250 to $1,000, depending on the bank and how long the term is.

The interest you receive from the CDs will be one or two percentage points higher than that of the regular bank savings accounts (occasionally more than this). For example, if regular savings were paying at a rate of 5%, six-month CDs might yield 6%, twelve-month CDs 6.5%, and two-year CDs 7%. Different banks and credit unions will have different interest rates for their CDs—it pays to shop around.

The rates *offered* by the bank will change with the prevailing interest rates, but once you have purchased a CD, your interest rate will be locked in until the expiration date (this is why CDs are fixed-income investments). These days, there are a few exceptions to this rule—some CDs have interest rates that fluctuate—so be sure to check.

When prevailing interest rates are low, it's not a good idea to lock yourself in to a long-term (two- to five-year) CD with a low return. The prevailing rates are likely to go up before the CD expires. You won't be able to take advantage of these new, higher rates, though, because you will be charged a fee if you withdraw your money before your CD matures (this fee may be as high as 90 days' interest on CDs with a term of a year).

CDs are a better place to park your extra money, or part of your emergency fund, than regular savings accounts. Not only will you receive a higher interest rate, but because of the CDs' early withdrawal fee, you will probably think twice before making any "impulse" withdrawals from your savings.

Like regular savings at almost all banks, CDs are covered up to $100,000 by the Federal Deposit Insurance Corporation (FDIC). You should be absolutely sure that your bank *is* covered by the FDIC. This means that if the bank should fail, you will receive all the money you have on deposit, up to $100,000.

MONEY MARKET ACCOUNTS

Another way of lending your money for interest is to open a money market account. These days, almost every financial institution has some form of money market account.

Just what is the "money market"? The federal government, banks, and large corporations all have a need to borrow money for the short term—less than a year. The government issues Treasury bills (T-bills) and Treasury notes, banks borrow by way of very large CDs ($100,000 and up), and large corporations put out IOUs called "commercial paper." It's not possible for the average investor to invest in most of these "money market securities," but banks and other institutions buy them by pooling depositors' money.

What does all this mean to the individual investor? By having a bank invest your money in the money market, you can earn substantially more than with a regular savings account. You may earn a bit more with a CD, but CDs have less liquidity. You can always withdraw funds from a money market account. You can even write three checks a month.

Banks usually set a minimum of $1,000 to $2,000 on money market deposit accounts (MMDAs). If your bank is insured by the FDIC, you are covered in the MMDAs up to $100,000.

Money market interest rates can fluctuate dramatically, unlike those of CDs. Once you've invested your money, you may earn more interest one month and less the next. In the spring of 1990, the return was about 7.5%; by the spring of 1992, it was down to 4% or less. Because of this fluctuation, MMDAs cannot strictly be called fixed-income investments.

The going interest rates on most money market accounts are pegged half a percentage point below the rate of U.S. Treasury bills.

So which is better, CDs or MMDAs? This depends on a couple of considerations. Longer-term CDs may give a slightly higher return, but money market accounts have more liquidity. CDs lock in a rate of interest for a given period, but if interest rates go up during that period, you'd be better off in an MMDA.

This is one of those decisions that can give people headaches—but really don't matter all that much. Over the long term, one or two percentage points can make a large difference, but over the short term, you can always transfer your money if one or the other kind of account looks better. They're both insured and they're both better than regular passbook savings accounts, if you can meet the bank's minimum deposit requirements.

These days, many banks have minimum deposit requirements even for passbook savings. You may find that you are being charged a monthly fee if your account is less than $500—and that this fee often amounts to more than the interest you are being paid! What this means, if you are a small depositor, is that you are better off squirreling your money away in a piggy bank until it reaches the level where you will not be charged a fee. Open a savings account then, but as soon as you can meet the minimum, take your money out of regular savings and open a money market account or buy a CD.

CREDIT UNIONS

Unlike banks, credit unions usually welcome small savings accounts—and without any monthly fees. Credit unions are an excellent alternative to banks. Because they are cooperatives, owned by their members, they are usually smaller, friendlier, and more sympathetic to the small borrower. In addition, you have the satisfaction of knowing that your savings allow the credit union to lend money to your neighbors or coworkers.

If you have access to a credit union where you work or in your community, I would strongly recommend you give it a try. The interest rates are usually comparable to those of

the banks, and your money is insured by the federal government (at most credit unions—be sure to check). These days,
many credit unions offer the same services as banks: CDs,
auto loans, credit cards, and checking accounts.

There are now 14,650 credit unions across the country,
with $200 billion in assets and 62 million members. For
help in finding one near you, you can contact the Credit
Union League in your state. Look in the phone book in
your city or the nearest city. If you can't find the league office
in your state, you can write the Credit Union National
Association, Public Relations Dept., Box 431, Madison, WI
53701. They will put you in touch with the closest league
office.

A growing number of community development credit
unions lend to such groups as small, inner-city, and minority businesses. To find one near you, you can contact the
National Association of Community Development Credit
Unions, 29 John St. Suite 903, New York, NY 10038, (212)
513-7191. This is an excellent way to put your savings to
work in a socially active manner.

BONDS: HOW TO LEND MONEY TO GENERAL MOTORS

You become part owner of a corporation by owning its
stock. But suppose you *lend* money to this same corporation—or to the federal government. This is also a type of
investment, because you will receive payments for the use of
your money.

The way you lend money is to purchase *bonds* issued by
corporations and governments. Bonds are essentially IOUs
that give you interest payments in return for the rental of
your money. Corporations figure they can make more than
the 7% to 10% they pay you by investing your loan in their
own operations. About 80% of their borrowed money comes
from issuing bonds.

Unlike stocks, whose dividends may fluctuate according to the fortunes of the company, bonds are fixed-income investments. This means the interest payments you receive will stay the same during the life of the bond. You don't gain more profit when the firm issuing the bonds does well, but neither do you receive less if the company falls on lean times.

Fixed-income investments offer the advantage of a stable return. You don't have the chance to make a large profit, as you do with riskier investments, but neither do you leave yourself open to a major loss. Fixed-income investments are the Volvos of the World of Investment: not terribly exciting or stylish, but extremely safe and dependable.

Other fixed-income investments besides bonds are long-term certificates of deposit, which we will discuss later in the chapter, and mortgages. The interest income you receive from these investments stays the same over a period of years.

For local, state, and national governments, bonds are an alternative to taxes as a way of raising money. Unlike the corporations, however, governments usually do not invest their bond income in money-making endeavors. Bonds are a way for governments to borrow at less interest than a bank would charge them for a loan.

You can buy and sell bonds through stockbrokers, very much the way you buy and sell stock. Just as with a stock, you will receive a certificate, which you can keep in a safe-deposit box or at your broker's.

Bonds are issued with a specific interest rate and a specific date at which they will "expire" or "mature." At this "maturity date," the borrower must pay back the entire amount of the bond—the so-called *face value.*

Most bonds are similar to "interest-only" loans, in that the principal is not paid off until the loan comes due. This is different from the amortized mortgage loans discussed in Chapter 10, where each payment includes a small amount to reduce the principal.

Instead, the issuer of the bond will pay you interest, usually every six months, then repay the amount of your original loan on the maturity date. (There are exceptions to this, as you will see in Chapter 21 on individual bonds.) The face value, interest rate, and maturity date are all printed on the bond certificate.

Bonds are generally regarded as extremely safe investments, especially those issued by the federal government and large corporations. There are, however, bonds with a low safety rating. Buyers of these bonds receive higher interest than they would for top-rated bonds, but run the risk of default by the issuing company (a default in payments means your bond could end up worth nothing).

The bonds with high safety ratings, however, can provide a good balance to stocks in a portfolio. Bonds yield a steady return—substantially higher than the dividends from most stocks—which you can either use as income or reinvest.

One reason bonds are safe and stable is that interest on a company's bonds must be paid before any dividends to stockholders. And, though bond prices do fluctuate, they do so much less than stocks. Bonds as a category, then, come out a notch or two lower than stocks on the risk-reward thermometers.

There are many different types of bonds, each with different characteristics. And the factors that make individual bonds and the bond market go up and down are generally different from those that affect the stock market. You will find descriptions of the different types of bonds and how to buy them in Chapter 21.

Most of these details, however, are useful only to more experienced investors. Individual bonds, like individual stocks, are generally not appropriate investments for the new investor. Mutual funds that hold their assets in bonds are a much better place to put your money.

The Rule of 70

There is a simple way of determining how long it will take your money to double at any compound rate of interest. Take the interest rate and divide it into 70: the result will be the number of years for the amount to double.

For example, suppose you invest $10,000 at 7%: 7% into 70 = 10. It will take approximately 10 years for your $10,000 to double at a rate of 7%, compounded each year. If your rate of return was 12%, however, your money would double in $5\frac{5}{6}$ years, or 5 years and 10 months (70 divided by 12 = 5.833, or $5\frac{5}{6}$). This will not be an exact number, but it's useful for quick figuring.

HOW COMPOUND INTEREST WORKS

Just as a CD or a money market account will earn you 1% to 3% more than a regular passbook savings account, a bond mutual fund will usually earn 1% to 3% more than a money market account.

But are a few percentage points of interest worth the trouble of taking the money out of your local bank and investing it in some mutual fund? If a certificate of deposit is giving 8%, why try for 10% with a corporate bond fund? The extra 2% would mean only $200 more a year, if you were investing $10,000. After all, your money is fully insured at the bank, and—at least in a money market account—you have immediate access to it.

The answer to this question is contained in the compound-interest chart in Appendix E. Referring to this chart, notice that at 8%, your $10,000 will become $20,000 in nine years, assuming that all the interest is reinvested at the end of each year—"compounded annually," in bank terminology. But notice that at *10%* compounded annually, the $10,000 has doubled itself in only a little over *seven* years!

This example illustrates how important two, or even one, percentage points can be over the long term. In 30 years, your $10,000 will have grown to almost $175,000 at 10%. At 8%, however, it would be only just over $100,000. Not a bad chart to remember when you're investing for long-term objectives like college educations or retirement. (Remember that in this scenario, growth is the only objective; you don't receive any spendable income from your investment—all of the interest is reinvested.)

Why do these one or two percentage points make such a difference? Because when you "compound" interest, you add it on to the principal. The next time you figure the interest, you figure it from this new, larger number.

For example, you invest $10,000 in a bond fund from which you receive an annual return of 10%. Interest is usually paid either quarterly or every six months, but for the sake of simplicity in our figuring, we're going to add it on at the end of the year.

On December 31, then, 10% × $10,000, or $1,000, will be credited to your account. You now have $11,000. *Next* year, the 10% interest will be paid not on the original $10,000, but on this *$11,000*. 10% × $11,000 = $1,100, which gets added to the total, making $12,100.

The third year, the 10% is figured on the $12,100, giving you $1,210. Adding it on, you now have $13,310.

Notice how the interest payments keep getting bigger as the principal amount gets bigger. When you get up to 10 years, the principal amount has grown to about $25,900. This means the interest payment will be $2,590. The larger interest payments mean the principal will grow at a faster clip each year.

If, however, you're getting 8% instead of 10%, the amount will grow more slowly. At the end of 3 years, $10,000

Compound Interest and Mutual Funds

Compound interest is one of the reasons most mutual funds don't perform quite as well as the overall stock market, as measured by stock indexes such as the Standard and Poors 500. Even no-load mutual funds have management fees, which subtract about 1% a year from the total value of the fund you own.

Suppose the stock market, as a whole, goes up 10% in a given year. If your mutual fund performs as well as the stock market, your gain will be only 9% after the 1% management fee is subtracted. If the fund has other expenses, like the 12b-1 fees mentioned in Chapter 6, your gain will be even less—maybe only 8%. We have just seen the difference between growth at 8% and growth at 10%.

What this illustrates is the importance of buying mutual funds that charge low management fees and very low or nonexistent additional expenses, such as 12b-1 fees. It also illustrates the importance of choosing the very best mutual funds—the ones that will equal or outperform the overall market. We'll learn how to do this in Chapters 14 and 15.

invested at 8%, compounded annually, will have grown to about $12,600. At 10 years, it will be $21,600, substantially less than the $25,900 at the 10% interest.

At 20 years, the difference has become dramatic: $46,600 for the 8% fund, $67,200 for the 10%. Such are the wonders of compound interest. This is why people get excited over a few little percentage points.

Stocks versus Bonds

While we're on the subject of compound interest, this is a good time to talk about why so many people invest in stocks instead of choosing the relative safety of bonds. Bonds—especially U.S. government bonds and top-rated bonds from the giant corporations—are about as rock-solid safe as investments get. Furthermore, though they may fluctuate in value, bonds are not likely to take the kind of dive as stocks did in 1987. So why risk your money in the stock market?

The answer is that while stocks are indeed riskier over the short term, in the long term they have outperformed bonds hands down.

From 1970 to 1990, inflation charged ahead at an average yearly rate of 3.36%. Regular savings accounts didn't stay very far ahead of inflation: $10,000 invested in 1970 and compounded over the years would have grown to $45,000 in 1990. If you subtracted the value of the dollar lost to inflation during that period, you would be left with only $11,400—a total profit of just $1,400.

In the same 20 years, $10,000 invested in corporate bonds would have topped out at $56,000. Stocks, however, as measured by the Standard and Poors 500 Index, would have made $10,000 grow to $82,500.

If you turn to Appendix D, "Fifty Years of Returns," you can see that the figures for the previous 30, 40, and 50 years are even more impressively in favor of stocks.

The table shows that $10,000 invested in corporate bonds in 1948 would have grown to $73,100 by 1988; $10,000 invested in stocks, though, would have amounted to almost a million dollars! (All of these figures assume that all earnings are reinvested.)

It's important to remember the twin demons of inflation and taxes in figuring total returns. If inflation is growing at an average rate of 4% and taxes take a bite of another 2.8% out of your total portfolio, then a 6.8% growth in your investments will amount to no growth at all.

Let's look at how the tax bite works. Suppose you receive 10%, or $1,000 on a $10,000 investment, and are taxed at the rate of 28% on this income. Your tax is $280 a year ($1,000 × 0.28 = $280). So your after-tax return is only $720. Another way of looking at this, however, is that your capital amount—the $10,000—has been decreased by $280, or 2.8%. So while inflation is busy lowering the value of your capital by decreasing the amount it can buy, taxes attack your capital head on. Added together, their total damage comes to 6.8%. Your tax rate may be higher or lower and the inflation rate may vary from year to year, but these figures are close to average rates over the last 20 years.

This is just one more reason the stock market needs to be a part of an individual portfolio: Stocks are among the few investments that have beaten the tax and inflation bites with plenty to spare.

Bond Mutual Funds

So now we have to ask another question: Why invest in bonds at all, if stocks have done so much better? The answer is that in the World of Investment, it's good to have as many bases covered as possible. We just don't know how stocks will perform in the 1990s. In Chapter 15, we'll go into more of the reasons for diversifying a portfolio of investments. Right now, let's consider mutual funds that invest in bonds.

As you will see in Chapter 21, the various factors to consider when buying individual bonds can get quite complex. Bond mutual funds, also known as "fixed-income funds," make it much easier for the new investor. The managers of the funds decide which bonds to buy and sell—and the best times to do so. All you have to do is choose the best fund. The great majority of investors have chosen this route: individual investors in bond mutual funds outnumber holders of bonds by about 25 to 1.

Like stock mutual funds, there are many different kinds of bond funds, with different investment purposes. There are super-safe funds that own only U.S. government securities, speculative funds that invest in junk bonds, and a whole spectrum in between. Here, we are interested in bond funds primarily for the safety and steady income they provide; for this reason, we're going to avoid the more speculative funds and deal only with the conservative ones.

These conservative funds buy government securities and high-rated corporate bonds. In the mutual funds section of Appendix A, we list a few fixed-income funds that are not only the safest, but have also given good returns over the years. These are the kinds of funds we include in our model portfolio in Chapter 14.

Resources

Credit Union National Association. Public Relations Dept., Box 431, Madison, WI 53701. (800) 356-9655.

If you would like to join a credit union but can't find any near you, this is the organization to call. They will put you in touch with your State Credit Union League (found in all 50 states). The State League will help you find an appropriate credit union for your needs.

CHAPTER 8

FINDING AND INTERPRETING FINANCIAL INFORMATION

The individual investor needs two kinds of information: descriptive and analytical. You need to know what's happening and, especially if you're a new investor, you have to know what it means—how you should respond to the information. And, of course, you have to get acquainted with the terminology: what is this Dow you're always hearing about? What do all those numbers and letters mean in the stock tables?

In this chapter, we will talk first about the best places to learn what's happening in the financial markets *and* where to find the best interpretations of these events. Then we'll get into the terminology and discuss such things as the various stock markets and stock indexes.

One of the greatest challenges to the new investor is tackling the vast amount of information and opinions pertaining to investing, and not just in the media. Everyone from your Uncle Fred to your next door neighbor seems to have some stock to recommend or some little nugget of

absolutely essential advice. New investors can often be swayed by what they read or hear, particularly if it is presented in an authoritative manner.

In fact, the inexperienced investor reading a financial paper can sometimes seem like a drunk in a department store. "Consolidated has a new chairman who has saved six other companies from bankruptcy" (check out Consolidated); "Analyst says gold has made a bottom and is ready to take off" (I've always wanted to buy gold—I guess now is the time); "Oil prices rise sharply" (Hmm, don't stocks usually go down when oil rises? Maybe I should think about selling some stocks), and so on, lurching from one possibility to the next.

How do you deal with this mountain of material? After all, we do need at least some of this information to make intelligent decisions.

First, remember where you are. You're not in Kansas anymore—you're in the Wonderful World of Investment, where all things seem possible. Each helping of information must be taken with several grains of salt. Remember, if that gold analyst were right even 60% of the time, she wouldn't need to be writing for *Barron's*. Remember, oil prices often go up and down like a bungee jumper and the stock market may or may not be affected.

What will help the most, however, is focusing yourself on the areas that appeal to you. As you set up an investment plan, you will then gravitate naturally to the information that pertains to your interests.

But where is the best current information and analysis? For general current information, you have your pick of the financial papers: the venerable *Wall Street Journal,* or the upstart *Investor's Business Daily.* If you tend to be overwhelmed by the quantity of information in the dailies, you can subscribe to the weekly journal *Barron's*.

Your best bet is to go to your local library and read the different papers. You should be able to sense pretty quickly which one suits you best. The stock tables are definitely easier to read in *Investor's Daily,* but the manner in which the rest of the news is reported is really a matter of personal taste. They all give the necessary information.

What about the magazines for individual investors? *Money, Financial World, Personal Investor*—all the slick monthlies with their color illustrations, charts, and easy-to-read articles? Or how about the heavyweights for business-people—*Forbes, Fortune,* or *Business Week?*

Again, you might consider a trip to your public library to sample the various publications; if you find one you like, cut-rate subscriptions are usually available for new readers.

Unlike the financial newspapers, which focus almost exclusively on stocks and bonds, magazines are more likely to run articles about all areas of investment and finance, from real estate to personal money management to business cycles. There are certainly some useful articles in the financial journals, but it's usually necessary to sift through a good deal of other information that may not interest you. These are, after all, written for as broad a base of readership as possible.

In our information-oriented society, it is now possible to tune in the radio or TV almost any time of day and hear discussions of the discount rate or the possibility of a rise in the silver market. During the day, CNBC-FNN carries up-to-the-minute news of the markets, as well as interviews and analysis. Many public broadcasting channels carry the *Nightly Business Report* in the evening. On Friday evening, Louis Rukeyser brings you his financial experts on *Wall Street Week*, and various segments of the economy are discussed on *Adam Smith's Money World*, both on PBS.

Whether these programs are useful has to be your own decision. I have heard insightful discussions and gotten interesting information from all these sources. A good thing to remember, though, when you're listening to the "experts" is that there is almost certainly another "expert" whose view is diametrically opposed to the one you're hearing. You won't have to look very far to find her, either—just listen to a discussion on the same subject on another program the next day.

Perhaps the best way to refine and limit the information you receive is to subscribe to a few good financial newsletters. When you decide on a specific advisory service, you have already begun to specialize in the kind of investments that interest you. The information you then receive is pertinent to your situation and your portfolio.

As for analysis of the economy and the specific markets, in my experience the advisers who write the newsletters do the best job—at least this is true of the advisers recommended in this book. It can be useful to read a weekly paper like *Barron's* for up-to-date reporting of financial events, but you may find that most of the analytical investment information you need is contained in your monthly or bi-monthly advisory newsletter.

Investors who buy and sell individual securities with some frequency may choose to subscribe to one of the daily financial papers. For the long-term investor, however, the time span of a few weeks between newsletters is just about right.

READING THE TABLES

Even though we recommend that the new investor stick to mutual funds, it's a good idea to know a few more things about the stock market—like how to read the stock tables. (The majority of funds are made up of stocks, after all.)

To begin with, what do all those funny-looking numbers and letters mean? The various financial papers may have the numbers arranged differently, but if you look at any stock table you will find these figures:

(1)		(2)	(3)	(4)	(5)	(6)	(7)	(8)	(9)
52 wk									
Hi	**Lo**		**Div**	**Shares**	**Yld**	**P/E**	**Hi**	**Lo**	**Last**	**Change**
40⅜	29	AT&T	1.32	6982	3.3	15	40	39⅝	39⅞	+⅛

(1) The high and low prices per share over the last 52 weeks. These are interesting figures. Overall, 75% of listed stocks fluctuate by more than 50% over a period of a year.

The prices of all stocks will fluctuate as the overall market goes up and down. Some, however, will rise and fall much more sharply than the market, and some less. This comparison of a stock's volatility compared to the market's volatility is called its *beta coefficient*. A stock with a beta of 1.00 tends to vary in price exactly as much as the overall market.

Eastman Kodak, for example, has usually had a beta of about 1.00. AT&T, like most utilities, has had a much smaller beta—around 0.65. Risky new technology stocks, on the other hand, may have betas as high as 2.00. A general rule is the higher the beta, the higher the risk. Some stock tables list betas, though you will usually see them only in more comprehensive descriptions of stocks.

(2) The total amount of dividends per share over the last year, in this case $1.32 per share. This does not necessarily mean the same dividend will be given during the next year. The larger companies tend to have more stable dividends than the smaller ones. The dividend is not the same as a company's total earnings. (See Chapter 4 for more about dividends and earnings.)

(3) The total number of shares traded that day, in 100s. This means you add two zeros to the number shown. On this particular day, 698,200 shares of AT&T were traded. Stock analysts watch these figures very closely. A sharp increase in the number of shares traded combined with a price increase means that a number of individuals and/or institutions are bullish on the stock. The reverse is true, of course, for a high volume of shares and a price decrease.

(4) The yield is the dividend divided by the stock price, expressed as a percent. In this case, $1.32 divided by $39\frac{7}{8}$ = 3.3%. This means if you invest in AT&T at the current price, you will get a cash return of 3.3% of your investment. This figure does not include the stock's increase or decrease in price over the past year—only the dividends.

(5) A company's earnings for the year divided into the current stock price results in a very popular figure called the *price-earnings ratio*, or P/E ratio. This number is watched very closely by many analysts. The idea is that if a firm's stock price falls but the earnings remain high, the stock is likely to rebound. In analyzing any stock, however, remember that the P/E ratio is only one of a number of things to consider. ("Earnings," you'll recall, refers to *total* yearly earnings, not dividends.)

(6), (7), (8) The high, low, and closing prices the stock traded at during the day. After these numbers, you will see the net change from the previous day (in *Barron's*, the numbers are weekly figures instead of daily).

The stock markets have not quite made it into the decimalized 20th century: prices are still quoted in fractions. To do any figuring on calculators, you must convert prices into decimals. A price of 20½ means $20.50 per share—or $2,050 for 100 shares; 20⅛ translates into $20.125; 100 shares at this price would be $2,012.50 (100 × $20.125). Prices of the costlier stocks will go up and down by quarters and eighths. The lower-priced issues often move in sixteenths, thirty-seconds, and, occasionally, sixty-fourths. See Appendix C for the decimal equivalents of the fractions.

(9) The net change in price from the previous day. In this case, one share of AT&T rose just an eighth of a point (12.5 cents) from yesterday's closing price. Notice, however, that during the day the price ranged from a low of 39⅝ to a high of 40.

Abbreviations

The papers have begun to improve on this score, but it can still be difficult to find a given company in the stock tables. Each firm has a code name called a *ticker symbol* in addition to its full name. General Electric is GE, for example, Apple Computer is AAPL, and so on. You need to use these symbols when ordering stock from your broker.

Unfortunately, the newspapers use neither the full names of the companies *nor* the ticker symbols, preferring instead to employ their own, often unintelligible combinations of the two. For example, *Barron's* lists Northeast Utilities (symbol NU) as NoestUt, Atlanta/Sosnoff (ATL) as AtalSos, and First Bank System (FBS) as FtBkSy. To make things more confusing, in searching for First Bank System in alphabetical order, you don't look for "FtBkSy," you look for "First": the listings are in the alphabetical order they *would* be in if the full name were used.

To their credit, the editors of *Investor's Business Daily* have made a real effort to list the company names intelligibly. Now, if the other papers would only follow suit, life would be made much easier for all of us, especially for the new investor trying to find GTE Corporation (GTE) in its proper alphabetical order. What they don't tell you is that companies whose names consist only of capital letters are listed at the *beginning* of their alphabetical letter. You will find GTE near the beginning of the G listings. You will *not* find IBM at the beginning of the I listings, however, because that company's name is still officially International Business Machines—you'll have to look under "International."

Scattered among the company names and assorted numbers in the stock listings are various letters: pf, n, s, wt, x, and many more. There are boxes at the beginning of the tables listing the various letter symbols and their meanings. These symbols are important. "Pf," for example, means preferred stock, which is quite different from common stock; "b" (in *Investor's Daily*) means the company is bankrupt, a rather significant thing to know if you're thinking of investing in it. Unfortunately, some of these letters mean different things in different papers—another good reason for finding one paper you like and sticking with it.

You will need to know the ticker symbols for each company when you watch the price quotes on the electronic display at your broker's or on the financial channels on TV. These displays are still called tickers after the old machines in the brokerages that would tick as they printed out the latest stock prices. (The paper tape from these machines was the same ticker tape that used to be thrown from windows of skyscrapers for parades. The tape made wonderful streamers.)

The ticker has a few more abbreviations. Here's an example of a ticker describing transactions on the New York Stock Exchange.

This display would be read as follows:

T	IBM		GE		T	PE	
40¼	5s	98	2,000s	75½	40⅜	2s 21¾	⅝

One hundred shares of AT&T (symbol: T) were traded at the price of 40¼ ($40.25 per share). When no quantity of shares is listed, you assume that it is 100 shares. In the next quote, IBM is trading at 98; "5s" means 500 shares were traded. Moving on, 2,000 shares of General Electric went for 75½. A hundred more shares of AT&T were traded, now at the price of 40⅜. Finally, 200 shares of Philadelphia Electric were traded at 21¾, followed by 100 more at 21⅝. In this case, the ticker has omitted the 21 because it's clear from the previous quote that the amount is 21⅝. The quantity of shares has been omitted, so you assume that it's 100 shares.

Occasionally, the ticker will fall behind; at these times, only the fractions will be displayed. You are expected to know that "T ¼" actually means "T 40¼."

STOCK MARKETS

The New York Stock Exchange (NYSE), the American Stock Exchange (AMEX), and the NASDAQ (National Association of Securities Dealers Automated Quotation system) are the markets listed in the papers. You may also see a regional exchange if there is one located nearby; for example, newspapers in the San Francisco Bay region list stocks of the Pacific Stock Exchange located in San Francisco.

The NYSE and the AMEX list about 3,000 stocks, NASDAQ another 3,000. The New York Exchange (sometimes called the "Big Board") accounts for about 80% of the volume of shares traded on the organized exchanges (excluding NASDAQ). These days, however, the over-the-counter (OTC) market, which includes the companies listed on NASDAQ and other small company stocks, accounts for a higher dollar volume of securities than the exchanges.

There are about 11,000 other stocks that you will not find listed in the newspapers. These make up the other part of the over-the-counter market. Most of these are so-called penny stocks—low-priced stocks of small companies. Brokers receive what are called pink sheets listing the daily prices of these stocks.

Many fine small companies are among those listed on the pink sheets, but there are also quite a few marginal ones. Unless you have personal knowledge of a specialized field or the prospects of a specific small company, it would generally be wise, as a new investor, to steer clear of the pink sheet stocks.

There are a couple of good reasons for this. First, it can be very difficult to measure risk in many cases, because of limited information about the small companies. In addition, a number of stock manipulations and other funny dealings have been associated with these lightly traded issues. Yes, the next Xerox or Apple Computer may be hiding among these issues, but it's a better bet that it's among the NASDAQ stocks.

If a pink sheet company starts to grow, it can apply for a listing with NASDAQ. This requires a certain amount of earnings, net worth, and a minimum share price now set at $3 a share (after listing, the price may drop below $3 without losing its listing).

If our former pink sheet company grows quite large, it can apply for admission to the American Stock Exchange or the New York Stock Exchange. Each has more stringent requirements for admission, with the New York Exchange being the most exclusive. The NYSE is where the big boys—General Motors, IBM, General Electric—hang out, though there are some very large, newer "blue chip" companies, like Apple Computer, that have elected to remain with NASDAQ.

BID AND ASK

When you buy almost any of the NASDAQ stocks, and quite a few of the thinly traded stocks on the exchanges, you will come across what is called the *spread:* the difference between the current price at which you can buy a stock and the price you can sell it for. These are the *bid and ask prices.* In the stock tables, you will see only one price—the "bid" price.

International Remote Imaging Systems (IRIS, NASDAQ) may be listed in the paper at $^{11}/_{16}$ (68.75 cents per share, or $68.75 for 100 shares). That $^{11}/_{16}$ is the bid price—the price "bid" by the broker who specializes in trading IRIS stock. This is the price you can sell it for if you already own it.

If you want to buy IRIS, you will be quoted another price when you call up your broker, in this case $^{13}/_{16}$ (81.25 cents per share, or $81.25 for 100 shares). This is the "ask" price—the price demanded by the specialist. This is the lowest price at which you can buy the stock.

The spread, in this case, is the difference between $^{13}/_{16}$ and $^{11}/_{16}$, or $^{2}/_{16} = ^{1}/_{8}$. This amounts to 12.5 cents per share, or $12.50 for 100 shares ($12.50 is the difference between the ask price of $81.25 and the bid price of $68.75). This $12.50 goes to the specialist; it does not go to your broker—the brokerage office gets its own commission from you. If someone wants to sell 100 shares of IRIS, this specialist will buy them for $68.75 and sell them to you for $81.25, pocketing the difference (not a bad business, eh?).

This spread is important to know about because it can add up to a substantial amount. If you bought 10,000 shares of IRIS, for example, your broker's commission would be about $300 (with a discount broker), but the spread would come to $1,250 ($8,125 minus $6,875). This means your IRIS stock will have to go up by about $^{3}/_{16}$ for you to recoup your $300 commission and the $1,250 spread. When buying a bid-and-ask stock, you need to think of yourself as already in the hole for whatever the spread is. Some spreads are as high as half a point (50 cents a share), some even more.

When buying the heavily traded stocks on the exchanges, and many on NASDAQ, you will buy and sell at the one quoted price—no need to worry about bid and ask.

INDEXES

"The Dow Jones Industrial Average rose ten and one-half points today in heavy trading, the S&P fell half a point, while the Major Market Index . . ."

Dow Jones averages? S&P? Major Market Index? Are these truly useful things, or simply more gobbledygook to confound the new investor?

Yes, the market indexes are important, because they show in which direction the markets are heading. And, unless the stocks or mutual funds you own are very unusual, they will be sensitive to the ups and downs of the market. Each index covers a different sector of the market.

The Dow Jones Averages

First of all, the granddaddy: the Dow Jones averages, started by Mr. Charles Dow in 1884. You will notice in the papers that there are actually four Dow Jones averages: the Industrial Average, the Transportation Average, the Utility Average, and the Dow Jones Composite Average, comprising the 65 companies included in the first three.

The Dow Jones Industrial Average (also known as DJIA, the DJs, or simply the Dow) is the one most often quoted. The DJIA is made up of 30 of the largest industrial companies from different sectors of the economy (such as IBM, AT&T, Sears, Exxon). Each day, the closing prices of these 30 stocks are added up and the numbers manipulated by a special formula. If the prices of the majority of these stocks rise during the day, then the DJIA will also rise, and the market will be said to have "posted a gain."

Many analysts are critical of the Dow as being too narrow a measure of the stock market. Some of the other indexes include many more companies, but for the purposes of most investors, the Dow is a good general indicator of where the markets are heading. With occasional exceptions, the other indexes head in the same direction—up, down, or sideways.

Other Indexes

- The Standard and Poors 500 (S&P 500) is a composite of four indexes monitoring 400 industrial, 20 transportation, 40 utility, and 40 financial companies. These 500 corporations account for approximately 75% of the total amount of equities in the U.S. market.

  The S&P 500 is made up of large companies on the American Exchange and NASDAQ, as well as the New York Exchange, so it gives a much broader indication of the market than the Dow does. It is the index that analysts always seem to use when making comparisons—for example, "This mutual fund outperformed the S&P 500 for the last five years."

- The AMEX Market Value Index measures the performance of more than 800 companies on the American Stock Exchange.

- The NASDAQ Composite Index keeps track of the over-the-counter stocks listed on NASDAQ (not the pink sheet stocks). This is the index that most often goes in a different direction from the Dow Jones Industrials. Investors often feel differently about the prospects for the smaller, more speculative companies listed on NASDAQ than they do about the giants monitored by the Dow.

- The Value Line Index and the Wilshire 5000 are the most inclusive indexes, including companies from the major exchanges and NASDAQ.

- In the financial papers, you will also find indexes for the major international stock markets. Among the most quoted are the British Financial Times

Industrial Index, the German DAX Index and the Japanese Nikkei Index.

The newspapers publish all kinds of statistics relating to the indexes: the percentage change from the previous day, the change over 12 months, graphs and charts showing the rise and fall of various averages over 30-year periods, charts of the volume of stocks traded and how this relates to the averages, etc., etc., *and* etc.

Serious investors will want to study these statistics to discover which ones are useful to them, and to get a better overall sense of the markets. The sheer volume of numbers, however, should persuade you to do this gradually. Don't get overwhelmed—it's not cost-effective.

What the new investor wants to achieve is a feel for the averages, and what makes them go up and down. In Chapter 20, we'll go into some of the reasons the stock market rises and falls. Right now, though, you can begin to get a feel for the market by watching the averages and noting the reasons the analysts give for the ups and downs.

Though it's useful to stay aware of the fluctuations in the stock market, it's also important for the long-term investor to take these fluctuations in stride. No matter how good the company or mutual fund, it will almost always be sensitive to a drop in the overall market. It is also true, however, that a good fund is likely to recover quickly when the market turns around. Don't get discouraged and sell at a loss simply because your stock fund has been dragged down by a bear market. Like the South, y'all gonna rise again!

OTHER KINDS OF INFORMATION

General economic and political information can be just as important as specific information about a company. Say

"The Market"

Analysts speak of "The Market" as if it were an entity unto itself. Everyone always seems to be trying to figure out what "The Market" is going to do. What the stock market actually *is*, of course, is no more than a vast conglomeration of individual investors, traders, and institutions driven by hopes, fears, and rumors.

It can be useful, though, to think of this monster as a separate entity, because not only is it affected by its investors, they, in turn, are affected by the market's ups and downs.

As an example, suppose IBM comes out with a very poor quarterly earnings report. Many investors decide to sell their IBM stock, and this causes the stock price to drop sharply. Because IBM is the largest corporation selling computers, other investors decide that IBM's poor earnings may be indicative of a slump in the entire industry and start selling stocks of other computer companies.

The Dow Jones Industrial Average starts to go down, because IBM is a major component of that index, and this makes investors wary of the entire market. Buying drops off and selling increases, driving the Dow down even further.

What has happened here is that some individuals and institutions reacted to the drop in IBM, and this reaction drove the market down. *Other investors then reacted to the fall in the market itself.* "The Market"—not IBM—was affecting these investors. This is why it's helpful to view the market as an individual entity.

this hot computer company is expanding its markets in China and the prospects look terrific. But what if there are signs that the political climate is changing in China and that American companies may be excluded? Similarly, what good will it do to research the best energy mutual fund if there is a growing oil glut which will depress oil prices and oil stocks?

Before long, by paying attention to national and international news, you will find yourself understanding and even occasionally anticipating market reactions. You will know, for example, that those strikes in the South African gold mines will probably drive gold prices up.

One thing that can discourage new investors, however, is how quickly the markets react. Before you can buy gold, or gold-mining stocks, you may find that the prices have already risen. Sometimes they rise weeks in advance in anticipation of an event. If many investors believe that the miners are going to go on strike, they will quickly bid up the price of gold.

One of the best things you can do is to keep your eye out for information that other people are not likely to see. For example, what area of the economy does your job or your interests make you an expert on? If the company you work for is involved in the wholesale food business, you might notice a growing number of orders for low-sodium, "healthy"-type foods. You can then begin to research which companies are producing these kinds of foods. You'll be surprised at the number of areas where you have a natural advantage over other investors simply because of your specific knowledge.

Just a further clarification about buying with the help of specific knowledge about a market, in this case the wholesale food market: This is *not* the kind of illegal "insider trading" you may have heard about. The illegal kind relates to buying or selling stock with inside knowledge of specific actions a company will take. For example, an officer of a corporation might know that his or her company is about to make an offer to buy another firm. If this person buys the second company's stock in anticipation that it will rise when the offer becomes public, that's illegal insider trading.

If you want information more quickly than the next day—if you plan to do the kind of hands-on investing that requires up-to-the-minute quotes—then you will be interested in the material in Chapter 22 on computers and data-retrieval systems. If you don't have and don't want a computer, there are various telephone data systems that will give you quotes on trades as they happen. These systems tend to be costly—$1 a minute is an average price. They can be extremely useful, though, if you're out and about but need to stay in touch with the markets.

Resources

Forecasts and Strategies, Philips Publishing Inc., 7811 Montrose Road, Potomac, MD 20854. (800) 777-5005. Mark Skousen, editor. Monthly. $139/year (but ask about special rates). Extras—additional books and articles—are usually included with subscriptions.

Mark Skousen is an economist and university professor. He was formerly an economic analyst for the CIA, however, and is a member of the White House press corps. Despite his Washington connections (or perhaps because of them!), he has quite a few unkind words for the policies of the Congress, the president, the IRS, and other government entities.

Skousen cuts through a lot of economic and political myths. I have found his newsletter to be a real breath of fresh air. The mix of economic analysis and excellent investment advice is exactly what new investors need. Highly recommended.

CHAPTER 9

FINANCIAL ADVISERS

S o . . . after reading this book and other materials, consulting with your friends and family, and considering the whole subject for a few months, you decide you would like to hire a financial adviser. What do you do now? The next step is to decide whether you want someone who will deal with your complete financial picture, or just your investments.

A *financial planner* will go over your entire financial life with you: your goals, your income, outgo, and possible budgets, insurance needs, tax planning, as well as investment strategies to reach your goals. Such a process can be extremely useful. If your finances have seemed like a mess, you'll be amazed at how good the ordering process can make you feel. A friend of mine once likened it to financial therapy.

Money is one of the two areas of life that people think and worry about the most. If this area is out of control, it can profoundly affect the rest of your life. There's no guarantee that putting it in order will help the other most common concern, i.e., love and sex, but it *is* a fact that money is the major source of disputes among couples.

In addition to helping you look at your overall financial picture, a planner may also manage your investments, if you choose. Or you can simply ask the planner to assist you in getting your financial house in order, then invest for yourself.

Suppose, on the other hand, you feel capable of handling your personal finances, but would like someone to manage only your investments for you. In this case, the person you would go to is an *investment manager*. After discussing at length your goals, investment preferences, and risk tolerance, the manager will invest your money for you and charge a fee for the service (the different kinds of fees are discussed below).

Your third alternative is to invest for yourself, but hire an *investment adviser*. With an adviser, you will do all the buying and selling; the adviser's role is just to provide information and advice.

The only fee charged by investment advisers comes from providing advice on various types of investments. As such, they need to be differentiated from the multitude of other people who may fill the role of adviser, such as stockbrokers or insurance agents. The difference—and it can be an important one—is that these latter two will get commissions if you buy on their advice.

Financial planners and advisers go by many different names and are licensed differently in different states. Whether they are called certified financial analysts, chartered financial consultants, registered investment advisers, or something else, however, they will generally fall into one of the above three categories.

HOW TO CHOOSE

Obviously, choosing a good financial adviser is not something to be undertaken lightly. There are two main things to consider when making this choice, in addition to a few technical considerations.

To begin with, of course, you want to be absolutely sure that the adviser you choose is competent and honest. There are some real turkeys in the profession, ranging from inept to out-and-out crooked. The first and best step is to get referrals from friends, family, or business associates. If someone you know well has dealt with an adviser for a few years (at least) and found this person to be honest and skillful, you're off to a good start.

But even though an adviser may come highly recommended by friends, *you* have to decide for yourself what you think about this person. Do you feel comfortable talking about your finances with him or her? Does it seem that the adviser is really listening? Do you *like* this person? It's important that you listen to your feelings, and not decide simply because you have heard how much money your friends have made. If you're comfortable with your adviser, the relationship is more likely to last and be fruitful.

If you are searching on your own, a good place to start is with the Social Investment Forum, listed in the Resources section in Chapter 12. In addition, the Funding Exchange, listed in the Chapter 2 Resources, will also help you find an adviser in your area. The individuals recommended by these organizations may be described as socially conscious advisers, but in reality they deal with all kinds of investments.

The reason I mention these places is that they subject their recommended advisers to an ongoing screening process. If a number of clients were to complain about any adviser, he or she would be dropped from the organization's list.

It's a good idea to interview a few different advisers (we are using the term "adviser" here for convenience—substitute "planner" or "manager" if that's who you are interviewing). Here are the questions you will want answers to:

1. Who are the adviser's clients? Are they roughly similar to you? Some advisers deal mostly with large institutional accounts; smaller accounts might be neglected because the profit to the manager would be less. If you know nothing about the adviser, you could ask for a few client names and phone numbers.

2. What professional registrations does the adviser have? Many states require that advisers demonstrate competence by taking various tests. In addition, the Securities and Exchange Commission (SEC) requires advisers to tell you in writing of their experience and education, the kind of work they do, and the manner in which they are paid. These things, together with information on any violations of the law, or bankruptcies, are contained in a document called the *ADV Form*.

   You can ask to see the adviser's ADV Form or you can send for a copy of it from the SEC, Public Reference Branch, Stop 1-2, 450 Fifth St. NW, Washington, DC 20549. Phone: (202) 272-7450.

3. How is the adviser compensated? By the hour? A fixed fee? Or is the fee based on a percentage of your assets to be managed? Fees can vary greatly and may depend partly on the size of your portfolio. Annual fees of 0.5% to 3% of total assets are common. Hourly rates may range from $50 to $300. However the fees are calculated, advisers who are paid by fees are called *fee-based advisers*.

   Advisers may also be compensated by commissions: they're called *commission-based advisers*. If the adviser charges only a small fee, or none at all,

Insurance "Advisers"

Recently, certain financial "advisers" have appeared on the scene whose main job is to sell insurance. These people are given a minimum of training by insurance companies and then sent out to masquerade as financial planners or advisers. You will recognize them by their great emphasis on all kinds of insurance.

Other planners will deal with insurance, too, but it will be only part of a balanced financial plan.

for a financial plan or for advice, it is probable the adviser will be receiving commissions from the companies he or she recommends.

For example, many of the large financial-planning firms and stock brokerages have their own in-house mutual funds and insurance programs. These mutual funds usually have fees, or loads, to buy in to them—which you will pay. Your adviser may get part of this load money as a commission. This is how you pay for his or her services, instead of paying an hourly fee.

There is nothing wrong or illegal about this, though the possibility for a conflict of interest exists here, as you may be directed toward the investments that pay the highest commission to the adviser.

For this reason, many people prefer to deal with advisers whose only income is based on fees. The reasoning is that such advisers will be more likely to concentrate on the best investments for the client, not on what will gain them the greatest commission.

My belief is that you should not rule out the commission-based adviser if you feel comfortable with him or her, think the planning program is a good one, and believe your interests will come first. Do take care to check out the recommended investments, though. That's why you're reading this book —so you can do this knowledgeably!

Smaller advisory firms or individual advisers are more likely to be fee-based, the ones in the larger firms commission-based. You will need to decide whether you want to deal with a large firm or a small office. This is essentially a matter of personal taste. Some feel more secure dealing with a large company, while others believe they will get more personal attention from a small firm or an individual.

4. If you opt for an investment *manager*—someone who will handle all your investing for you—you have to decide just how much control this person will have over your money. A *discretionary account* gives the manager the right to invest your assets without first obtaining your approval. With a *nondiscretionary account*, either you or the manager may decide on an investment, but you have to approve that it be carried out.

The new investor should know that the most flagrant abuses in the field come from managers who have been entrusted with their clients' money. In many states, financial planners and managers operate with a minimum of government supervision or certification. This is changing, but slowly; many people who call themselves "planners" or "managers" have actually had very little training or experience. Others are nothing but con artists. The North American Securities Administrators Association estimates that investors are cheated out of $500 million a year by dishonest financial managers.

This means that extraordinary care must be taken in investigating and choosing someone to

whom you will entrust your money. Alarm bells
should start sounding in your head if a planner:
a. insists that you open a discretionary account
b. promises high returns from risky investments
c. is not registered with the state regulators
d. is evasive about educational background or
experience

5. Finally, when interviewing advisers you will want to
discuss your investment preferences. You must be
sure, for example, that your adviser understands
your personal tolerance for risk. In the process, you
can ask about the adviser's performance record with
the kind of investments you choose.

If you are discussing investing in a portfolio of
mutual funds, for example, ask to see the past performance of the funds the adviser has chosen for
other clients' portfolios. The performance of the adviser's past recommendations should be compared
to that of other funds in the same investment categories.

If you are interviewing several managers or advisers, you can compare their performance figures.

One of the best ways of choosing a financial adviser is
by noting whether this person speaks *intelligibly*. Some
advisers will purposely make things sound difficult, so that
the client will feel confused and in need of advice. Others are
simply not good at making themselves clear.

Either kind of adviser is someone to avoid. Whether or
not you are managing your own portfolio, you absolutely
need to understand what's going on.

I think you will agree that finding a good adviser or manager is one of the more important steps you can take in becoming an investor. If you choose this route, the information
here should assist you in making a good choice.

Resources

Here are two excellent sources for financial advisers or planners:

The Social Investment Forum. See Resources, Chapter 12.

The Funding Exchange. See Resources, Chapter 2.

CHAPTER 10

REAL ESTATE: OWNING A HOME

"They ain't makin' any more of it."
—WILL ROGERS, ON WHY LAND
IS A GOOD INVESTMENT

W hat do you think of when you hear the words *real estate*? Hucksters? A safe place to invest? Or a good way to get rich? For years, real estate has been extremely popular with the average investor. Millions of people are investors simply through owning their homes.

There is a great deal to learn if you are interested in real estate, either as a home owner or an investor. The place to begin, though, is determining *whether* real estate is the right investment for you. We're going to start you off on that track in this chapter. If you decide you want to go ahead, the Resources at the end of this chapter and the next chapter list several recommended books and an excellent newsletter.

More people have invested in their own homes than in any other type of investment. Is owning a home for you?

Owning a home has generally been an excellent investment. Will Rogers might have added that in contrast to the breakdown in the land-producing industry, the people-creating industry is doing just fine. Once more, this is a question of supply and demand, so property has generally appreciated—and faster than the rate of inflation.

There are, of course, other factors to be considered—factors that the financial gurus like to call "intangibles"—such as the satisfaction of owning your own place. For every intangible on one side of the ledger, however, there is another one on the other. Many people, for example, consider being able to call up the landlord when the water pipes are spraying all over the kitchen to be a very important intangible. With the homeowner, the buck stops here—and there can be lots of bucks involved.

So should you invest in a home? There is much to be said for the financial advantages, but this is one of those decisions that depend a great deal on the intangibles. The important thing is not to rush into buying a home because everyone, especially your father-in-law, says you have to. "Look at all the money you're pouring down the drain in rent" is usually the argument.

Certain people are very happy owning their home and other people would rather rent. And even though they require more discipline than making monthly house payments, there *are* other excellent ways to invest your money.

Try making a list of all the things you would like about owning a home—and another one of the things you know you wouldn't like. Have you always dreamed of owning a home? Do you like to putter around trimming hedges and fixing odds and ends? (I believe that enjoying puttering is a prerequisite to happy home ownership, unless you can afford to hire people to maintain everything for you.)

You need to make a list of the finances involved, too. At today's high real estate prices, many individuals or couples find themselves with very large monthly payments—much more than rent for a comparable property. On the other hand, there are some excellent tax advantages to owning a home. In the next few pages, we'll discuss some of these pros and cons.

FIX-UP

Many people dream of buying an older home, fixing it up while living in it, then selling it and buying a more expensive one. I have done this and seen other people do it. It can work *if* you're willing to do much of the work yourself. If you have to hire contractors, the increase in value will generally not match the expense.

There are exceptions to this rule: In a rapidly appreciating real estate market, improvements can bring good returns. And a run-down building purchased at a very low price can also show a profit, even with professionals doing much of the work. The finances of such a project, however, need to be carefully worked out.

If you are reasonably skilled, enjoy this kind of work, and have enough spare time, you will probably do well—given a stable or appreciating real estate market. If you are inexperienced at fix-up work, have a full-time job, children, or other commitments, beware! Living in a construction zone and working on weekends is a good definition of a high-stress situation.

MORE PROS AND CONS

An argument can be made that buying a house is a kind of enforced savings account: you can't take your down payment out, and even though the monthly mortgage payments may be high, you are gaining *equity* by gradually paying off your loan. (Equity is the amount of the property you actually own. If you made a 20% down payment, you have a 20% equity in the property. The bank owns the other 80%.)

As the amortization schedules show, however, this equity buildup is significant only if you hold on to the house for a number of years. If you tend to move every few years, you won't gain very much equity, especially with a 30-year loan, because most of your payment goes toward the interest on the loan. This is important, because the average holding time for residential property these days is less than five years.

An argument can also be made for getting into a rising real estate market, even if you plan to move. If you buy a house and the prices in your area go up, you are able to buy another house more easily, because you can sell yours for more.

But buying in a high-priced housing market can be riskier than is generally believed. Suppose you pay $250,000 for your house, putting 20%, or $50,000, down. This will mean a loan of $200,000. A 30-year loan at 9.5% will leave you with payments of $1,680 a month plus about $250 in taxes (depending on your area) and $50 insurance, for a total of $1,980 a month.

Depending on your credit history, amount of debt, etc., etc., the bank will want your income to be at least $6,000 a month, or $72,000 a year. The general rule of thumb is that no more than one-third of your income should go to house payments ($1,980 is about one-third of $6,000).

On the plus side, there are important tax advantages to owning a home. The greater part of your mortgage payments in the early years of the loan go to pay interest on the loan. This interest is a deductible item on your federal income tax, which can mean substantial savings on your tax payment.

If you have a secure, high-paying job, or income from other sources, you may not worry about your ability to meet your mortgage payments. In the recession of 1990–91,

How an Amortized Home Loan Works

It's pretty simple. Each month you make the same payment; part of it goes to pay interest on the loan to the bank, and part of it goes to pay off the principal (the total amount you owe). At first, most of your payment will go toward the interest, but each month more and more will go to pay down the principal.

For example, if you borrow $100,000 at 10%, to be paid back over 30 years, your first monthly payment will be $877. Of that, $830 will go to pay the interest and $47 will go to pay down the principal.

Next month, however, the total amount you owe will be only $99,953, because you have paid off $47 of the loan. So, since you are charged 10% interest only on the amount you owe, the interest part of your payment will be slightly less. This time, you will still pay $877, but of that, $829.60, instead of $830, will be interest. This means $47.40 will go toward paying down the principal. The principal has now been reduced to $99,905.60.

This doesn't sound like much of a change, but it builds up over time. By the end of the second year, the principal has been paid down to $98,700. This means of your $877, $819.21 will go toward interest and $57.79 will be subtracted from the principal. The principal gets reduced very slowly on a 30-year loan.

Here's how the loans progress over a period of years. The dollar figures are the amount of the principal left to pay at the end of each year (the original principal being $100,000).

Year	2	5	10	15	18	20	25
20-yr	$96,300	89,300	72,000	44,400	20,300	0	
30-yr	$98,700	96,200	90,200	80,500	72,100	65,000	40,000

Notice how slowly the principal decreases during the first few years. And notice how much faster the 20-year loan gets paid off. At the end of 25 years, there is still $40,000 owing on the 30-year loan.

Monthly payments on a 20-year, $100,000 loan are $965, about $100 more than the $877 for the 30-year loan. But because the 20-year loan gets paid off 10 years earlier, you end up paying many thousands less in interest. At the end of 20 years, you would own the house free and clear, while a 30-year person would still be making payments.

This should make it clear that *if you plan to hold on to a house for a number of years, a shorter-term loan is in your best interest*. In fact, you will do better with the 20-year loan if you hold the house longer than five years. The amount of the loan you will pay off will more than offset the larger monthly payments.

At your local bookstore, in the section on real estate, you can probably find a small booklet that will tell you the monthly payments for an amortized loan of any amount at the prevailing interest rates. Ask for a payment table for monthly amortized mortgage loans. If you can't find a booklet there, you can contact Contemporary Books, 180 N. Michigan Ave., Chicago, IL 60601, (312) 782-9181. Ask for their *Monthly Interest and Amortization Tables* ($5.95).

however, a fair number of people lost their jobs and couldn't make their payments, and thus lost their homes and their equity when the banks were forced to foreclose on the loans and repossess the houses.

There were also those who wanted to move, but were caught in the falling real estate market. A common sight in

Is It for You?

Pros	Cons
Traditionally a good investment	Can be very expensive: payments, repairs, etc.
Enforced savings	Time consuming
Helps credit standing	Greater responsibility
Can borrow against equity	Ties up capital; in a down market, a house can be difficult to sell
Mortgage interest deductible on income tax (large item!)	Equity buildup is negligible if you move often
Personal satisfaction and other intangibles	More difficult to move quickly
Equity buildup	Risk of losing equity if you can't make payments
More freedom: remodeling, pets, gardens, etc.	
Greater security: can't be evicted at owner's whim	

those days was "For Sale" signs in front of houses with several asking prices crossed out and new, lower prices added.

So when I say that owning a home has generally been an excellent investment, I mean that *over time* residential property has tended to appreciate. Like the stock market, the real estate market experiences a good many ups and downs. If you're planning on buying and holding, these fluctuations won't bother you much. If you need to move often, they may interfere with your plans.

There is, as you can see, much to be considered in buying a house of your own. There is even more to consider if you are thinking of building. If you are leaning in either of those directions, I hope you will read some of the excellent literature listed below. These books will tell you how to go about buying or building—all the practical things to consider, once you've made your decision.

But I would like to emphasize again that, regardless of what your father-in-law says, it is *not* necessary to own a house to be financially stable or smart. There are arguments to be made on each side, and much comes down to the so-called intangibles—which really translate into personal preference.

Resources

Money Guide: Your Home by the editors of *Money* magazine. Andrews and McMeel, 1990. $6.95 (paperback).

This is my kind of book: short, easy to read, full of good information, but not overwhelming. All the necessary topics are covered: what to look for in a house, how to buy, how to finance, remodeling, selling. Some health considerations are also included: how to look for such things as asbestos and formaldehyde insulation. If you are thinking of buying, you can learn much of what you need to know in a couple hours.

How to Get a Mortgage in 24 Hours by James E. A. Lumley. John Wiley & Sons, 1990. $12.95. (paperback).

You don't have to need a mortgage in 24 hours to find this book useful. You will learn the essentials about the different kinds of loans available and where to find them.

If you finally decide that you want to buy a house, get this book before you start looking. Not only should you shop around for the best loan, you should get the whole process started before you actually find a house. The lender will want to check out any house you find, of course, but it's a good idea to establish relationships with prospective lenders in advance, have them look at your credit history, find out how much you can borrow, and so on.

That way, you can make an offer on a house, knowing you will be able to buy it. Desirable properties can sell very quickly; often, you need to be able to make an offer on the spot.

How to Plan, Contract and Build Your Own Home by Richard M. Scutella and Dave Heberle. McGraw-Hill, 1991. $16.95 (paperback).

This is a thorough treatment of the title subjects, enhanced by numerous illustrations. The book has a roomy quality to it: plenty of white space, with no clutter or confusion, kind of like a well-designed house. A very useful book for the prospective home builder.

CHAPTER 11

REAL ESTATE AS AN INVESTMENT

RENTAL PROPERTY

"HOW I MADE 10 MILLION DOLLARS IN REAL ESTATE WITH NO MONEY DOWN WHILE HOLDING TWO JOBS AND RAISING SIX CHILDREN—YOU CAN DO IT TOO!" It used to be that the hucksters in real estate were out selling swampland in Florida. Now they're selling get-rich-quick schemes. Their books, seminars, and home study courses make great profits seem ridiculously easy to obtain. And because there is usually at least some truth to their claims, they have an air of plausibility.

You can indeed make money in real estate. It takes quite a bit of time, energy, and, perhaps, a certain knack, but there are people who do it. The advantages of buying rental properties as investments are readily apparent. You can borrow up to 80% of the cost, sometimes more, and this gives you very high leverage. (*Leverage* is a favorite word in the investment world. A "highly leveraged investment" is simply

126 THE FIRST BOOK OF INVESTING

one in which you put down a small percentage of the purchase price and borrow the rest. Remember your high school physics? Using a lever, you can lift large weights with a minimum amount of energy.)

What this high leverage means is that you can buy a property worth $100,000 using only about $20,000 of your own money and borrowing the rest from a bank. This means that if the property should appreciate 20%, to $120,000, you would realize on paper a 100% appreciation on your investment of $20,000.

During the 1980s, when the value of property was rising fast in many areas, it was not unusual for property owners to realize this kind of increase or more in just a few years. You should note, however, that by 1990, in most areas, real estate appreciation had slowed dramatically and in some cases reversed. In the past, the appreciation has always come back, but sometimes you have to wait a few years for an increase in value.

There are certain substantial tax advantages to owning rental property. For example, on the assumption that your building decreases in value as it gets older, you are allowed to deduct this "loss"—or *depreciation*—from your income each year. In addition, if you make improvements, thereby increasing the value of the property, you can deduct the expense of the improvements from your income. Real estate can, therefore, be a good *tax shelter*, especially if you have a high income.

So why isn't everybody investing in rental property? Why aren't people beating down the doors of the real estate offices? One answer is that the great appreciation in real estate values has left rental income in the dust. In other words, in many areas, the yearly income from rents is no longer enough to cover the mortgage loan payments and other expenses.

Except in the areas where property values have not kept pace with the rest of the country, it is becoming difficult to buy a house, apartment building, or commercial property where the rents will cover expenses. This means out-of-pocket payments each month for the owner—something few people are prepared to do.

Being a Landlord

It takes a good deal of time, energy, and skill not only to acquire a good property but to manage it successfully. It also helps to have some knowledge of building repairs, or at least to know some good repairmen.

But most important, unlike stocks, bonds, or most other kinds of investments, rental property gets you directly involved with people. As a landlord, you suddenly find yourself mixed up in people's lives—and this can include their finances, their bad habits, or their occasional dishonesty.

I once owned several rental properties, and it was never easy. It was always something: So-and-so couldn't pay the rent because he lost his job; the sewer pipe had to be replaced, which meant the toilets and other fixtures couldn't be used for a week. I had to get a court order to force out one tenant who hadn't paid rent for six months. (In response to abuses by some landlords, the courts have made it difficult to evict tenants quickly, even for nonpayment of rent.)

Yes, you can check tenants' backgrounds, and yes, you can even get a management company to do it all for you (for a handsome fee). But you cannot control all the variables when you are dealing with people. Often you find yourself struggling with moral questions: Should you evict the family whose breadwinner just lost a job and can't make the rent payment? Or should you wait a month? Two months? Since you are probably depending on the rent to cover the mortgage payments, you can imagine the possible dilemmas.

I never enjoyed all the various difficulties that came with owning rental properties, and I'm happy to be out of the business. To my friend Bob, however, being a landlord was an entirely different experience. With a minimum of capital and a maximum of wheeling and dealing, Bob managed to acquire half a dozen different houses, some of which he divided into two or more units. He had skills as a designer, carpenter, and general handyman, so he was able to do much of the remodeling and repairs himself.

What made him even more suited to the rental business, though, was that he *enjoyed* it. He was your basic hands-on landlord; I remember driving around with him in one of his beat-up cars to visit a few properties. He would fix a water heater at one place, dicker about rent with a tenant at another (in the process, getting into a long, totally unrelated conversation), then meet with a prospective tenant at yet another. He had his own unorthodox style that worked well for him.

It's not necessary to be a character like Bob to succeed in the property rental business, but you should enjoy dealing with people. It also helps to have some understanding and patience with such things as stoves, furnaces, and leaky roofs.

RAW LAND

Sounds kind of unappetizing, doesn't it? But I prefer this term to "undeveloped land," because the latter makes it sound as if development is inevitable. Whether raw land is an appealing addition to your holdings depends on your needs.

Buying land is like making any other investment in that plenty of research is necessary. It's not enough to buy and hold, hoping that population growth will eventually drive the price up. You could wait a long time in the states that are losing population.

The best places to buy, of course, are in the areas that appear due for development. The price of land can appreciate dramatically when developers get interested.

While good returns are possible with this strategy, the new investor needs to know that it is not always easy to pick which areas are going to grow. There are experienced speculators who lose their shirt trying to do this. A city's expansion may turn in another direction, or the economy may go sour, putting developments on hold. In the meantime, the landholder is stuck with payments on a loan, taxes, and no income from the investment. A risky business, this.

As with other real estate investments, then, buying land should be something you do after you have learned a good deal about it, done the necessary research, and feel comfortable with the risks.

IF IT STILL LOOKS GOOD TO YOU . . .

If the prospect of owning real estate—income property or land—still looks good to you, do take note of the Resources section at the end of the chapter. If you are thinking of buying rental property, a subscription to John Reed's newsletter is a good place to make your first down payment.

We have covered just a few basic things here; there is much more to know and consider. Find a friend or acquaintance who owns property and make a nuisance of yourself by asking every conceivable question. If you are thinking about buying either a home or an income property, you will need to consult with a tax expert on your specific tax situation.

It's a good idea to decide what kind of building you want, what areas you like, and how much you want to pay *before* you start talking to real estate agents. Most agents I have known have been straight, honest people, ready to help you find the right piece of property for your needs. As salespeople, though, they have their own agendas: they have properties they are interested in selling, and may steer you toward them.

If you are sure of what you want, however, you are much more likely to be shown only those properties that fit your needs and your budget.

Those who inherit a piece of real estate are often unacquainted with the market in the area where it is located. Under these circumstances, it's a good idea to have the building appraised by an independent real estate appraiser. This should be done before approaching a real estate agent about selling the property.

OTHER WAYS OF INVESTING IN REAL ESTATE

REITs

There are real estate investments that involve less responsibility and fewer hassles than rental property or raw land. These methods are good for people with less money to invest. For example, *real estate investment trusts*, or *REITs*, are essentially closed-end mutual funds that invest in specific areas of the real estate market. They are listed on the exchanges and on NASDAQ and can be purchased through a stockbroker.

REITs may be *equity trusts*, which buy, sell, and rent out properties, *construction and development trusts*, which give short-term loans to developers, or *mortgage trusts*, which give long-term loans to real estate investors.

Remember that even though you may be relieved of the responsibilities of direct management, your success as an investor in an REIT still depends on the general market for real estate—and on the skill of the managers. Many REITs have not done well over the last decade and have, therefore, achieved a bad reputation in much of the investment community.

There are some sound ones out there, but you need to check certain things very carefully. All the following questions should be answered to your satisfaction before investing money in a trust or partnership:

Have the distributions or dividends been paid on time— and have they been up to the original projections?

Has the cash flow increased?

Are the economic conditions good in the areas where the properties are located?

Are the properties themselves of a high quality?

In a partnership, does the management have an active repurchase plan so that you can sell your shares if you want to? (very important!)

Are the managers reputable, skillful businesspeople?

I think a well-run REIT is an appropriate place for a small amount of a portfolio. It makes for a healthy diversification into real estate, without the kind of day-to-day management details of owning property on your own. The answers to the above questions *must* look good, however. Too many people have lost money because they didn't ask them.

Partnerships

It is also possible to invest in a *real estate general partnership*. This is organized by a *general partner* who buys and manages the properties. You, as an investor, are a *limited partner*. As such, your liability is usually limited to your original investment, though you will share in the profits and losses. There are some tax advantages similar to those for owning your own property, but these are complex enough that you should consult with a tax expert.

Public partnerships are registered with the Securities and Exchange Commission; you can buy them through your broker. Watch out—there will be a "load" to get in. There are also private partnerships, which you can learn about from brokers, from newspaper advertisements, or by word of mouth.

Real estate partnerships have fallen into disrepute in recent years because of abuses by some general partners. The regulatory agencies are trying to make it more difficult for investors to be cheated, but until that happens you would do well to avoid investing in a limited partnership.

Mutual Funds

As you might imagine, there are real estate mutual funds—though only a few. These differ from the REITs in that they are open-end mutual funds which invest in many different kinds of firms associated with real estate. A real estate fund portfolio might include real estate brokerage companies, building companies, and different kinds of REITs.

You would buy in to a real estate fund if you expected the construction and sales of homes and commercial buildings to do well. You might also buy in, however, simply because a fund has performed well—and shows good prospects for the future. For example, since the real estate downturn started in 1989, the managers of the Fidelity Real Estate Fund have managed to focus their investing on areas of the market that *are* doing well, such as REITs specializing in health care properties. In spite of the generally depressed market, this fund has done well during the last three years.

If you feel bullish about the real estate market, a real estate mutual fund is a good place for a new investor to start. As you learn more about the market, you could expand into the more specialized REITs.

Low-Income Housing

For those who can benefit from tax credits, the government still offers a break to investors in partnerships that build or refurbish housing for low-income tenants. The annual tax savings from these partnerships can be as much as 13% to 15% a year, depending on your tax situation. And this is on top of any income you may receive from the partnership.

There are rules about who is eligible for the tax credits. You will need to check with a tax adviser to see if you could benefit. And whether these credits will still be around in a few years is anyone's bet—again, a good tax adviser will be able to tell you if they are still in existence.

These low-income housing projects should be of special interest to those wishing to invest in a socially responsible manner. You will be helping to provide housing for people in need. Some (not all) of the housing complexes are operated on a nonprofit basis. But all of them must keep their rents at a low-income level for 30 years; after that, they may be kept at those levels or increased.

Remember that list of questions in the section above on REITs? In buying in to these partnerships, you need to ask the very same questions. Be sure you get good answers.

Second Mortgages

Another way of getting at least halfway involved in real estate is to lend money to those needing to finance properties. Banks or other institutions are usually the holders of the main loan on a house, the "first" mortgage. Home buyers sometimes need additional financing, however, and take out a second loan, using their house as collateral. This loan is called a second mortgage. Second mortgages are often held by individual investors who are attracted by their relatively high rate of return.

In larger cities, it's possible to invest in second mortgages through finance companies, which guarantee the loans. This is a relatively safe way of getting 10% to 13% on your money—if you are satisfied that the finance company is sound and well managed.

The only problem could arise in a severe recession that caused many people to default on their mortgage payments. This could put a strain on the company that guarantees the loans.

It's also possible to get 15% or more on your money by buying second mortgages directly from other lenders. Often a holder of a second mortgage will want to cash out and will sell the contract at a discount. If you buy the contract, you will then be the one to receive monthly payments from the homeowners who are paying off the loan. Needless to say, this requires thorough research into the value of the property and the creditworthiness of the homeowners. Anyone lending money for second mortgages should have a good knowledge of real estate and be wealthy enough to absorb possible losses.

Resources

John T. Reed's ***Real Estate Investor's Monthly,*** P.O. Box 27311, Concord, CA 94527. (800) 635-5425. Monthly. $121/year.

If you are thinking of buying property as an investment, then you need John T. Reed's newsletter, which has received good reviews from such well-known financial writers as Jane Bryant Quinn, who calls him smart and witty. It's a good bet that any aspect you can think of concerning the buying, managing, and selling of income property has been or will be covered in the newsletter.

A subscription to Reed's newsletter gets you a list of the topics covered in back issues. You will also receive a description of the various books and cassette tapes written or recorded by Reed, such as *How to Manage Residential Property*, *Real Estate Investment Strategy*, *Aggressive Tax Avoidance for Real Estate Investors*, and *High-Leverage Real Estate Financing*. There are others, all of them very useful to the would-be investor.

Reed can be quite outspoken in support of issues he feels strongly about. You may not agree with everything you read in the newsletter (I don't). But you don't have to agree with his opinions to follow his excellent advice on practical matters.

The subjects covered in the newsletter, the books, and the tapes are the nuts and bolts of real estate investing. They stand in sharp contrast to the dubious books and seminars that claim making a fortune in real estate is easy. It's not.

PART 2

INTERMEDIATE INVESTING

CHAPTER 12

SOCIALLY RESPONSIBLE INVESTING

A friend of mine recently decided to become a socially responsible investor. He realized that while he was donating money to organizations dedicated to saving marine mammals, he owned stock in a company that was killing dolphins with its fishing practices.

Socially responsible investing—also known as ethical investing, socially conscious investing, or simply social investing—has been around for most of this century. In the mid-1970s, however, growing concern about social issues and the environment caused a large number of people to look closely at what they were investing in. The movement has developed during the last 15 years into a major force in the investment world.

The social investor seeks out companies that are concerned with the social and environmental consequences of their manufacturing and marketing practices. This investor avoids companies that pollute the environment, produce products damaging to health (such as tobacco, alcohol, or weapons of war), neglect the welfare of their workers, or support repressive regimes (such as those that do business with South Africa).

In a sense, investing is, by itself, a socially responsible thing to do. By taking the money out from under your mattress and providing capital for businesses, you are helping to provide jobs and increase the general prosperity. Socially responsible investing simply carries this idea one step further.

Businesses dedicated to preserving or enhancing the natural and social environments will tend to increase the general prosperity over the long term. Businesses whose operations damage the natural, political, or economic environments, however, create problems that will cost us all dearly in the future.

Operations that threaten the environment can damage the company as well. Witness the massive debts piled up by the utility companies that built nuclear power plants without adequate research into the dangers of a breakdown, or the proper disposal of nuclear waste. Investors in these utilities took a bath when the public began to become aware of the dangers and influenced state governments to prohibit the operation of the nuclear facilities.

On the other hand, care and foresight in the areas of social concern seem to be the same skills that help a company grow. This is not surprising: A work force in tune with management will generally be more productive; a company employing successful techniques in dealing with environmental problems probably has the same kind of talented people working on its technological innovations.

In addition, many companies have discovered that an increasingly aware public will snap up their environmentally friendly products. Conversely, firms perceived as being careless with the environment (such as Exxon after the Valdez oil spill) find themselves dealing not just with expensive cleanup operations, but public boycotts and angry regulatory agencies.

RESPONSIBLE = PROFITABLE

For years, the myth circulated in the conservative investment community that social investing meant giving up good profits. Socially conscious investors were dismissed as do-gooders or even anti-business radicals.

With this in mind, Ritchie Lowry, the editor of the *Good Money* newsletter (see Resources), started a *Good Money* Industrial Average. To be parallel with the Dow Jones Industrial Average, which is made up of 30 large, blue chip corporations, he also chose 30 large corporations for his index. *These* corporations, however, were chosen for their positive social and environmental records.

Lowry started this average in 1981, but figured the averages back to 1976. During the 15 years from 1976 to 1991, the Dow Jones Industrial Average increased by about 200%. The *Good Money* Industrial Average, however, went up by a dramatic 600%! Score one for the do-gooders!

The success of companies with good social and environmental records has not gone unremarked by the forces of conservative investing. Nothing makes Wall Street sit up and take notice like investments that beat the averages.

Fortune magazine, which once sneered at socially conscious investing as "insignificant do-good nonsense," now runs articles like "Environmentalism: The New Crusade." It reports how "smart companies" are realizing unexpected profits by responding to environmental concerns.

Nothing speaks louder than success. Socially responsible investing has come into its own.

CHOOSING CONSCIOUSLY

Investing in a socially conscious manner can sometimes be difficult. If you want to avoid companies that invest in countries like South Africa, employ unfair labor practices, produce weapons, or damage the environment, you will have to research them very carefully. For example, that utility company building a solar electric plant may also own several nuclear power plants. The corporation that deals so fairly with its employees may also be a large military supplier.

How about smaller companies? Many of these may be suppliers of parts for military hardware built by the large corporations. Certain small companies in the biotech sector have done very well for their investors during the past few years. Biotechnology, however, usually means testing new products on animals—a process that can involve cruel, often torturous techniques.

Each new investor needs to decide what is acceptable to him or her. These days, there is a lot of help available— the books and newsletters listed at the end of the chapter will inform you about the social and environmental stances of the companies they consider to be socially responsible.

One thing the new investor needs to know is that the various socially responsible mutual funds use quite different "screens" to determine which companies to invest in. You will have to decide by reading a fund's prospectus whether you agree with the managers' philosophy.

You also need to be aware that some funds calling themselves "environmental" actually invest in some of the largest polluters. The *Good Money* newsletter publishes a *Social Funds Guide* that will help you choose the funds which invest in companies with a true social conscience.

THE POWER OF THE BALLOT

Some investors feel their investment choices become too limited when they leave out all the companies that are not entirely socially conscious. Many of the larger corporations, for example, have areas where their social concerns are lagging.

There is, however, yet another way of exercising your social concerns. When you buy equities, you become part owner of the firm. As such, you have a vote in the affairs of the company. (Only holders of common stock can vote; preferred stock or bonds carry no right to vote.)

If you have owned at least $1,000 worth of stock for 12 months, you are eligible to vote. Within a year of buying stock in a company, you will get a notice of the next shareholders' meeting and the issues being put to a vote. Often, some of these issues have to do with social or environmental concerns.

You can usually vote by mail—you don't need to attend the meeting in person. The issues up for voting are usually placed on the agenda by individual shareholders who have formed groups, or blocs, large enough to have some influence. Your number of votes is almost always equal to the number of shares you hold. So your 100 shares in General Electric may not seem like much, but by joining a bloc of a few thousand other shareholders, you can have a major impact.

Do you think GE is placing too much emphasis on marketing its nuclear technology? Do you believe nuclear power is not only a danger to the environment but a bad investment for the corporation? Well, so do quite a few other shareholders. So far, in this particular case, there haven't been enough who feel this way to change company policy, but who's to say what might happen in a few years?

As you can see, then, there is an alternative to completely avoiding companies involved in activities you disagree with. More and more people are coming to believe that the private sector must take greater responsibility for the social and environmental problems it helps create. As this number grows and includes more shareholders, even the great multinational corporations will be strongly affected.

The Securities and Exchange Commission regulates the procedure by which shareholders can place an issue on the ballot for the annual shareholders meeting. To learn this procedure, send for "The Shareholders Proposal Process," a 16-page guide distributed by the United Shareholders Association, 1667 K St. NW, Suite 770, Washington, DC 20006, (202) 393-4600.

SOCIALLY CONSCIOUS SOUL-SEARCHING

Socially responsible investing may prompt you to do more than a little soul-searching. There are many ways in which we, as investors, can express our concerns. Just how socially conscious do you want to be with your money? Are there areas you feel more strongly about than others? How would you feel about investing in a company that was involved in a practice you disagreed with?

What about investments that might be termed socially neutral, such as rare coins? Do you want any neutral investments, or do you want all your money to be at work in socially conscious ways?

Do you want to lend money to the federal government by buying government bonds, thereby encouraging further deficit spending? Do you want to put your savings in a large bank, where it might be lent to socially irresponsible corporations? Or would you rather it be in a community-based credit union?

There's a lot to consider when contemplating socially responsible investing, but the knowledge that your money is at work in a manner helpful to the world, or at least undamaging to it, can be a powerful source of satisfaction. And, as we have seen, it can also be of great benefit to your portfolio.

Resources

The socially concerned investor can count on a large and growing number of individuals and organizations who will lend moral support and practical advice. In the Resources section of Chapter 2, you will find a listing for the Funding Exchange. This is a national network of foundations whose concerns include socially responsible investing.

Contacting a member foundation near you will put you in touch with most of the resources you will need to get started. These resources include advice, reading material, contact with other concerned investors, and names of investment advisers and brokers who specialize in responsible investing.

Good Money: The Newsletter for Socially Concerned Investors, Good Money Publications Inc., Box 363, Worcester, VT 05682. (800) 535-3551. Bimonthly. $75/year. Subscriptions include an annual index, occasional supplements and reports, and *Netback*, a newsletter of "opinion, controversy, and networking announcements."

Good Money also publishes various handbooks at additional cost, such as *Good Money's Social Fund Guide*. This guide shows how the managers of the ethical mutual funds choose the companies for their portfolios, which is very useful if you plan to invest in funds, because the methods for choosing fund portfolios are often very different. And, of course, you will want to know which funds have been the most successful.

Good Money is a handsome, well-put-together newsletter, full of helpful information for the socially responsible investor. With all their additional supplements, it's a real bargain.

Good Money: A Guide to Profitable Social Investing in the 90s by Ritchie Lowry. W. W. Norton, 1991. $19.95 (hardcover).

Ritchie Lowry, the president of Good Money Publications, is a pioneer in the field of social investing. This is an inspiring book, partly because the goal—the preservation and improvement of life on Earth—is so worthy, partly because responsible investing is already beginning to have some success in moving the business community toward that goal. Lowry takes the reader through some of the history and goals of the movement, then turns to the practical task of identifying which investments are truly responsible—and which are likely to be the most profitable. There is even a chapter on the growing international social investing movement.

If you really want to know more about this subject, this is your book.

Social Investment Forum. 430 First Ave., North, Suite 204, Minneapolis, MN 55401. (617) 451-3252. Membership: $35/year. Membership includes their Guide, which lists all members, including 250 financial professionals, ethical mutual funds, and other information pertinent to responsible investing. Members also receive a quarterly newsletter.

The Guide—and the newsletter, which provides updates on new members—are good places to find a financial adviser or manager with social concerns. The Forum also holds quarterly meetings on such topics as "Clean and Green" (environmental investing).

Chapter 13

International Investing

F or years, only the very rich invested in foreign countries. But recently, with what the economists like to call the "globalization" of world markets, it has become much easier to put money into foreign assets. This is fortunate, because most of the major world economies have done much better than the U.S. over the past two decades; some, like those of Japan and other Asian countries, have risen at an astonishing rate. Even during the bull market of 1985 to 1990, the U.S. stock market finished 16th out of 18 major world stock markets.

It's my opinion that any medium to large portfolio should be invested at least 15% to 20% in foreign assets. Investing only in the U.S. has the same disadvantages as investing in only one stock; that is, you don't have enough diversification in your portfolio. During the 1970s, for example, after correcting for inflation, the U.S. stock market as a whole was actually worth less at the end of the decade than at the start. A balanced portfolio that included investments in the major foreign economies, however, would have ended up comfortably on the plus side.

To be an international investor these days, it's not necessary to open an account in London or Zurich (although you can, if you like the idea). There are several ways to put money into foreign corporations and other investments without going any further than your own stockbroker. The first, and easiest, way is by means of our friends, the mutual funds.

MUTUAL FUNDS

International funds and global funds—that's what you're looking for. The international funds are more truly international; the global funds may have as little as 25% of their assets in foreign securities—be sure to check the prospectus. There are a growing number of these funds and they invest in all sorts of different markets. There are funds that invest in the Pacific Basin, some that specialize in Japan, others in Europe, and quite a few that invest in companies all over the world. Some invest only in stocks, some in bonds, others in both.

You can find the best-performing international funds the same way you find the best domestic funds (see Chapter 6). You will also find a few suggestions in the realm of international funds in Appendix A. Again, however, be aware that the best-performing funds over the last year or 10 years may not be the ones to buy now.

Good examples of the wisdom of this warning are the funds that invest heavily in Japanese stocks. During the 1980s, buyers of these funds made out like bandits because the Japanese economy was on its way into orbit. In 1990 and 1991, however, the stock market came back down to earth —hard. At one point, the Nikkei stock index had lost almost half its value from a year earlier. Needless to say, the own-

ers of the Japanese-based mutual funds were extremely un-
happy. So do your best to look to the future and not just the
past.

These days, the European funds look promising. As
Europe moves toward greater economic unity and Eastern
Europe opens up, the prospects seem excellent for Western
European corporations. Right now, however, this rosy picture is clouded by the war in former Yugoslavia, and the possibility of unrest in the former Soviet Union. If you do invest
in European equities in any form, keep your eye on the international news.

CLOSED-END COUNTRY FUNDS

Most mutual funds are known as open-end funds because
there is theoretically no limit to the amount of shares they
can sell. Closed-end funds are similar to the open-end
mutual funds in that they are investment companies which
own a portfolio of stocks in different companies. The closed-
end funds, however, sell only a limited number of shares,
like most corporations, and the shares are traded on the
stock exchanges. For this reason, they are called "publicly
traded funds."

Some closed-end funds invest in a portfolio of American
stocks. Others—the "country funds"—invest in stocks of a
certain country. There is a closed-end fund for almost every
country with a major economy and some for smaller
economies, like the Irish Investment Fund. The share prices
of these funds may be found among the stock listings; the
financial papers also list them in a special section, usually after the open-end mutual funds.

The country funds provide a way of investing in individual world economies, but they are ornery investments,
kind of like untrained horses. A case in point: You see that
the Korean economy is doing well, so you buy 100 shares of

the Korea Fund at $25 a share. Almost immediately, the Fund shoots up to $35 a share and you are accepting congratulations all around. But then, a month passes and you open up the paper one day to discover that the share price has dropped to $22. "Impossible!" you exclaim, but, over the next couple of weeks, the price continues to fall, bottoming out at $12.

"What happened?" you demand of your broker, or whoever is handy. "Did I blow it in researching the Korean economy?" No, Korea still looks like a winner. Lots of Hyundais and computers. What happened was this: suddenly, a large investor (a) decided he had made a good profit and it was time to sell his shares in the fund; (b) read an account—along with other investors—of how other Asian economies were challenging the Koreans; or (c) learned that his friend's Hyundai had just broken down.

When this investor sells his 50,000 shares and the stock begins to fall, other investors decide somebody must know something they don't, and begin to sell *their* stock. Pretty soon, everyone's jumping ship and nobody wants to buy except at a very low price—so the stock goes down to $12 a share. In such ways are financial decisions often made in the World of Investment.

This kind of thing can happen with any volatile stock, but it seems to happen with regularity among the country funds. The figures above are not fictitious; in 1990, shares in the Korea Fund had a high of $37 and a low of $11. Meanwhile, the Korean economy, despite a few ups and downs, remained generally strong.

How to Buy Something for Less Than It's Worth

As we explained in Chapter 6, the net asset value of an open-end mutual fund is the total value of its assets divided by the number of shares outstanding. A greater demand for shares does not increase the net asset value because new shares are issued as more people buy in to the fund. There is an unlimited supply of shares. The story is different, however, in the case of closed-end funds.

Closed-end funds figure their net asset values in the same way as the open-end funds. But in the financial tables, you will notice *two* prices listed after these funds—the net asset value and the share price—and these prices are usually different. This means that often you can buy shares of a fund for *less* than their net asset value.

How can this be? It can be because we're back to supply and demand again. These funds are called "closed-end," remember, because they issue a limited number of shares. If investors decide that the Korea Fund is a hot property, there will be more buyers for this limited number of shares—and their price will be bid up, regardless of the net asset value.

In the closed-end listings, you will notice yet a third figure, after the NAV and the price. This is the percent of difference between the net asset value and the price per share. If the price is 10% more than the NAV, it is said that the fund is trading at "10% over net asset value"; if the price is 10% less, it is trading at a "10% discount to net asset value."

The Korea Fund has been so much in demand at times that its price has been 150% over net asset value! On the other hand, in November 1990, the NAV of the Turkish Investment Fund was $11, but the price of a share was only $7.75. The fund was trading at about a 30% *discount* to net asset value.

There are two things to consider, then, when buying a closed-end fund: whether the companies it owns will do well *and* what investors *feel* about the chances for the fund. This is an excellent example of what the new investor (or any investor) needs to consider in making any purchase. An individual company, for example, may have a fine balance sheet and terrific prospects, but the price of its stock won't go up until the investment community decides it's a good buy.

In the case of the closed-end country funds, their prices will go up according to how well their country's economy is performing *and* whether investors believe that economy will perform well in the future.

Some advisers will tell you to jump at the chance to buy funds trading at discounts to their net asset values, but I have reservations. I see the situation as no different from that of any good company whose share price has been driven down by fears and misperceptions. Such companies can be sound investments, especially if you're willing to wait a while, but their stock will start to rise only when investor sentiment changes.

If you are willing to wait and take a little risk, watch for the funds of countries with strong economies that are currently in disfavor with investors. When the shares start trading at a 10% discount to net asset value or more, that's the time to do some research on the country in question.

If the prospects for the economy look good, then take a look at the share prices and the net asset values of the fund over the last few months. Is the present price higher than the lowest price during this period—or is the fund still on its way down? If it's turned the corner, now is the time to buy if you're interested. All you need is a little luck and a change in investor sentiment.

The luck is often easier to come by than a change in sentiment. The investing public as a whole is not always known for its rationality. The meteoric rise and fall of the country funds provides one of the best illustrations of how *perceived* value can often be more important than *real* value in determining what people will pay for a given stock in the marketplace.

For the new investor, open-end mutual funds are the best places to start your international investing career. As you begin to get a feel for the international markets, a few well-researched country funds would be appropriate for a small amount of your portfolio.

Eventually, however, if you find that you enjoy sending your money on world tours, you will want to invest in individual companies. One simple way of doing this is to buy ADRs.

ADRs

In order to make it easy for Americans to invest in them, many foreign corporations—large and small—trade shares on American stock exchanges. These shares are called *American depository receipts*, or ADRs.

Despite a rather complex arrangement between international banks that makes this possible, buying ADRs is very much like buying any other stock. The advantage to buying in to a foreign corporation in this way is that you avoid such difficulties as transferring your money abroad, and foreign taxes on dividends and on capital gains.

There are over 600 ADRs traded in this country. The financial papers list those of the larger corporations. Your broker should have a more complete list, if you are interested.

It's important to remember that whether you buy an ADR or stock in the same corporation on an exchange in its own country, you are buying in to that country's economy. In unstable political climates, economies can change overnight. If you buy shares of Benguet Corporation, for example, you are speculating not only on gold-mining and engineering projects in the Philippines, but also on the often violent politics in that country. A revolution would almost certainly bring about economic turmoil, resulting in a sharp fall in the Philippine peso as well as a sharp devaluation of stock prices.

Such factors also have to be considered when buying open-end mutual funds that specialize in only one or two countries, and in buying the closed-end country funds. As you might imagine, the First Philippine Fund is one of the most volatile of the country funds.

TRADING IN INTERNATIONAL MARKETS

It is possible to open a trading account almost anywhere in the world. Through brokerage houses and banks, you can buy securities, foreign mutual funds, precious metals, and real estate—in short, just about anything you can buy in this country. Some international investors open savings accounts in countries where interest rates are higher than in the U.S. and/or the currency seems likely to appreciate against the dollar.

Opportunities are excellent for those who know what they're doing. There is a fair amount to learn, because international investing involves certain complexities that are necessary to know about: Tax rates, rules about taking money out of a country, different investment procedures, and, of course, different languages are just a few of the things confronting the international investor.

This is not to discourage you, however. I think foreign markets are eminently worth knowing about. The material listed at the end of this chapter will give you a good start, if you're interested. It's not all that difficult to learn—it's just a good idea to know as much as you can before putting down any real money.

As you become more knowledgeable about and comfortable with international markets, you can start looking for a good international broker. As a rule, only the large brokerages such as Merrill Lynch and Dean Witter have international divisions. Once you have found a broker, he or she can trade securities for you on exchanges in almost any country. And because these are full-service brokers, you can discuss your proposed purchases with them, or consider their recommendations.

CURRENCY

The new international investor needs to know that each country's currency is constantly going up or down in value compared to other currencies, because of the performance of a country's economy relative to the economies of other countries.

If you make an investment in a foreign country, you have to buy units of that country's currency with dollars. Should the value of that country's currency go down relative to the dollar, the value of your investment also goes down. When you come to sell your investment and change the foreign currency back into dollars, you will get fewer dollars than you put in.

The reverse is also true. If you had bought German marks in 1988, used this money to invest in German stocks, and then sold them two years later, you would have realized a 20% profit on the currency exchange alone because during that time, the German mark appreciated 20% against the dollar. The stock of the companies you bought was priced in marks, and in 1990, changing these marks back into dollars gave you 20% more dollars.

This means that when you invest abroad, you need to consider more than just the type of investment. You need to have a feeling for how well that particular foreign currency is likely to do against the dollar.

Some investors buy foreign currencies simply because they think they will appreciate against the dollar. There are different ways of doing this, but the complexities of international currency speculation go beyond the scope of this chapter. *The Global Investor*, listed in the Resources section,

has an excellent chapter on currencies and exchange
rates.

Starting out in mutual funds that invest internationally
avoids this whole problem. You don't have to worry about
the currency exchanges, the managers of the funds do.
That's what you're paying them for.

INTERNATIONAL SOCIAL INVESTING

The number of environmentally aware corporations and investors is growing all over the world. The movement is particularly strong in Europe.

For those who want to carry their social concerns into
international markets, Ritchie Lowry's book *Good Money*,
listed at the end of Chapter 12, discusses social investing in
other countries. Lowry lists the organizations the socially responsible investor can contact in each country.

Don't let the seeming complexities of foreign markets
keep you from the opportunities. Investing abroad can be
not only profitable but fascinating. Suddenly, you may find
yourself listening to the BBC, or reading some obscure journal on the economies of the Far East. International investing
is a constant reminder of how interdependent the world has
become, as well as how fast it is changing.

Resources

Dessauer's Journal, Limmat Publications Inc., P.O. Box 1718,
Orleans, MA 02653. (508) 255-1615. Twice monthly. $195/year;
$35/two-month trial.

John Dessauer is one of the better-known advisers on international investing. His journal includes general articles on the
world economy and short updates on stock markets in various
countries. Dessauer also has a portfolio of recommended stocks
from around the world (including the U.S.). This journal is an

excellent place for the new investor to enlarge his or her knowledge of world markets.

TAIPAN, Agora Inc., 824 E. Baltimore St., Baltimore, MD 21202-4799. Monthly. $79/year.

If you subscribe to just one international newsletter, it should be *TAIPAN*. Whether they are discussing the buying opportunity in the Thai stock market, the market in rare documents, or the best way to purchase land in Greece, the reports make for fascinating reading. On the first of the year, they send out a thick report on the political and economic situation in various countries throughout the world.

The newsletter also reports on various opportunities and developments in this country. The investments recommended are generally more for the experienced investor; I mention *TAIPAN* for new investors more for the information and fine reporting. This kind of reading is one of the best ways to become a more knowledgeable investor. When you feel ready, you can start actually acting on the advice.

The Global Investor by Thomas R. Keyes and David Miller. Longman Financial Services Publishing, 1990. $19.95 (hardcover).

A good solid book on the various aspects of international investing. I found the chapters "Currency" and "Avoiding Pitfalls" to be especially clear and well written. You will need a book like this if you get interested in investing in more than international mutual funds.

Chapter 14

The Model Portfolio

U p to this point, I've been giving you an overview of the most important areas in the World of Investment. In this and the following two chapters, I'm going to ask you to start thinking about how *you* might fit into this world. This does not mean it's time to start buying. It's simply time to consider what kinds of investments would meet your needs.

To make these decisions easier, we're going to look at a model portfolio—a group of investments created with a specific purpose in mind, in this case *long-term growth*. This chapter outlines the investments that make up the model. In Chapter 15, using the model as an example, we'll talk about what goes into the building of a successful portfolio. And then, in Chapter 16, you'll be able to look at the portfolios of a few individuals, and, perhaps, compare your needs and goals with theirs.

As I have emphasized throughout this book, it is usually wise for the new investor to start out investing in mutual funds. The diversification already present in their portfolios adds to the safety we are looking for. In addition, the performance of the fund managers against the overall market can be easily checked.

Over time, some investors will stay with the funds; others, as they gain experience, will want to begin buying individual securities. The model portfolio is presented as a place to start for both kinds of investors.

Let's take a look at the categories included in the model portfolio.

Equity Income/Balanced Funds.   We begin with this category for the sake of the good income and stability these funds provide. There is also good growth potential in stocks that yield a high dividend. (*Yield*, remember, refers only to yearly income, not appreciation in value. A "high-yielding" stock is one with a large, yearly dividend.) Remember that in figuring the overall growth of a stock or mutual fund, we are including the reinvestment of dividends. If a dividend amounts to 5% to 8%, the reinvestment of it will cause an investment to grow much faster than a dividend of only 1% to 3%.

Most of the companies that give large dividends are utilities, so this is what you find in most equity income funds. Utilities are an excellent way of adding safety to any portfolio, because their stock prices don't fall as far as others in bad times, and usually rebound more quickly. This is because the utility companies usually continue to pay good dividends, even in bad times.

Balanced funds emphasize preservation of capital as well as growth and income. They will often have much of their stock portfolio in utilities—and the bonds in their portfolios will also provide good income.

High-income stocks are a specialty of the two conservative newsletter advisers recommended in this book. Richard Band's newsletter *Profitable Investing* is listed in the Resources section for Chapter 4, and Richard Young's at the end of this chapter. Young shows that investing in the highest-yielding stocks in the Dow Jones Industrial Average would have provided a much greater return over 30 years than investing in the lower-yielding Dow stocks.

Similarly, from 1981 to 1991, $10,000 invested in the stocks that make up the electric utilities index would have grown to $70,000 with all dividends reinvested; the same $10,000 invested in the S&P 500 would have become only $48,500.

The first 20% of our capital will, therefore, be invested as follows: 10% in the best equity income fund we can find, 10% in the best balanced fund.

Growth Funds.   Certain funds have been star performers over the last 10 years—and show every sign of continuing their success. These are in the fund categories of "growth" or "aggressive growth." We have listed a few in Appendix A. Take a look at these, but do some research on your own, too. We're going to put 20% of our model portfolio into the two growth funds with the best record *and* the best prospects, 10% each.

International Funds.   The major international stock markets have handily outperformed the U.S. market over the last 20 years. The large, no-load international funds have been among the star performers of the last decade.

Whether this will continue into the 1990s is unclear. The Japanese stock market stumbled badly in 1990–91, and the European markets have been up and down. The economies of both Japan and the Common Market, however, are still in better shape than the U.S. economy, in many ways. In any case, investing abroad provides excellent diversification for our portfolio.

Eastern Europe needs to be watched very closely for possible unrest or civil war, which could adversely affect the Western countries. But should peace prevail, the further economic unification of the Common Market countries should bring great benefits to all the economies involved.

Considering these facts, we're going to invest 5% of our capital in a European growth fund and 10% in another, similar fund that invests all over the world. We'll invest in the two no-load funds with the best records and best prospects.

Small-Cap Stocks. These are stocks of smaller companies. "Cap" is short for "capitalization"—companies that have a small capitalization have relatively few shares of stock outstanding. They are generally low-priced issues. "Low-priced" in this case means $10 a share on down, with special emphasis on those under $5 a share.

During most of this century, small-company stocks, as a whole, have handily outperformed those of the larger corporations, including the blue chips (see Appendix D, "Fifty Years of Returns"). This was not true during the 1980s—the blue chips were stronger then—but there has been a strong small-cap revival in the 1990s. (In 1991 the mostly small companies on the NASDAQ Industrial Average were up by 65%, compared to the blue chip Dow Jones Industrials rise of 20%.)

The stocks of individual small companies tend to fluctuate more than those of the large corporations. They are vulnerable to downturns in their sectors and in the greater economy. Owning a group of them in a diversified mutual fund, however, spreads out the risk. We'll put 15% of our portfolio into two mutual funds whose holdings include a number of top-performing small companies in various fields.

Small-cap stocks are discussed in more detail in Chapter 19.

Bonds (Fixed Income). Because of their low risk and steady return, bonds provide a good balance for a portfolio composed mostly of stocks. Unlike stocks, individual bonds will not usually appreciate much in value, but their yield in yearly interest is greater than that of most stocks. As this money is reinvested and compounded, the bond fund will grow in value. We're going to invest 10% in a bond fund with a portfolio of government bonds and AAA-rated corporate bonds. An additional 10% will go to a fund specializing in international bonds.

Cash. We're going to keep the final 10% of our money in a money market account, either at our broker's or at the same office as one of our mutual funds. This money market cash will give us interest, too—not as much as the bond funds, but normally anywhere from 3% to 9%, depending on the credit markets.

In actuality, we will have substantially more than 10% of our capital in cash, because the managers of stock and bond mutual funds commonly hold 5% to 20% of *their* assets in cash. The percentage of fund assets invested in the stock and bond markets depends on the fund managers' perception of the condition of these markets. If the managers see a rocky road ahead, they will sell some of the fund's securities and keep the proceeds in cash for a while.

Buyers of individual stocks will want to keep at least 15% to 20% of their capital in cash. This not only provides added safety but allows an investor to take immediate advantage of any buying opportunity.

Our portfolio now looks like this:

20%	Equity income/Balanced
20%	Growth
15%	International
15%	Small companies
20%	Bonds
10%	Cash
100%	

We own 10 separate funds, plus the money market fund. This is not a difficult number to keep tabs on, particularly because this is to be treated as a *buy-and-hold* portfolio.

Beating the Averages

In the stock market sector of the World of Investment, a great premium is placed on "beating the averages." What this has come to mean is making better profits with your stocks, or stock funds, than the overall stock market does. If the market, as measured by the S&P 500 Index, increased in value by 10% in a given year, then an 11% increase in your portfolio would constitute beating the averages.

The kind of enthusiastic advertisements for investment advice you see in the newspapers suggest that it's easy to do better than the S&P 500. This is not the case: In any given year, the S&P 500 outperforms the majority of professional financial managers and advisers.

It's possible to place too much emphasis on beating the averages while ignoring other important factors. The stock funds in the model portfolio were chosen partly because their investment categories have often done better than the overall stock averages. They were also chosen, however, because together they provide the kind of balance the new investor should look for. Safety and balance will create a portfolio that will shine in a good market, but will also weather the recessions.

ABOUT THE MODEL PORTFOLIO

The model portfolio is directed toward long-term growth, not income. What income there is, from dividends or interest, would be automatically reinvested in the fund that produced it. The investments are also strongly directed toward safety: the preservation of capital. Except for the

small-company funds, all the categories are quite conservative, with a heavy emphasis on blue chip stocks, domestic
and international. The overall risk-reward temperature of
the portfolio is right in the middle, which is a good place for
it to be for the new investor.

We are emphasizing long-term growth here. The investment categories we have chosen have done extremely well
over the years, but these years have included many ups and
downs.

Investing in these same categories with the intention
of buying and selling for short-term profit would send the
readings on all of the risk-reward thermometers right to the
top. Even bonds, despite their safe and secure reputation,
can fluctuate sharply in value over a few months or a year.
And stocks (and stock mutual funds) must be considered
risky investments in the short term. They go up and down
according to the economic winds and the whims of fickle
investors. The only factor that lowers their risk is that, as
a whole, the trend in their value has always been upward
over time.

Be aware, then, that the risk-reward thermometers you
see in this chapter are for investments held for a number
of years.

Modifying the Model

As we will see in Chapter 16, it's very easy to modify the
model portfolio to provide an income and even greater
safety—or to emphasize more growth. And because we are
investing in mutual funds, it's easy to vary the amounts invested to fit the needs of large or small investors.

As new investors evolve into experienced investors
over time, these categories can also be modified to satisfy
socially conscious criteria. For example, for our international category, it's now possible to find socially responsible mutual funds based in foreign countries. If you become

The Rule of 10%

New investors are often confused about what rate of
return to expect from investments. This confusion is not
helped by the ads that promise a safe return of 50% a
year—or by Uncle Joe who boasts about how he doubled his money in three months with a hot stock.

A 10%-a-year return on your money is a good place
to start. The new investor who invests carefully should
feel pleased if a 10%-per-year return is gained overall.
Some funds may not make 10%, but others may balance
them out by making more than 10%.

Don't be discouraged if you make less. Some years
may simply be bad ones for the securities in your portfolio. You may show a growth of only a few percent, or
even a minus; the bad years, however, should be balanced out by times of exceptional growth.

Your eventual goal is to make more than 10%, while
maintaining the same level of safety. As you get more experienced in managing your portfolio, this goal can become a fine challenge. But 10% is a good benchmark to
start from.

comfortable with international investing, you may want to
move in this direction.

If you decide to use all or parts of the model portfolio,
you will find in Appendix A a list of appropriate, high-
performing mutual funds in each category. You should be
aware, however, that funds change over the years—and
promising new ones come into existence. For this reason,
you should check each fund carefully before you buy. The
sources and advisers recommended in this book should help
you make your own informed, up-to-date choices. In the

next chapter, we'll go into how to choose the best funds in more detail.

Resources

Richard Young's Intelligence Report, Philips Publishing Inc., 7811 Montrose Road, Potomac, MD 20854. (800) 722-9000. Monthly. $177/year (unless Philips is having one of their frequent specials which often includes bonuses of pamphlets written by Young for new subscribers—inquire when you call).

Young is your basic conservative investor: His specialties are bonds, utilities, and high-yielding blue chips. He also recommends mutual funds. Young is a good adviser for new investors. He writes clearly and concisely and frequently restates his investment philosophy and methods. *And* his subscribers have done very well with his recommendations.

CHAPTER 15

BUILDING A
SUCCESSFUL PORTFOLIO

"An investment operation is one which, upon thorough analysis, promises safety of principal and an adequate return. Operations not meeting these requirements are speculative."

—*BENJAMIN GRAHAM, NOTED INVESTOR AND AUTHOR OF INVESTMENT BOOKS*

Just a few, important elements are required to set up a portfolio that will ensure a good return *and* will let you weather the various financial storms. These are general factors that should go into the building of any successful group of investments.

In setting up the model portfolio, we considered three major factors, and we will add a fourth—performance—in this chapter:

- Design. What purpose is the portfolio designed for?

- Quality. How to buy the best investments.

- Diversification. Keeping a good balance among your investments.

- Performance. After the portfolio is set up, the final factor is keeping tabs on how it performs.

PORTFOLIO DESIGN

The design of a portfolio depends on your purposes and your goals. The model portfolio in Chapter 14 was designed for long-term growth, with a strong emphasis on safety—the preservation of capital. Though the overall value of the investments may fluctuate with the markets, we are aiming for as rapid an increase of our principal as we can, while still maintaining the necessary safety.

If our purpose was to get more income, while still cultivating some growth, we would buy more bond and utility funds, fewer small-company funds, and fewer low-yielding blue chips. On the other hand, a need for even greater growth—accepting the added risk—would have us buying just the opposite: more small companies, fewer bonds, and less cash in the money markets.

BUYING THE BEST—AND HOLDING ON

In Chapter 19, we're going to talk about a few more advanced methods of investing. Right now, though, let's deal with the only buying system employed by the model portfolio: the venerable *buy-and-hold strategy*.

You are in excellent company with the buy-and-hold method of investing. Such noted investors as John Templeton, Warren Buffett, and Peter Lynch all subscribe to this way of building a portfolio. If it seems too boring, just remember that the reason these men are respected is because they made great pots of money for those who invested with them or followed their advice. Making money is not usually boring.

Buy and hold is just as it sounds—though you might not hold an investment forever. If, over a period of a year or two years, a mutual fund or a security is not performing as well as the rest of its market category and its prospects don't look good for the future, then you sell it.

The key to a successful buy-and-hold strategy is selecting the best investments. If you choose companies or funds on the basis of their excellent past performance *and* their excellent prospects for the future, you can afford to watch their prices fluctuate. If your choices are good, these are the investments that will recover the quickest after a recession and appreciate the most in good times.

Choosing the Best Funds

In Chapter 6, we discussed a few ways of choosing the best-performing mutual funds. Spending enough time selecting the best ones will pay off handsomely in the long run.

Using one of the books or journals recommended in the Resources section of Chapter 6, find the three funds in the category you want that have performed the best over the last five years. Then check out what the funds invest in (the books will have this information, too).

Say you're looking at international funds. After finding the three funds with the best records over the past five years, you see that the two top funds are heavily invested in Japan. Now, suppose that when you are looking, the Japanese economy is having a bad time, with no immediate prospects for recovery. The third fund, on the other hand, has diversified investments all over the world. This is the one you want.

The next step is to call the fund's 800 number (listed in the books and journals) and ask for a prospectus. This prospectus will give you all the details about investing in the fund; it will also describe the fund's investment policy and the securities it owns. If you like what you see, then you're ready to invest.

While the buy-and-hold strategy means generally ignoring the ups and downs of the market once you own a security, you *do* need to be aware of market conditions when you are buying. If the stock market appears very shaky, keep your money in cash until things improve.

You also need to be aware of future prospects. If there is good evidence that the Japanese economy is improving—and that the stock market is beginning to reflect that improvement—then you will want to take another look at those first two international funds.

DIVERSIFICATION

The model portfolio was set up with diversification as a primary objective. Whatever your portfolio looks like, diversification gives it balance and stability. If some of your investments go down in value, they will be balanced by others that don't go down, continue to give you income, or even go up.

For example, if stocks should fall and your stock funds lose value, you would continue to get income from the bond funds. The funds investing in utility companies will also most likely continue to pay dividends. And the international equity funds may not go down with the American market. The total value of your portfolio may be reduced, but you should ride out the storm easily until the stock market turns around.

When it *does* turn around, it is sometimes the blue chip stocks that go up the fastest, sometimes the small-company stocks. This is why it's a good idea to have a blue chip fund *and* a small-company fund in your portfolio.

Chapter 14 lists the various categories of funds, their investment objectives, and their risk-reward thermometers. It's a good idea for the new investor to build a portfolio of funds with temperatures that *average out* to the middle of the scale. A low-risk bond fund, for example, would balance out a higher-risk small-company fund.

Your choices, however, need to be high-quality investments. Buying three risky, high-temperature funds, such as a junk bond fund, a small-company biotech fund, and a precious-metals fund, is *not* the kind of diversification that will help you ride out the storms.

Even if you have only a small amount to invest, it's still important to diversify. If you have $2,500, you can put $500 each in five different funds, then add a couple more funds as you get more to invest. Anywhere from five to ten funds is a reasonable number for the new investor to own. (See the next chapter for a low-income portfolio.)

PERFORMANCE

It's a good idea to check the value of your funds at least once a week, and do a major evaluation of your portfolio once every six months. If your portfolio is being managed, then you will want to talk it over with the manager every six months.

The *Portfolio Simplifier* recommended at the end of this chapter is an excellent way of keeping track of your various investments. Alternatively, if you are comfortable with computers, you can buy one of the many software programs that help you organize your finances (see Resources in Chapter 22).

What you are watching for is the increase or decrease in value of your funds compared to other funds in the same investment category. Even though the share price of a fund may have increased, if it is doing noticeably less well than other funds in the same category it may be time to sell yours and buy a better-performing one.

For example, if your aggressive growth fund has gained 8% over two years, but the *average* gain for the category of aggressive growth funds has been 15%, it's time to consider selling, and buying one of the funds that topped 15%. (The financial papers publish quarterly retrospectives on the performance of different categories of funds and individual funds.)

If, on the other hand, your fund has done brilliantly but the economic situation has changed, it may also be time to think about selling. Suppose, for example, your European small-company fund has appreciated an average of 18% a year during the last three years. Recently, however, tensions in the Middle East have aroused fears of an interruption in the oil supply. The resulting higher oil prices could throw Europe into a recession—and small-company stocks are usually the most vulnerable in recessions.

So . . . it may be time to let go of your prize fund. You could sell it all, or you could sell 70% or 80% of it and hold on to the rest. This would lock in a good profit, but allow you to keep at least some of the fund, in case the political tensions evaporate.

Though buying and selling should generally be based on performance over a period of at least a year, there are times when you may need to move faster. For example, if it was clear that the situation in the Middle East was deteriorating rapidly, you would not want to wait for your six-month review to sell your European fund.

Unless your investment objectives have changed, you need to maintain the original balance of investment categories in your portfolio. For example, if your small-company funds have been such star performers that they now account for 25% of your assets instead of the original 15%, it's time to think about taking some profits. It may be difficult to bring yourself to sell such winners, but remember that small-company funds can also be big losers in any recession.

How *much* you sell depends on the economic climate and whether the funds are continuing to rise. If they still look good, you could sell enough to bring this category down to just 20% of the whole. If the trend upward has stalled, though, sell more and spread the proceeds around to your other funds, so that the original balance is regained.

Resources

Profitable Investing Portfolio Simplifier by Richard E. Band. Profitable Investing, Philips Publishing Inc., 7811 Montrose Road, Potomac, MD 20854. (800) 777-5005. $25. Band's *Profitable Investing* newsletter is listed in the Resources for Chapter 4. If you subscribe to the newsletter, you get the *Portfolio Simplifier* free ($149/year, including telephone hotline—often a special subscription rate is offered).

Unless you plan to use your computer to organize your portfolio, you will need something like this booklet. There are five sections: Getting Organized, Tracking Your Portfolio, Year-End Tax Planner, Targeting Your Retirement, and Sources and Records. It's all laid out very clearly, and the author gives some useful advice in each section.

Jay Schabacker's Mutual Fund Investing, Philips Publishing Inc., 7811 Montrose Road, Potomac, MD 20854. Monthly. $99/year. Subscription includes hotline service and booklets on mutual funds.

Jay Schabacker has had an excellent record picking mutual funds. He will also give you background information on *why* certain funds look the best (good managers, low fees, balance against bad times, etc.). No trial subscription is offered, but Philips will send you a back issue for review.

**NoLoad Fund*X. Russ Building, 235 Montgomery St., Suite 662, San Francisco, CA 94104. (800) 323-1510. Monthly. $114/year. Ask about discounts and bonus publications.

**NoLoad Fund*X is one of *Hulbert's* top performers from 1980 to 1991. They use a modified buy-and-hold method, which involves buying top-performing funds when the funds you are holding begin to lag. This is an extension of the methods outlined in this chapter; it shows excellent results, but is simple and safe to use for new investors. Highly recommended.

Morningstar Mutual Funds. (See Resources, Chapter 6.)

CHAPTER 16

INDIVIDUAL PORTFOLIOS

One advantage to the model portfolio presented in Chapter 14 is that it's easily modified to suit individual needs. In this chapter, we're going to look at a few financial scenarios and how the model can be tailored to each one.

The model is presented simply as a place to start from. As you will see, some people include real estate as part of their portfolios; one woman invested heavily in the stock of the company she worked for; another used a small amount for speculation. By comparing the situations of these people to your own, you should begin to see more clearly what your own portfolio might look like.

Whether you use the model as a starting point, however, or set up your own portfolio, you need to ask yourself a few questions:

1. To what extent do you want to manage your portfolio? There are basically three kinds of investors: those who give the management of their assets to a financial professional; those who manage their own

portfolios, but minimally, adopting a long-term buy-and-hold strategy and reviewing their portfolios only occasionally; and the "hands-on" investors, who keep tabs on things daily, and trade more often.

2. What personal goals do you want your portfolio to help you reach? College for the kids? Retirement? Extra income? Deciding on these goals will determine the design of your portfolio. For example, do your goals mean investing for long-term growth only, or do you need income from your investments?

3. How much risk are you willing to take? Risk comes with the territory in the World of Investment, but you need to determine the amount that seems right for your situation—*and* for your nervous system. If you're lying awake nights worrying whether International Skeet Management is going to drop another 10 points, then perhaps you need a less risky investment.

The portfolios described below are the result of each person or couple answering these questions. I hope that pondering these examples will bring you closer to deciding what your own portfolio will look like. There's no reason to rush it, though: the World of Investment isn't going anywhere, except up and down.

JIM: EXTRA INCOME AND LONG-TERM GROWTH

Let's start with my friend Jim, the sculptor. After moaning for years that American society doesn't support the artist, Jim finally sold a major work for $25,000. We'll forget the few hundred he spent to celebrate and assume he has $25,000 to invest.

Now, one of Jim's complaints was that he had to do odd jobs to earn a living, which took him away from his art. So he wanted to invest the $25,000 in a way that would give him some income and keep the principal safe. (Jim already has $5,000 set aside in a certificate of deposit for emergencies, and he has health insurance.) Jim, who is 35 and single, is also interested in establishing a fund that might grow over a period of years. Artists don't get pensions.

Proposed portfolio: Two no-load bond mutual funds, one investing in international securities yielding 10.5%, the other in corporate bonds yielding 9.5%—$10,000 in each.

This is $20,000 with an average return of 10% a year = $2,000 a year, or about $165 a month. This might not seem like much, but to Jim, who makes a business of living as cheaply as possible, it's almost one-seventh of his total monthly living expense of $1,200. The extra $165 means he can avoid odd jobs for two or three more days each month and concentrate on sculpting.

These two or three days mean more than just the satisfaction of working at what he loves; they also mean Jim has more time to produce art that might sell. So by investing in funds that give him extra income, he is essentially investing in himself—in his own business.

The remaining $5,000 was divided equally among five no-load stock mutual funds in the following categories: (1) international conservative growth stocks, (2) utilities, (3) environmental (large companies), (4) small-company growth, and (5) a stock index fund based on the S&P 500. These funds had been averaging 12.5% growth a year including the reinvestment of dividends.

Jim is aware that past performance doesn't guarantee future results, but *if* these funds continue this kind of growth, in 10 years he will have about $16,200; in 20 years, $52,750; and in 30 years, when he will be thinking about retirement, a nice sum of $171,000.

In addition, Jim will still have the $20,000 in the bond funds. While the value of these funds may fluctuate over the years, it will probably not increase or decrease by any appreciable amount. The amount will not grow because Jim is *using* the income, not reinvesting it. Of course, if his sculpture becomes the rage, he might not need the income from those funds and could invest more for growth.

Jim says artists never really retire, but that it's good to have some money put away for old age. Because of inflation, the income from the $171,000 won't go as far as it does today, but it will still be a very nice addition to a Social Security check. And the total amount will give Jim some backup funds for any medical emergencies or long-term care.

SUSANNA: GROWTH AND EARLY RETIREMENT

Jim needed the income to live on. Let's look at investing the same amount in a very different scenario. Susanna, 28, has done well as an assistant buyer for a chain of clothing stores. With her salary and occasional bonuses, she has accumulated $25,000. She doesn't need extra income, so she would like to invest the entire $25,000 for growth over the long term. Susanna is not particularly interested in managing investments on a day-to-day basis; she would like to invest the money and just check it occasionally.

Because she is young and the prospects for future earnings look good, Susanna is willing to invest some of her portfolio in riskier mutual funds, with a likelihood of growth. She would also like to retire early—in 15 or 20 years.

Proposed portfolio: Susanna's company has an attractive stock ownership plan for its employees. For every four shares an employee purchases, management kicks in an extra fifth. Susanna has an insider's knowledge of the company and thinks its future looks promising—and that she can contribute to its success. So she invests $8,000, which buys $10,000 worth of stock, under the company's plan.

The remaining $17,000 is placed as follows: $5,000 in two international growth funds (investing all over the world); $2,500 in a European aggressive growth fund; $5,000 in two U.S. environmental funds, one specializing in large companies, the other in small companies; $3,000 in a utility equity fund; and $1,500 in a corporate bond fund, currently yielding 9%. All the funds are no-load and all dividends and interest are to be reinvested.

Let's suppose that, overall, Susanna's funds, and her company's stock, grow at an average rate of 12% a year—not an unreasonable expectation if all the income is reinvested. Ten years will see her $25,000 grow to $78,000; 20 years, $241,000; and 30 years, about $750,000.

The income from $241,000, after 20 years, would not be enough to support the kind of lifestyle Susanna would prefer. She would like to have at least $500,000: this amount, invested for income at 10%, would give her $50,000 a year to live on, which she considers the absolute minimum.

With the help of a compound-interest table (see Appendix E), Susanna figures that if she can invest an additional $800 a quarter, or $3,200 a year, in 20 years she will have $257,000, assuming the same 12% growth rate. This, added to the $241,000 from the other account, will give her almost $500,000. If, in the meantime, her earnings continue to go up, she will be able to invest more, thus pushing her retirement closer to 15 years away.

Just to illustrate the importance of a few percentage points, if Susanna had invested the $25,000 in government bonds with a return of 8.5%, the total would amount to only $128,000 in 20 years and $289,000 in 30 years. If, on the other hand, her company's stock and the riskier growth funds do well, causing her portfolio to grow at an overall rate of 15% a year, she would be looking at $410,000 after 20 years, and $1,655,000 after 30 years. This last figure is more than double the amount at the 12% rate—such are the wonders of compound interest.

JANET: LONG-TERM GROWTH AND SPECULATION

Janet is doing well as a cardiovascular specialist, though up to two years ago, the majority of her earnings went to supporting her three children and putting them through college. Now, however, they are grown and earning incomes of their own.

Janet is 52 and divorced. She has accumulated $100,000 in savings, and the prospects for continued earnings look excellent. She has backup savings and all necessary insurance, and she will almost certainly continue to generate a surplus that she can continue to invest. She would like to put $50,000 in a safe place where it would start growing and compounding, since she doesn't need the income. She looks on this as her retirement fund and plans to add to it in the future. The other $50,000 she wants to invest and manage herself.

Proposed portfolio: First $50,000: the model portfolio. This long-term-growth portfolio provides the kind of growth and safety Janet wants. This $50,000 Janet will essentially leave alone, just checking every week to see whether the funds she chose are performing well. The only change she will make in the model is to put $5,000 into a real estate mutual fund.

Now for the other $50,000. Janet has purchased a data-retrieval service for her computer that gives her real-time quotes from the various markets (see Chapter 22). She has the computer at her office and checks her investments during lunch hour and occasionally between patients. (Now you know why you have to sit so long in the waiting room.)

She invests $35,000 in 20 growth stocks she chose from the newsletters she subscribes to and then researched further on her own. She is especially partial to small pharmaceutical and medical research companies, because she has an educated feeling for what products will be successful. She also places $5,000 in rare coins, after carefully researching the market. She checks on the stocks every day,

though she may buy and sell only a few over the course of a
few months. She hopes the rare coins will appreciate over a
few years.

Janet uses the remaining $10,000 for pure speculation.
After caring for others for 25 years, as a wife, mother, and
doctor, she has suddenly discovered a financial speculator
emerging as part of her personality. She trades stock options, index options, a few junk bonds, and futures options
on gold. These she buys and sells from day to day, finding the
process absorbing enough to divert her attention for a while
from arteries and heart valves.

PETE AND MARILYN: BUILDING A PORTFOLIO

Pete and Marilyn, both in their early thirties, are anxious to
build up a college fund for their two children, ages 3 and 1.
They also want to start investing for their retirement. Pete
works as an estimator and carpenter for a construction firm;
Marilyn works part time in a day-care center and full time
as a homemaker. Their combined earnings come to $32,000
after taxes, and almost all of this goes for living expenses.

By saving $250 a month ($3,000 a year) for several
years, they were able to get together a down payment on a
three-bedroom house. Now, even though there are added expenses with the two children, Pete's salary also goes up a
bit each year. So they decide they can still invest $250 a
month.

With part of this $250, Pete is able to start an individual
retirement account (IRA), contributing $165 a month for the
yearly limit of $2,000. Because the IRA is a "tax-advantaged"
account, Pete and Marilyn can deduct the $2,000 from their
income on their tax statement. (For more on the advantages
of IRAs, see Chapter 17.)

The other $85 goes to paying down the mortgage on
their house. According to an agreement worked out with

Real Estate

Some investors may want to include real estate in their portfolios. Many people already own real estate in the form of a home; a few may own income properties. For those who are unable to own real estate, or don't wish to, a real estate mutual fund is a good way of including this category in your portfolio. These funds (as discussed in Chapter 11) invest in the securities of real estate brokerage companies, real estate investment trusts (REITs), and property development companies.

As far as the risk-reward balance of your portfolio, the real estate funds are about a 7 on a scale of 1 to 10, with 10 being the riskiest. *Long-term* investments in high-quality homes or income property should be seen as a relatively conservative investment (the risk-reward thermometer would be just under the midpoint). Short-term investing for a quick profit, however, especially in lower-quality properties, sends the thermometer right up to the top.

For further ways of investing in real estate without actually buying property, see Chapter 11.

---

the bank that holds the mortgage, when Marilyn makes the $775 mortgage payment each month, she will add $85 to it.

This additional $85 a month means that their 20-year mortgage of $80,000 will be paid off in 15 years. Over the years, this will save a total of $31,500 in interest on their mortgage.

In 15 years, their firstborn will be ready for college, followed in two years by his sister. By that time, Pete and Marilyn will no longer be making house payments, which means they will have extra cash to contribute to both children's tuition and expenses. If they need to, they can also take out a small loan against the house. They hope to contribute about $10,000 a year to each child for four years, for a total of $80,000.

This amount of money will not be nearly enough to pay tuition and expenses at a private college (especially with the expected increases during the next 15 years). At the state university, though, $10,000 will amount to a large percentage of the children's expenses, with student loans and summer jobs making up the remainder. A less expensive alternative would be for them to start out at the local community college, while living at home, and transfer to the state university after two years.

Pete is a very conservative investor uncomfortable with the ups and downs of the stock market. He placed the IRA in a bond fund and planned to buy a few other bond funds over the years. Marilyn finally convinced him to buy at least one balanced fund and a utility fund to add some diversity to the portfolio.

Conservative investments mean conservative growth rates: Pete and Marilyn's funds should grow at about 10%. In 20 years this would mean $125,000 in the account; in 30 years, $373,000.

After they no longer have to pay for college expenses, Pete and Marilyn will use their extra cash to build another fund. They would like this money to go toward a down payment on a house or small apartment building. Either Pete will fix it up and sell it, or they will hold on to it as part of their portfolio.

There are a couple of noteworthy points in Pete and Marilyn's story. The first is that by contributing a small amount each month, you can accumulate a healthy sum over a number of years.

The second point is that if you are a homeowner, you have invested in real estate and your home should be considered as part of your portfolio. By putting the $85 toward paying down the mortgage, Pete and Marilyn were investing more in their home.

For them, the house is a good diversification of their portfolio—but not absolutely necessary to their plans. If they had lived in an area where a house was too expensive for them to buy, they could have started another account with the $85 a month. At the end of 20 years, at a growth rate of 10%, this account would have been worth $64,500; in 30 years, $192,140. They could have used—or borrowed against—this fund for their children's education.

MIKE AND SARAH: INHERITANCE USED FOR INCOME AND STARTING BUSINESSES

Mike and Sarah have inherited a total of $1 million from their respective families. Because neither of them particularly likes their jobs, they want to leave them and use their inheritance to give them a living income. Mike wants to write a novel and Sarah wants to start a dress shop. They are both in their early forties.

Because they are aware that novels and new businesses are chancy things, they want to set aside a large percentage of the money to provide an income while they work on their new projects.

Sarah's inheritance came only recently, from her father, so she is in mourning and realizes that she is in no shape to make important investment decisions right away. Mike had inherited a year earlier from a distant uncle, so his emotions are not involved, but both of them realize they need time to acclimate themselves to their new lives.

With this in mind, they buy six-month CDs at their bank and let the money sit there gathering interest. Sarah leaves her job, but Mike stays on at his for six months, providing an income during this period. In the meantime, they start reading books on investing and asking their friends and relatives for advice.

At the end of six months, they have come to some conclusions. Their main decision is that because they want to
concentrate on their various projects, neither of them is particularly interested in managing their investments. So, on the
recommendation of a good friend, they make an appointment with a woman in a reputable financial-planning firm,
first establishing that they will *both* have to like this person
and agree on her recommendations before working with her.

The planner goes over all of Mike and Sarah's financial
needs, from various kinds of insurance to tax considerations, from retirement planning to investment possibilities.
The process is time consuming, but both of them agree that
it is worthwhile.

In the end, the planner, having gotten a good idea of
Mike and Sarah's investment preferences, recommends a
portfolio of diverse stocks and stock funds for growth, and
bond funds for income. Because both of them have strong
social concerns, emphasis is placed on funds investing in socially and environmentally responsible companies. The planner recommends that they meet again in six months to
review the portfolio.

At the same time, Mike's father asks him to invest
$100,000 with him in an apartment complex. Because Mike's
father has several successful property investments, the planner approves this, saying it will provide more diversity and
good income.

From the $800,000 invested with the financial planner,
Mike and Sarah get a yearly income of about 6% from dividends from the stock funds and interest from the bond
funds. This comes to $48,000 ($800,000 × 0.06 = $48,000).
This is income only—it does not count any appreciation in
the value of the funds. They get an additional 10% from the
$100,000 real estate investment—$10,000—so their total
yearly income comes to $58,000.

Sarah takes the remaining $100,000 to start her dress
shop. Although she has high hopes, she realizes that she
shouldn't expect any net income from the shop for at least

a couple of years. The $58,000 is enough for them to live on in the meantime, although after taxes, they will hardly have a sumptuous lifestyle. For the present, though, they are more interested in following their dreams.

For more information on investing in yourself by starting a business, you can look at Chapter 23. For now, it's important to note that Sarah and Mike have enough that they can afford to lose the $100,000 going into the dress shop. They have their finances worked out so that they don't need the $100,000 to live on. I mention this because starting a business should be considered a high-risk investment. Ideally, it should be done with money you are not depending on for income.

It's also important to realize that, except for the apartment building, the couple have not locked themselves in to any long-term investments. If their situation should change and they should want more income, some of their growth stock funds could easily be sold and reinvested in higher-yielding stock or bond funds. Or if Sarah's dress shop became a hit and Mike wrote a best-seller, they would not need as much income from the portfolio. In that case, they would want more of the portfolio in growth investments with the possibility of greater long-term gain. In any case, they have left their options open.

LOW-INCOME INVESTING: CREATING A PORTFOLIO

Except for Jim, the sculptor, everyone else described in these scenarios was fairly well-off. (We will present a scenario for a retired couple in the next chapter.) Pete and Marilyn were certainly not rich, but they could contribute $250 a month to build their portfolio.

Many people, however, have incomes too low to invest more than a few dollars above their monthly expenses. If they are able to contribute these small amounts to an

Savings versus Investment Capital

You will want to keep a certain amount of extra cash accessible and safe from market fluctuations in case you need it for an emergency. One way of determining the amount is to figure how much you (and your family, if you're married) would need in monthly expenses if something should happen to the major wage earner. It's a good idea to keep at least three months' expenses on hand in readily available cash.

The first two months' worth of this amount should be in a money market account at your bank where it is immediately accessible. Make it a joint account, with both you and your spouse able to write checks. Further amounts can go into one-year certificates of deposit (CDs) at your local bank. This money is also readily accessible, though the bank will charge you a fee if you withdraw it before one year.

Extra money in these amounts should be looked on not as investment cash but as backup money. There are a couple of reasons not to invest this money in stocks or bonds. First, a sale of securities can take up to a week to clear and you may need the cash immediately. Secondly, your securities may be down in value when you have to sell; you could easily come out with less money than if you'd left it in the bank.

When you accumulate more than you need for emergencies, that is the time to start thinking about investments. Carefully chosen investments will almost always appreciate, but they need time. Investment capital, therefore, should be money that you can leave for at least several years.

investment plan, however, the money can grow into much larger amounts over time. I have developed a program for low-income investors that combines safety with growth.

The first thing any investor needs to do is to set up an emergency fund. As described in the box on the previous page, this fund is considered as savings, not investment capital.

Any amount you can save—$50 a month, $75, $100—should go into this fund. If you can't find any money at the end of the month, try thinking of it as a tax and set it aside when the paycheck first comes in. Another way is to set aside a dollar or two a day.

Your goal is to build up a savings account equal to at least three months of expenses. Suppose your total monthly expenses came to $1,350; your savings would need to amount to about $4,000 ($1,350 × 3 = $4,050). This money is left in the bank or credit union to earn interest and be at the ready for any future emergency. The money should be in a money market account or a CD in an institution that is insured by the Federal Deposit Insurance Corporation (FDIC), or the credit union equivalent, the National Credit Union Administration (NCUA).

You will have some help in building up this fund from the interest earned from your savings. Without interest, $50 saved every month would amount to $600 a year, or $2,400 over four years. Adding in a 7% compounded interest rate on what you save, however, will give you $2,760 after four years, $3,580 after five years. Seventy-five dollars a month at 7% would give you the needed $4,000 after three years and nine months.

Once you have the necessary savings for emergencies, *then* you can begin to make the money work for you. While the principal amount—in this case the $4,000—has to stay in the bank, the *interest* earned by the $4,000 can now go toward investing. Four thousand dollars at 7% will earn you $280 a year. If you can continue to put aside $50 a month,

you will have $880 to invest each year: $600 from your continuing monthly savings and $280 from interest on your
emergency account.

As soon as you accumulate $500, you can invest it in
a mutual fund. Start out with your first $500 in a bond
fund that invests in AAA-rated corporate bonds and government bonds, the second in a bond fund that invests
in bonds of foreign governments. Then you can graduate
to a utility fund, a socially responsible balanced fund, and
a blue chip stock fund. Finally, round out your portfolio
with a conservative international fund and a small-company
fund.

In less than four years, you will have $3,500 invested in
seven different funds—and probably more than that, if your
funds have increased in value. You can now send your
money to each fund alternately, every month or every quarter, whichever is easier. Your $880 a year would come to
about $73 a month or $220 a quarter.

Here's how your investment would grow if the markets
act as they have in the past: At a growth rate of 11% a year
(with all dividends and interest from the funds reinvested),
after 5 years, $73 a month would amount to about $5,800;
after 10 years, it would be $15,800; 20 years, $63,200; and
after 30 years, you would have a grand total of $205,000. Not
bad for an out-of-pocket outlay of $50 a month.

A couple of additional notes for this kind of portfolio
building: You can set up your mutual fund accounts as individual retirement accounts (IRAs). This will allow you to
deduct the amount you invest from your earned income, so
that you don't pay taxes on it until you retire. The interest
and reinvested dividends will also be tax-deferred. Mutual
funds will charge a small yearly fee for managing IRA accounts; be sure you know what this fee amounts to. For
more on IRAs, see Chapter 17.

If you plan to use this money before you retire, IRAs are
not such a good idea, because the government will charge a
stiff fee for withdrawing it before retirement.

Investors of small amounts need to invest directly with mutual funds. The commissions charged by brokers take too big a bite out of the monthly contributions. If you feel you need assistance with your investing, most banks employ an investment counselor for the benefit of their depositors. This person can answer questions about IRAs and help you set up your mutual fund accounts.

This chapter opened with some questions you need to ask yourself before setting up a portfolio of investments: your management style, goals, and risk tolerance. If, for example, you need an income, like Jim, the sculptor, you will need more bond and utility funds. If you are well-off and are investing for long-term growth only, your portfolio will look more like the model. But if the whole idea of putting your hard-earned money in stocks makes you cringe because your grandfather lost everything in 1929, then you may want to invest more in real estate and bonds, like Pete and Marilyn.

The other things that make a portfolio work are always the same, whether you start with a million dollars or invest a dollar a day: designing your portfolio based on your goals, taking care to choose the best investments, diversifying, and keeping tabs on your portfolio.

Ideally, this chapter has helped you to focus on your investment goals and the best ways to achieve them. The situations described above, while certainly not identical to your own, may be similar enough to help you organize your investments.

When you get ready to invest, the model portfolio—or your personal variation of it—is a good place to start. Some will choose to stay with mutual funds and manage their investments in the manner described above. But even if you plan to be a more active investor, the model is a good place to begin. You can get your footing and develop a feel for different areas before you start trading in more complex markets.

If you do begin to buy individual securities, starting with the model will help you keep your portfolio balanced and diversified. You would simply substitute individual securities for a fund in the same investment category. For example, you could sell a utility fund and buy stock in three utility companies. To maintain diversity you might buy in to a gas company, an electric utility, and a telephone company.

CHAPTER 17

RETIREMENT

O ur culture has traditionally divided life into the working phase and the retirement phase. Many people, though, have begun to rethink this artificial division. Quite a few younger people don't want to wait until age 65 to be free to pursue interests other than their work. And many older people enjoy continuing to be productive. Ideally, it should be possible to be productive at things you enjoy, while still having plenty of time to pursue other interests. Time to read, play music, travel, or be with your children or grandchildren should be available at any age—35 or 85.

Some people are happy with their jobs; others simply like the security of working until the normal retirement age. Still others, however, would like very much to retire early and pursue a different lifestyle or cultivate new interests. In the Resources at the end of this chapter, these people will find a book and a seminar created especially for them.

INCOME AND INVESTMENTS

In Chapter 16, we suggested several ways of building up a portfolio for your retirement years. The earlier you start, the more you will have when you get ready to retire. Either by investing a lump sum, putting away a certain amount each month, or both, you can build up quite a large amount in 20 or 30 years.

The total return on your investments will be much greater if you invest as much as you can in a tax-deferred retirement plan. These plans are explained later in the chapter.

You can get income from this fund; if you are a later retiree, you may also have a pension, and you will get Social Security. To find out how much you will get from Social Security, you can ask for a Personal Earnings and Benefit Estimate Statement (Form 7004-PC) from your local office, or by calling (800) 234-5772. This is a record of your earnings and an estimate of your retirement benefits based on your past and expected future earnings.

Investment during retirement is really not that much different from before. There is simply a greater emphasis on income and on safety—more bonds, more utilities, fewer small-growth companies. Even if you are retiring in your mid-sixties, however, it's a good idea to keep at least 25% of your portfolio in growth stocks. There's a good chance that you may live at least another 20 years, and you need the growth to counter inflation.

GLEN AND ALICE: A WELL-PLANNED RETIREMENT

Let's look at a portfolio for a newly retired couple who have planned carefully for their retirement. Even though they are retiring at 65, their portfolio is pertinent to anybody on a fixed income. The difference, of course, is that early retirees wouldn't have a pension or Social Security. They would, therefore, need a larger amount to invest to give them an income—unless they plan to live very modestly.

Glen and Alice have just retired at age 65. They have Glen's Social Security (Alice worked as a homemaker), his pension, and $100,000 in savings. The pension and the Social Security provide a comfortable income, their house is paid off, and they have health insurance. They also have long-term-care insurance, in case either of them has to go into a nursing home (see box on page 198). If they decide to live in a retirement community in a few years, they will sell their house and buy in with the proceeds.

They would like to have extra income to travel, and they want to set up a fund to help with college expenses for their four grandchildren. The oldest won't be ready for eight years, so they have a little time to work on this.

Proposed portfolio: First of all, $5,000 goes into a money market account for readily available emergency cash. In addition, they purchase a certificate of deposit with another $5,000. Glen's pension and Social Security would continue to support Alice if he should die, but this CD they have earmarked for expenses surrounding either of their deaths, such as the cost of a funeral.

Of the remaining $90,000, $70,000 goes into a mix of bond mutual funds and high-yield stock funds, with an emphasis on utilities. The average return on the $70,000 is 8%, or $5,600 a year. Of this, Glen and Alice will take $4,000 a year for traveling and other extras and reinvest the remaining $1,600. They could get a slightly higher yield by investing exclusively in bonds, but they expect the stock funds to appreciate over time.

Glen has decided to manage the remaining $20,000 himself in an attempt to increase the contribution to the grandchildren's college fund. He starts reading the books recommended in this book, talking with friends, and subscribing to a few of the best newsletters. He finds he enjoys this, and within a year he is fully invested in stocks of well-established companies with good growth potential and a record of secure dividends. Because of the importance of the fund and the limited amount of capital, Glen avoids the smaller, riskier growth companies.

Glen and Alice are securely set up for their later years. Many people who are retired or approaching retirement, though, are unfortunately not so well prepared. For these people, I would urge purchasing the books and seminar recommended at the end of this chapter. The authors of this material are experts at teaching creative ways of getting the most out of your income. And for the best ways to invest small amounts of capital, you can review the section on low-income investing in the preceding chapter.

TAX-DEFERRED RETIREMENT PLANS

Elsewhere we have recommended using tax-deferred investment plans wherever possible. Now we're going to talk about why. The benefits of these plans can be dramatic, as you will see.

Over the years, the federal government has created various ways of encouraging people to save for retirement. The incentives are centered around taxes: If you contribute to a retirement plan, you will get a break on your taxes. The incentives have worked. Hundreds of billions of dollars are now invested in different kinds of retirement plans.

It's interesting to note that the benefits of these savings work not only for the individuals who own them but also for the national economy. Whether invested directly in stocks and bonds or in bank savings accounts, the money is used as capital for economic growth.

There are various plans that will give you tax breaks if you put away money for your retirement. There are individual retirement accounts (IRAs), Keogh plans for the self-employed, simplified employee pension plans (SEPs) and 401(k) plans for employed people. The basics of these plans are all similar: You are allowed to put a certain amount of money away each year and deduct that amount from your income.

You not only save on your yearly taxes by this deduction, you also save on taxes on the income from the account you set up. *Any interest or dividends on these monies is not taxed on a yearly basis.*

These are called "tax-deferred plans" because when you eventually withdraw the money, you *do* have to pay the taxes on it then. But the idea is that you will withdraw the money in small increments over a period of years when you retire—and you may well be in a lower tax bracket at that time.

Are these plans good? They're terrific! First of all, they provide a real incentive to set up a solid retirement savings plan. If you need further incentive, though, take a look at the box "Double Your Money." This shows the difference between a Keogh plan and a straight investment plan.

While the idea behind these plans is simple enough, the rules surrounding them are quite complex (the Internal Revenue Service is involved, after all)—and they keep changing. For example, the money you invest in a tax-deferred retirement plan must be *earned* income: no Social Security, interest, dividends, or money from rentals. You may consider that your business is in managing your investments, but it's no go. The IRS considers any money you make to be investment income, not earned income.

How much you can contribute yearly is strictly controlled. At present, you can put $2,000 a year into an IRA, though as this book goes to press, there are proposals to raise this to $2,500. Depending on how much you earn and whether you have other retirement plans, you can deduct this $2,000 on your tax return.

If you are self-employed, you can invest in a Keogh plan; this allows you to contribute as much as $30,000 a year or 25% of your income, whichever is less.

Double Your Money

Suppose you are able to put $500 a month into a Keogh plan. That adds up to $6,000 you can deduct from your yearly income. If you are in the 28% tax bracket, this amounts to a savings of $1,680 every year ($6,000 × 0.28 = $1,680).

If your investments grow at a rate of 10% a year, compounded monthly, in 20 years you will have $379,684. This is assuming that all interest and dividends will be reinvested.

If, on the other hand, you invest the money without the benefit of a retirement plan, the $6,000 will be taxed as income. This means you will start off with only $4,320 to invest yearly: $6,000 minus $1,680 (the tax on the $6,000) = $4,320. In addition, any interest or dividends generated by the account will be taxed at the 28% rate.

How much slower would a taxed account grow? Well, $4,320 divided by 12 months = $360 a month. The tax cuts into the amount you have to reinvest each month, so the fund grows at a slower rate. At the end of 20 years, you will have $192,157, roughly half what you would have in the Keogh account.

The manner in which you can withdraw money from your retirement plan can be quite complex. If you withdraw money before you reach the age of 59½, there are penalties—except in certain cases. I encourage you to find out all you can before you invest in any one of these plans.

Mistakes can cost you money. For example, after you reach the age of 71½, the IRS says you *have* to start withdrawing a certain amount from your IRA. If you don't, you get socked with a penalty of half of what you should have withdrawn! So do read the recommended tax book and/or consult with a tax adviser. The money you save will be your own.

Where to open an IRA account? You will find that banks, credit unions, brokerages, and mutual funds will fall all over themselves for the privilege of managing your IRA. There is nothing financial institutions like better than money that stays with them for a long time! You can contribute to the account however you wish—monthly, quarterly, yearly, or whenever you feel like it.

You can buy CDs at your bank, or you can invest in securities at a brokerage in an IRA account. Buying and selling stocks goes on just as it would in a regular account. The only difference is that you can't take any money *out* without the IRS charging you a penalty.

If you open an IRA account at a mutual fund office, you can invest in different funds within that family of funds. However, all the financial institutions will charge you a small yearly fee for managing your IRA account. It is, therefore, worth your while to keep your IRA at one or two fund offices instead of opening a lot of IRA accounts in different places. A number of those fees could put a dent in your yearly return.

Keeping your IRA at a brokerage allows you the greatest amount of investment options—and you will be charged only one management fee.

Insurance companies sell tax-deferred savings plans called *annuities*. These are similar to mutual funds and resemble IRA accounts in that the *earnings* from the investments in the account are not taxed until they are withdrawn. However, *contributions* to deferred annuities are *not* tax deductible. You can, however, contribute as much as you want each year.

Deferred annuities will pay you a certain amount monthly once you retire—how much depends on how much you have contributed over the years and how well the investments have done.

Extended-Care Insurance

One important kind of insurance that is often overlooked
is extended-care insurance. This will pay for care for a
long-term disability such as Alzheimer's disease or rehabilitation from an accident or stroke. Many health insurance plans pay only for intensive hospital care and a
minimum of rehabilitation. But continued rehabilitation
or quality nursing home care is extremely expensive.
Long-term care for many couples, therefore, has meant
the loss of all their assets.

Extended-care insurance is not expensive if you
start at age 40. But even though the expense is greater
later on, it is still a vital thing to have. There is quite a bit
of difference between policies. Some are very expensive
but limited in their coverage (some provide for home
care, for example, while others do not). You need to
compare policies very carefully.

To learn more before you buy, contact the American
Association of Retired Persons (AARP), 1909 K St. NW,
Washington, DC 20049, (202) 728-4355. Ask for their
two booklets "Making Wise Decisions on Long-Term
Care" and "Before You Buy: A Guide to Long-Term Care
Insurance."

The financial soundness of the insurance company is a
critical factor here. Many large insurance companies have
been experiencing difficulties in the last few years. Investi-
gate carefully before you buy. You might do better setting
up a retirement account on your own with the help of a financial consultant.

PLANNING—AND A LITTLE CAUTION

No matter what your age, there are various things you can begin right now to make your wishes come true. In the preceding chapter, we dealt with how to set up various portfolios so that they will grow over time, and we discussed how one person might achieve an early retirement. The number of things to consider, however—for an early or later retirement—go beyond the scope of this book. For further reading (or listening), I believe you will find the material listed in the Resources very helpful.

Retirement—early or late—should be a time of fulfillment. Getting your finances squared away can leave you more time to do the things that really interest you.

One last word. Older, retired people are often seen as easy marks by con artists or unscrupulous advisers. You have probably read stories about crooks who convinced a group of retirees to put their money in a "surefire investment"—and then disappeared. In a recent version, someone persuaded a number of people that his company could convert the black sand of a Caribbean island into gold!

Sometimes, the villain may not even be dishonest, but rather an incompetent adviser or manager. This is one reason you are reading this book: to be able to recognize such people. If you are an older retiree, caution is even more important, because you may not be able to earn more to replace the losses. You will find information on how to choose a good investment adviser or financial manager in Chapter 9.

Resources

The Retirement Letter, Peter Dickinson, editor. Philips Publishing, 7811 Montrose Road, Potomac, MD 20854. (800) 777-5005. Monthly. $87/year, but, as usual, Philips will probably be offering a discount rate with bonus books by Dickinson.

This is the newsletter written specifically for those in retirement or actively planning for it. Dickinson has also written some useful books, some of which you get as subscription bonuses. *Doing Retirement Right* and *Late Starter's Guide to a Successful Retirement* are two good ones. Philips offers a money-back guarantee, so you can take out a subscription and see whether you find the newsletter useful.

Cashing In On the American Dream: How to Retire at 35 by Paul Terhorst. Bantam Books, 1988. $16.95.

This is a great book for all would-be retirees—not just those wanting early retirement. This book is essentially about how to live very well on an income most people would consider low. The author travels extensively with his wife, writes, plays saxophone in a jazz band, and generally enjoys himself. There are sections on the cheapest and nicest places to live abroad, and a chapter on how to retire with kids. Easy and fun to read.

The seminar recommended in Resources in Chapter 3, **"Transforming Your Relationship with Money,"** contains much good information on how to retire early.

How to join the **American Association of Individual Investors (AAII)** is described in Resources, Chapter 1. Not only does the AAII monthly journal run useful articles on retirement, the group organizes seminars covering such topics as estate planning and investment strategies for retirement. Joining is also a good way of contacting other investors. If you plan to be an active investor, you may want to join an investment club.

Just because your company has hired professional managers to invest your pension fund doesn't necessarily mean they are doing a good job. There are other dangers too: occasionally, when corporations are taken over by new owners, the pension fund is raided to procure extra cash. Know your rights and be aware what goes on with your pension! **The Pension Rights Center** is a private watchdog organization that keeps tabs on pension funds. It puts out a handbook: *Protecting Your Pension Money: A Pension Investment Handbook.* $6. 918 16th St. NW, Suite 704, Washington, DC 20006-2902. (202) 296-3776.

CHAPTER 18

GOING FURTHER WITH STOCKS

$500,000—RISK FREE!

Hey, how would you like $500,000 to play around with? For $100, you can. This is the National Investment Challenge—not only can you have some fun, you can learn about investing in the stock market without any risk. Reading this book and a few others may be the first step, but hands-on experience is definitely the next.

Your $100 buys you an "account" of $500,000. You are assigned an account number and given an 800 telephone number that connects you with one of the contest "brokers." Over a period of three months, you can make up to 100 imaginary trades, buying and selling whatever stocks you choose. At the end of the contest, the contestants whose portfolios have appreciated the most are given cash prizes.

Whether you win a prize or not, this is a great way to learn. No stocks are actually bought or sold, but the contest gives you a real feel for the markets, and stimulates you to

learn what you need to know to buy and sell. Nothing moti-
vates like possible gain or loss of money—even play money.
The Challenge is easy to enter. The number to call is listed in
Resources.

If you decide to buy stocks in individual companies,
there are a few things more that you need to know. We will
cover them in this chapter.

PREFERRED STOCKS

If you consult the stock listings in the financial pages, you
will occasionally see two listings for a stock; the second will
have a "pf" after it. (Occasionally a company will show a
list of "pf" stocks at varying rates of interest.) These are so-
called "preferred stocks" (in contrast to the regular "common" stocks), so named because the dividends are given
preference, or priority, over common-stock dividends. In
other words, if a company is having a bad year, it must reduce its dividend on its common stock before it does so on
the preferred.

This sounds good, until you realize that, like bonds, preferred stock has a fixed dividend payment. Common stock
dividends fluctuate according to the fortunes of the company. With preferred stock, however, you will get a certain
amount of income each year. If the stock sells for $50 a share
and the dividend is set at 10%, you will get $5 per share—no
more, no less.

This means the price of the preferred stock will stay
pretty much the same, unless overall interest rates change.
The reason for buying preferred stocks, then, is not that you
think they will increase in value, but that you want a steady
income and a higher dividend than most common stocks
provide.

As you look through the "pf" listings, you will see some
with spectacular dividends: 15%, 18%, and more (normal

return from preferreds is 8% to 10%). These are usually companies in trouble. The investment community believes there is a good chance the company will default on its payments to the preferred stockholders, so the price of these shares has gone down (as the share price goes down, the percentage of return to a buyer goes up—*if* the company continues to pay the dividend).

So this is yet another instance where you would have to decide how speculative you want to be. Remember that even though owners of the preferreds will be paid before holders of common stock, they come *after* the bondholders.

One more thing about preferreds: Most of them are "callable"; that is, the company can tell you at any time to turn in your shares at a set price. This price is something to be aware of should you buy this kind of stock—especially if it is lower than the market price of the stock.

In my opinion, there are safer ways for the new investor to get a steady income and better ways of speculating. An exception are the *convertible preferred* stocks. These are preferred shares that you can convert into shares of common stock in the same company at any time. Because of this factor, these "convertibles" go up and down with the market price of the common stock. The dividend rates are not as good as those for straight preferreds, but substantially better than for common stock.

Like convertible bonds, convertible preferreds are a good way of getting substantial dividends, but also investing for growth.

ODD LOTS

Brokers like to trade stock in denominations of 100 shares. If you buy less than 100 shares of an equity, you will be buying what is called an *odd lot*. This should not dissuade you from buying, say, 10 shares of IBM at $120 a share, if it looks like a good buy (100 shares would cost $12,000—too much for some people).

But if you can afford it, it's generally better to buy 100, 200, or 500 shares at a time, rather than 162 or 305 shares. This makes it easier for you to figure the value of your holding, as well as easier for the brokers to make a trade. Two hundred shares of a $36 stock, for example, is simply 2 × 36 = 72, plus a couple of zeros, or $7,200.

STOCK PRICES

The price range of stocks over about $10 a share is not necessarily related to the underlying value of its company. IBM at $120 a share is not worth three times as much as General Motors at $40 a share. For reasons of their own, different companies prefer to have their stock trading in a certain price range. IBM has been an expensive stock for a long time. On the other hand, Philadelphia Electric, a major utility, costs only $15 to $20 a share.

If the price of a company's shares increases over a period of time, perhaps doubling in value, often the company will engineer a stock split.

STOCK SPLITS

When a company splits its stock, it will ask you to send in your shares; it will then send you twice as many shares in return, each worth half as much. General Electric split its stock several years ago when it was selling for about $120 a share. If you had owned 100 shares, you would have traded them in and received 200 shares, each worth $60.

A stock split is generally welcomed by shareholders. They see it as an indication that the company is doing well, and the hope is that the lower price will attract more buyers, thereby sending the stock up again. Splits of 3 for 1, 4 for 1, or higher are not unknown, though not as common as the standard 2 for 1. Occasionally, a company will make a *reverse split*, giving one share for two at double the value.

Ex-Dividend

As you read through the stock tables, you will occasionally see an "x" in front of a stock. This means the stock is about to issue a dividend. About a week before the dividend is issued, the stock, in market lingo, "goes ex-dividend." If you buy the stock during this time, you will not receive the dividend. You will pay less per share, however; the stock price will be lowered during that week by the amount of the dividend. If the dividend were a dollar per share, the stock price would be lowered by a dollar.

LIMIT ORDERS

In Chapter 5 we described how to buy and sell stocks, using what is called a *market order*. To buy or sell "at the market" means you are simply asking your broker to get you the best possible price.

You can, however, specify the price at which you want to buy. "I want to buy a hundred shares of AT&T at no more than thirty-five dollars a share" is what you would tell your broker. This is called a *limit order* and you can make it just for the day (a "day order"), or specify that it is "good till canceled" (GTC). If you make it GTC, the order will stand unless you cancel it; the broker will buy the 100 shares as soon as the stock goes down to $35 or less.

Similarly, you can sell stock with a "limit order to sell." For example, you might tell your broker you don't want to sell until AT&T reaches at least $40 a share.

STOP ORDERS

Say you succeed in buying AT&T for $35 a share. You chose well, because over the next few months the stock climbs to $42 a share. You hope it will go higher, but at the same time, you don't want to lose what profit you have. You're a busy person and don't have the luxury of keeping track of the hour-by-hour changes in the stock. So you tell your broker to sell your AT&T stock if it goes down to $40.

This is called a *stop order* (short for "stop-loss order"— you are stopping any possible loss). Like the limit orders, it can be a day order or good till canceled. With your stop order at $40, you have locked in a profit of $5 a share, should the stock start to go down from $42. If it goes up, you can always sell at a higher price.

It's important to know that a stop order is not always a sure thing. If a stock suddenly plummets, your broker may not be able to sell at your specified price, and you will be sold out at a lower price.

SELLING SHORT

Suppose you have it on good authority that Consolidated Bobsleds is about to go downhill fast. What you want to do is sell it, of course, but the trouble is that you don't *own* any Bobsleds stock. Difficulties like selling something you don't own, however, have never hampered people in the World of Investment.

All you have to do is call your broker and say that you want to "sell short" Consolidated Bobsleds stock (or, simply, to "short" it). The broker then "borrows" the stock from someone who owns it and sells it to a buyer at the market price. You are obligated to buy it back sometime in the future; this is called "covering your short position." The broker then "returns" it to the lender. (You don't have to understand these machinations—all you need to know is that you make money if the stock goes down, lose if it goes up.)

If the stock goes down, you can buy it back at the lower price and keep the difference. If it goes up, then so do you—up the creek! At some point—it's your decision when—you will have to buy back the stock and take a loss.

Selling short is more complex than buying stocks. You have to have a margin account with your broker, for one thing (see the next section). You have to pay the stock dividend to the lender of the stock, and your broker will hold on to the money from the short sale and charge you interest on it.

MARGIN ACCOUNTS

Now wait, all you people who believe you can't understand anything involving arithmetic, don't space out! I have tested this chapter on people who started spacing out in math class in third grade, and they gave it a thumbs up. So hang in there!

You may not be aware that if you own $10,000 worth of stock, you can purchase $10,000 more for free. Well, not exactly for free; the brokerage will charge you interest on the $10,000 you borrow. Low interest, to be sure—these days it is around 9% to 10%—but interest nonetheless.

When you open an account, the broker will ask you whether you want a *margin account.* "Margin" in this case simply means collateral; the broker will hold your shares of stock as collateral for a loan. ("Collateral" is something of value held by a lender in case you can't pay back your loan. Your house, for example, is collateral for your mortgage loan.)

If you have a margin account, you can use your stock as collateral to buy more stocks or bonds, up to double the amount you own—in this case, $10,000 more. This is called "buying on margin."

It's pretty clear that if you use your margin, or collateral, to buy more stocks, they had better increase in value more than 10% over the course of a year (you will have the benefit of any dividends, too, of course). If their price stays the same or goes down, you are out the 10% interest on whatever you borrowed—$1,000 in this case, if you borrowed the full $10,000.

Buying on Margin: An Example

Suppose you own $10,000 worth of General Electric stock and have $2,000 cash in your margin account. You use the stock as collateral to buy shares worth $10,000 more—still

GE, for simplicity's sake (the security bought on margin does not have to be in the same company). But GE has a so-so year, and the stock is selling for the same price a year later. You still own $20,000 worth of stock, but you are out $1,000—the interest on the $10,000 you borrowed from the broker. It has been deducted in increments each month from the $2,000 cash in your account.

The next year, you think things look better for GE; it is expanding its markets in Eastern Europe and the prospects seem promising. So you hold on to your "margined stock" (the $10,000 worth you bought with the borrowed money), and yes, indeed, the stock does go up very nicely—25% by the end of the year. So . . . your original $10,000 is now worth $12,500 and your $10,000 of margined stock is also worth $12,500, making a total of $25,000 worth of stock.

At this point, you decide to sell the whole shebang, and $25,000 is credited to your account. From this is deducted the original $10,000 loan, leaving $15,000. In addition, you have paid a total of $2,000 interest on the loan, $1,000 each year. This leaves $13,000. You have made a $3,000 profit in two years.

It's interesting to compare this $3,000 with how much you would have made with only the original $10,000 worth of stock. No margin loan—no interest costs. A 25% increase in value would have left you with $12,500, or $2,500 in profits, minus commissions—not that much less than the $3,000, but with less risk.

What these figures say is that you have to believe a stock is going to go up by at least 15% to 20% a year to justify the added risk of buying on margin.

One more note: A stock you can borrow against is called a *marginable stock*. To be marginable, a stock must be selling for at least $5 a share (according to present rules) and be traded on a major U.S. exchange like the New York or the American Exchange. Some over-the-counter stocks are marginable; be sure to check with your broker before you buy. Some brokers allow mutual funds to be used as margin, others don't; this is something to consider when finding a broker if you plan to buy on margin.

Margin Calls

So buying on margin is chancy—chancy enough for the new investor to avoid. The value of a stock has to increase quite sharply to make it worthwhile. Your opportunities for a greater profit increase, but should the stock take a real dive, your losses will double. In short, the risk-reward ratio has moved up sharply.

And there is one more thing: Suppose the stock you bought for $20,000, with a $10,000 margin loan, should go down by $7,200 to a new total value of $12,800. Your collateral now only amounts to $2,800 ($10,000 minus $7,200). But your broker wants you to bring your collateral up to 50% of the *new* value, that is, $6,400 ($12,800 × .50 = $6,400). This means a *margin call*—the broker tells you to bring in $3,600 ($3,600 added to your $2,800 = $6,400).

Brokerage firms can set their own margin levels, but this level cannot be more than 75%. Most firms set their levels at 65% to 70%. This means you will get a margin call if the value of your stock falls to less than 65% or 70% of its original value.

If this happens, you can now do one of two things: You can pony up the needed $3,600, or you can sell enough of the stock to cover the shortfall. Experienced investors will usually choose to sell, even though the price is down. If the stock has dropped sharply, they feel they don't want to throw good money after bad. Only if they are certain that a rise is imminent will they put up more money.

If you fail to do anything, the brokerage will act for you by selling *twice* the amount of stock necessary to cover the margin shortfall.

1929

Of course, if the stock price continues its downward spiral, you will get another margin call, because your collateral will have again decreased. A bad situation.

As a matter of fact, this downward spiral is what compounded the disaster of the 1929 crash. In those days, you needed only $10,000 worth of stock to borrow $90,000 more. As you can guess, quite a few people did just this—they borrowed the limit. If they had only $1,000, they borrowed $9,000; if they had a million dollars, well, they borrowed 9 million more!

A $100,000 portfolio with a $10,000 cash outlay looks pretty good—as long as the stocks continue to go up. When they go down, however, watch out! If the value of the stocks falls to $80,000, you have a situation where the total value is less than the $90,000 that was borrowed—$10,000 less, to be exact. So that $10,000 would be the amount of the margin call.

Because so many shareholders had borrowed up to the limit, they had no way of meeting the margin calls with cash. They had no choice, therefore, but to sell some of their stock. Everyone selling their stock at once tended to depress prices even further, leading to *further* devaluation of the stocks—and more margin calls! A deadly spiral. It is easy to see why the Federal Reserve Board now sets the amount you can borrow at a much lower level. (Margin requirements change from time to time. They have been at their present levels for more than a decade.)

Modern Margin Calls: Watch Out!

In addition to borrowing on margin to purchase stocks and bonds, you can also use your securities as collateral for a personal loan. For these personal loans you can borrow up to *half* the value of your portfolio. If you own $10,000 worth of stocks (or bonds), you can borrow $5,000.

The larger brokerages make it very easy to write checks or use Visa cards as a loan against your balance—too easy, if you're not careful. Brokerage Visa cards are different from the charge cards you are accustomed to. They are called *debit cards*. If you have a cash balance in your account, your brokerage Visa purchase will be charged against that balance—*it will not be a loan*. Only when you have no cash in your account are your card charges—and the checks you write—lent against the collateral of the securities in your account.

A loan with such low interest can be very seductive, especially since you need to make *no payments*. The 10% interest is automatically deducted each month from the cash in your account—or added to the amount owing, if there is no cash (the actual interest charged may vary, depending on the prevailing interest rates).

Another difference from regular bank loans is that if you should sell some stock, the resulting cash will immediately go first to pay off any outstanding margin loan.

The main thing to watch for here is borrowing too much, because, just as in the case of buying stocks on margin, you can get a margin call for this kind of loan, too. Suppose you owned $10,000 worth of securities, and that you borrowed your limit, in this case half the $10,000, or $5,000. Now, if the value of the stock goes down to $7,000, you will get a margin call asking for $1,500. With a collateral of only $7,000, your borrowing limit has decreased to half this $7,000, or $3,500. You are being asked to come up with the difference between the $5,000 you borrowed and your new $3,500 limit. This can be a very nasty shock if you're not prepared for it.

To prevent this kind of upset, if you do borrow a good move would be to set your borrowing limit at half your actual limit. In this case, with $10,000 worth of stock, that would be $2,500. This allows quite a bit of leeway and should prevent margin calls in all except truly disastrous dives by your stocks or bonds.

Resources

The National Investment Challenge. $100 for three months of trading with an "account" of $500,000. Call (800) 545-1990. The managers will send you a brochure with all the information you need to enter. There are now professional and amateur divisions to the Challenge.

Value Line. The Value Line Investment Survey, 711 Third Ave., New York, NY 10017-4064. (800) 883-0046 for credit card orders. $525/year; $55/10 weeks (introductory offer).

No chapter on buying individual stocks would be complete without a reference to Value Line, one of the oldest and most respected stock evaluation services. For your $55, you will receive a 2,000-page folder with detailed information on 1,700 stocks. Then, each week, you will receive updated information on 130 stocks.

Over the years, the top-rated Value Line stocks have generally outperformed the market very nicely. Even if you don't buy in to the companies they recommend, however, the folder is an excellent basic reference for stocks. Many public libraries also subscribe to Value Line.

Louis Navellier's MPT Review, 824 Baltimore St., Baltimore, MD 21202. (800) 223-1982, ext. 415. Monthly. $129/year.

Mark Hulbert, the editor of *Hulbert Financial Digest,* which tracks the best newsletters, calls the *MPT Review* "far and away the best-performing newsletter" for the six years up to June 1991. Be aware, however, that these are risky stocks.

National Association of Investors Corporation. P.O. Box 220, Royal Oak, MI 48068-9972. Membership: $32/year. Includes subscription to *Better Investing* magazine (monthly; $17/year without membership), and an Investors Manual, Club or Individual Edition.

4

Some 7,500 investment clubs are members of the NAIC. If you are interested in getting together with other folks and pooling your money and investment savvy, this is a good place to start. Even if you're not interested in joining a club, the organization's magazine is one of the best I've seen for new investors. It even runs a monthly "Beginner's Corner." The clubs and the magazine are mainly for investors in individual stocks.

CHAPTER 19

BUYING METHODS

In 1973, an economist named Burton Malkiel planted a bomb on Wall Street. No, not a terrorist bomb, but something much worse, as far as the stockbrokers and professional money managers were concerned. The bomb was a book titled *A Random Walk Down Wall Street.*

According to the *Random Walk* theory, a portfolio of stocks picked at random has just as much chance of success as one selected by most stockbrokers. In other words, a group of chimpanzees throwing darts at the *Wall Street Journal* would hit as many winners as most professional advisers (or individual investors).

The reason is what Malkiel terms the "efficient market." The idea is that any information about a company will be immediately picked up by the market, causing the stock price to rise or fall too soon for most investors to profit from the news.

Malkiel has since revised and updated his book, but he has changed few of his assertions. During the 1970s and 1980s, according to Malkiel, the stock market as a whole, as measured by the S&P 500 Index, outperformed two-thirds of the managers of large institutional funds.

The implications of these figures for the individual investor are quite dramatic. They say that in selecting winning stocks, in the majority of cases, you are better off investing in a stock index fund that covers the overall market than in giving your money to a manager or listening to a stockbroker's recommendations. And the same may be true, according to Malkiel, of trying to pick stocks on your own.

The professionals might give you other useful advice, of course—the chimps won't know about your tax situation or the balance in your portfolio. Our model portfolio, for example, takes into consideration more than just increase in value in the stock market—balance, diversification, and safety of principal are weighed. The *Random Walk* theory deals only with stocks that go up in value.

There *are* exceptions to the *Random Walk* theory—even Professor Malkiel admits this. The advisers who write the books and newsletters that I recommend in this book, for example, beat the averages more often than not—some of them dramatically. There *are* ways to optimize your chances of coming out ahead.

The buying methods presented in this chapter are among those that have helped investors to beat the averages. These are the kinds of techniques you can use in setting up and working with your portfolio. We'll start out with the famous method of *dollar-cost averaging*.

DOLLAR-COST AVERAGING

What it all comes down to, of course, is "buy low, sell high." Buying methods are simply various ways of doing this—or trying to. The question is, how do you tell when the highs and lows occur? The first method—dollar-cost averaging—

doesn't even try to guess. But it very neatly has you buying more shares at low prices, fewer at the highs.

What you do is invest a given amount each month, say $500, in a security or mutual fund. Over a period of a year, on the 20th of each month the price of shares in a mutual fund might vary like this:

Jan	Feb	Mar	Apr	May	Jun	Jul	Aug	Sep	Oct	Nov	Dec
$12	14	15	14	12	12	10	8	9	8	10	12
41	37	33	37	41	41	50	62	55	62	50	41

The figure below the price per share is the number of shares purchased by $500 (rounded off). Each month, your $500 is divided by whatever the price per share is at the time; the resulting figure is the number of shares you purchased. Over the year, you invested $6,000 ($500 × 12 months), and bought 550 shares of the fund. Notice that you bought more shares in months when the price was down, fewer when the price was up.

Notice also that the fund returned to its original price of $12 a share on December 20. If you had taken the $6,000 and invested it all in January, you would have bought 500 shares of the fund ($6,000 ÷ $12 = 500 shares). By December, after some ups and downs, you would be back exactly where you started: you would own 500 shares at $12 a share = $6,000.

But, using the magic of dollar-cost averaging, by December you would own *550* shares, worth $6,600 (550 × $12 = $6,600), even though you invested the same $6,000. This happy difference is the result of buying more shares when the price was down, fewer when it was up.

Dollar-cost averaging is an excellent way of creating a portfolio if you have only monthly income to invest. As we discussed in Chapter 16, putting in a small amount each month will eventually result in a large amount. We have chosen a time period of a month, but you could, of course, put money in every week or two weeks, or every quarter—whatever is most convenient for you.

Even if you have a lump sum to invest, you may want to do it using dollar-cost averaging—especially if the stock market has been acting like a person on a trampoline. By investing each month over a year, you will avoid putting all your money in at the top of the market, and have a better chance of coming out ahead, as in the example above.

There are a few postscripts to this explanation. The first is that you will do much better buying directly from the mutual fund than paying a broker $20 or more commission for each purchase. The funds are very fond of dollar-cost people and make it easy for them. After an initial investment of $500 or $1,000 (depending on the fund), most funds encourage monthly additions of as little as $50, at no charge (for no-load funds). This makes dollar-cost averaging perfect for the small investor wanting to build a portfolio.

Buying individual stocks with this method can be expensive because of the commissions—and this is true of almost any investment that charges a commission. No-load mutual funds are the preferred vehicle for dollar-cost averaging.

You will do even better if you make your dollar-cost averaging part of an individual retirement account (IRA). The advantages of IRAs are explained in Chapter 17. Most funds allow smaller initial investments and smaller monthly additions for IRA accounts.

The final postscript is that with stocks or stock funds, you will do best over the long run by putting in your monthly investment on or about the 20th of the month. The large institutions tend to do their buying around the early part of the month, driving prices up. Around the 20th is when much of the selling occurs, so prices are driven down. This also means that the first two or three days of the month are good days to *sell*, statistically speaking.

Fundamental Analysis

Fundamental analysis evaluates the stock of a company starting with the company's financial statements. You want to know the general financial health of the company as well as its position in its industry, and its ability to cope with ups and downs in the economy. A detailed description of all the methods used in fundamental analysis is beyond our scope here. For active investors, the way to pick the best companies by doing your own fundamental analysis is described thoroughly in the two books listed in Resources.

Technical Analysis

Technical analysts attempt to predict the direction of a stock by studying what is actually happening to it in the market. Forget the financial statements. Are people actually *buying* the stock? If so, is the daily volume of stock trading going up? What does the graph of the stock's price over the last year look like? Are the large institutions buying the stock? In his book cited below, William O'Neil goes into the most important technical factors in choosing a stock.

Technical analysis can also be performed on the entire stock market, using a variety of indicators: the direction of the market, the volume of stocks traded, the volume of short selling, whether the mutual funds are buying or selling, what the majority of investment advisers are saying, etc., etc.

The technical analysts are trying to "time" the stock market—to ascertain just *when* the market is going to move, and in what direction. (For more on market timing, see Chapter 24.)

Though this will vary from month to month according to market direction, statistically speaking, prices will be marginally lower during the days around the 20th. A small thing, but one that will add up over the years.

LOW-PRICED STOCKS

When we speak of low-priced stocks, we are discussing small companies with good prospects; we are not including larger corporations whose stocks have fallen because of bad times or bankruptcy. For example, in January 1991, after Pan Am filed for bankruptcy, you could have bought its stock for ⅜ (37.5 cents) a share. Buying companies in dire straits, however, is an entirely different—and risky—buying method (Pan Am eventually went out of business).

During most of this century, stocks of small companies, as a whole, have done significantly better than those of large companies. To see how *much* better, take a look at Appendix D, "Fifty Years of Returns."

Unless you have specific knowledge about a small company, it's generally wise to stick to those stocks listed on the major exchanges or NASDAQ. As we discussed in Chapter 8, the unlisted ones—the "pink sheet" stocks—are too volatile and uncertain for the new investor's portfolio.

Within those restrictions, though, low-priced, small-company stocks can be an excellent addition to a portfolio. Investors who are just starting out can buy mutual funds specializing in small companies, as recommended in Chapter 14.

As you gain experience, however, you may want to buy individual issues. This is, after all, where the Apple Computer or Adobe Systems of tomorrow is to be found.

One attractive feature of the low-priced issues is that when they go up in price, the percentage gain is usually greater than for the higher-priced stocks.

For example, if you buy a stock in a company for ¾ a share (75 cents a share) and it goes up ¾ of a point to 1½ ($1.50 a share), you have doubled your money. Yes, it could also go down and you could be a large percentage loser on paper, but you don't have to sell. If you have done your research and the company is a good one, there is a good chance it will go up again.

Another attraction of low-priced issues for the adventurous investor is that it's possible to buy a large number of shares. For an investment of $1,250, plus commission, you could buy 1,000 shares of a company's stock selling at 1¼ ($1.25 a share). If this company should hit the big time and the stock go to $10 a share or higher, your 1,000 shares will suddenly look like gold.

It is true that occasionally even the best research doesn't do the job, or a company encounters unexpectedly difficult times. There is risk here—these are small companies, and a couple of bad years can be disastrous.

Most investors are well aware of these dangers, so the stocks tend to be traded much more lightly than those of the big companies. When the demand is low, the price of the stock will stay down. If the company begins to do well, however, you have a situation where investors are bidding for a relatively small number of shares. This can drive the price up quite dramatically.

If a small company catches your eye in a newsletter or elsewhere, you can do your own analysis of the company's fundamentals. You can call up the management, ask for recent quarterly reports, and follow the price of the stock for a while in order to get a feel for the company and its prospects.

This can be fun as well as profitable. Investing in a small company where you have spoken with the managers and learned about its history and field of operations makes for a stronger involvement in your investment than with a large, impersonal corporation. If you are acquainted with the type of business carried out by the company, perhaps you will make suggestions to the management. This is the way investment used to be carried out. Investors in the 17th and 18th centuries usually involved themselves intimately in the companies they bought into.

Research and diversification will help you tilt the odds in your favor when investing in small companies. Diversification becomes even more important with riskier investments. If you invest in small-company stocks, it's good to own at least a half dozen. This prepares you for an occasional loser in your portfolio.

The third way of limiting your risk is simply to put only 10% to 20% of your portfolio into low-priced issues. That way, the risk-reward thermometer of your portfolio will stay in a comfortable range, but you will have a good chance of seeing some real winners emerge, given a reasonable economic climate.

To further increase your chances of success, try the three small-company newsletters listed in Resources. These will give you a running head start in the field of low-priced stocks.

CONTRARIANISM

Sounds like a political faction, doesn't it? It's actually the method used by many of the sharpest investors to buy low and sell high. This is one way the less-experienced investor can successfully imitate the pros.

What it means is just what it sounds like: being contrary. While everyone else is following the high fliers—investing in the bright, successful companies that have captured the public's attention—the contrarian is off in a little room studying the companies that have been left behind.

This studious contrarian is looking for the success stories of the future: companies with great balance sheets,

---

Things to Watch For: Overmanaging

Overmanaging a portfolio can cause as much trouble as not giving it enough attention. "Has the stock gone up one point? Perhaps we should sell now before it goes down!" This kind of excessive concern can lead you to sell prematurely.

Appreciation in a portfolio is generally something that happens over a period of years. The more volatile, smaller companies may require more attention. But if you choose quality investments, you are usually expecting them to appreciate over the long term.

Being a successful investor often involves being aware of your internal responses and correcting for them. In this case, you might need to be aware of your tendency to overreact.

---

a large percentage of the market in their field, good management, or perhaps an exciting but unpublicized product.

These companies either have not yet been discovered by the investment community, are currently out of favor because of a bad year or two, or have simply been eclipsed by the high fliers. Their stock, then, is currently trading at a low price relative to earnings or projected future earnings.

Even entire market groups can be food for contrarian diets. Those investors smart enough to buy small-company funds in the autumn of 1990 saw their investments go up by 30% to 50% in six months. These funds had performed poorly relative to blue chips for several years, but some contrarians realized that the small companies were undervalued—and underpriced.

Usually, however, being a contrarian involves buying stocks of individual companies. If you decide to be an active manager of your portfolio, this is one excellent method of picking potential winners.

The good newsletters often recommend stocks for contrarians. One newsletter that specializes in small companies with good prospects is listed in Resources. You can also find such companies on your own by doing the kind of fundamental analysis explained in the recommended books.

Perhaps the most difficult part of contrarian investing is bringing yourself to invest in a currently unpopular stock. We are social animals, often given to believing that the safest course is to follow the herd. If you invest in a popular issue and it takes a dive, you will, at least, have a lot of company. If you're wrong with your contrarian investments, you'll be wrong alone. It can seem like a risky business.

This perception of risk is usually a false one, however. Contrarian investors—at least the ones who really do their homework—have traditionally been among the most successful in the investment community. The courage it takes to listen to a different drummer is, more often than not, rewarded.

Resources

Newsletters

Newsletters like the ones listed here are generally for those investors who have decided to actively manage their portfolios. These advisers are good, but following their recommendations will require keeping constant tabs on the changes in the market and in your portfolio.

The first two advisers have done extremely well, both at market timing and portfolio advice. The second pair are two of the best small-company specialists.

Zweig Forecast, P.O. Box 2900, Wantagh, NY 11793. (516) 785-1300. Published every three weeks with occasional special bulletins. Includes hotline phone service. $265/year. $155/six months.

Zweig Performance Ratings Report. $205/year.
Martin Zweig is one of the better-known investment advisers. He has been very successful both with his stock picks and his mar-

ket timing. The *Performance Report* lists 1,500 stocks rated by Zweig. His No. 1–rated stocks have done extremely well over the years; the lower-rated stocks are the ones to avoid.

Because the market can move up or down very quickly, some newsletters give their subscribers hotlines to call. These are recorded messages that inform you of any up-to-the-minute changes advised for the portfolio recommended in the newsletter. In Zweig's case, he will also give you his opinion on where the market is headed. His hotline is recorded Monday, Tuesday, and Thursday.

Sy Harding Investor Forecasts, P.O. Box 352016, Palm Coast, FL 32135-2016. Published every three weeks. Includes a hotline recorded twice a week. $195/year.

Harding is one of the most accomplished market timers. And, like Zweig's, the investments he recommends have also done very well. The newsletter features three portfolios: Buy and Hold, Mutual Fund Switching, and Short-Term Trading. The hotline updates subscribers on buy and sell recommendations and gives Harding's latest opinion on the direction of the market.

The Acker Letter, 2718 E. 63rd St., Brooklyn, NY 11234. 8–12 issues a year and occasional special bulletins. $85/year. $25/3-issue trial.

The Acker Letter is one of my favorite newsletters. Bob Acker puts it out himself, with his wife as business and production manager, using a typewriter at their kitchen table. There is a kind of capitalist class struggle going on in this newsletter: the individual investor against the "big boys"—the large investors who ignore or look down on the small companies recommended by Acker. With each stock recommendation that succeeds, Acker triumphantly headlines: "Score one for the Good Guys!"

The "Good Guy" subscribers who buy stock in the companies recommended in the newsletter have done very well over the last few years. Acker is not only a small-company specialist but a contrarian. These are companies with a special product that have been overlooked by most investors, or basically sound firms whose stock has been driven down by a couple of bad years.

The Bowser Report, P.O. Box 6278, Newport News, VA 23606. (804) 877-5979. Monthly. $57/year.

If you are interested in small-cap stocks, this is the newsletter you want. Not only do you get the letter every month with buy recommendations and articles, you get a very useful booklet on the best ways to buy low-priced stocks. For an additional $2.50, you can buy *Bowser's Notebook*, a glossary of stock market terms and articles geared to the new investor.

New Energy Report: Investing in the Environment, 84 Canyon Rd., Fairfax, CA 94930. Monthly. $45/year. Free sample.

The *New Energy Report*, edited by Sam Case (the author of this book), profiles promising small companies whose products or services are aimed at solving the great environmental problems of the day. Companies focusing on alternate energy, non-polluting transportation, recycling of wastes, and naturally-produced food stand to make dramatic gains in the 1990s.

Books

How to Make Money in Stocks by William J. O'Neil. McGraw-Hill, 1988, revised 1991. $9.95 (paperback).

O'Neil is the founder of *Investor's Business Daily* newspaper and a well-known figure in the investment world. This book lays out his methods for choosing stocks in a clear, readable manner. In the process, he gives pointers to new investors and tells stories about his own experience as an investor. A good read for the serious, hands-on investor.

One Up on Wall Street by Peter Lynch. Penguin, 1990. $8.95 (paperback).

Lynch was the manager of the immensely successful Fidelity Magellan Fund, one of the equity mutual funds that consistently beat the market during the 1980s. He advocates investing in areas where you have special knowledge—the subtitle of the book is "How to Use What You Already Know to Make Money in the Market." You will also learn what he looks for in the companies he investigates. This book reads easily—very good for the new investor.

Chapter 20

Bad Times

Iraq invades Kuwait! . . . Middle East in turmoil . . .
oil prices soar! . . . dow loses 300 points.
Who could forget these headlines in early August 1990?
Investors are not likely to. The Dow Jones Industrial Average, which had been as high as 3,000 in July, lost 20% of its value in a matter of weeks. And this was just the average loss of the blue chip stocks; many of the smaller, over-the-counter stocks went down by 30%, 40%, or 50%. Many analysts had felt that the market was due for a "correction" (a move against the upward trend), but the prospects of war and high oil prices turned the correction into a rout.

Real estate prices began to turn down in most areas, to the dismay of homeowners and speculators alike. Younger property owners were especially distressed; for those who had started buying in the mid-1970s, it had seemed as if real estate went in only one direction: up!

What is the individual investor to do in a case like this? Many stockholders sold at a loss and got out of the market entirely. This was particularly hard on the investors who had watched stocks climb during the bull market earlier in the year. They had decided in June or July that they should get on board, even at inflated prices, lest they be left behind altogether. So they ended up doing what investors are always warned against—that is, buying at the highs and selling at the lows.

But what were the alternatives? Some analysts were talking about a possible 50% drop in the market and were even raising the specter of the crash of 1929. Wouldn't it be better to preserve what capital was left and get out?

This, as you might guess, is a source of much disagreement among investment advisers. Some will tell you to sell and then buy again when the market reaches its lows. Others will tell you to grit your teeth and hold on; don't sell while prices are declining.

"HARD TIMES, COME AGIN NO MORE . . ."

Before we get into practical measures to deal with economic downturns, let's look at how bad times have manifested since the Second World War.

The fear of another 1929-type crash and subsequent depression has colored the thinking of individual and professional investors for 60 years. Perhaps this fear goes back even further in the common memory. Throughout the 19th century and into the 20th, devastating boom-and-bust cycles were commonplace.

Although the recessions of the post–World War II era can look grim to those who lose their jobs or see their assets plummet in value, these downturns have actually been very mild compared to the bad times of yesteryear. Modern-day recessions generally last only about six months to a year and are now seen as simply part of the normal business cycle.

Guns and Money

War, despite persistent beliefs to the contrary, is *not* good for capitalist economies. It disrupts the flow of goods, upsets energy supplies, and directs money and manufacturing away from consumer goods into weapons.

During the 19th century, there was more reason for Karl Marx and others to believe that increased government spending on war, or preparation for war, had stimulating economic effects. Nowadays, however, there is already so much government spending that the main effect of increased outlays for defense is simply to add to the national debt.

The enormous government debt in this country is almost entirely related to the massive cost of our defense establishment, which was set up to fight the Cold War. Paying the interest on this debt and continuing with new military expenditures is one of the main reasons the U.S. economy is having such difficulties. A chief cause for the collapse of the Soviet Union was its economy's inability to carry the burden of its enormous military establishment.

Witness the booming economies of Germany and Japan, which have spent much less on defense since World War II than other major countries. Witness also the meteoric rise of the stock market in January 1991, when it appeared that the Mideast war would soon be over. Investors know that peace means prosperity.

Why is this? Economists point to a better understanding of fiscal and monetary policy by government leaders and central banks. There are various actions a government can take to revive a slumping economy, and during the 45 years since the end of the war these actions have succeeded in smoothing out the old boom-and-bust cycles in most modern economies.

To John Dessauer, the well-known adviser on international investing (see Resources, Chapter 13), the constant concern about the state of the economy is a good sign—when the concern is coupled with positive action. He points out that the Great Depression of the 1930s came about partly because of the general consensus in the 1920s that prosperity was here to stay. The few economists who disagreed not only saw their warnings go unheeded, they were accused of being unpatriotic! Dessauer believes that our ongoing anxiety about the economy makes an economic catastrophe less likely to happen.

From this point of view, the doomsayers who write books with titles like *How to Profit from the Coming Collapse of Western Civilization* are actually performing a useful service. At least some of the failings in our economy that they describe so graphically are indeed things we should be concerned about. But the new investor needs to know that so far, the great majority of such books have been mistaken in their predictions of major economic disasters and great depressions.

There have been 14 major bear markets in stocks since World War II ended. Some of these downturns lasted several years, some only a few months. The average decline in value of the overall stock market during these times was 25%.

The market traditionally rises substantially, then goes to unrealistic limits where stock prices reflect speculation rather than real value. A "correction" inevitably follows and the market goes down anywhere from 7% to 30%. A bottoming-out process then occurs in which stocks stay at roughly the same low prices for several months. And, finally, a new rally begins. This pattern has been repeated over and over throughout the years.

Why Do Markets Go Up and Down?

What makes the stock market—or any financial market—go up and down? This has been the subject of an extravagant amount of research, speculation, and fancy mathematics. Much of this research has been directed at trying to discern the exact time a market is going to move; if you know this time, you can then get in or out before the crowd. When the crowd gets in or out, the market reacts to the massive buying or selling, the law of supply and demand kicks in, and the market goes up or down, often violently.

Traditionally, the stock market goes down in times of recession and up in good times. Other things that tend to drive it up: buying by foreign investors, lower energy prices, lower interest rates, good performance by an important sector of the market, and (in the short term) program buying by large investment firms (buying large quantities of stocks according to signals generated by computer programs).

The opposites of the above things tend to drive the market down; in addition, wars are generally bad for the market, as are political upheavals. Even the president being in ill health can send the market into a tailspin.

It's not just real situations that affect investors, however; *rumors* of any of the above can send the financial markets up or down. The futures markets are especially sensitive to rumors, but the stock and bond markets are vulnerable too. Sad to say, these rumors are occasionally started by unscrupulous people for their own trading reasons. The effects of such rumors are usually short-lived, but they illustrate how easy it is to frighten investors and traders, and how important it is not to buy or sell on rumor.

As you can readily see, there is much more at work here than the calm, rational assessment by experienced investors that, perhaps, their money might earn more in another place. The main focus of attention is not on the problem—the economy, for example—but on the *perception* of the economy by other investors. Is the news bad enough that people will get scared and start to sell?

I see the financial markets as excellent examples of self-fulfilling prophecies. If people *think* other people are going to sell, then *they* will sell, and the market will indeed go down. It is a situation where everyone is doing his or her very best to figure out what everyone else is going to do.

It reminds me of army ants—the jungle ants that go out in hordes, devouring everything in their path. For years, entomologists tried to discover which of these ants were leading this march of destruction. They were finally forced to conclude that there *were* no leaders—that the ants in front were simply being pushed by those behind.

The key to understanding markets is that there is a limited amount of capital in the world. This capital flows to whatever market looks the most profitable at any given time. If it appears that the stock market is going down, many individuals and institutions will sell much of their holdings.

These shares, of course, are bought by other buyers, who take advantage of the lower prices brought about by the selling. But soon, the buying and selling slows down and the prices stay at depressed levels. The majority of stocks and the market as a whole are now worth less than before, because so much capital has been withdrawn.

Where has all the capital gone that was invested in these stocks? It has gone into anything that appears safe: savings accounts, money market funds, or so-called cash equivalents like government bonds. Some may go into corporate bonds, certain foreign stock markets, or currencies, thus driving these markets up. If investors perceive the stock market to be a bad bet over the long term, some money may go into real estate, sending prices up there.

Finally, when whatever situation scared people out of the stock market looks to be improving—an economic recession starts to turn around, for example—then the owners of capital begin to look at stocks again. This process, wherein investors try to decide exactly *when* to start buying, is wondrous to observe. It's like a cat getting ready to spring—quivering with anticipation, but waiting till just the right moment!

Everyone is keyed in to the slightest indication that
everyone else might be ready to make the plunge, but no
one wants to buy first and expose himself to another
downturn. Some market analysts warn that it may not be
quite the right time yet—that the bear market has a ways
to go yet; others urge buying while the prices are still
low.

Finally, the buying begins, the market reacts to the
increased demand, and the prices go up. Before long, the
speculation will turn to whether investors will be both-
ered by the speed of the advance and start selling . . . and
the cycle goes on.

The stock market usually goes up and down with up-
swings and recessions in the economy. Stocks are often a
good predictor of a downturn: prices will head south before
the other economic indicators point to a recession. And they
will usually start back up in advance of a recovery. The crash
of 1987 was an exception to this link—that was a solo performance by the stock market. The recession that many
analysts predicted never happened, and the market gradually recovered.

After each of the postwar bear markets, the market
recovered and went on to make new highs. Long-term
investors have done well with a buy-and-hold strategy.
Rather than worry about every downturn, many people opt
for this strategy of buying stock in quality companies and
simply sitting it out.

PLANNING AND ACTION

The key to success with a buy-and-hold strategy is *diversification*. Some investments will go down sharply during a

recession, others will weather it better, and some may even go up. In Chapter 15, we discussed keeping your portfolio diverse enough to handle the inevitable ups and downs of the market. A balanced group of investments, such as the model portfolio, is designed to do this.

But what action should you take if you—and the advisers you respect—feel strongly that a fall in the market is imminent? Generally, no action. The model portfolio is designed to be bought and held, not traded or timed with the market. The great danger of selling your stocks or stock funds is that you will be out of the market when it makes a major advance.

If you feel you just have to do something, one move is simply to *alter the balance* of your portfolio, so that the risk-reward thermometer goes down a few degrees. This can be easily accomplished by selling a few of the higher-risk investments—like small-company stocks or mutual funds that invest in them—and buying low-risk bond or money market funds. The bulk of your portfolio, however, should remain intact.

Actions like this should be planned in advance of any recessions; it's a good idea to know what you might sell or buy before the time for action arrives. What you need to watch out for is unwarranted panic at a market downturn.

The classic mistake made by inexperienced investors is to panic and sell all their stocks after a market crash. Those who hold on, however, and ride out the storm almost always do better than those who sell. Remember that stocks have always recovered and gone on to new heights. Barring a major change in the economic structure of the country, this pattern of recovery is likely to continue.

DEFENSIVE ACTION IN REAL ESTATE

If you have invested in a home or in income property, you have already chosen a buy-and-hold strategy, whether you like it or not. Real estate is generally difficult to sell fast enough to protect you from a downturn in property values. You can take comfort, though, in the fact that real estate, as a whole, has always recovered its value and gone on to new heights.

The way to avoid trouble from a real estate bear market is by exercising as much foresight as possible. When you buy a home or income property, do your best to arrange things so you won't have to sell at a loss. Obviously, this may not always be possible, but imagining a few worst-case scenarios could help you avoid them—or, at least, prepare for them.

INVESTMENT WORLD ANOMALIES

As a new investor, you are, perhaps, beginning to follow news of the economy more closely. Suppose that over a period of a few weeks, the newspapers report grim news. Many of the major economic indicators look bad: The negative trade balance is getting worse, consumer spending is down, and corporate earnings have not been good. Then the unemployment figures come in, looking even worse than expected . . . and the stock market responds by going *up* 50 points! What's going on here?

This is one of those things that can leave the newcomer to the World of Investment wondering whether she's ever going to get back to Kansas. In this case, because unemployment is up sharply, investors believe that the Federal Reserve Bank will now be forced to lower the discount rate—the interest rate at which it lends money to member banks—in order to stimulate the economy. With cheaper money being lent to them, banks will then be able to make loans to corporate clients and consumers at lower rates— and this usually stimulates the economy.

See? It's all very clear, isn't it? Bad news is really good news. . . .

Now that we've cleared up that little matter, let's go on to individual stocks. Say you bought some shares of International Widget Software a few months ago and the stock has taken off. You're up 25% from your purchase price and feeling pretty good. You feel even better when you read that earnings are up a dazzling 20% from the previous quarter—until the next day, when the price of the stock goes down 15% in heavy selling. Over the next week, it drops even further, until it's close to where you bought it.

Wha' hoppen? Does somebody know something you don't about the demand for widget software? Probably not. More likely, IWS disappointed traders with an earnings increase of "only" 20%. The price of the stock had gone up over the last few months as these traders anticipated a truly stupendous earnings gain. So in this case, good news is really bad news.

What do you do? Hold on! You're an investor, remember, not a trader. You think in terms of years, not weeks. You buy on value and you researched IWS carefully before you bought it. You didn't buy it just because the price was going up and everyone said it was a "hot stock" (did you?). Its earnings have been increasing for several years; the company has sound management and a good position in the widget software market.

So hold on. Don't let the strange doings of the market get you down. The people who make money, ultimately, are those who are aware of the fluctuations in a market, but hold fast to their method of buying and selling.

AWAKE AND AWARE

So what's ahead for the 1990s? As you might guess, there are roughly an equal number of bulls and bears speculating on the U.S. and world economies. In the same newspaper, you can find predictions of the stock averages doubling in the next five years right next to predictions of total disaster. The disaster scenarios usually include a collapse of the banking system and a debt crisis, brought on by the massive amount of private, corporate, and government debt.

The new investor should be aware that there *are* serious problems in the U.S. economy. Bullish advisers will argue that there have always been serious problems, and the trend has been upward anyway. This may be true, but the job of the individual investor is to stay awake and aware. In addition to the dangers we know of, unforeseen events, like the 1990 crisis in the Middle East, can happen at any time, with devastating effects on the economy.

The keys, then, to dealing with bad times are preparation, preparation, and . . . more preparation. A well-planned, balanced portfolio will help you ride out the storms. Deciding in advance what to buy and sell in a downturn will allow you to act quickly, if you need to. And, most of all, resolving to stick to your plans and remain cool during any bad times is the kind of preparation that will help you act like a seasoned, successful investor.

CHAPTER 21

BONDS

Bonds are also known as fixed-income securities, debt securities, debt instruments, or debentures. You don't need to remember all these terms, but the writers in the financial papers will sometimes use them.

In Chapter 7 we talked about what bonds are and why they are useful investments. Now we're going to discuss the different kinds of bonds. This chapter is not just for those who may invest in individual bonds. Those who plan to buy bond mutual funds still need to know about what kind of bonds the funds are investing in.

CORPORATE BONDS

In order to raise new capital, corporations can issue stock, or they can borrow by selling bonds. These "issues" of bonds are available for purchase through your stockbroker. You can buy them when they are first issued by the corporations, or later on, on the open market (the so-called secondary market).

Corporate bonds are almost always issued in denominations of $1,000. Most of these bonds are called *debenture bonds* or simply *debentures*. Debenture bonds are not backed by any tangible assets (as, for example, a home mortgage is backed by the tangible asset of the house). They are backed only by the good credit and financial strength of the issuing corporation.

The safest, highest-rated bonds currently return about 7% to 9% to the investor. This would mean a return of $70 to $90 a year on a $1,000 bond. The return on corporate bonds is generally higher than that for government securities, because they are considered a little riskier. Historically, however, the top-rated bonds issued by the major corporations have been extremely safe.

Corporate bonds have terms of anywhere from 1 to 20 years until they "mature." At that time, the holder of the bond receives the $1,000 back from the corporation.

U.S. GOVERNMENT SECURITIES

Treasury bonds, or *T-bonds*, can be purchased in denominations from $1,000 up to $1 million. T-bonds have terms of 10 to 30 years; the 30-year bond is called the *long bond*.

You can buy T-bonds through your broker or through your bank. The income from all the government securities is exempt from state and local taxes, but not from federal taxes.

Treasury notes (T-notes) have shorter terms than T-bonds—from 2 to 10 years. Like corporate bonds, all the government securities can be bought and sold on the open market and, like corporate bonds, they will rise and fall in price with the prevailing interest rates (why fixed-income securities rise and fall in value is explained below).

Treasury bills (T-bills) are issued for periods of three months, six months, and a year. They come in large sizes only: $10,000 and up, with $10,000 being the standard amount. T-bills don't pay interest in the same way as other bonds; instead, you buy them at a discount and then receive the full $10,000 when the bill comes due. For example, a T-bill may be quoted at $9,400. If you buy it, you will receive $10,000 when it matures (comes due): a profit of $600. On a 12-month investment of $9,400, $600 would mean a return rate of 6.38% ($600 divided by $9,400 = .0638 = 6.38%).

The main advantage to all the federal securities is safety. Regardless of what you might think about the size of the national debt, the government has not yet defaulted on any of its bonds. In return for this safety, you get less return than from the corporate bonds, though this difference can vary a good deal.

Another advantage is that the market of buyers and sellers is large. Some corporate bonds can be difficult to sell because there aren't enough people wanting to buy them. This feature makes government issues "liquid." Liquidity can be an important thing to consider in any investment; if you want to get out for any reason, ease and rapidity of sale are an attractive feature.

MUNICIPAL BONDS

Municipal bonds, also known as "municipals" or "munis," are issued by your own city hall, often for a specific purpose, such as new schools or sewers. These are the "bond issues" you vote on in your local elections. The majority of these bonds—the so-called *public purpose bonds*—are *tax free*. The interest income you receive is free from federal income taxes and, in many cases, from state and local taxes as well (be sure to check this out before you buy). State governments issue public purpose bonds, too.

The yields on the tax-free bonds are less than for other types of bonds, but the tax-free aspect makes them attractive to individuals in high tax brackets. By not paying taxes on the income from the bonds, you effectively receive 2% to 3% more income from munis. Whether they would be right for you is something to discuss with your tax accountant.

Munis come in a few different forms. The most common are general obligation bonds and revenue bonds.

General obligation bonds are repaid from tax revenues. If a municipality has a good tax base, these are considered the safest bonds.

Revenue bonds are issued by states and cities to fund income-producing projects, such as toll bridges or sports stadiums. The interest and principal will be paid by income from the project. These bonds are somewhat riskier; if the project doesn't produce the expected income, the bondholders may be out of luck.

Municipal bonds as a whole have become a little chancy in recent years. A few cities have actually defaulted on their bonds. You need to take note of the bond ratings (explained below) before you buy.

Alternatively, you can put your money in a mutual fund specializing in municipals and let the fund managers worry about such things. Depending on the kind of municipals the fund owns, the income is free from federal taxes and sometimes state taxes, just as with the individual bonds.

ZERO-COUPON BONDS

Remember how we have discussed reinvesting all the income from an investment when growth is the only objective? Zero-coupon bonds do this for you. The interest is simply added to the principal twice a year. You get the face value (usually $1,000) when the bond matures.

Zero-coupon bonds (also called simply "zeros") get their name from the fact that they pay out no yearly interest in cash—all the interest is reinvested. Bonds used to have detachable coupons (a few still do), which the holder clipped and sent in when the interest payment was due. "Coupon," therefore, has become synonymous with "interest" in bond jargon. Zero yearly interest payment = zero coupon.

The interest is nevertheless subject to taxes each year, even though you don't get this income until the bond matures. This makes zeros good for tax-deferred accounts like IRAs and Keoghs (see Chapter 17). They are also good presents for a child with college education in mind, since up to $1,000 of the interest is tax-exempt until the child reaches 14.

Zeros are cheap, especially those with maturity dates 20 or 30 years away. This makes them attractive to small investors. A 30-year zero, for example, might cost as little as $50 to $60, depending on the going interest rates. In 30 years, you would receive the full $1,000 face value of the bond.

Zeros are bought and sold on the open market, but their prices are even more sensitive than those of regular coupon bonds to changes in the prevailing interest rates. And some may be redeemed—"called"—by the issuing company before they mature, at less than face value. This is an important thing to check ("calling" a bond is explained below).

CONVERTIBLE BONDS

The trouble with owning bonds instead of stocks is that if the corporation issuing them starts to do well, you will get no benefit from this success—you just continue to get your 9%. If the company does poorly, though, and the rating on your bonds goes down, your portfolio will lose value; if the company goes bust, you can lose it all. Convertible bonds attempt to remedy at least part of this situation.

Convertible bonds are similar to other coupon bonds in most ways, except that their interest rates are not as high. The dramatic difference is that at any time, you can convert the bonds into the common stock of the corporation at a fixed rate. For example, your bond might be convertible into 50 shares of company stock. If the stock is selling at $25 a share, your bond will be worth at least $1,250 (50 × $25). This is called the *conversion value*.

The bond will probably be worth a bit more than its conversion value because it gives a higher interest rate than the common stock. It is hardly ever advisable, then, to actually make the change. If the stock goes up, the price of the bond will rise right along with it. If the stock price should go down, the bond will also, but you will continue to get your 6.5%, or whatever the interest rate is.

Convertibles are a neat way of dealing with the risk-versus-return dilemma. They are safer than common stocks in that their interest payments always take precedence over the dividend payments of the common. They give a good return, so in bad times you might not fret so much if the price is down. And in a bull market, their prices will rise with that of the common stock.

Naturally, you need to research a company in the same way you would if you bought its common stock. Even convertibles can lose their interest payments if a company is on the skids. To lessen your risk, there are—you guessed it—mutual funds dealing only in convertible bonds.

JUNK BONDS

Junk bonds are also called "high-yield" bonds—just to confuse new investors. "High-yielding" *stocks* are in companies that pay a high dividend and are among the safest and best stock investments. High-yield *bonds*, however, have acquired a negative connotation, because so many of them are risky investments.

High-yield bonds were formerly issued by smaller companies that used the higher yields to attract investors. Because these yields were usually several percentage points higher than those of the top-rated bonds, some investors were willing to take a chance. There was always the danger, however, that the company might not be able to meet the interest payments, and this caused the bonds to be graded very low by the ratings services (hence the "junk" label).

In the 1980s, larger, more established companies began to issue high-interest bonds as a way of paying for takeovers of other companies. This method of financing takeovers was developed by a former Drexel Burnham executive, Michael Milken, about whom you may have heard in connection with other creative (and illegal) manipulations of large sums of money.

These so-called leveraged buyouts were not illegal, but they were often ill-advised, as corporations were left with troublesome amounts of debt in the form of their high-interest junk bonds. When the recession hit in 1990, many companies were unable to meet the payments on these bonds. In that year, 8.5% of the junk bonds, with a value of $24.6 billion, were in default.

When a class of investments, such as the junk bond market, starts to look shaky, investors begin bailing out. This selling then drives down the total value of the whole market—even the better-quality investments. This happened to the junk bond market in 1989 and 1990, leaving many portfolios worth substantially less than a few years before.

This kind of loss can be very hard on individual investors. When the junk bond portfolios belong to large institutions, however, you have the makings of a world-class crisis.

The collapse of the junk bond market made the savings and loan crisis much worse, because many of the S&Ls had bought large quantities of these bonds. And if you have heard rumblings about troubles in the insurance industry, these too can be traced partly to an investment diet too rich in high-yield bonds.

The massive amount of corporate debt created by the issues of junk bonds has left some analysts worried about the ability of many corporations to function effectively. Money that goes to pay high-interest debt is money that is not funding the kind of research and development needed to compete in today's world markets.

These difficulties are part of the legacy of the 1980s, when a certain air of unreality enveloped much of the financial marketplace. This departure from reality resulted, to a large extent, from indifference to the traditional risk-reward ratio by financial managers who were supposed to know better. They believed they could get high returns in junk bonds and still retain the necessary safety. By 1990, the risk-reward ratio had reasserted itself, and the bills had come due for ignoring it.

All this underscores the importance of paying attention to the risk-reward ratio, as pictured by our little thermometers throughout the book. For a while, in good economic times, risky investments may do well. But the reasons they are known as risky can make themselves apparent with a vengeance when times turn bad.

Yes, there are mutual funds that deal mostly in junk bonds—and no, they are not recommended for the new investor. Returns of 12%, 15%, and higher can look awfully good, until you consider the possibility of default and further loss of value on the part of the junk bonds. You would think that most people would be warned off by the name. . . .

RATINGS

Nowhere are there clearer illustrations of risk versus return than in the bond market. From the absolutely safe govern-

Bond Ratings

Moody's	Standard & Poors	Quality
Aaa	AAA	Highest quality
Aa	AA	High quality
A	A	Upper medium grade
Baa	BBB	Medium grade
Ba	BB	Speculative elements
B	B	Speculative
Caa	CCC, CC	Default possible
Ca	C	Default—partial recovery possible
C	D	Default—recovery not likely

ment bonds to the junk bonds, the story is the same: greater return = greater risk. (Government securities are not even rated—they are considered risk-free.) The bonds that receive a lower grade from the rating services will give you a higher return, but the risk will be measurably bigger. Junk bonds give you the highest yields, but are extremely risky.

So how can you learn which bonds are the most highly rated? For years, Standard and Poors ratings and Moody's ratings have been the industry standards. You can find their books in the business reference section of your public library, or you can subscribe. The Resources section of this chapter tells how to subscribe to Standard and Poors stock and bond ratings.

A warning is in order here. Ratings can change—sometimes drastically. A friend of mine was dismayed to find that the AAA top-rated Occidental Petroleum bond he had held for just a year had been downgraded to BBB, a "medium grade" rating. The rating services didn't like the looks of the latest balance sheets at Occidental. Unfortunately, a drop in ratings almost always means a drop in value for the bond, and this case was no exception.

This is another argument for investing in bond mutual funds instead of holding individual bonds. The large quantity of bonds in the funds' portfolios means that any risk is spread out; if one bond loses value, another may rise. For added safety, in this book I recommend buying mutual funds that invest only in bonds rated A or better.

Junk bonds, incidentally, have a rating of BB or lower—almost always lower, in fact. Many are not even graded by the rating services.

UPS AND DOWNS IN THE BOND MARKET

Unlike savings accounts or certificates of deposit in a bank, bonds can increase or decrease in value. This is true of anything you can buy or sell: the markets will determine the price. If you need to sell a bond, there is a good chance it will have gone up or down in price since you purchased it.

A decrease in the value of a bond does *not* mean its interest rate will go down. Your interest payments will stay the same, barring something drastic like a default on bond payments by the corporation—a very rare occurrence in high-rated bonds. (Some bonds have variable interest rates, but these are rare.)

If you are invested over the long term, you don't need to worry too much about market fluctuations; you just hold on to your bond until it matures and continue to collect your interest payments.

Two things can cause a bond to decrease in value: the downgrading of the rating or an increase in the interest rates paid by newer bonds. Even government bonds fluctuate with the prevailing interest rates. The reasons for this decrease are pretty clear. Who wants to buy a bond yielding 9% when the new ones are giving 10%? The only thing that would make a 9% bond attractive would be to lower its price.

Say you bought a General Motors bond for its face value of $1,000, maturing in 10 years and yielding 9%. This 9% is called the *coupon interest rate* or *coupon rate*. You will be getting $90 a year, or $45 every six months. But now suppose that after a year, interest rates on new, comparable bonds have risen to 10%. Your 9% suddenly looks kind of shabby.

But if the price of your bond were lowered to $900, it would then yield 10% to whoever bought it at this new, lower price. The bond would still be *yielding* $90 a year in interest, but this $90 would be *10%* of the $900 price to the new buyer. This new interest rate of 10%, based on the $900 price, is called the *current yield*—as opposed to the coupon rate of 9%. What this means is that having bought the bond for only $900, the new holder will continue to get an effective yield of 10% until the bond matures.

In addition, this new buyer will get the full $1,000 face value when the bond matures. This gives rise to the term *the yield to maturity*. This yield adds the extra $100 the buyer will realize when the bond matures.

Conversely, if the new buyer paid more for the bond than the face value, you would *subtract* the difference to get the yield to maturity. If the bond was purchased for $1,100 and was going to mature in four years, the buyer would receive the $1,000 face value at that time—but this would be $100 *less* than was paid for the bond. The yield to maturity would then reflect this $100 difference.

Yields to maturity are computed according to a fairly complex formula. Your broker can provide you with a bond's yield to maturity before you buy it.

Of course, you don't have to sell your bond just because the interest rates change—if you hold on to it, you will continue to get your 9% for the next 10 years. But if you do decide to sell when interest rates have risen, you will get less than you paid for the bond.

How the Federal Reserve Bank Controls Inflation and How This Affects Interest Rates

When credit is easy to get, the large amount of borrowed money tends to stimulate growth in the economy. Businesses have more to spend on expansion, and consumers support business by purchasing more on credit. This growth, however, can also lead to an increase in inflation; with more people buying, the increased demand causes prices to go up. To prevent inflation from getting out of hand, the Federal Reserve Bank (also known as "the Fed") can restrict the total amount of money in the economy. Less money = less borrowing = less growth = less inflation.

The Federal Reserve can also make loans more expensive. It does this by raising the interest rate at which banks can borrow money from the Fed (this is called raising the *discount rate*).

Because banks have to pay more for their money, they must charge their borrowers more. As a result of the increased cost of loans, corporations and individuals will borrow less. Less borrowing means less spending, which means economic growth will be slowed down— and this, in turn, will put a damper on inflation.

The increase in the cost of money from the Fed coupled with the decrease in the money supply makes *your* money more attractive to banks and corporations. They will pay you more if you deposit money in savings or buy bonds. Interest rates will rise.

When the economy is in recession, the Federal Reserve will *lower* the discount rate, thus making borrowing easier. Cheaper money from the Fed means banks can charge less interest on the loans they give their customers. And this means the banks will pay less for the use of your money. Interest rates paid on your savings will go down.

And yes, happily, the reverse can be true. Interest rates might fall to 8%, in which case you could be proud of your 9%. And the value of your bond in the market would increase.

There is, however, one more thing about bonds that could ruin your delight over any increase in value due to falling interest rates: Corporations don't like paying 9% when the prevailing rate is 8%. They would rather issue new bonds at the lower rate. So if interest rates drop sharply, the company issuing your bond may *call* it—that is, it can tell you to send the bond in so it can pay you the face value now, instead of when the bond matures. This feature, known as *callability*, is something to check carefully before you buy a bond. You will get your original investment back, but you'll have to go looking for 9% elsewhere—and in an 8% market. Even government T-bonds are callable these days.

When you buy a bond on the market, it's a good idea to check out the callability. If you buy a $1,000 bond for $1,100, it will not be to your advantage to have it called at the $1,000 face value in a year or two. Even after figuring in your interest payments, the $100 loss will make your total return look like Wile E. Coyote after an encounter with the Roadrunner.

Again, of course, the reverse could be happily true. Buying the bond at $900 would leave you very content to have it called at $1,000.

How to Read the Bond Tables in the Newspapers

(1)	(2)	(3)	(4) Cur Yld	(5) Vol	(6) Last	(7) Net Chg
PG&E	$8\frac{1}{2}$	09	8.9	70	$95\frac{5}{8}$	$+\frac{1}{8}$

(1) The name of the company, in this case, Pacific Gas and Electric.

(2) The coupon rate, or yearly interest this bond will pay: $8\frac{1}{2}$%. A bond with a "par value" (or face value) of $1,000 would yield $85 a year at $8\frac{1}{2}$%.

(3) The maturity date, when the face value of the bond will be paid back. Only the last two digits are given. In this case, the maturity date is 2009. If the date reads 96, the bond will mature in 1996 (not 2096!).

(4) The current yield. Because the value of this bond has declined, a buyer will actually be receiving 8.9% on his or her money, rather than the coupon rate of $8\frac{1}{2}$%.

(5) Yesterday's volume. Add three zeros and a dollar sign. Unlike the stock tables, where the volume refers to the number of shares traded, bond volume is figured in dollar amounts. In this case, there were $70,000 worth of PG&E bonds traded.

(6) The last price at which the bonds traded. This figure is a *percentage* of $1,000—the face value of most corporate bonds. A bond trading at $95\frac{5}{8}$ will cost $962.50 ($95\frac{5}{8}$% = .95625 × $1,000 = $962.50). This PG&E bond is trading "at a discount." Sometimes bonds will trade "at a premium" to their face value. If you see a price listed as "102," this means a buyer will have to pay $1,020 for the bond.

(7) The net change in price from the previous day. If you look at the bond tables on any given day, you will usually see either a great majority of plus signs, or of minus signs. The price of bonds is very sensitive to changes—or rumors of changes—in the interest rates. A few bonds will run counter to the majority, because of a revision of their rating, or good or bad information about the company that issued them.

(Occasionally, you will see an "s" between the coupon rate and the year of maturity: for example, "7s99." The sole function of the "s" is to separate the two numbers, so you don't read them as "799.")

So . . . are bonds a good investment? Bonds are good for investors who need a safe source of income over the long term, or those who need to balance and diversify their stock portfolios. And again, the bond mutual funds are probably the best bet for safety and stable return.

This is a good time to assess again the amount of risk you are comfortable with. If you want no risk at all, you will buy Treasury bonds or notes, or mutual funds that invest in them. A little more risk tolerance will put you into corporate bonds, then convertible bonds, and finally common stocks.

Or perhaps by now you're bored with bonds and blue chips and are ready to consider Cousin Jack's Australian gold mine. . . .

Resources

Standard & Poors Bond Guide, Standard & Poors Corp., 25 Broadway, New York, NY 10004. Monthly. $176/year. To subscribe, call (800) 221-5277.

The *Bond Guide* is a quick reference booklet to over 7,000 bonds, mostly corporate, but some foreign and municipal bonds are also included. An essential reference for anyone wanting to invest in individual bonds.

For bond mutual funds, check Resources, Chapter 6. The books listed contain not just stock mutual funds, but also bond mutual funds. The statistics on past performance will help you choose the best funds.

CHAPTER 22

USING YOUR COMPUTER

As I write this book on my personal computer, I can, if I wish, push a few buttons and display the latest quotes for the stocks I own. I pay a monthly fee for a financial data service connected to the same cable that brings in the television and FM signals. I prefer this to systems that use a modem to connect the computer with the telephone, because this leaves the telephone free.

With the software provided by the service, I have set up a list of the stocks in my portfolio and can stare at them as they change in price from minute to minute (a hypnotic thing). If I wanted to, I could buy more expensive software programs that would perform technical analysis on any company I was interested in—or inform me which companies I *should* be interested in.

If you are comfortable with computers and plan to keep close tabs on your portfolio, such a data-retrieval service can be very valuable. If you don't work well with computers and/or plan to employ a buy-and-hold strategy with only occasional trades, then the quotes in the financial papers will be enough for you. Those who are invested in mutual funds over the long term will have little use for such services.

If, however, you are interested in being an active manager of your portfolio, you will want to be aware of the various ways you can use your personal computer to follow the markets and help you decide what to buy. There are software programs that will provide you with fancy graphs and charts to assist in the analysis of various markets or of individual stocks. Other software gives historical information on securities, and tracks the records of futures or options.

You can type out your buy and sell orders using a phone modem connected to your broker's computer. You can even have your computer call you up if a trading situation develops when you're out of the house. ("Yo, Alex, this is Hal, the computer. Hey, time to get into that Adobe Systems stock, pronto!")

There is also software for portfolio management, and computer-generated spreadsheets for tax and financial planning.

And this is just the more mundane software. Much more complex and expensive programs are available for the experienced investor. There are even services that will develop personalized software to work with your own trading strategies.

In short, a sometimes bewildering array of investment-oriented software has sprung up just in the last few years. If you are interested in finding a good program to suit your needs, I highly recommend the book and newsletter listed in Resources.

A note about hardware: The great majority of investment software is designed for IBM and IBM-compatible computers. The amount of software for Macintosh users is increasing, but if you are in the market for a computer, this is something to consider. Get one with at least a 386 chip.

DATA RETRIEVAL

In order to use much of this software, you will have to connect to a *data-retrieval service*. The prices of the various data services depend mostly on how many markets you want to watch and how current you need the information to be.

You can get day-end quotes of stocks and mutual funds for as little as $40 a month. If you want real-time stock and option quotes, you can pay as much as $500 a month. ("Real time" means you are quoted the price of the last trade as soon as it happens. Because prices can change so quickly, this can be valuable information if you are at the point of buying or selling.) Quotes from other markets, such as futures, are at additional cost. All this information becomes the database for the various software programs.

The data-retrieval services connect to your computer through your phone line or TV-FM cable, or via satellite communication. In the latter case, the company will send you a small satellite dish (about two to three feet in diameter) which you can mount on your roof or in an open space.

After struggling with a three-foot dish on my roof, I have to recommend going with a system that transmits through a cable, if this is possible in your area. Many subscribers use satellite dishes, but the reception is not as reliable as with cable—and it may not work at all if you live in a valley.

Two of the better-known data-retrieval systems are listed below. Being fairly new technology, data-retrieval systems still have bugs to be worked out. Because of this, even though some of the smaller outfits tend to charge less, I would recommend going with one of the larger, more experienced companies. In addition, much of the investment software is designed to be employed with the more widely used systems.

Resources

Computerized Investing, American Association of Individual Investors, 625 N. Michigan Ave., Chicago, IL 60611. A monthly, 24-page newsletter.

See Resources, Chapter 1, for information on joining AAII. With membership ($49/year), a subscription to *Computerized Investing* costs $30/year. It's $60/year for nonmembers.

This is the newsletter you want if you plan to use your personal computer for investing. It includes how-to articles, reviews and descriptions of the latest investment software, and evaluations of data-retrieval systems and financial databases. It also puts you in touch with local AAII computer groups, if you and your IBM 386 are feeling sociable.

A subscription to *Computerized Investing* includes a free gift of ***The Individual Investor's Guide to Computerized Investing.*** For members of AAII, this constantly updated book costs you $18 if you decide not to subscribe to the newsletter; it's $22.95 to nonmembers.

The *Guide* offers descriptions of more than 400 software programs and 100 financial databases. These cover stocks, bonds, mutual funds, futures, options, and real estate. There is also good information on various data-retrieval systems.

Data Broadcasting Corporation. 1900 S. Norfolk St., San Mateo, CA 94403. (800) 367-4670. This is one of the most widely used data-retrieval systems. In most areas you can get it by cable. Various packages are available, from inexpensive, end-of-day stock quotes to expensive, minute-by-minute stock, options, and futures quotes. Call for brochures.

S&P Comstock. (800) 431-5019. Comstock has many services comparable to Data Broadcasting, but it also includes quotes from exchanges around the world. This is the service you will want if you plan to invest in foreign stocks and bonds. The data comes through the phone lines or by satellite connection. Call for information.

PART 3

HIGH-RISK INVESTING

CHAPTER 23

INVESTING IN YOURSELF: STARTING YOUR OWN BUSINESS

To some, there is no vision so enticing as starting a business. Just think! (says that small, seductive voice). You'd be doing exactly what you want to do. You'd be your own boss. And you'd make a lot of money besides. Now that you have some capital, moreover, you don't need to wait; you can *Just Do It!* After all, doesn't investing in your own business automatically make more sense than investing in someone else's?

The answer to that question is a definite *maybe*. Starting a business of your own is a noble ambition, but one that is hard to achieve. This chapter will help you think about whether you really want to pursue it—and if so, what to do first.

TWO QUESTIONS

For starters, you need to ask yourself two fundamental questions. Despite what would-be entrepreneurs sometimes think, the answers to these questions are not obvious.

First: *Why do you want to be in business for yourself?* Because it somehow seems more secure than working for someone else? If so, forget it—the great majority of new businesses fail. Because you like the idea of taking an hour (or a day, or a week) off any time you feel like it? Forget that reason, too. Entrepreneurs as a group work harder than almost anybody. The hours, quipped one veteran, are 7 A.M. to 7 P.M., six days a week, plus worrying time in the evenings and praying time on Sunday (just a *little* help, dear Lord, in meeting the payroll next week).

As for making a lot of money, it's true that starting a company offers a possible road to riches. (Look at Bill Gates, the boy wonder who created Microsoft Corp.; he now counts his net worth in the billions of dollars.) But not only is the road risky, it sometimes leads in the wrong direction.

Let's say you open a restaurant because you love to cook. To make big money, however, you'll have to run not just one restaurant but many—a chain. And once you head down that path, you won't be spending much time at the stove. I have a friend who began a cabinetmaking business. It was successful, and pretty soon he had six employees. The employees built the cabinets (a task my friend enjoyed) while he bid new jobs (a task he didn't enjoy at all).

Essentially, there are only two good reasons for starting your own business. One, you have something you really want to do, and you can plausibly imagine doing it in your own company. Two, you think you'd enjoy the incredible variety of tasks involved in starting a business: handling the money, hiring the help, dealing with customers, etc., etc. If neither statement applies to you, you'd better find another place to invest your money.

Ladies and Gentlemen, I think it's clear that the market
is trying to tell us something about this product.

But suppose you do pass that first test. Now you have to
answer the second fundamental question: *How much money
do you propose to invest—and is it enough?* No single investment can eat through a portfolio faster than a struggling
small business. You set yourself up, and you begin to get a
few customers. You're not making money yet, but you think
you will fairly soon, so you invest a little more. And a little
more. And a little more . . .

Granted, you can read plenty of stories about entrepreneurs who withdrew their life savings, mortgaged their
houses, and sold all their worldly possessions to fund their
companies and are now multimillionaires. What you *don't*
hear about are the entrepreneurs who withdrew everything,
mortgaged everything, and sold everything . . . and wound up
in bankruptcy court because their companies failed anyway.

So unless you're the devil-may-care sort (and if you are,
then why are you reading this book?), you should figure out
what you need for peace-of-mind money—a nest egg,

college funds, insurance, whatever—in case your business goes belly-up. After you determine how much you need, the remainder is the amount you have to invest in your business. Now you can begin to research the cost of getting started in your chosen field.

This peace-of-mind money is part of a "Plan B" that all people who invest in themselves should have. If the worst happens and the new business has to fold, will you still be able to pay the rent? Will you be able to get a job similar to the one you had or go back to your old profession?

Despite your best efforts, "Plan A" may fail because of factors totally beyond your control. You may do everything right in starting up your business and then, a year later, suddenly find yourself in the middle of an economic recession. Even well-planned, well-run firms can founder in a turbulent economic environment. A good Plan B can help you conduct an orderly retreat instead of being subject to a rout.

PLANNING

Okay, suppose starting a business of your own really *is* your dream. Your motivations withstand scrutiny; the money you have available to invest seems like enough. So you decide to plunge in. You're going to buy (or create) that restaurant, set up that shop, hang out your shingle as a computer programmer or graphic designer or furniture builder. Maybe you even want to start a company capable of rapid growth, such as a temporary-personnel agency or an environmental consulting firm.

Whatever your business, remember that entrepreneurship, like investing, isn't magic, it's a skill. Like any skill, it can be learned, and like any skill, it's sharpened by experience. To start, what you need is a little information-and-experience gathering. There are three basic steps to this.

1. Immerse yourself in the culture of entrepreneurship. Read books about starting a company (see Resources). Subscribe to *Inc.* and *Entrepreneur* magazines. Talk to people who have started businesses—friends, relatives, neighbors, local shopkeepers. You'll find that most are glad to share their experiences.

2. Learn everything you can about the industry you propose to enter. You wouldn't dream of starting a computer company without knowing something about computers—so don't imagine you can set up a travel agency just because you like to take trips.

   If you've never worked in the business, take a job for a year or two. Subscribe to some of the trade magazines for the industry. Contact the industry's trade association and ask whether they have any materials for new entrepreneurs. Again, go talk with people who have started companies in this field. Some may not give you the time of day, but others will be only too happy to advise an enterprising newcomer how to proceed. After all, they were once in your shoes.

3. Write out a business plan and ask a few knowledgeable people to critique it. Putting your plan down on paper forces you to confront questions that a lot of novices prefer to avoid. Exactly what do you intend to sell, and to whom? Who is the competition, and what will your company offer that your competitors don't? How do you propose to make prospective customers aware of your existence? What do you think revenues will be after six months? After a year? When will you start turning a profit?

   You can get guidance on writing a plan from the books and tapes listed in Resources, but the fundamental idea is simple. The plan should explain, in detail, why and how your business can succeed.

Once you've drafted the plan, search out a few sympathetic readers—maybe a lawyer, an accountant, or just friends with relevant business experience. You can be sure they'll poke plenty of holes in it, but it's better to plug them in the planning stage than to wait until you've launched the business.

Capital

Since this is a book about investment, we'll leave the details of how to do market research, how to set up a corporation, and so forth, to others. But you should know a little about where to look, aside from your own portfolio, for money for your enterprise.

Venture capital—that is, money from organized venture capital partnerships—is probably not for you. Venture capitalists typically fund new companies that have huge growth potential, and that are managed by executives with substantial business experience. Probably less than 1% of all new companies started in the United States each year are plausible candidates for venture money.

Bank loans are hard for new companies to get . Typically, banks require collateral (a mortgage on your house, for example) or a personal guarantee (you'll pay back the loan even if the company goes broke) or both. In some circumstances new companies may qualify for so-called SBA loans, which are bank loans guaranteed by the federal government's Small Business Administration, or for similar state-guaranteed loans. Consult some local bankers.

Friendly money—that is, loans or equity investment from parents, other relatives, or friends—is probably your best bet. Sometimes you can even find a successful local entrepreneur (an "angel") who invests in new companies as a sort of hobby. Ask accountants and other businesspeople.

Buying a Business

A good way to maximize your chances for success in business is to buy a going concern in a field you already know about—and care about. Consider this example.

Ernie and his brother Jim had each worked in the natural-foods industry for 15 years. Between them, their experience covered most aspects of the field. When a small natural-foods store in their town came up for sale, the two brothers moved fast. With the help of a state-guaranteed bank loan to add to their personal capital, they were able to swing the deal. The state agency was impressed with their experience in the field and this helped in obtaining the loan guarantee.

The store was already profitable, but with their experience, Ernie and Jim improved certain aspects of the business and a year later were bringing in even more customers. One visit to the store shows you why. The produce bins are filled with ripe, flawless organic fruits and vegetables, the shelves are neatly stocked with a variety of fine products, the clerks are friendly and helpful—in short, this is a very pleasant place to shop. It's clear that the store is run by people who care about their customers, and about natural foods.

New entrepreneurs might consider starting off by buying an operating business, like Ernie and Jim did, instead of starting from scratch. If you add experience and a real interest in the field to this equation, you have a formula that can substantially increase your chances of success.

One caution: The same rules apply to investments from parents and friends as apply to any investment. Spell out exactly what they're getting for their money (so much of the company's stock; a loan at 6% interest due in three years—whatever). Ask a lawyer to look over the language. You need to treat them as you would any investor, explaining the risk and keeping them honestly informed of your progress. Families and friendships have been torn apart by business misunderstandings. It isn't worth it.

DREAMS

Dreams, enthusiasm, and a positive attitude are fundamental to any business venture. Some people hesitate to do the necessary planning for fear that cold facts will chill their optimism. "If I think about it too much, I'll never do it!" is the argument. Planning, however, is not the same as worrying. Planning is the process of bringing dreams down to earth— of testing them against reality as thoroughly as possible.

Lest you think we have thrown unnecessary amounts of cold water on your dreams in this chapter, remember that the landscape is littered with business failures that tried to operate on enthusiasm alone. Success in business emerges from a *balance* of positive thinking and careful planning. This is not a guaranteed formula, but it is a powerful one.

You owe it to yourself to treat your dreams with care. Test them well against reality in the planning stage before exposing them to the hard knocks of the real world.

This chapter is by John Case, a senior editor at *INC.* magazine who has written extensively on the successes and failures of various small businesses. He has also written several books on more general topics relating to business and the economy. His latest is *From the Ground Up: The Resurgence of American Entrepreneurship.* Simon & Schuster, 1992. $23 (hardcover). This is the book you need if you want to know what has been going on in the American economy for the last 20 years. It is of special interest to would-be entrepreneurs because it deals with the growth of the

small-business economy at a time when many of the
giant corporations have been in decline. It should also
be of interest to new investors who want an overall
view of the economy written in plain and enjoyable
English.

Resources

Inc: The Magazine for Growing Companies, Subscription
Service Dept., P.O. Box 51534, Boulder, CO 80321-1534. Monthly.
$19/year.

Inc. publishes articles on start-ups, the ins and outs of running a small company, and many fascinating stories of successful
and not-so-successful entrepreneurs.

In addition, it offers a number of books and videos with titles
like *Anatomy of a Start-Up, How to Really Start Your Own Business* (book and video), *Inc. Guide to Creating a Successful Business Plan,* and others. Subscribing will bring you a complete list of
titles. To get the list of titles without subscribing, call (800)
372-0018, ext. 4125.

***In Business: The Magazine for Environmental Entre-
preneuring,*** 419 State Ave., Emmaus, PA 18049. 6 issues/year, $23.

In Business covers the growing number of small businesses
in the environmental field. If your interests run in that direction,
this is for you. A recent issue featured articles on the natural-
clothing trade, franchise opportunities in the environmental field,
Ben & Jerry's Ice Cream (a socially conscious company), retail
sales for solar systems, nonpolluting cars, and getting in on the
ground floor of the water conservation industry.

Growing a Business by Paul Hawken. Simon & Schuster,
1987. $9.95 (paperback).

This book addresses the philosophical side of starting a business—initially of equal importance to the practical. It deals with
the mental and emotional work you need to do when your business is in the planning stage. Hawken believes that an idea for a
business should start from deep inside you.

Hawken has successfully started several small businesses himself, so the practical advice in the book is drawn from
experience.

I think every prospective entrepreneur should read this book. My feeling is that one of the main reasons new businesses fail is that their owners don't have a clear idea of what they want to achieve. Instead of the business beginning from a deep place inside of them, it starts from a surface idea: "Video stores seem to be making a lot of money, so let's start one." That kind of thing.

CHAPTER 24

CAVEAT EMPTOR:
LET THE BUYER BEWARE

SHORT SKIRTS AND SUPER BOWLS

A lot of people were disappointed on December 31, 1990. For the first time in 23 years, an NFL team had won the Super Bowl in January (of 1990) but the S&P Industrial Average had failed to make a gain for the year. In every other year since 1967, an NFL win had meant an up year, an AFL win a down year. (Well, actually, in 1984, the average went from 184.24 to 184.36, even though an AFL team won, but who wants to split hairs?)

Other "analysts" have noted that in years when women's hemlines have gone up, the markets have also gone up. Investors usually smile when they talk about such theories, but there is always a touch of "who knows, maybe it's true" in their smiles. Many investors are willing to listen to virtually any theory if it has a good record.

Quite a few of them also seem to be willing to respond to the direct-mail solicitations and the ads in the journals for various buying methods and advisers with "systems." I know this is true because the number of these ads and solicitations seems to increase daily.

"230% profit in ONE YEAR!" "Easy to carry out!" "Hasn't failed in 20 years!" And the phone solicitors are even less restrained. In the process of writing this book, I responded to a bunch of ads and solicitations. "Did any of them sound good?" you ask. Let me tell you, they *all* sounded good! Take the silver salesmen (please!).

The silver salesmen called to tell me that the precious metal had reached a new low and that knowledgeable investors were buying. They, of course, had a method for buying silver that would maximize my profits. Every time— *every* time—silver had reached a new low in the past, buyers had made thousands of dollars. Did *I* want to make thousands of dollars, or was I (they implied) one of those schleps who let great opportunities pass them by?

It sounded terrific. The only thing that gave me pause was that I was acquainted with the silver market, and silver was continuing to go down. I finally got rid of the silver-tongued salespeople and over the next few months watched the price of silver decline steadily: 5%; 10%; it was down 20% the last time I looked.

My father used to say that the more you knew about a subject, the more you realized how biased and inaccurate was the reporting of it in the newsmagazines. This observation translates beautifully to the hard sells aimed at the individual investor. The more you know about a market, the more likely you will see through the sales pitches.

Many salespeople depend on the inexperience of the average investor. They are experts at putting out just enough information to make an investment sound unbeatable. If you are acquainted with the market they're working in, you may be able to see flaws in what they're saying. But if you don't know about it, then there's all the more reason to leave it alone. Investing in a market you're not familiar with is little more than gambling.

Don't try to argue with them—just tell them you're not interested and hang up. Salespeople try to make it sound as if there's no tomorrow for the opportunity they're offering. But there are always opportunities in the World of Investment, and the best ones are caught by those knowledgeable enough to recognize them.

LET'S LOOK AT THE RECORD . . .

Concerning the ads in the journals and the direct-mail flyers, the new investor needs to realize that the majority of strategies for buying and selling have been around for years in one form or another. If you see something that looks really good, it needs to be put to several tests:

1. Is the historical data that supports the strategy real or hypothetical? Anyone can figure out a system and then backtest it with selective historical data. Anyone can, and does—the ads are full of such systems. Buying and selling in the real world, however, is a different proposition. This is not to dismiss these methods entirely—some of them may have value, but they need to be checked out thoroughly, and looked at in the light of the markets of the present day.

   This is especially true in the early 1990s because we are just coming off one of the great bull-market decades in history. Most of the performance records you will see are based on material from these years. But the systems that did the best under those favorable market conditions are often the ones that will do worst in a bear market.

   Whether the '90s will repeat the amazing performance of the '80s is the subject of much speculation, informed and otherwise. Good times or bad, though, the new investor needs to be wary of the winning records displayed so enthusiastically. In this case, past performance is not only no guarantee, it may not even be an *indication* of future results.

2. How easy is it to carry out the system? Some methods require constant attention to the markets, something not all investors are willing to do.

3. What risks are involved? As you begin to get on mailing lists, you will receive direct-mail flyers advertising futures-related systems. Some of these systems cost as much as $3,000 but promise fantastic returns. In these cases, you have to ask yourself the obvious question, i.e., why do they even bother to sell these systems if they work so well for *them?* The sellers try to anticipate this question by protesting that they want to "share" these systems with others. Such generosity! Such altruism! Only $3,000!

So caveat emptor! The fact that the admonition "Let the buyer beware!" has been around since Roman times says a lot about sales methods through the ages. Nowhere do you need to "caveat" more than with solicitations for investment systems and strategies.

THE GREATEST DANGER

The greatest danger for the new investor—or any investor—is not, as you might think, the sharpies trying to get hold of your money or the big, bad bear markets. It's something much closer to home: It is his or her belief that it's possible to attain great returns in a short period with little risk.

After all, you hear about people making a killing in this or that all the time. "So why not me?" you ask. This is the question that leaves you open to the clever salespeople or the occasional dishonest adviser.

The Crash of '87

When Charles II was restored to the throne of England in 1660, he quipped that he was unable to find anyone who wasn't delighted to have him back.

In a similar vein, since the stock market crash of October 1987, it's extremely difficult to find even one adviser who didn't predict this debacle. You will see the ads for these advisers, if you haven't already: ". . . out of stocks in May of 1987 . . ." ". . . advised readers to get into the money markets in early October . . ." ". . . sold all equities in August of 1987 . . ."

So *many* advisers seem to have predicted this crash, in fact, it leads one to the inescapable conclusion that it was actually they who *caused* it. If the accounts you read are accurate, there must have been at least several hundred advisers telling their thousands of readers and followers to get out of stocks—certainly enough to cause the massive sell-off of October 19. . . .

The media are no help in this area. Success stories make better copy than failures, unless a spectacular scam is exposed. You're much more likely to hear about the lady who made $50,000 in six months buying distressed real estate than about the guy who bought gold futures on a sure bet and lost $10,000 in two weeks. The media are biased this way—and even your friends are more likely to tell you about their successes than their failures.

Inexperience coupled with this kind of misinformation can lead to investments that are too risky. It's important to point out here that it's not necessarily "desire" or "greed" that gets people in trouble, in spite of what traditional moralists might say. Everyone desires the best return on his or her money with the lowest possible risk. And "greed" is simply desire run amok. The thing to watch for is a tendency to believe that *you* can find an exception to the risk-return ratio and come out a big winner in a short time. With a belief like this, you have already done 90% of the work of the salespeople. All they have to do now is turn you in their direction and give a little push. . . .

This does not mean you shouldn't ever be adventurous or try occasional investments with some level of risk. What we're talking about is simply putting the odds in your favor—and this happens when you research an investment carefully.

For example, buying stocks of selected small companies, as described in Chapter 19, can bring large returns with a manageable degree of risk. For those who want to go after the "big money," this is the kind of place to look—at least for a small percentage of your portfolio.

GOING BROKE WITH BROKERS

It sometimes seems as if there are quite a few things to watch out for in the field of investing, doesn't it? I think this is because anywhere you find money, you find people who are willing to stretch the truth—or ignore it altogether—in order to get hold of more money.

The version we are dealing with here is stockbrokers who put themselves first and their clients a poor second. As noted in Chapter 5, there are so-called full-commission brokers and discount brokers. A discount broker gives no advice on what to buy, whereas a full-commission broker is like a personal financial adviser specializing in securities.

If you choose a full-commission broker, he or she should have a clear picture of such things as your tax situation, your personal risk-reward ratio, and your goals for your portfolio. The investments the broker recommends should be made taking these factors into consideration. A feeling that these factors are not being considered should set off some alarm bells.

A few other practices that should also set the alarms ringing: Because brokers are paid from commissions on buying and selling securities, some brokers have been known to recommend trades simply to gain those commissions. This practice is called *churning* an account. I knew a broker who would call up a client and recommend that he buy more of a certain stock. When the client demurred, saying he had enough shares of that company, the broker might then recommend that he *sell* some of the same shares. This is churning.

A broker who is constantly coming up with "hot tips" is someone to watch out for. He or she may promise unrealistic returns or ignore your risk-reward ratio by recommending investments that are too speculative for you.

Brokerage houses will sometimes agree to "make a market" in a new issue of a stock; this means they will be looking for buyers. It's a good idea to establish with your broker from the start that whenever he or she is recommending a company in order to make a market, you want to know about it. The company making the new issue may indeed be a good investment, but you have to know where the advice is coming from.

Occasional bad advice is not a basis to sue or go to arbitration. Obviously, your broker isn't going to hit all winners, but if you feel you have gotten consistently bad advice, the best thing to do is to take your business elsewhere.

There are certain offenses, however, for which you should seek recourse. These include the abovementioned churning, as well as lying, or executing trades improperly in a way that hurt you financially.

Most brokerage houses require that you sign a paper agreeing to submit disputes to arbitration. The large stock exchanges and NASDAQ hold hearings to mediate disputes between customers and brokers. These hearings are generally very fair to the individual investor; to ensure impartiality, the majority of people on the arbitration panel are drawn from outside the securities industry. This is your recourse if you feel you have been wronged.

The majority of stockbrokers are honest and most have the interests of their clients at heart. Whether they are skillful at choosing the best investments is something else again; if you are going to pay the extra commissions to get their advice, then the advice had better make you more money.

I know many people who are very satisfied with their brokers and who have developed a friendly relationship with them over the years. If you don't feel comfortable with your broker, however, or feel you've been getting bad advice, you shouldn't hesitate to try someone else—or, perhaps, make your investment choices yourself, buying through a discount broker.

SWITCHING WITH THE MARKET TIMERS

Suppose you could invest in a good equity mutual fund when stocks were going up, sell the fund when the stock market and the fund started going down—and then buy back in at a lower price when things started looking better again. And suppose you could do this at little or no cost.

This is what many investors attempt to do with the help of certain market analysts known as *market timers*. Using every economic indicator known since the beginning of recorded history (including, in some cases, astrology), the market timers perform "technical analysis" of the stock market. They are trying to predict which direction the market is headed and to what degree.

Timing the markets is actually a more respectable method than many of the risky systems you see advertised. Deciding when a market is due to rise or fall is a skill employed successfully by only a minority of advisers—but their recommendations are often accurate enough to be useful to experienced investors.

A lot of high-powered selling of timing systems has been directed at naive investors, however. This is why we include the subject in this chapter. Following the predictions of market timers is not an appropriate tactic for the new investor, but you need to know what all the talk is about. And you need to be prepared for the onslaught of advertisements and direct-mail flyers with rosy-sounding timing statistics.

The goal of investors who follow the predictions of the market timers is to sell their stocks and stock funds when the market has reached its peak, stay out of the market during its decline, and then buy back in at the bottom. This is the opposite of a buy-and-hold strategy: instead of ignoring the ups and downs, the goal is to use the cycles to make as much profit as possible.

Getting in and out of the market, however, can be an expensive proposition if you have to pay commissions on buying and selling a portfolio of stocks. Though many kinds of investors do this, market timing has been especially popular with mutual fund investors, because many mutual funds allow their investors to switch their money, at no cost, from stock funds to money market funds—within the same family of funds, of course.

Thus, if you, or your favorite market timer, felt that the market was about to head south—and take your Fidelity Low-Price Stock Fund down with it—you could call up the Fidelity office and ask to have your money switched to the Fidelity Cash Reserve Fund. Switching simply means you sell your Stock Fund, with its portfolio of small-company stocks, and buy in to the Cash Reserve Fund. With your money in this money market fund, you are protected from any downturn in the stock market.

Now you are out of the stock market and are hoping, of course, that the market will go down over the next few weeks or months, so that you can switch back into the Stock Fund when its shares are selling at a substantially lower price.

If, however, the market should confound you and go *up* instead, you will be left behind. The market has a nasty way of doing just this kind of thing—which is why so many people stick to the buy-and-hold strategy. With all their buy and sell recommendations, only about 10 market timers have consistently done better than the stock averages over the last five years.

Many mutual funds are becoming less lenient with their switching policies. So many people have been switching their money in and out of equity funds that the managers have had difficulty holding on to the stocks in their portfolios.

Many funds have, therefore, cut back to allowing only a few switches a year, while others have taken to charging a fee. Some timing newsletters, however, have dictated as many as 14 switches a year.

Some investors adopt a *modified* buy-and-hold strategy. If the market timers predict a bear market, these investors modify the balance of their portfolios by switching out of those funds likely to fall the most—such as the small-company funds. They sell these funds and put the cash into bond funds or money market funds.

The managers of most equity mutual funds try to be market timers themselves. They will sell many of their stocks—especially the more volatile ones—in a market downturn. As support for the buy-and-hold strategy, however, it's important to note that the majority of these funds— where the managers try to time the market—don't do as well as the overall market, as measured by the various stock indexes. What this illustrates is the great difficulty of timing the ups and downs of the markets.

GAMBLING

When experienced traders invest in risky markets, they are speculating. When inexperienced investors go into the same markets looking for a quick return, they are simply gambling.

A fair number of investors use the markets as a place to gamble. They try their hand at futures trading or junk bonds or timing the markets—anything for a little excitement. The kind of tried and true buying methods discussed in Chapter 20 can seem very staid and boring to them.

If you're well-off and risking only a small portion of your portfolio, a gambling spree won't do much harm. If you're not, then I'd like to suggest the obvious, which is that the World of Investment is not the best place to go looking for thrills. Try the racetrack, or take a few hundred to Vegas or Atlantic City. But keep your capital intact—these days, this is already a venture with plenty of challenge and risk.

The investments described in this section of the book— Part III—are really not suitable for the new investor. Why are they included? A few reasons:

1. General information and interest. You may have wondered about rare coins or the futures markets. You deserve to have them explained in a simple, straightforward manner.

2. Forewarned is forearmed! The riskiest investments are the ones that are sold the hardest. You're going to hear and read a great deal about rare coins, fortunes in the futures markets, and the wonders of options. The salespeople are skillful at their presentations

and often depend on your naïveté to sell their
product.

3. You may be interested in or have a need for these
   markets in the future. Many businesspeople and investors use certain futures and options as a way of
   buying "insurance" on their investments. (This is described in Chapters 26 and 27). Or you may get interested in a certain kind of collectible at some time
   in the future.

CHAPTER 25

PRECIOUS METALS, RARE COINS, AND OTHER COLLECTIBLES

GOLD!

Gold, indeed! If this book were being written anytime up to a few hundred years ago, it would concentrate *mostly* on gold, with maybe a few chapters on precious gems and real estate.

Not only does gold have historical prestige, it echoes through the stories we heard as children. What did the king give the young hero as a reward for killing the monster? What was buried under the witch's cottage?

Gold, then, has an emotional appeal that transcends its real investment value in today's markets. Many new investors feel they "should" own some gold. Doesn't it hold its value? Don't the billionaire sheiks in the Middle East own a lot of it? And isn't it a hedge against inflation or a stock market crash?

The facts are, sadly, that in the last decade, gold has lost much of its allure, at least as an investment. Yes, for a long time gold was used as a hedge against bad times. During wars or great upheavals, the price would be driven up by buyers seeking a safe haven for their money. And gold used to go up when the stock market went down.

But no more. When Iraq invaded Kuwait in the summer of 1990, gold took a brief spurt upward. By September, however, it was declining; by January, the price was down to $365 an ounce—$50 lower than a year earlier. Even a shooting war couldn't get it out of the cellar.

So what has happened to gold? In 1980, gold stood at an all-time high of $800 an ounce, and some advisers were predicting prices of $1,200, $1,500, even $2,000 an ounce! What happened was that high oil prices—and the inflation they were helping to cause—were brought under control. In addition, the large, institutional investors found a new way of hedging against a downturn in the stock market—in a word, *currencies.*

If things look bad for the U.S. markets, the big investors will simply buy Swiss francs or Deutschemarks or Japanese yen—whatever economy looks good at the moment. These transactions are carried out instantaneously by computers—a much simpler process than buying gold, which has to be transported and stored.

A further reason for gold being in the dumps is that while demand has stayed relatively flat over the past decade, supply has increased. Unless gold cuff links come back into style, demand is not likely to increase markedly (jewelry is the largest use for gold). So, barring the return of double-digit inflation or serious upheavals in the world economy, the best analysis has the price of gold remaining weak during the 1990s.

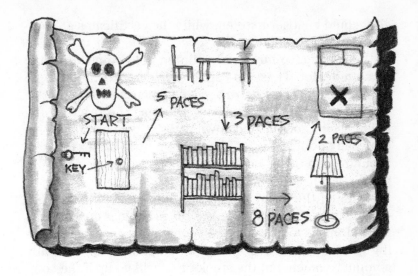

Buying Gold

You say you still want to put some of your assets into gold?
Okay, here are several ways of doing this.

First, you can actually buy gold bullion—bars of gold,
like the kind they have in Fort Knox. You can get these in
various sizes—up to 25 pounds each—or you can buy thin
wafers of gold weighing as little as 1 gram. Banks and gold
dealers will sell them to you, with a 3% to 10% commission
(!) added on. You can then take the gold home with you and
hide it in the mattress or bury it in the back yard (be sure to
make a good map!).

If, however, you have a waterbed or live in an apartment
without a proper yard, the bank will be delighted to store the
gold for you and give you a certificate of ownership in return. This is the preferred method of holding gold these
days, as hiding the certificate in the mattress doesn't make
for such an uncomfortable lump as the gold bar does. Seriously, the certificate is a safer way of holding the gold. The

gold could be lost or stolen, while the certificates are protected by registration.

You can also buy newly minted gold coins at a bank
or coin dealer. These so-called *bullion coins* need to be
distinguished from the *rare coins* discussed below. Rare
coins have their own market, whereas the price of the
bullion coins goes up and down with the gold market. Coins
are easily bought and sold and are a little easier to carry
around than gold bars. Commissions range from 2%
to 4%.

One of the disadvantages of holding gold is that you
don't get any return on it, unless the price goes up. One way
around this is to buy shares in companies engaged in mining gold. Dividends from these companies don't usually
amount to much, but the stock price will go up if the company makes a big strike in one of its mines. The price will
also go up if the price of gold goes up—usually. If the company itself is on the skids, of course, an increase in the price
of gold may not help.

Gold-mining stocks are among the riskier ventures, as
you might guess. If you want to spread out your risk, try buying shares in a mutual fund owning shares in gold-mining
companies. If you must invest in gold, this is probably the
least risky way of doing it, though I must warn you that these
mutual funds—and the companies they own shares in—are
still very high-risk investments.

Finally, if you have it on unassailable authority that the
price of gold is about to make a meteoric rise, you can invest
in gold futures (see Chapter 26 on futures trading). This is
combining a very volatile commodity with a very risky trading method, so you'd better be pretty darn sure. As you will
discover when you read the chapter on futures, they are generally something for the new investor to avoid. I mention
them simply to round out this information on the different
ways of buying gold.

... AND SILVER

If you have read the section on gold, then you know most of what you need to know about silver. Silver is another metal with a history, not quite so distinguished as that of gold, but just as long. And silver too is currently depressed in price.

The silver market is an excellent example of how buying methods that have worked in the past may fail when new situations develop. In the past, when silver fell drastically in price many traders would buy, and eventually the price would rise. For the last several years, salesmen have been urging people to buy silver because it has reached new "historic lows." But the silver market has responded by making even *more* historic lows.

The reasons for this are simple enough: The market for silver has changed—demand has flattened out while the supply has increased. And, as with gold, investors who once used silver for hedging against bad times have found new and better ways of doing this.

The various methods of buying silver are similar to those for gold: bullion, coins, stocks in silver-mining companies, and mutual funds. The mutual funds will often buy stocks in both gold and silver mines—it's hard to find a fund specializing in silver only. And, yes, there is a silver futures market.

Unless the world economy and the silver market change radically, however, I would invest only in silver jewelry; there, at least, its beauty is undiminished.

At some point during the decade, gold and silver will probably rise in value; this will finally give those who have been pushing precious metals a chance to say "I told you so!" Remember, though, that most of them have been predicting a rise for years and years. The increase in value will have to be pretty impressive to make up for all the losses suffered by gold investors during the '80s and early '90s.

In the same vein, Harvard economist Robert Reich (now Secretary of Labor) tells a story on himself. In early October 1987, he recommended on a radio talk show that his audience sell their stocks immediately. Two weeks later the market crashed, and Reich found himself beset with investors wanting his advice. What they didn't know, as he recounted later, was that he had been predicting a bear market since 1981!

Both these examples should make the reader pause when he or she hears enthusiastic claims of successful market predictions. You have to ask how many times the "guru" was mistaken before finally being right.

RARE COINS

If you read the financial journals, you have seen the ads. On the Financial News Network they come on about every 10 minutes. "Rare coins have outperformed the stock market over the last twenty years! Wall Street about to invest in rare coin market! Coins could double in the next year! Only fools and greenhorns are not investing in rare coins!" (Well, they may not actually make that last statement, but it's not hard to catch their drift.)

Even as a new investor, you are probably already aware of the quantity and variety of advertising aimed at you. The investment industry is immense. The people we pay to buy and sell remind me of the people who came to California in 1849 not to look for gold, but to sell mining equipment and other necessities to the miners. It may not have looked as glamorous or exciting, but these people almost always did well.

That fact should give pause to anyone listening to the advertisements. Yes, there are certainly people who make money with investments, but there are also ones who lose. The people selling the picks and shovels, however, make money either way.

This is especially true in the rare coin industry, where the difference between the dealer's price and the customer's price can be as much as 25%. This difference is called the *spread*. It means your coin must go up 25% in value before you can sell it back to a dealer for the price you paid for it. There are a few dealers who claim to have smaller spreads, but it's up to the buyer to compare prices.

Just as the merchants to the forty-niners had a lock on the market, the rare coin dealers seem to have a lock not just on the coins, but on information about the rare coin market. It is difficult to find material other than what the industry puts out—though there is plenty of that, and it's very self-serving. You will find a few unbiased sources listed in Resources.

What makes the market in rare coins different from the markets in other collectibles, such as fine art or comic books? The coin dealers have made a big effort to standardize their products.

Since 1986, coins have been "graded" by independent organizations according to their general appearance and lack of blemishes. They are then encased in clear plastic, where they *stay*—woe to any hapless buyer who takes a coin out of its case.

Gone are the days of collectors showing off their precious gold coins to admiring friends. Indeed, it is estimated that true collectors make up less than 5% of the coin market nowadays. Instead, you have the somewhat surreal situation where investors buy a coin encased in plastic, put it away in a dark place, and hope that another investor will eventually pay more for it. It has become a market based almost entirely on perceived value, and while you can argue that this is true of any collectible, at least with works of art you can display and enjoy them while waiting for their value to go up.

The coin market is extremely volatile. It is the kind of investment for only a small percentage of a portfolio—and even then, only for those investors willing to make a real study of the market. Buyers should be prepared to hold coins for a few years—emotionally as well as financially prepared. It can cause a bit of stress to watch the value of your investment decrease by half in a few months. Yes, the coin market overall has done well over the last 10 years, but we know by now about past performance and future success. Furthermore, the market's performance has been based largely on certain groups of coins.

GRADING OF COINS

Which coins tend to appreciate in value the most? There are two factors in the value of a coin: its rarity and its condition—its *grade*, in the system set up by the dealers. A coin can have a rating of 1 to 70. The coins most traded are uncirculated; that is, they were never in general circulation and have retained their Mint State condition.

These Mint State (MS) coins have ratings in the mid-60s. The coins you want to buy are the MS64s, MS65s, and MS66s (a rating over MS66 is very rare). Of these, you want the ones with the lowest populations—in short, you want the rarest and highest-quality coins you can afford. These are the ones that increase the most in value. One MS64 1910 Indian head $10 gold piece is worth fifty MS64 1881 Morgan silver dollars, not because of its greater beauty or quality, but simply because there are very few coins of this quality from this particular year in existence.

There are a few things to watch out for if you decide that the rare coin market looks good. Once you start dealing with one firm, the word somehow gets around to other dealers that there's a new dude in town, and soon you're

Three Kinds of Valuable Coins

1. **Bullion coins.** With the American Eagle in 1986, this country joined other countries that mint gold coins. These coins are not used in general circulation as gold was up to 1933. They are bought by people wanting to invest in gold (as we discussed above). There are also silver bullion coins.

   These are not "rare coins." Their value goes up and down with the gold and silver markets.

2. **Generic coins.** These might be termed "semi-rare." Examples are those silver dollars you've had in your desk drawer for 20 years that you've been wondering what to do with. There are gold coins, too, minted before 1933, which were in general circulation and are not terribly unusual. These coins do have some rarity value, however; their prices are partly tied to supply and demand, partly to the precious-metals markets.

3. **True rare coins** look pretty much the way they did when they were minted. They were never in circulation, and populations are usually in the hundreds or low thousands. The market for rare coins is not generally tied to the precious-metals markets, though if the price of gold doubled, you would see some movement in rare gold coins.

getting phone calls—lots of them. You might be able to prevent this by asking your dealer not to circulate your name, but I have my doubts. It could be that simply subscribing to the *Wall Street Journal* gets your name and number on the mailing and calling lists.

Aggressive salesmanship is alive and well in the coin market. You will do yourself a big favor by learning as much as you can from independent sources before you start talking to the coin dealers. Their salespeople are fonts of information—torrents! So be firm. Don't let them make you feel like a fool because you don't immediately realize that these recently discovered 1914 Russian gold pieces from the *Czar's personal treasury* will skyrocket in value in a matter of months. They, of course, have only a limited number of these treasures and can't be responsible for what might happen if you should wait till the next day. . . .

Incidentally, speaking of foreign coins, most of the trading in this country is done with American coins. Venturing into foreign coins greatly increases the already speculative nature of the game.

OTHER COLLECTIBLES

If my mother hadn't thrown out my comic books from the 1950s, I'd be extremely rich today. The number of comic book collectors and investors is on its way up. Dealers in the fine arts claim that the arts outperformed the stock market 4 to 1 in the 1980s, but this is another market with extreme volatility. Precious gems are used for investment as well as for decoration.

The most recent collectibles are '50s and '60s pop records. The compact disc is turning the old-fashioned 45 and $33\frac{1}{3}$ rpm records into rarities; some of the older, more unusual ones are now worth hundreds of dollars; a few are worth thousands.

The tendency of some new investors is to jump at such statistics. Here is something they can understand! No complicated market structures, no research or legwork needed. Just a regular old comic book—buy low, sell high.

One useful thing to remember, though—and not just in

the collectibles market—is that when you come up with a dynamite investment idea, chances are 99 to 1 that a bunch of other smarties came up with the same idea 10 years ago. In this case, it's the comics dealers who buy low, sell high— a 50% to 100% spread is not unusual.

Respectable Collectibles

The older, more "respectable" markets deal with art, antiques, and other fine collectibles. Silverware, china, antique dolls, toys, miniatures—there are about 70 recognized categories of collectibles. If you are interested in learning more about a certain type of collectible, several sources are listed at the end of the chapter.

If you have inherited some fine antiques or, perhaps, a collection of miniature animals carved in ebony and are wondering what to do with them, the books in Resources will get you started. Trade associations will help you find a reputable dealer or appraiser; two of these are listed in Resources.

It's a good idea to get clear in your mind whether you are going to be predominantly a collector or an investor— whether you're in it for love or money. It is possible to be both: for example, I have a friend who is a world-renowned authority on Egyptian revenue stamps—but dealing in these stamps is his chosen occupation. For someone to whom it is only an interesting sideline, it's a different game. Do you love those antique dolls for their beauty or because they're valuable? If you're going to spend the kind of money required to have a fine collection, it's something to think about.

If you decide to be an investor, be sure to research how fluid any given market is. The rare coin dealers have made it easy for you to buy and sell (although with a large spread in their favor). But when you come to sell your 19th-century Shaker rocking chair or your 1958 Elvis album, are there going to be buyers at hand? The ability to move in and out of a market can be worth a good deal if that particular market is going nowhere and you want to put your money elsewhere.

In case you haven't guessed, by now, it's probably not a good idea for a new investor to rush out and buy rare coins or other collectibles. You have a much better chance of coming out ahead in the stock market.

I don't like to dismiss a market out of hand, however. When you have gained experience as an investor, you may be drawn to a market because of some interest or expertise in the field. Perhaps your mom didn't throw out your old comics or baseball cards, or you have inherited some beautiful antiques.

If you simply feel drawn to collectibles, the best idea is to pick an area where you have a real affinity or background. Then learn as much as you can about it and start to deal in a small way.

Resources

American Numismatic Association. P.O. Box 2366, Colorado Springs, CO 80901. (719) 632-2646. Membership $26/year, $32/first year. Membership includes a subscription to *The Numismatist,* a monthly magazine with articles of general interest about coins. You also receive a resource directory, listing all the various services provided by the ANA.

The ANA concerns itself with everything you ever wanted to know about coins. Their library dealing with coins is the largest in the world; as a member you can take out books and videos. The association presents workshops, coin shows, and seminars on investment advice and other topics. A good place for the new rare coin investor to start.

Coin Dealer Newsletter, P.O. Box 11099, Torrance, CA 90510. (213) 370-5579. Weekly. $50/six months, $89/year, $147/ two years.

The so-called "gray sheet" (yes, its pages are actually gray) will give you the current bid and ask prices for all U.S. rare coins.

PRECIOUS METALS, RARE COINS, AND OTHER COLLECTIBLES 295

It also covers trends in the market for coins. The gray sheet is primarily for coin dealers, so the trade language takes some getting used to. If you begin to trade coins seriously, though, this paper is a necessity.

Donald Kagin's Personal Guide to Rare Coin Investments by Donald Kagin. Prentice Hall, 1984. $15, hardcover, $9.95, paperback.

This is still the best book for the beginner. Everything you need to know about investing in rare coins plus historical and other related information.

It's easy to find information on the fine collectibles, but harder to find material on things like baseball cards and comic books. One source for popular *and* fine collectibles is **Collector Books,** P.O. Box 3009, Paducah, KY 42001. (800) 626-5420. They will send you a free catalog listing the more than 130 books they publish on all kinds of collectibles.

Ralph and Terry Kovel are perhaps the best-known experts on antiques and collectibles. They have written 14 books; 2 of the most popular are:

Kovels' Know Your Antiques by Ralph and Terry Kovel. Crown Publishers, 1981. $14.95 (paperback). Information for the new collector on all kinds of antiques.

Kovels' Know Your Collectibles by Ralph and Terry Kovel. Crown Publishers, 1981. $16.95 (paperback). A guide to various kinds of fine collectibles. How to buy and sell, determine their value, origin, etc.

If you want to know the value of something you own or have inherited, you will need a good appraiser. The **International Society of Appraisers** will recommend reputable appraisers in 130 categories. The ISA may be contacted at P.O. Box 726, Hoffman Estates, IL 60195. (708) 882-0706. They will send you a pamphlet listing their services and the various categories of appraisers they can recommend. An excellent resource.

CHAPTER 26

FUTURES

The big, bad futures markets! There seems to be a general consensus about the futures markets: (1) They are absolutely unintelligible; (2) they are of use only to cutthroat speculators out to make a fast buck; and (3) it's possible to make or lose a lot of money in a very short time. Of these assumptions, only the last is accurate.

It takes a little concentration, but futures contracts are not that difficult to understand. No, really! If you have ever made a financial agreement or a business contract, you have made an agreement that something will be transacted in the future. That's all a futures contract is: an agreement to deliver a set amount of a commodity of a certain quality at a given date.

Such contracts started in this country in the mid-19th century as a way for farmers and large buyers of farm produce to stabilize the agricultural markets. Then, as now, the prices of grain and other commodities were always changing as supply and demand changed. This was hard on the producers. One year, a farmer might grow a bumper crop of corn only to find that all the farmers in the region had similar crops. The resulting surplus drove the price of corn way down—often causing much of it to be dumped.

The next year, everyone had learned his lesson. Nobody grew very much corn, and the wholesale buyers couldn't supply their customers. The price was way up, but few of the farmers had much to sell.

It was at this point in one of the cycles that a farmer—we'll call him Smith—saddled up his horse and rode to his buyer's office in the city.

"In one month, I can deliver two hundred bushels of corn to you if you'll give me ten cents a bushel," Smith told the buyer, whose name was Frank Middleman.

The buyer, who had several customers willing to pay him 15 cents a bushel, agreed on the spot. This was a futures contract—not the first one, for the Japanese had contracts for rice delivery in the 17th century. But this contract and others like it began to stabilize the agricultural markets in this country.

It's easy to see the benefits of such contracts: Farmer Smith and the other growers had a price they could depend on, the buyers had a supply they could depend on, and the retailers and general public were assured of a steady supply of corn and other grains. Before long, the times of the contracts were extended. Farmer Smith could make contracts in the spring for delivery in the fall; that way he knew how much to plant, not just of corn, but of other grains as well.

"All very well," you say, "but what about the speculators?" Well, after Farmer Smith left, Joe Sharp dropped by his friend Frank's office. Joe was a financial speculator and when he heard about Frank's contract with Farmer Smith, he saw an opportunity. Joe believed that because there was a shortage, the price of corn was going to go even higher.

"Look, Frank," he said, "when Smith delivers that corn, I'll buy it from you at fourteen cents a bushel—twenty-eight dollars for the two hundred bushels. We'll put it in writing, if you like—make a contract."

"But what about my customers?" Frank protested. "I can get fifteen cents a bushel from them. If I pay Smith twenty dollars for his corn and sell it for thirty, I'll make ten dollars."

"If you sell it to me, you'll only make eight dollars," answered Joe, "but it's a sure thing. A lot can happen in a month, you know. If the price of corn goes down to eight cents a bushel, do you think your buyers are going to give you fifteen? You don't have contracts with them, remember."

Frank thought it over. The price of corn might go up, in which case he would make more than the 15 cents a bushel. But Joe was right—it could go down and he was locked in to buying from Smith at 10 cents a bushel. He was not a rich man and the prospect of an assured $8 looked good. (Remember, we're talking 1840 here, when a dollar was a day's wages.) "You got yourself a deal," he told Joe, and the futures market was born.

Frank Middleman was happy, not only because he was going to be $8 richer, but because Joe had relieved him of any risk—risk he couldn't afford to take. Farmer Smith was still happy: he didn't care who ultimately got his corn as long as he got his 10 cents a bushel. And Joe Sharp was delighted with his new investment idea. He had enough money to take a little risk for the possibility of a big gain. If the price of corn went up to 20 cents a bushel in a month he could sell the 200 bushels for $40. Subtracting the $28 he would pay to Frank, he would realize a $12 profit.

A few days later, Joe got another brainstorm. He was beginning to worry about the price of corn. If the price dropped below 14 cents a bushel, he would be stuck with a loss.

His bright idea was to go to one of Frank Middleman's customers, a woman named Jenny who ran a bakery. Jenny was greatly in need of corn and Joe was able to make a contract with Jenny to sell her 50 bushels of the corn he was due to receive from Farmer Smith. He simply told her the obvious—that the price of corn was very volatile these days and that locking in a price of 16 cents a bushel was in her interest.

Joe had now made both kinds of contracts that are available in the futures markets: contracts to sell a commodity and contracts to buy it. Both these contracts were based on future delivery of the corn; hence the name *futures contracts* or simply *futures*.

As it happened, the following week one of Joe's other business deals went sour. He now needed the $28 he was going to give to Frank Middleman for the corn. Luckily, he knew another speculator, John, who believed that the price of corn was headed higher. After explaining his agreement with Frank, Joe convinced John to take on the contract— John would now be the one to buy the corn from Frank Middleman.

This kind of transfer is the way futures contracts are traded today. You don't actually "buy" a contract, you take it on, or assume it. You deposit a certain amount of money with a commodities broker in order to assume a contract.

If the price of corn had gone up, the contract to buy Farmer Smith's corn would have become more valuable. Joe would have bought 200 bushels of corn at 10 cents a bushel, and could have sold at least the remaining 150 bushels of it at a much higher price, say 20 cents a bushel, to other buyers (not to Jenny—she has her price locked in on her 50 bushels). Therefore, the value of the contract would also have gone up—and so would the price.

If corn had gone down, on the other hand, the contracts to *sell* would have become more valuable. Joe could have bought 50 more bushels of corn from another farmer for, say, 6 cents a bushel and sold it to Jenny for the agreed-upon price of 16 cents a bushel.

If you think the price of corn, or any commodity, is likely to go higher, you will take on a contract allowing you to buy corn (in market terminology, you will "buy corn" or "go long on corn"). Conversely, if you believe the bears are in the corn, and the price is on its way down, you will "sell

corn"—that is, take on a contract to sell it. This will make
you "short on corn." In either case, if you're right in your
assessment of the market, the value of your contract will go
up and you can sell it for more than you paid.

Those are the basics of the futures markets. Contracts
are salable items. Futures contracts may be traded many
times before the actual date for delivery. And, no, you don't
actually have to deliver or receive 5,000 bushels of corn (the
amount of present-day contracts). You simply sell your contract sometime before the last day of trading—the day when
the contract comes due. Someone who has the capability
will handle the actual delivery. The futures exchanges—the
organizations that handle and regulate futures trading—see
that delivery is made when necessary.

MODERN FUTURES CONTRACTS

In order to trade futures contracts, you need to open an account with a *commodities broker;* stockbrokers do not handle futures. Depending on which markets you wish to trade,
you will be asked to deposit a certain amount of "margin"
capital at the brokerage office.

This margin money is not to be confused with the kind
of margin required by stockbrokers (discussed in Chapter
18). This margin is "upfront money"—to show your good
faith in honoring any contract you may assume. It is similar
to the money you might deposit with a title company when
you make an offer on a house.

There are full-service commodities brokers, who will
give you advice on what to buy, and there are the discount
brokers, who will simply execute your trades. Needless to
say, the selection of a commodities broker is an important
decision. You should expect to be called by commodities
brokers looking for new accounts; they will expand on the
marvelous profit possibilities in the futures markets. Don't

listen to them. Instead, read Jake Bernstein's chapter on how to pick a broker (see Resources).

These days, you can buy futures contracts for any number of agricultural commodities, for metals, and even for currencies. These contracts all have their uses for different people, but their greatest value is in *the transfer of risk to speculators*. In the story above, Frank Middleman transferred his risk to Joe Sharp, who was better able to afford it. The markets may be different nowadays, but the concept is the same.

Suppose, for example, you had a business that dealt in fine china. You have a contract to buy plates from a British firm for $100,000 in three months. In order to actually make the purchase, you will have to change your $100,000 into the equivalent amount of British pounds—you will have to "buy" pounds with dollars.

Now if, during those three months, the pound appreciates against the dollar, say by 5%, you will need *more* dollars to buy the required number of pounds—$5,000 more, in fact ($100,000 × .05 = $5,000). There is a chance, of course, that the pound might go down against the dollar, in which case you would do well, because you would need fewer dollars to buy pounds. But you are a businessperson, not a speculator. You don't like the risk, so what can you do?

What you can do is "hedge" your purchase by taking on a futures contract for the pound. In this case, you take on a contract to buy pounds, which means you will make money if the pound goes up (you are "buying" pounds—you have taken a "long" position on pounds sterling or, more succinctly, you are "long on sterling.")

Now, with this contract, if the pound should go up by 5%, you will make back the $5,000 you lost by having to buy the more expensive pounds to complete your business contract (actually, you would even make a little more than $5,000—see below).

The contract for the pounds sterling is essentially no different from the contract for corn that Joe Sharp sold to his investor friend, John. In this case, though, instead of 200 bushels of corn for 10 cents a bushel, you are agreeing to buy 62,500 British pounds for $2 a pound. A 5% rise in the pound over three months would mean it would then take not $2, but *$2.10* to buy one pound ($2 × .05 = $.10) Your contract would have gone up in value by $.10 a pound, or $6,250 (62,500 × $.10). Sell it!

Of course, the pound could have decreased in value, in which case you would have lost money on your futures contract. You would have gained most of it back, however, because when it came time to pay for the British china, your dollars would buy more British pounds.

So you don't make or lose much either way—and that's the whole point! Your concern is with china, not international currencies. That's the job of the speculators who are creating the currency markets by buying futures contracts in the British pound and other currencies. By assuming a futures contract, you have successfully transferred most of the risk involved in your china transaction to these speculators.

It is also possible to take on a contract to *sell* pounds whereby you would make money if the pound went down against the dollar. (In this case, you would be "short on sterling.") The manufacturer of the china in England might want a contract like this. It is in his or her interest that the dollar not go up against the pound.

The futures markets, then, are of great importance to individuals or firms wanting to hedge against possible losses in the purchase or delivery of their product. As noted above, one of their main functions is the transfer of risk from businesspeople to speculators. In agricultural commodities, the hedgers are the large wholesale buyers and the farmers themselves.

In recent years new futures markets have been created. Bankers can now hedge with interest-rate futures. Managers of mutual funds can hedge against large drops in the stock market with stock-index futures.

If you want a fuller explanation of the different kinds of futures markets, see the books cited in Resources. They will also give you the essential details you need to know to invest in futures. My purpose here has simply been to give you some idea of what these contracts are and to demonstrate the importance of the futures markets. If you own a business, you may someday find yourself hedging against losses with futures contracts.

SPECULATION

If you decide to speculate in these markets, you should remember that at least one of the myths about the futures markets is true: It is indeed possible to lose large amounts of money in very short periods of time. You saw, for example, how a profit or loss of $6,250 was possible with just a 5% rise or fall in the value of the British pound.

This kind of percentage change can and does happen much more quickly than in three months—sometimes too quickly to get out of the market soon enough to prevent a big loss. It's very easy to lose thousands of dollars on just one futures contract—it happens all the time. The majority of speculators in the futures markets lose money each year. (Hedgers and businesspeople don't usually lose—just those who trade purely for speculative purposes.)

These markets are attractive to speculators because of the possibility of large profits and because they don't need a large amount to get started. (Cousin Jack *loves* futures!) To enter into the contract for British pounds, for example, the broker would have required only $2,025 to be deposited as "margin." You would get this deposit back when you sold the contract—*if* you came out ahead. If you lost money on your trade, say in the amount of $3,000, you would sacrifice your margin deposit *and* have to pay an additional $975. The (discount) broker's commission would amount to about $50 to $75 for both trades.

There *are* ways of minimizing your risk—Kelly Angle explains these methods thoroughly in his book, listed below. I hope you will read it and the other recommended book before you think about putting any money down on futures, either as a hedger or a speculator.

Resources

One Hundred Million Dollars in Profits by Kelly Angle. Windsor Books, 1989. $45 (hardcover).

Despite the lurid title, this is quite a conservative book. Angle's father was actually the one who bought gold futures at just the right time and made all the money. After telling his father's story—which really involved more luck than skill—the author then proceeds to tell us the *right* way to go about trading futures. Angle is a conservative trader—he emphasizes the preservation of capital. The book reads easily. Before you know it, you are thinking in terms of volatility indexes and trend lines.

How the Futures Markets Work by Jake Bernstein. NYIF Corporation (a division of Simon & Schuster), 1989. $15.95 (paperback).

This is a more comprehensive book than Angle's. It gives the history of the futures markets and explains how they operate in the present day. It also includes all the practical information you need to get started trading. Clear and well written.

CHAPTER 27

OPTIONS

"Anybody who plays the market without inside information is like a man buying cows in the moonlight."

—DAN DREW, LEGENDARY TRADER

O ptions? Options? In my experience, discussing the concept of "buying an option" tends to draw as many blank stares as the idea of futures contracts. But you may have already bought an option of sorts. As a young man, I bought an option without even knowing I was doing it.

When I was 21, I decided it was time I found myself a *real* car, as opposed to the junkers I'd been driving. The first one I looked at was a red '55 Ford convertible, to my eyes a most lovely piece of machinery. Having just started my search, however, I wanted to see what else was out there. At the same time, I didn't want someone else to buy the car.

"Look," I said to the owner, "I like the car, but I want to look around some more. I'll give you twenty-five dollars to hold on to the car until ten tomorrow morning. If I don't buy it, you keep the money."

"Okay," he said, "but at ten o'clock, out she goes."

I had just bought an option. And he had just sold an option. As it turned out, there was nothing on the market even close to this paragon; I came back the same afternoon, paid him $300, and drove off at a high rate of speed.

In this case, I got my $25 back. When you purchase an option to buy stock, you're not so lucky; the person who sold you the option keeps the money. What you're hoping, when you put out money for an option, is that the stock will go up enough to cover the price of the option and give you a profit.

CALL OPTIONS

Say you decide IBM is about to make a move upward. The stock has been down recently but their new personal computer looks like a winner, and you think the price will rise maybe 10 points ($10 a share) or more over the next few months. Right now, however, the price of the stock is $120 a share and you can't afford to buy 100 shares. You could buy 20 shares for $2,400, but then a 10-point rise would bring you only a $200 profit, which would just cover your commissions to buy and sell.

In the options section of the financial pages, however, you find an item one day in early January that looks interesting. It's very succinct: "IBM March120 call 9." Translation: For $9, you can purchase an option—a right—to buy 1 share of IBM, or 100 shares for $900 (options are sold in 100-share blocks). "March120" means that at any time before the third Friday of March you have the right to buy these 100 shares at the price of $120 a share.

Why would you buy this option? You would buy because you believe the price of IBM stock is going to go up.

Buying a *call option*, or simply a *call*, means you are betting the stock will rise. A call option is a right to buy 100 shares of a certain stock at a given price, at any time during a set period of time.

The seller of the option, also called the *option writer*, is the one who collects the $900 cost of the option. The transaction takes place through your stockbroker, but all the broker gets are commissions on the purchase and sale, paid for by the buyer—in this case, you.

This option writer is hoping IBM stock will *not* go up. If you decide to exercise your option, this writer is the one who must sell you the 100 shares of IBM stock at $120 a share. If IBM remains at $120, or goes below $120, it would not be in your interest to exercise your option.

If, on the other hand, the stock should rise to $125, you could buy the 100 shares from the option writer for $120 a share and sell them on the market for $125. This would allow you at least to recoup $500 of your $900, less commissions. The writer of the option would still keep the $900, but he or she must buy IBM stock at $125 and sell it to you at $120— so the writer is minus $500 of the $900.

If the stock should go up to $134 before the third Friday of March, then you would be in great shape. You would have the right to buy 100 shares of IBM at $120 a share, or $12,000, and could sell them at $134, or $13,400. This would give you a profit of $1,400 ($13,400 minus $12,000 = $1,400). Subtracting the $900 price you paid for the option would then leave you $500 to the good, less whatever broker's commissions you paid for selling the stock (you could, of course, hold on to the stock if you wished).

In reality, relatively few options contracts are actually exercised in the manner described above. This is because a rise in the price of a stock will cause an immediate rise in the price of an option based on that stock. Like a futures contract, an option is also a contract and, as such, is a salable item. Salable contracts will go up and down according to the demand for them on the market.

Say you got lucky and IBM went up to $125 just a few
days after you bought the March120 option. Next day, the
price of the option might look like this: IBM March120 call
13. Your call option has gone up in price by 4 points, from
9 to 13. Four points means a profit of $400, if you should
decide to sell the option.

This means some people out there are willing to buy
your call option for $1,300 because they think IBM is likely
to go even higher before the option expires in March. It also
means you do not have to hold on to the option until it
expires.

Now you have the pleasant task of deciding whether
you want to sell your option and take your profit, or hold on
to it a while longer, in case IBM goes up further. If you sell
it, you will have made $400, less commissions ($1,300
minus $900 = $400). The commissions will be about $40 each
way—$80 in all—with a discount broker, and subtracting
the $80 will leave you with a $320 profit. Not bad for a few
days, with a $900 investment.

If you decide to hold on to your option for a while, however, watch out! Options "expire" on the third Friday of the
month listed in the paper—in this case, March. This means
by that date you either have to exercise your option to buy
the underlying stock, or sell the option. As their expiration
date approaches, options have a nasty habit of "decaying"
in price. If IBM stock goes back down to $120 a week
before the expiration date, your $900 option will be worth
almost nothing. Nobody wants to buy an option that enables
them to buy stock at the going market price.

So the best bet would be to sell your option if you get a
nice profit in it. If the stock goes down and your option with
it, you may also decide to sell before it goes down too far. If
IBM goes down a few points below 120 in January, your option will also go down a few, but it will still retain some
value—this is called "time" value, because there are still two
months wherein the stock might go up.

If the price of IBM goes down in *March*, however, close to the expiration day, the option will have no time value at all. As in most decisions relating to when to buy and sell, there are no rules here. It's up to you and how much risk you want to take.

The advantage to options, then, is that you get the possibility of large profits with a relatively small outlay. The majority of options are less expensive than the IBM options; many cost less than $100. This means your risk is limited. If the bottom fell out of the market and IBM dropped 20 points, a holder of 100 shares of IBM stock would see the stock drop $2,000 in value. You, however, would have lost only your $900.

The advantage of stocks over options is, of course, that the stockholder's loss is only a "paper" loss. He or she could hold on to the IBM shares in expectation that they would go up again (they always have). You, on the other hand, would never see your $900 again.

PUTS

If you believe a stock is about to take a dive, there is a way to invest in that, too. You can buy what is called a *put option* or, more simply, a *put*. This is similar to a call, except that instead of enabling you to buy a stock over the next few months, it enables you to *sell* it.

"How can you sell something you don't own?" you ask. Don't forget: This is the wonderful World of Investment. As in the case of short selling, minor details such as nonownership are easily overlooked.

Puts are listed with calls in the financial pages. They are designated as "puts" or may simply have a "P" after them. For example: IBM March120 Put 8. This means that for $800 you can buy the right to *sell* 100 shares of IBM at the price of $120 until the third Friday in March.

If you buy this put, and IBM drops 20 points before the third Friday in March, you can buy 100 shares on the open market for the new price of $100 and sell them to the writer of the put option for $120. Profit: $2,000, less $800 for the option, less commissions for buying and selling the stock.

Rather than go through all this, of course, it would be easier to sell the option on the open market. It will have appreciated anywhere from 10 to 25 points, depending on how close it is to the expiration date. You will make a very nice profit.

Buying options is a risky business, though. You can make good profits or you can very easily lose your entire investment. Like futures speculators, the majority of options traders lose money over the course of any given year. If you sell or "write" the options, you are also opening yourself up to high risk. In the case above, where IBM dropped 20 points, the writer of the option would have come out $1,200 to the downside ($2,000 less the $800 received for the option).

There are ways of minimizing this risk, but these methods are beyond our scope here. If you're interested, Ken Trestor's book listed in Resources explain these methods in detail.

A FEW MORE DETAILS

For now, here are a few more things you need to know about buying options.

You can buy options that have expiration dates anywhere from one to nine months. The most common options you see listed have lives of two to three months. Recently, options called *leaps* have been introduced—options with an expiration date two years away. The longer the life of an option, the more expensive it is, because the stock has a longer period in which to go up or down (the "time value" is greater). Leaps, therefore, are the most expensive of the options.

You can, of course, buy options on the open market that have expiration dates just a week or even a day away. This kind of trading is engaged in by some speculators with a very high tolerance for risk (or a subconscious desire to lose).

The price of the stock at which you can exercise the option is called the *strike price*. In the examples above, the strike price of the options—$120 a share—was "on the money," meaning it was the same as the present price of IBM stock.

The strike price can also be "in the money," meaning the strike price is less than the present selling price of the stock (the stock price is still $120). For example: IBM March 115 call 16. Notice that the price of this "in the money" call option—$1,600—is more expensive than the "on the money" option because you have an additional five points given to you.

An "out of the money" option has a strike price that is higher than the present selling price. These are the options the speculators like to use because they are the cheapest. For example: IBM March 130 call 2. For $200, you can purchase an option to buy 100 shares of IBM at $130 a share. The speculators know it's not necessary for IBM to go up all the way to $130 for them to make a profit. If it only went up to $125 in a few weeks, the option would probably go up a point or two—enough for them to make a profit. (Speculators often buy a large number of a certain option. If 10 were purchased, for example, a rise of one point would mean a profit of $100 on each option, or $1,000.)

Some options are thinly traded. This means you may not be able to sell when you want to—an important consideration. In the options quotes, you will see a column headed "Open Interest": these figures are the number of options traded during the previous day. Occasionally, you will see

"No trade," meaning there are options of that kind on the market, but there were no buyers at the price they were offered at.

Warrants are a kind of call option. They give you the right to buy a certain stock at a given price in a given time frame. Unlike most options, however, warrants are created by the companies whose stock they are based on.

Corporations making new issues of stocks or bonds will often offer warrants as a further inducement to buy the securities. Warrants usually have lives of a few years instead of a few months, but they should be considered in the same speculative class as regular options.

Buying options—puts and calls—takes some getting used to. Before you get into it with real money, I would strongly recommend trying the National Investment Challenge, Options Division (see Resources, Chapter 18). Watch how quickly you can gain or lose a few hundred thousand dollars with options. It's easy! It's fun!—especially when it's Monopoly money.

If you decide to use real money, however, this is one of those areas where it would be wise to start very small. Buy a few options for $50 or $100 and see how you feel holding them. Buying options with expiration dates a few months away will give you a longer time to decide whether this is the right market for you.

INDEX OPTIONS

Remember the stock indexes described in Chapter 8—the market indicators based on the prices of certain groups of stocks? Did you know you can buy options that are based on many of these indexes? In fact, the most widely purchased options are those based on the S&P 100 Index and the S&P 500 Index. These are called, respectively, "OEX" and "SPX" options. These are the options you would purchase if you were certain an entire segment of the stock market was due for a rise or fall.

Index options are similar to stock options in that there are puts and calls, different strike prices and expiration dates. When you exercise an index option, however, you cannot buy the stocks that the index represents. These options are settled in cash, the amount of which is based on the value of their index on the expiration date of the option.

For example, suppose you paid $500 for an OEX call option in June, with an expiration date on July 20. The index is currently at 358.50 and your strike price is $360. Because the expiration date is a month away, the option still has time value, which is why it is selling for as high as $500.

By July 20, the index has risen to 362—two points above your strike price of $360. These two points mean you will receive $200 as a settlement. You're out $300, because you paid $500 for the option.

In actual trading, you would probably have sold your option when it still had some time value. As with stock options, most people sell their index options before they expire.

These index options are a favorite tool of speculators. Some investors, however, use index options as a kind of "insurance" on their stock portfolios. If they believe the stock market is about to tumble, they can purchase put options on one of the major indexes. Then, if the market does indeed go down, their stocks may lose value, but their put options will gain in value.

Options on Futures

Yes, you can actually purchase options to buy futures contracts! How about a call option to buy a soybean contract with a strike price of $6.25 a bushel, expiration date in June? Just as with a stock option, if the price of soybeans goes up, the value of your option will go up and vice versa. And just as with stock options, there are puts and calls, different strike prices and expiration dates.

To deal in these options requires a pretty fair knowledge of the futures markets. For each commodity there is a different contract, and the options are based on these contracts. As with futures contracts, futures options are purchased from a commodities broker, not a stockbroker.

Futures options as a speculative tool provide most of the profit potential of the futures themselves, but with much of the risk eliminated. You can lose only the price of the option. Like futures, however, they should be considered to be in the realm of the speculative trader, not the investor.

For the businessperson who has a need to hedge some commodity or currency, a futures option is often a simpler, less expensive way of hedging than a futures contract.

Futures and Options—Why?

I include these speculative methods of trading partly for the few who will want to pursue them further. But I also want to dispel the air of mystery that surrounds futures and options, and show their real uses and value in the business world.

My other reason for including such things in a book for new investors is simply that they are important for you to know about. As we mentioned in Chapter 24, much of the high-pressure sales efforts directed at investors describes various techniques for dealing in futures—with promises of enormous profits. You need to know that any "enormous profits" will probably be made only by the sellers of such systems.

Even if you choose to have someone else manage your finances, knowing about futures and options will enable you to make informed decisions. Suppose, for example, your investment manager told you that he planned to invest half your portfolio in futures contracts. You need to know not just that futures are risky, but *why* they are risky, and just *how* risky. Otherwise, the adviser might be able to argue you into it. You need to know enough to immediately take your money out of his control—and, perhaps, notify the agency in your state that licenses such managers.

The above warning is not a fantasy. Every year I hear stories about naive clients whose managers lost their money in futures, gold mines, options, or high-risk stocks. One couple ended up actually *owing* $6,000 on a futures contract—after losing all their money. With a little knowledge and care, such nightmares need not happen.

Resources

Trestor Compleat Option Report, Target Inc., P.O. Box 25, Pleasanton, CA 94588. (800) 877-7833. Monthly. $295/year. Weekly updated hotline included.

If you insist on buying options, you can at least turn yourself from a gambler into a knowledgeable speculator. Subscribing to this newsletter is a good start. Ken Trestor also has a book and video on the subject; the cost of each of these is reduced for subscribers. And if you *really* want to get into options, Trestor gives a seminar on the subject. You can inquire about seminar dates, cost, etc., at the same address.

CHAPTER 28

STARTING TO INVEST

This book is meant for those who plan to do their own investing *and* for those who decide to hire a professional adviser. If you were undecided when you started, I hope that reading the book has given you a better idea which path is right for you.

Of those who wish to handle their own investments, many will decide to stick with mutual funds and follow the program we presented in Chapters 14, 15, and 16. We laid this out not only as a way of getting started, but also as a continuing method of investing. This program should work very well for those who want to invest in a conservative, buy-and-hold manner.

Once your portfolio is set up, the main task of you conservative investors is to keep tabs on it. Watch for underperforming funds, and buy and sell as necessary at the time of your six-month review.

I hope that those of you who choose to manage your investments more actively will arrive at a method of investing that feels right to *you*. Just as there are no sure things in the World of Investment, neither is there one right way to invest. A close look at successful investors will reveal a different method employed by each.

Much of the investment world is a win-win situation. You buy corporate bonds: you get interest payments and the corporation uses your money to invest. If a market increases in value, everybody comes out ahead—except those who were playing it short.

If you start to trade actively, however, you begin to play zero-sum games in which if you win, somebody else loses. In order to compete with professional investors, you need to improve your odds in any way you can. Playing your strong suits—that is, investing in areas you know about—is the best way of doing this.

If your job makes you knowledgeable in a certain field, then you have an advantage over other investors. You'll be likely to spot the companies that are producing the new products your industry really needs.

Another thing you can do is get the pros on your side. Learn as much as you can about a field by reading or listening to the experts recommended in this book. Hire some top-notch advisers by subscribing to the recommended newsletters. Go to a few seminars on topics that interest you. The American Association of Individual Investors sponsors some good ones; so do many of the foundations that make up the Funding Exchange (see Resources, Chapter 2).

The third way to tilt the field in your direction is to do what the professionals do: Avoid investing in areas you are not expert in. As we have pointed out, investing without knowledge of or a real feel for a market is not even speculating—it's gambling.

Investing is not for everybody. One way of judging whether it's for you is by taking a good look at whether you enjoy it or not. If Martin Zweig's economic predictions bore you, if the roller-coaster markets make you queasy, or if you simply love your own job so much that you don't want to be distracted (lucky person!)—then forget the whole shebang.

Find a good financial adviser or manager and let him or her worry about the price of oil, or whether the Federal Reserve will lower the discount rate. Just remember to keep an eye on things.

RECOMMENDATIONS: THE FIRST AND BEST THINGS YOU CAN DO TO START OFF RIGHT

This book was conceived as a way of condensing the vast amount of information about investments so that the subject would be more manageable. Even in this book, though, we have dealt with a pretty sizable amount of material. This section, then, is an attempt to summarize even further. What are the most important things you, as a new investor, can do to get off to a good start?

Because your investment strategy must necessarily depend on your individual circumstances, most of the advice and recommendations for further information in this book are presented for you to pick and choose from. There is much that new investors have in common, however; there are certain things you can do that can greatly improve your chances of success. Here are a few final suggestions.

1. Take a good look at your attitudes toward money and finances. What problems do you have dealing with them? What are your financial goals? As an invaluable aid in considering these questions, I recommend Joe Dominguez's seminar on audiotapes: *Transforming Your Relationship with Money and Achieving Financial Independence* (Resources, Chapter 3). A good investor needs to know where he or she is going and needs to be in a state of internal agreement about these goals. If you are investing with a spouse or a partner, you need to be in a state of external agreement as well.

2. Be sure that your personal finances are in good order. The best investments in the world will all be for nothing without reasonable spending habits, adequate insurance, and good tax planning. If you want to do this yourself, consult a book on financial planning. There are several excellent ones on the market; look them over at your local bookstore (probably not the library—these books have to be up to date). The clearest and most readable one I've found is *The Price Waterhouse Book of Personal Financial Planning,* cited in Resources, Chapter 3.

   If you feel the need of help in this area, financial planners and advisers are available. You can find an honest and competent one with the help of the information in Chapter 9. Be sure the adviser comes with good recommendations and that you like and feel comfortable with him or her. It's likely to be a long relationship.

3. Give yourself time! If you've just come into some money, or just started investing, you need some time to get used to this state of affairs. Don't rush out and buy the first stock you get a hot tip on. Take at least six months to a year to study, talk with friends, practice, and generally test the waters. It's a good idea to do this even if you plan to go to an investment adviser or manager. Buy some certificates of deposit at your bank and just let the money sit and gather interest. Don't worry if the stock market is on a roll or real estate is skyrocketing. There will always be opportunities, and you'll be much more likely to capitalize on them once you know what it's all about.

   If you are anxious or nervous about suddenly coming into money, be assured that you're not alone. If you feel unable to cope with your distress about inheriting or being richer than your friends, try getting together with others in the same boat and talking about it (Resources, Chapter 2).

You can also give yourself the gift of counseling if you are conflicted or confused about dealing with money. Counselors and psychotherapists can be expensive, but it may turn out to be the best investment you will ever make.

4. Start practicing. There's no substitute for actually doing it: buying and selling and watching your purchases—and your emotions—go up and down. Fortunately, at least in the case of securities, you can do this without risking any money. The National Investment Challenge allows you to buy and sell $500,000 worth of stocks (or options in the options division) for three months, for an entry fee of $100 (Resources, Chapter 18). Your winnings and losings may be Monopoly money, but the experience you gain is real gold.

If you're interested in real estate, you can start looking at buildings. With the help of the recommended reading material (Resources, Chapter 11), it's easy to figure out a balance sheet on any given property. How much do you need to invest, how much will the loan payments be, the expenses, the income, etc?

After doing a number of these balance sheets, and tramping through buildings checking out roofs, foundations, furnaces, and asbestos in the walls, you will begin to get a feel for possible good investments. Or you may decide that real estate is not for you—a decision that will make the time spent no less valuable than if you had gone ahead.

Whatever you decide to invest in, it's a good idea to do it first on paper. Pretend you've bought something, then follow your investment for a few months. If it goes up, don't kick yourself for not investing real money—there are always new opportunities; if it goes down, you can congratulate yourself on your prudence.

5. Start out small. Once you're using real money, it's a good idea to invest relatively modest amounts at first, then build up as your confidence and your feel for the markets increase. Remember the importance of balance in your portfolio, as we discussed in Chapter 15.

6. Don't push the river—let it flow by itself. There is a certain rhythm to investing. It takes time for things to appreciate in value; if you get impatient and try for large profits in a short time, you run a good chance of getting into trouble.

   Remember the Rule of 10% (Chapter 14). If you, as a new investor, are getting 10% on your money per year, you're doing well. If you are getting more than that and still investing safely, you're doing extremely well. If you shoot for 30% or 40% or more, however, you've left safety behind and have entered the realm of speculation and gambling.

A SAMPLE SCHEDULE

Here is a schedule for those who like schedules. It is, of course, approximate; some will want to progress faster or slower. But this should give you a general idea of a time frame for getting involved with investing.

First month: Read this book. Start thinking about what you want from your investments and what your personal risk-reward thermometer might look like. If you have just come into some money—a lot or a little—it's time to get used to having the extra amount. Put the money in the bank and leave it. Talk it over with your spouse and family.

Second month: Now that you know a little, start talking with friends and family about what *they* invest in—but don't act on any advice yet. Start reading the financial pages in the newspaper. Borrow from the library or buy one or two of the recommended books. If you have inherited real estate, or think you might want to buy a home or income property, subscribe to John Reed's newsletter (Resources, Chapter 11). If you have inherited antiques or other collectibles, look at Resources, Chapter 25.

Third month: Subscribe to one or two of the recommended newsletters—trial subscriptions, if they have them. Continue to talk to friends and read. Consider joining the American Association of Individual Investors (Resources, Chapter 1).

Fourth month: Try buying single copies of various financial newspapers and magazines to see whether any of them appeal to you. Sample a few more trial subscriptions to the recommended newsletters, but don't act on their suggestions yet. Advisers in newsletters and magazines have a way of making certain investments sound urgent, but excellent opportunities will always be available. Right now, you are still in the process of taking in information and sorting it out. Actual investing should wait for a while.

Fifth month: Okay, now you're getting ready to test your wings—but without any risk. If you're leaning toward making real estate a part of your portfolio—home or income property—try doing some balance sheets. See how the income and expenses come out on various properties. The recommended books and newsletters will show you how to do this. Start driving around by yourself (no real estate agents yet) and seeing what's available.

Mutual fund investors, start working out your own model portfolio. Without focusing on specific funds, decide whether you want long-term growth or income or both, and modify the categories of the model in Chapter 14 according to your needs and goals.

Sixth month: Take $100 and buy $500,000 to "invest" in the National Investment Challenge (Resources, Chapter 18). Even though this is more like speculation than investing, it will help you to feel what it's like to actually risk money.

Continue to work on your model portfolio—and read and discuss investing with friends.

Seventh to ninth months: Now we're getting down to business. By now, you have noted quite a few mutual funds recommended in the various magazines and newsletters. Make a note of the ones that look the best to you. Take out a trial subscription to *Morningstar Mutual Funds* (Resources, Chapter 6). See how they rate the funds you have on your list. Look at their top-rated funds (the five-star list at the front). Generally, you should invest in the funds that are rated four-star or five-star by Morningstar.

You should have an idea by now whether you want to do your own investing or engage the help of a professional adviser or manager. If you feel you want to hire someone, consult with friends and associates and do some research on your own. Remember, you can interview as many advisers as you want to find one you really like.

By the end of the ninth month, you should have your model portfolio pretty well worked out. You should also have come to some conclusions about real estate. If you're leaning that way, ask friends and associates whether they know of a good real estate agent. Start arranging for financing.

Tenth to twelfth months: Investing! Finally! Start out slow. Decide whether to buy directly from the funds or through a broker (Chapter 15). In either case, send for the prospectuses of the various funds you're interested in. The reports in *Morningstar* will tell you most of what you need to know, but you should look over the prospectuses, too.

A good way to begin if you're buying directly from the funds is to dollar-cost-average your investments (Chapter 19). This method is too expensive if you're buying through a broker because of the commissions. Start with the conservative funds first and work your way to the riskier ones.

Now that you've done your homework in the real estate area, it's time to engage a real estate agent. By now, you should be able to tell the agent just what kind of property you want, including the price range. Don't jump at the first likely property, but do be prepared to put down money if you find exactly what you're looking for.

First year and continuing: Once you're fully invested in mutual funds, remember to do your review every six months. If you have decided to invest in individual stocks, now is the time to begin your research. When you're ready to buy a stock, you can sell some of your mutual funds in the same category; for example, if you're buying a small company, then sell part of a small-company fund. That way, your portfolio will stay in the same balance you started with. Keep some of your mutual funds—not only is this a good diversification, but you can compare your stock picks against the performance of the funds.

Constant vigilance is a necessary quality of the successful investor. You may give the wheel to someone else—an investment manager, perhaps—but you need to stay aware of this person's state of mind. Is he or she driving well?

Thousands of other people may have driven the road you're on; you may have road maps and the best directions. But this day, a bridge may have washed out and all your directions are no substitute for being alert and quick to react. You need to have a Plan B—an alternate route—for such contingencies.

Awareness is energy well spent. Money may not be able to buy you happiness, but it can mean greater freedom to pursue your goals and interests. And it can provide at least some security in an uncertain world.

Learning to deal with money successfully is the kind of experience that can empower you to handle other areas of your life more skillfully. Willingness to learn, to change, to take some risks, balance, perseverance—the factors that make for success in the World of Investment will inevitably carry over into other fields of endeavor.

Money is a central issue. The money you earn is the physical representation of the life energy you have expended to earn it. If you have inherited or won a lottery, it represents other people's life energy. Investing, then, is a way of making this energy grow so that you may benefit from it—and, perhaps, help others to benefit.

APPENDIX A

THE MODEL PORTFOLIO:
AN EXAMPLE

T he funds listed here should be considered only as an
example of what a model portfolio might look like.
Right now, these particular funds have been performing well, but you may be reading this some months later. As
we discussed in Chapter 15, it's necessary to choose funds
according to their recent performance as well as their performance over the last five to ten years.

Remember, this model is directed toward growth, with
all income reinvested. If your goal is more income or a lower
risk-reward temperature, you will need to buy more equity-
income and bond funds and fewer growth funds. Try to keep
some growth funds, though. Even if you're retired, you need
the growth to counter the effects of inflation.

Equity Income/Balanced	Portfolio Capital
Wellesley Income	10%
Pax World Fund*	10%
Growth	
Fidelity Magellan**	10%
Janus Twenty	10%
International Stock	
Harbor International	10%
Scudder Global***	5%
Small Cap	
Twentieth Century Ultra	10%
Schield: Progressive Environmental * **	5%
Bond Funds	
Vanguard Investment-Grade	10%
Scudder International Bond	10%
Cash	
Money market (bank, credit union, or mutual fund)	10%
	100%

* Socially responsible
** Low load. We will bend our no-load rule when the fund shows particularly fine performance and prospects.
*** The model calls for a European fund, but as of this writing, Europe did not look good. This demonstrates the need to always be ready to modify the model according to the current investment climate.

APPENDIX B

SOCIALLY RESPONSIBLE FUNDS

Although their criteria may differ, generally these mutual funds invest in companies with good records of occupational health and safety, a high regard for the environment, consumer protection, and nontoxic products. Another consideration is a product that helps solve environmental problems. The funds, however, do not confine themselves to environmental companies, but buy securities in firms in many different areas.

In evaluating the performance of these funds, remember to compare them with the other funds in their class. Pax World Fund, for example, is a balanced fund designed for safety of principal as well as growth. Its performance should not be compared with that of the growth funds. In the class of balanced funds, it's a star—*Morningstar Mutual Funds* gives it their top rating.

As a rule, these socially screened funds have performed better than average in their class. Some, like Pax World, have been standouts. Send for their prospectuses and give them an up-to-date evaluation. As the country becomes more environmentally conscious, these funds should do even better during the 1990s.

Several of the funds charge loads. Again, we are bending our general rule about buying only no-load funds because of the excellent performance of these funds and their social significance.

Note how much lower the minimum purchase requirements are for individual retirement accounts. This is true of most mutual funds.

Fund	Type	Minimum Initial Purchase and Minimum Subsequent Purchase	IRA
Dreyfus			
Third Century	Growth	$2,500	$ 750
(800) 645-6561	No-load	$ 100	no minimum
Green Century	Balanced	2,000	500
(800) 93-GREEN	No-load	200	50
New Alternatives	Growth	2,650	2,000
(516) 466-0808	5.6% load	500	500
(call collect)			
Parnassus	Growth	2,000	1,000
(800) 999-3505	3.5% load	100	100
Pax World	Balanced	250	250
(800) 767-1729	No-load	50	50
Schield			
Progressive	Growth	1,000	250
Environmental	4.5% load	100	50
(800) 826-8154			

APPENDIX C

FRACTIONS INTO DECIMALS

Since the stock market has not yet learned about decimals, here are the decimal equivalents of the fractions in which stocks are traded:

$\frac{1}{16}$	=			.0625	$\frac{9}{16}$	=			.5625
$\frac{2}{16}$	=	$\frac{1}{8}$	=	.125	$\frac{10}{16}$	=	$\frac{5}{8}$	=	.625
$\frac{3}{16}$	=			.1875	$\frac{11}{16}$	=			.6875
$\frac{4}{16}$	=	$\frac{1}{4}$	=	.25	$\frac{12}{16}$	=	$\frac{3}{4}$	=	.75
$\frac{5}{16}$	=			.3125	$\frac{13}{16}$	=			.8125
$\frac{6}{16}$	=	$\frac{3}{8}$	=	.375	$\frac{14}{16}$	=	$\frac{7}{8}$	=	.875
$\frac{7}{16}$	=			.4375	$\frac{15}{16}$	=			.9375
$\frac{8}{16}$	=	$\frac{1}{2}$		.5					

Appendix D

Fifty Years of Returns

Fifty Years of Returns (1939 through 1988)

	S&P 500	**Small Stocks**	**Long-Term Corporate Bonds**	**Long-Term Government Bonds**	**Treasury Bills**	**Inflation (CPI)**
Average Annual Compound Rates of Return (%)						
Last 10 Years	16.3%	18.9%	10.9%	10.6%	9.1%	5.9%
Last 20 Years	9.5	11.5	8.3	7.8	7.5	6.3
Last 30 Years	9.7	14.5	6.3	5.8	6.2	4.9
Last 40 Years	12.2	15.2	5.1	4.5	5.0	4.1
Last 50 Years	11.2	15.8	4.6	4.2	4.1	4.4
Growth: What $1 Invested Would Have Grown To						
Last 10 Years	$ 4.53	$ 5.65	$2.81	$2.74	$2.39	$1.77
Last 20 Years	6.14	8.82	4.93	4.49	4.25	3.39
Last 30 Years	16.08	58.10	6.25	5.43	6.08	4.20
Last 40 Years	99.93	287.14	7.31	5.82	7.04	4.99
Last 50 Years	201.95	1,532.60	9.48	7.82	7.46	8.61

Annual returns and growth figures include dividends and/or interest, but excludes taxes and transaction costs.

Source: Roger G. Ibbotson and Rex A. Sinquefield, "Stocks, Bonds, Bills and Inflation," 1982 ed., Institute of Chartered Financial Analysts, Charlottesville, Va.; updated by Ibbotson Associates, "Stocks, Bonds, Bills and Inflation 1989 Yearbook," Chicago.

APPENDIX E

COMPOUND INTEREST

Here's how much your $1.00 would grow over the years if the rate of growth was the same every year. Remember, with compound interest the profit from each year is added on to the principal. Then the next year's interest is figured from this new, larger amount. If you take any income out, the charts won't work.

Compound interest is pretty amazing stuff. If you left $150,000 to your great-grandchildren and it grew at a rate of 15% a year, in a 125 years it would be worth some $6.4 trillion. The great-grandchildren could help pay off the national debt and still have enough left over for one of them to run for president. . . .

To find the compounded amount for any sum of money, simply multiply the sum by the proper amount in the columns. Example: How much would $45,650 grow to, if compounded at the rate of 9% for five years? Go to the 9% column and follow it down to five years. Multiply 1.538 by $45,650 = $70,209.

$1.00 COMPOUNDED ANNUALLY

Years	5%	6%	7%	8%	9%	Years
1	$1.050	1.060	1.070	1.080	1.090	1
2	1.102	1.123	1.144	1.166	1.188	2
3	1.157	1.191	1.225	1.259	1.295	3
4	1.215	1.262	1.310	1.360	1.411	4
5	1.276	1.338	1.402	1.469	1.538	5
6	1.340	1.418	1.500	1.586	1.677	6
7	1.407	1.503	1.605	1.713	1.828	7
8	1.477	1.593	1.718	1.850	1.992	8
9	1.551	1.689	1.838	1.999	2.171	9
10	1.628	1.790	1.967	2.158	2.367	10
11	1.710	1.898	2.104	2.331	2.580	11
12	1.795	2.012	2.252	2.518	2.812	12
13	1.885	2.132	2.409	2.719	3.065	13
14	1.979	2.260	2.578	2.937	3.341	14
15	2.078	2.396	2.759	3.172	3.642	15
16	2.182	2.540	2.952	3.425	3.970	16
17	2.292	2.692	3.158	3.700	4.327	17
18	2.406	2.854	3.379	3.996	4.717	18
19	2.526	3.025	3.619	4.315	5.141	19
20	2.653	3.207	3.869	4.660	5.604	20
25	3.386	4.291	5.427	6.848	8.623	25
30	4.321	5.743	7.612	10.062	13.267	30

$1.00 COMPOUNDED ANNUALLY (*CONTINUED*)

Years		Annual Rate				Years
	10%	12%	15%	18%	20%	
1	1.100	1.120	1.150	1.180	1.200	1
2	1.210	1.254	1.322	1.392	1.440	2
3	1.331	1.404	1.520	1.643	1.728	3
4	1.464	1.573	1.749	1.938	2.073	4
5	1.610	1.762	2.011	2.287	2.488	5
6	1.771	1.973	2.313	2.699	2.985	6
7	1.948	2.210	2.660	3.185	3.583	7
8	2.143	2.475	3.059	3.758	4.299	8
9	2.357	2.773	3.517	4.435	5.159	9
10	2.593	3.105	4.145	5.233	6.191	10
11	2.853	3.478	4.652	6.175	7.430	11
12	3.138	3.895	5.350	7.287	8.916	12
13	3.452	4.363	6.152	8.599	10.699	13
14	3.797	4.887	7.075	10.147	12.839	14
15	4.177	5.473	8.137	11.973	15.407	15
16	4.594	6.130	9.357	14.149	18.488	16
17	5.054	6.866	10.751	16.672	22.186	17
18	5.559	7.689	12.375	19.673	26.623	18
19	6.115	8.612	14.231	23.214	31.948	19
20	6.727	9.646	16.366	27.393	38.337	20
25	10.834	17.000	32.918	62.668	95.396	25
30	17.449	29.959	66.211	143.370	237.376	30

INDEX

AAII Journal, 14
Abbreviations in stock tables, 97–99
Acker, Bob, 225
Acker Letter, 225
Adam Smith's Money World, 94
ADRs, 153–154
Advertisements, 271–274
ADV Form, 111
Aggressive growth mutual funds, 71–72
American Association of Individual Investors (AAII), 14
  on mutual funds, 74–75, 76–77
  retirement and, 200
  seminars by, 317
American Association of Retired Persons (AARP), 198
American depository receipts (ADRs), 153–154
American Numismatic Association, 294
American Stock Exchange (AMEX), 99–100
  Market Value Index, 103
AMEX Market Value Index, 103
Amortized home loans, 120–121
Angle, Kelly, 304
Annuities, 197
Antique doll collections, 293
Appalachian Community Fund, 31
Apple Computer, 100
A Random Walk Down Wall Street (Malkiel), 215–216
Arbitration agreements with brokers, 277–278
Arithmetic, 2
Attitudes. *See* Emotional issues
Automobile insurance, 20
  as personal finance issue, 35–36

Back-end load of mutual funds, 65–66
Bad times, 227–238
Balanced funds, 72
  in model portfolio, 159–162
Balancing checkbook, 35
Band, Richard E., 51, 159, 173

Banks
  buying and selling securities through, 57
  CDs in, 78–79
  money market accounts in, 80–81
  starting a business, loans for, 266
Barron's, 75, 93, 94
Bear markets, 11, 230
Beating the averages, 163
Bernstein, Jake, 304
Beta coefficients, 95–96
Better Investing, 213
Bid and ask prices, 100–101
Big Board. *See* New York Stock Exchange (NYSE)
Blue chip stocks, 46
  diversification and, 170
  dividends, 48
Bond funds, 72–73
Bonds, 41, 82–84, 239–253. *See also* Government bonds
  calling bonds, 251
  convertible bonds, 243–244
  corporate bonds, 239–240
  face value of, 83
  fluctuations in market, 248–251
  interest on, 83–84
  in model portfolio, 161–162
  municipal bonds, 241–242
  mutual funds investing in, 89–90
  ratings for, 246–248
  reading bond tables in newspapers, 251–252
  stocks versus, 88–89
  trading price of, 252
  zero-coupon bonds, 242–243
Bowser Report, The, 225–226
Bread and Roses Community Fund, 31
Breitbard, Stanley H., 39
British Financial Times Industrial Index, 103–104
Brokers, 54–59. *See also* Discount brokers; Full-commission brokers
  accounts with, 58–59
  call options and, 307
  choosing a broker, 56–57

churning an account, 277
  commissions for, 54, 55, 57–58
  commodities brokers, 300–301
  floor brokers, 43
  history of, 42
  mutual funds and, 63–65
  names for brokers, 56
  problems with, 276–278
  street name, holding securities in,
    59
Bullion coins, 286, 291
Bull markets, 11
Business, starting a, 261–269
  buying a business, 267
  capitalizing, 266–268
Business Week, 93
Buy-and-hold strategy, 162, 168–169
  market timers and, 280
  for mutual funds, 169–170
Buying methods, 53–60, 215–226
  dollar-cost averaging, 216–218

Callability of bonds, 251
Callable stocks, 203
Calling
  bonds, 251
  stocks, 203
  zero-coupon bonds, 243
Call options, 306–309
  warrants, 312
Capital
  for business, 266–268
  defined, 20
  inherited money as, 20–22
Carpenter, Donna Sammons, 39, 40
Case, John, 268–269
*Cashing In On the American Dream:
  How to Retire at 35* (Terhorst),
  200
Cash in model portfolio, 162
CDs, 78–79, 186, 187, 197
  long-term CDs, 83
  money market accounts compared,
    80–81
Certificates of desposit. *See* CDs
Charities, wills for leaving money to,
  38
Charles Schwab, 56
Checking accounts
  balancing checkbooks, 35
  with discount brokers, 57
China collections, 293
Chinook Fund, 31

Churning an account, 277
Closed-end country funds, 149–150,
  151–152
Closed-end mutual funds, 67
CNBC-FNN, 94
Coin Dealer Newsletter, 294–295
Coins. *See also* Rare coins
  bullion coins, 286, 291
  foreign coins, 292
  grading of, 292–294
Collectibles, 292–294. *See also* Rare
  coins
Comic book collections, 292
Commercial paper, 80
Commissions
  for brokers, 54, 55, 57–58
  for call options, 307
  for financial advisers, 111–113
  on gold sales, 285, 286
  mutual funds, discount broker
    commissions for, 64
Commodities brokers, 300–301
Common stock, 47
Community colleges, 28
Compound interest, 85–87
  mutual funds and, 87
  table showing, 332–334
Computerized Investing, 257
Computers, role of, 254–257
Con artists, 199
Conservative growth funds, 72
Construction and development trusts,
  REITS as, 130
Contrarianism, 222–224
Conversion value, 244
Convertible bonds, 243–244
Convertible preferred stocks, 203
Counseling on money, 28–30, 320
Country funds, 149–150
Coupon interest rate, 249
Credit cards. *See also* Visa cards
  with discount brokers, 57
  interest, 33–34
Credit Union National Association, 82,
  90
Credit unions, 81–82, 90
  National Credit Union Administra-
    tion (NCUA), 187
Crossroads Fund, 31
Currencies
  gold and, 284
  trading in, 155–156
Current yield, 249

Cyclical stocks, 46–47

Data Broadcasting Corporation, 257
Data-retrieval service, 256
Dean Witter Reynolds, 56
  international division, 154
Debenture bonds, 240
Debt, 36
Debtors Anonymous, 40
Decimals, fractions into, 330
Defensive stocks, 46–47
Deferred sales charge of mutual funds, 66
Depreciation, rental property and, 126
Design of portfolio, 168
Dessauer, John, 156–157, 230
Dessauer's Journal (Dessauer), 156–157
Dickinson, Peter, 199–200
Direct-mail flyers, 271–274
Disability insurance, 35–36
Discount brokers, 55, 276
  list of, 56–57
  for mutual funds, 64
  super discounters, 57
Discount rate, 250
  lowering of, 236–237
Discretionary accounts, 113
Distributions from mutual funds, 70–71
Diversification
  downturns and, 234–235
  and low-priced stocks, 222
  in portfolio, 170–171
Dividends, 47–48
  earnings distinguished, 47
  ex-dividend, 205
  from gold-mining stock, 285, 286
  from mutual funds, 70–71
  preferred stocks, 202
  in recession period, 60
DJIA. See Dow Jones Industrial Average (DJIA)
Dollar-cost averaging, 216–218
Dominguez, Joe, 30, 35, 318
Donaghue, Bill, 33
Donald Kagin's Personal Guide to Rare Coin Investments, 295
Dow Jones Averages, 102–103
  index funds tied to, 74
Dow Jones Composite Average, 102
Dow Jones Industrial Average (DJIA), 102–103

IBM influencing, 105
Downturns, 227–238
Drew, Dan, 305
Drexel Burnham, 245
Dreyfus Fund, 70, 329

Earnings distinguished from dividends, 47
E. F. Hutton, 56
Emergency funds, 186, 187
Emotional issues
  of inheriting money, 22–24
  of lottery winners, 25–27
  money and, 34–35, 318
Entrepreneur magazine, 265
Entrepreneurship, 261–269
Environment, investing for. See Socially responsible investing
Equities, defined, 54
Equity, 119
Equity-income funds, 72, 159–162
Equity trusts, REITS as, 130
European mutual funds, 149
Ex-dividend, 205
Extended-care insurance, 198
Exxon, 140

Face value of bonds, 83
Families, 16
Federal Deposit Insurance Corporation (FDIC), 187
  CDs, protection of, 79
  for money market accounts, 80
Federal Reserve Bank
  discount rate, lowering of, 236–237
  inflation and interest rate, 250
  margin requirements, 211
Fee-based advisers, 111–113
Fees. See also Commissions; Mutual funds
  for financial advisers, 111
  public partnerships, 131–132
Fidelity, 56
Fidelity Balanced Fund, 68
Fidelity Blue Chip Growth Fund, 68
Fidelity Group of Funds, 69–70
Fidelity Magellan Fund, 62, 226
Fidelity Real Estate Fund, 132
Fifty years of returns, 331
Financial advisers, 108–115
  commissions for, 111–113
  retirement and, 199
Financial managers, 2

Financial News Network
  Donaghue, Bill and, 33
  "Guru Review," 11, 13
Financial planners, 108
Financial World, 93
First Philippine Fund, 154
Fixed-income securities. *See* Bonds
Floor brokers, 43
Forbes, 93
Forecasts and Strategies, 107
Foreign currency, trading in, 155–156
Foreign investors, 44
Fortune magazine, 93
  and socially responsible investing, 141
401(k) plans, 195
Fractions into decimals, 330
Friendly loans, 266–268
From the Ground Up: The Resurgence of American Entrepreneurship (Case), 268
Full-commission brokers, 55
  commissions to, 57–58
  commodities brokers, 300–301
  in international markets, 154–155
  list of, 56
  mutual funds, commissions for, 65
  problems with, 276–278
Fundamental analysis of stock, 219
Fund for Southern Communities, 31
Funding Exchange, 24, 31–32
  for financial advisers, 110
Futures, 296–304
  options on, 313–315
  speculation in, 303–304

Gambling on the market, 12, 281–282
Gates, Bill, 262
General Electric, 100
  socially responsible investing and, 143
General Motors, 100
General obligation bonds, 242
Generic coins, 291
German DAX Index, 104
Germany, 229
Global Investor, The (Keyes & Miller), 155–156, 157
Globalization of world markets, 147
Gold, 283–286
  buying gold, 285–286
  futures, 285, 286

Gold bullion, 285
Gold-mining stocks, 286
Good Money: A Guide to Profitable Social Investing in the 90s (Lowry), 145–146, 156
Good Money Industrial Average, 141
Good Money newsletter, 141, 145
  Social Funds Guide, 142
Good till canceled (GTC) orders, 206
Government bonds, 10, 240–241
  callability of, 251
  fluctuations in market, 248–249
Graham, Benjamin, 167
Greed, 276
Green Century fund, 329
Growing a Business (Hawken), 269–270
Growth and income funds, 72
Growth funds, 72
  in model portfolio, 160
Growth stocks, 46
"Guru Review," 11, 13

Harding, Sy, 225
Hawken, Paul, 269–270
Haymarket People's Fund, 31
Headwaters Fund, 31
Health insurance, 20
  extended-care insurance, 198
  personal finance and, 34, 35–36
Heberle, Dave, 124
Hedgers, 303
High-yield bonds. *See* Junk bonds
High-yield stocks, 48
Home-ownership, 116–124
  amortized home loans, 120–121
Homeowner's insurance, 20
  as personal finance issue, 35–36
How the Futures Markets Work (Bernstein), 304
How to Get a Mortgage in 24 Hours (Lumley), 123–124
How to Get Out of Debt, Stay Out of Debt and Live Prosperously (Mundis), 40
How to Make Money in Stocks (O'Neil), 226
How to Plan, Contract and Build Your Own Home (Scutella & Heberle), 124
Hulbert, Mark, 51, 213
Hulbert Financial Digest, 50, 51

IBM, 100
    influencing the Market, 105
    investment in, 53–54
IBM-compatible software, 255
In Business: The Magazine for Environmental Entrepreneuring, 269
Inc. magazine, 260, 265
Income funds, 72
Income stocks, 46
Income taxes. *See* Taxes
Indexes, 102—104
Index funds, 74
Index options, 312–313
Individual Investor's Guide to Computerized Investing, 257
Individual Investor's Guide to No-Load Mutual Funds, 76–77
Individual issues, 220–221
Individual portfolio examples, 174–190
Individual retirement accounts. *See* IRAs
Industrial Average, 102
Inexperience, 275–276
Inflation
    bonds and, 88
    Federal Reserve Bank and, 250
    gold and, 284
    inherited money and, 21
Inheriting money, 19–25, 319
    emotional issues of, 22–24
    inflation and, 21
    portfolio example for, 183–185
In-house mutual funds, 112
Insider trading, 106–107
Institutional investors, 44
Insurance. *See also* Health insurance; Homeowner's insurance
    extended-care insurance, 198
    in-house insurance programs, 112
    issues, 20
    junk bonds and, 246
    personal finance issues, 35–36
Insurance advisers, 112
Interest. *See also* Compound interest
    on bonds, 84
    on convertible bonds, 244
    coupon interest rate, 249
    Federal Reserve Bank controlling, 250

rule of 70, 85
    on zero-coupon bonds, 242–243
International investing, 147–157
    currency, trading in, 155–156
    socially responsible investing, 156
    trading in markets, 154–155
International mutual funds, 73
    choosing the best, 169
    in model portfolio, 160–161
International Remote Imaging Systems (IRIS), 101
International Society of Appraisers, 295
In the money options, 311
Investment advisers. *See* Financial advisers
Investment bankers, 42
Investment capital, 186
Investment Home Study Course, 14
Investment managers, 109, 113
Investment software, 255
Investors
    defined, 9
    expectations of, 12
Investor's Business Daily, 93
    stock tables of, 97–98
IRAs, 188–189, 194–195
    with discount brokers, 57
    dollar-cost averaging for, 218
    in financial institutions, 197
    zero-coupon bond investment, 243
IRIS, 101
IRS publications, 71

Japan, 229
    mutual funds specializing in, 148–149
Japanese Nikkei Index, 104
Jay Schabacker's Mutual Fund Investing, 173
Journals, information from, 93
Junk bonds, 244–246
    in bond funds, 73
    diversification and, 171

Keogh plans, 194–196
    zero-coupon bond investment, 243
Keyes, Thomas R., 157
Kovels' Know Your Antiques, 295
Kovels' Know Your Collectibles, 295

Landlord responsibilities, 127–128
Leaps, 310–311
Leverage, 125–126
Leveraged buyouts, 245
Liability insurance, 20
Liberty Hill Foundation, 31
Library research, 93
Life insurance, 36
Limited partnerships for real estate
    investments, 131–132
Liquidity of government bonds, 241
Live Oak Fund, 32
Load of mutual fund, 65–66
Loans for starting a business, 266
Long-term CDs, 83
Lottery winners, 25–27
    emotional issues of, 25–27
Louis Navellier's MPT Review, 213
Low-income housing, investment in,
    132–133
Low-priced stocks, 220–222
Lowry, Ritchie, 141, 145–146
Lumley, James E. A., 123–124
Lynch, Peter, 226

Macintosh-compatible software, 255
Magazines, information in, 93
Malkiel, Burton, 215–216
Marginable stock, 209–210
Margin accounts, 208
    calls on, 210
    example of buying on margin,
        208–210
    1929 crash and, 211
    personal loans, 211–213
    for selling short, 207
Margin calls, 210
Market orders, 206
Market timers, 278–281
Marx, Karl, 229
Math, 2
McKenzie River Gathering Founda-
    tion, 32
Men and money, 16–17
Merrill Lynch, 56
    international division, 154
Microsoft Corp., 262
Military establishment, 229
Milken, Michael, 245
Miller, David, 157
Miniature collections, 293
Mint State (MS) coins, 290
Model portfolio, 158–166

diversification in, 170–171
example of, 326–327
for long-term growth, 163–164
modification of, 164–165
performance factor, 167, 171–173
Modems, use of, 255
Money, 93
Money Guide: Your Home, 123
Money management, 35
Money market accounts, 80–81
    CDs compared, 80–81
Money Masters, The (Train), 51–52
Moody's ratings, 247
Morningstar Mutual Funds, 77, 323,
    328
Mortgages, 83, 119, 120–121
    second mortgages, investment in,
        133–134
Mortgage trusts, REITS as, 130
Mundis, Jerrold, 40
Municipal bonds, 241–242
Mutual funds, 61–77. *See also* Interna-
    tional mutual funds
    advantages of, 63
    American Association of Individual
        Investors, guide by, 74–75
    back-end load, 65–66
    bonds, investment in, 89–90
    brokers, use of, 63–65
    buying shares in, 63, 65–67
    choosing the best, 169–170
    closed-end country funds, 149–150,
        151–152
    closed-end funds, 67
    compound interest and, 87
    discount, funds trading at, 152
    distributions from, 70–71
    dividends from, 70–71
    dollar-cost averaging for, 218
    families of funds, 69–70
    front-end load, 66
    general category funds, 71–73
    in-house mutual funds, 112
    for junk bonds, 246
    net asset value (NAV), 68
    open-end funds, 67
    past performance as indicator, 76
    price-setting for, 69
    prospectus of, 75
    reading mutual fund tables,
        67–69
    real estate mutual funds, 132
    reinvestments in, 70

sales load, 65–66
specialized funds, 73–74
stock-index futures, 302
timing the market, 278–281
12b-1 plans, 66

NASDAQ, 44, 99–100
Composite Index, 103
mediating disputes, 278
small-cap stocks in, 161
spread, 101
NASDAQ Composite Index, 103
National Association of Community
Development Credit Unions, 82
National Association of Investors
Corporation, 213–214
female investor clubs, 17–18
National Credit Union Administration
(NCUA), 187
National Investment Challenge,
201–202, 213, 320
Options Division, 312
National Network of Women's Funds,
32
Net asset value (NAV), 68
New Alternatives fund, 329
New Energy Report: Investing in the
Environment, 226
New issue of stock, 45
Newsletters, 49–51
contrarianism and, 224
New York Stock Exchange (NYSE),
99–100
listings on, 44
origins of, 42
Nightly Business Report, 94
1929 crash, 211
**NoLoad Fund*X, 173
No-load mutual funds, 65–66
Nondiscretionary accounts, 113
North American Securities Administra-
tors Association, 113
North Star Fund, 32

Odd lots, 203–204
OEX options, 312–313
One Hundred Million Dollars in
Profits (Angle), 304
O'Neil, William J., 219, 226
One Up on Wall Street (Lynch), 226
Open-end mutual funds, 67
Options, 305–315
call options, 306–309

expiration dates for, 310–311
on futures, 313–315
index options, 312–313
leaps, 310–311
in the money options, 311
out of the money options, 311
put options, 309–310
strike price, 311
thinly traded options, 311–312
warrants, 312
Option writer, 307
Out of the money options, 311
Overmanaging a portfolio, 223
Over-the-counter (OTC) market, 44,
100

Pacific Basin, mutual funds for, 148
Paine Webber, 56
Parnassus fund, 329
Partnerships, real estate investments
by, 131–132
Pax World Fund, 328, 329
Penny stocks, 46, 100
Pension Rights Center, 200
People's Fund, The, 32
Personal Earnings and Benefit
Estimate Statement, 192
Personal finance, 33–40
Personal Investor, 93
Pink sheet stocks, 44, 100, 220
Portfolio. See also Model portfolio
buy-and-hold strategy, 168–169
computer management of, 254–257
defined, 4
design of, 168
diversification in, 170–171
downturns and, 235
example of model portfolio,
326–327
individual portfolio examples,
174–190
overmanaging of, 223
performance factor, 167, 171–173
real estate in, 181
for retirement, 192–194
Practice investing, 320
Precious metals
funds, 73–74
gold, 283–286
silver, 287–288
Preferred stocks, 47, 202–203
Pre-owned stock, 45
Price-earnings ratio (P/E ratio), 96

*Price Waterhouse Book of Personal
    Financial Planning* (Breitbard &
    Carpenter), 39, 319
*Price Waterhouse Investors' Tax
    Adviser* (Carpenter), 40
Profitable Investing (Band), 51, 159
Profitable Investing newsletter
    (Band), 173
*Profitable Investing Portfolio
    Simplifier* (Band), 171, 173
Prospectus of mutual fund, 75
Prosperity consciousness, 30–31
*Protecting Your Pension Money: A
    Pension Investment Handbook,*
    200
Prudential-Bache, 56
Publicly held corporations, 42
Public partnerships, 131–132
Public purpose bonds, 241–242
Put options, 309–310

Quick & Reilly, 56
Quinn, Jane Bryant, 134

Rare coins, 288–290
    bullion coins distinguished, 286
    grading of, 290–292
    true rare coins, 291
Ratings for bonds, 246–248
Raw land, investment in, 128–129
Real estate
    downturns and, 235–236
    home-ownership, 116–124
    as investment, 125–135
    low-income housing, investment in,
        132–133
    mutual funds for, 132
    partnerships for investing in,
        131–132
    in portfolio, 181
    raw land, investment in, 128–129
    REITs, 130–131
Real estate general partnerships,
    131–132
Real estate investment trusts (REITs),
    130–131, 181
Real Estate Investor's Monthly
    (Reed), 134
Real-time stock and option quotes, 256
Recession, 227–238
    Federal Reserve Bank and, 250
    stock market and, 59–60
Record collections, 292

Redemption fee of mutual funds, 66
Reed, John T., 134–135
Reich, Robert, 288
Reinvestment in bonds, 84
REITs, 130–131, 181
Rental property investment, 125–128
Renter's insurance. *See* Homeowner's
    insurance
Retirement, 191–200. *See also* IRAs;
        Keogh plans
    discount brokers, planning with, 57
    planning, 36
    tax-deferred retirement plans,
        194–198
Retirement Letter, The (Dickinson),
    199–200
Revenue bonds, 242
Reverse stock splits, 205
Reward thermometers, 10
Richard Young's Intelligence Report,
    166
Rogers, Will, 116, 117
Rukeyser, Louis, 18, 94
Rule of 10%, 165
Rule of 70, 85

S&P Comstock, 257
Sales load of mutual funds, 65–66
Sample schedule for investing, 321–324
Satellite dish, use of, 256
Savings accounts, 186
Savings and loan crisis, 245–246
Schabacker, Jay, 173
Schedule for investing, 321–324
Schield fund, 329
Scudder Fund, 70
Scutella, Richard M., 124
Secondary issues, 46
Second mortgages, investment in,
    133–134
SEC Public Reference Branch, 111
Securities, defined, 54
Securities and Exchange Commission
    (SEC)
    and brokers' commissions, 55
    financial advisers, information on,
        111
    voting, regulation of, 144
Selling short, 207
Seminars
    on investing, 317
    for personal finance, 39
Shares of stock. *See* Stocks

Sharp, Curtis "Mack," 25–27, 28
Shearson Lehmann Brothers, 56
Silver, 287–288
Silverware collections, 293
Simplified employee pension plans (SEPs), 195
Skousen, Mark, 107
Small-cap stocks, 161
Small company stocks, 10
  diversification and, 170
  low-priced stocks, 220–222
Social Funds Guide of Good Money newsletter, 142
Social Investment Forum, 110, 146
Socially responsible funds, 73
  listing of, 328–329
Socially responsible investing, 139–146
  international investing as, 156
Social Security, 192
Software programs, 254–257
Solicitations, 271–273
South Africa, 140, 142
Specialist brokers, 43
Specialized mutual funds, 73–74
Speculators, 9
  expectations of, 12
  in futures, 303–304
  futures options, 314
  with options, 311
Spread, 101
  for rare coins, 289
SPX options, 312–313
Standard & Poors Bond Guide, 253
Standard & Poors 500 (S&P 500), 103, 247
  beating the averages of, 163
  index funds tied to, 74
State government bonds, 241
Stockbrokers. *See* Brokers
Stock certificates, 53, 59
Stock indexes, 74
Stock-index futures, 302
Stock market, 41–52, 99–100
  crash of October 1987, 275
  downturns, 227–238
  fluctuations, reasons for, 231–234
  gambling and, 281–282
  history of, 42–45
  as individual entity, 105
  international markets, trading in, 154–155
  method of trading in, 43
  1929 crash, 211

recession and, 59–60
timing the market, 278–281
Stocks, 206. *See also* Blue chip stocks; Dividends; Margin accounts; Options; Small company stocks
  versus bonds, 88–89
  buying and selling, 53–60, 215–226
  contrarianism, 222–224
  convertible bonds and, 244
  dollar-cost averaging for, 218
  fundamental analysis, 219
  growth stocks, 46
  income stocks, 46
  issuing stock, 41–42
  limit orders, 206
  low-priced stocks, 220–222
  method of trading, 43
  odd lots, 203–204
  over-the-counter market (OTC), 44, 100
  penny stocks, 46, 100
  pink sheets, listing in, 44, 100, 220
  preferred stocks, 47, 202–203
  pre-owned stock, 45
  prices of, 204
  secondary issues, 46
  selling short, 207
  small-cap stocks, 161
  socially responsible voting of, 142–144
  stock splits, 204–205
  stock tables, how to read, 95–99
  stop orders, 206–207
  in street name, 59
  technical analysis, 219
  types of, 45–47
Stop orders, 206–207
Street name, holding securities in, 59
Strike price for options, 311
Sy Harding Investor Forecasts, 225

T. Rowe Price, 70
TAIPAN, 157
Tax-deferred annuities, 197
Tax-deferred retirement plans, 194–198
Taxes
  effects of, 88–89
  home-ownership and, 119–120
  low-income housing investment credits, 133
  mutual funds, rules regarding, 71

personal finance issues, 36–37
on public purpose bonds, 241
rental property and, 126
shelter, real estate as, 126
on zero-coupon bonds, 243
T-bills, 241
T-bonds, 240
callability of, 251
Technical analysis of stocks, 219
Television, information from, 94
10% a year return rule, 165
Terhorst, Paul, 200
Therapy and money, 28–30
Thinly traded options, 311–312
Ticker symbols, 97–99
Timing the market, 278–281
T-notes, 240
Toy collections, 293
Traders, 9
Trading floor, 43
Train, John, 51–52
Transforming Your Relationship with Money and Achieving Financial Independence (Dominguez), 39, 318
Transportation Average, 102
Treasury bills (T-bills), 80, 241
Treasury bonds, 240
callability of, 251
Treasury notes, 80, 240
Trestor, Ken, 315
Trestor Compleat Option Report, 315
The Trick to Money Is Having Some! (Wilde), 30–31
Trust accounts with discount brokers, 57
12b-1 plans, 66
20th Century Growth Fund, 65

Undeveloped land, investment in, 128–129

United Science and Energy Fund, 65
U.S. government bonds. *See* Government bonds
Utilities
dividends of, 48
in model portfolio, 159
Utility Average, 102

Valdez oil spill, 140
Value Line Index, 103, 213
Vanguard funds, 70
Vanguard Index Trust 500 Fund, 74
Vanguard Public Foundation, 32
Venture capital, 266
Visa cards
from brokerage, 212
with discount brokers, 57

Wall Street Journal, 93
Wall Street Week, 18, 94
War, 229
Warrants, 312
Wilde, Stuart, 30–31
Wills, 20, 37–39
Wilshire 5000, 103
Wisconsin Community Fund, 32
Women
investor clubs, 17–18
and money, 17–19
National Network of Women's Funds, 32

Yield, 159
current yield, 249
Young, Richard, 159–160, 177

Zero-coupon bonds, 242–243
Zweig Forecast, 224
Zweig, Martin, 224–225, 317
Zweig Performance Ratings Report, 224–225

A unique story beautifully told by one of the most talented men I know. He shares his story bravely.... His willingness to give to others has been inspirational to me and to my family.... When you know Al Kasha, you know there's got to be a morning after.

> Dom DeLuise
> Motion picture actor/comedian

I found [*Reaching the Morning After*] to be fascinating, poignant and wonderful—impossible to put down.

> Dr. Irene Kassorla
> Best-selling author of
> *Go for It!*

Reaching the Morning After is *not* a book—it is a life experience. As I read it, I was living in old Brooklyn; I was struggling in the tough, creative world of the music business; I wrestled with personal problems within my family; I stood with an Oscar in my hand; and I felt the terror of agoraphobia and the unutterable joy of release and personal faith. You will be there—and you will love the involvement/reading of this beautifully written, truly unique book.

> Dr. Jess Moody
> Pastor
> First Baptist Church
> Van Nuys, California

Reaching
the
Morning After

Reaching
the
Morning After

by
A<small>L</small> K<small>ASHA</small> and J<small>OEL</small> H<small>IRSCHHORN</small>

THOMAS NELSON PUBLISHERS
Nashville • Camden • New York

3 4 5 6 7 8 9 10 11 - 97 96 95 94 93 92 91 90 89 88 87

Published in Nashville, Tennessee, by Thomas Nelson, Inc. and distributed in Canada by Lawson Falle, Ltd., Cambridge, Ontario.

Printed in the United States of America.

Library of Congress Cataloging-in-Publication Data

Kasha, Al.
  Reaching the morning after.

  1. Kasha, Al—Health. 2. Agoraphobia—Patients—
United States—Biography. I. Hirschhorn, Joel.
RC552.A44K37   1986   616.85'225   [B]   86-805
ISBN 0-8407-5509-0

_____ Dedication _____

To my wife, Ceil, who was always there. I couldn't have done this without her.

To my daughter, Dana, who is the joy and delight of my life.

To my brother, Larry, who went through the wars with me and tasted the sweet fulfillment of victory.

The Morning After

There's got to be a morning after,
If we can hold on through the night.
We have a chance to find the sunshine;
Let's keep on looking for the light.

Oh, can't you see the morning after?
It's waiting right outside the storm.
Why don't we cross the bridge together
And find a place that's safe and warm.

It's not too late—we should be giving.
Only with love can we climb.
It's not too late—not while we're living.
Let's put our hands out in time.

There's got to be a morning after;
We're moving closer to the shore.
I know we'll be there by tomorrow,
And we'll escape the darkness;
We won't be searching anymore.

By
Al Kasha
Joel Hirschhorn

Contents

Prologue
11

PART I BATTERED AND ABUSED
15

1 Broken Bottles
17

2 The Way Out
25

3 Binging
32

4 The Brooklyn Beat
39

5 Forced to Leave Home
43

PART II ACHIEVE! ACHIEVE!
55

6 Negative Voices
57

7 Up the CBS Ladder
65

8 Please, God, Let Me Sleep
73
9 Starting Over
83
10 Hollywood Lifeline
90
PART III BREAKING DOWN—WORKAHOLISM
99
11 Panic
101
12 Addicted
105
13 Oscar
112
14 The Towering Inferno
119
15 Escaping the Darkness
138
16 Running a New Road
156
17 Only with Love Can We Climb
168
18 The Morning After
179
Appendix
188

_____ Acknowledgments _____

Many thanks to those who have done such good work on behalf of child abuse and victims of phobic illness:

Dodie Livingston, commissioner, department of Health and Human Services, Washington, D. C.; Captain T. W. "Slim" Cummings of the Pan Am Flight Phobia Program; Christina Crawford, Survivor's Network; Dr. Arthur Hardy of Menlo Park, Calif. (TERRAP); Robert L. DuPont, M.D., director of Phobia Program of Washington, Rockville, Md., and president of the Phobia Society of America; Congressman Michael Bilirakis of Florida; Phobic Society of America's director of Public Education, Jerilyn Ross; Congressman Henry Waxman of California; Shervert Frazier, M.D., the director of the National Institute of Mental Health; Phobic Society of America (PSA) board member and spokesman Willard Scott; researcher David Sheehan, M.D.; the Oak Ridge Boys, honorary chairmen of the National Committee for Prevention of Child Abuse; Maralyn Teare, M.S., M.F.C.C. and clinical instructor of psychiatry, University of Southern California School of Medicine, Anxiety Disorder Clinic.

With gratitude to those whose love and support helped me to reach my new morning after:

Dom De Luise, Red Buttons, Happy Goday, Nell Carter, Irving Mansfield and Jacqueline Susann, Stuart Berton, Gene Kelly, Peter Engel, Ed Lubin, Terry and Moncita Botwick, Debby Boone, Gabriel Ferrer, Ernest and Tove Borgnine, Irwin and Jackie Mazur, Susan Munao and Jennifer Carter.

To all my talented friends from the Brill Building on Broadway, who lived the highs and lows with me:

Barry Mann, Cynthia Weil, Neil Diamond, Neil Sedaka, Howard Greenfield, Don Kirshner, Carole King, Gerry Goffin, Jack Keller, Burt Bacharach, Hal

David, Jerry Lieber, Mike Stoller, Bob Dylan, George David Weiss, Jackie Wilson, and Aretha Franklin.

For their spiritual wisdom, guidance and belief, my deepest love and gratitude to:

Dr. Jess Moody, Senior Pastor Jack Hayford, Dr. Robert Schuller of the Crystal Cathedral, Tim Timmons, Ken Day, Dr. Fred Price, Ed Neteland, Bill Underwood, Norman Newman, Donna Summer, Bruce Sudano, and Chuck Smith.

Thank you, Tom Thompson, Jahn Lutz, and Theron Raines, for believing in *Reaching the Morning After* from the beginning.

To all the people at Nelson Publications who helped make *Reaching the Morning After* a reality:

Bob Wolgemuth, Mike Hyatt, Sam Moore, Walter and Lori Quinn, Peter Gillquist, Bill Fox, Steve Hines, Victor Oliver, Joan Alford Boyle, Sara Fortenberry, Margaret Singleton, Trish Morrison, the fine sales force of Nelson, Bruce Nygren, and our terrific editor, Larry Weeden.

To Maureen McGovern, whose sincere and sensitive singing performance of "The Morning After" reached people all over the world, and to Russ Regan and Irwin Allen, who believed in the song before anyone else.

Most of all, *Reaching the Morning After* is dedicated to everyone helping the countless thousands of child abuse and phobic victims who suffer in silence.

Prologue

It doesn't matter if you win the Oscar tonight, I told myself. *All that matters is being nominated.*

As our rented limousine raced along the Hollywood freeway, I struggled to push beyond the cloud of anxiety that had settled over me. My wife, Ceil, chattered in an unnaturally cheerful voice, squeezing my hands and whispering words of encouragement.

"You'll win, Al."

I have to win.

Tonight, I felt, was crucial to my future happiness. I had been nominated for an Oscar for Best Song and the recognition and prestige it offered would make me a worthwhile person, a super achiever.

Look, Mom and Dad. I did it!

Mom and Dad would be watching from their small, cluttered apartment on Avenue M in Brooklyn. They would see that their son had made the right choice when he had chosen show business over engineering. Their criticism would be transformed into selfless devotion and pride. And their inexhaustible demands would finally be satisfied.

The limo lurched to a stop and I had a dark, simultaneous image of a belt cracking me across the face. My mind slid backward to the past, and I was caught up in a barrage of beatings. I felt my brain expanding to accommodate the ugly memories. My mother screaming, "Irving, don't please!"; dishes being smashed on the floor or hurled against the wall; my father's endless acts of brutality against his wife and sons.

"You okay?" My partner Joel's voice from the back seat broke into my thoughts. His hand squeezed my shoulder.

"Look, it's raining," said the limo driver. "Hope it's not bad luck."

"Don't say that," Ceil warned. "The boys are gonna win tonight for sure."

The driver parked; and we ran through the drizzle, past noisy fans clamoring for a look at their idols as they entered the Dorothy Chandler Pavilion.

The interminable evening began. Shelley Winters, considered a shoo-in for Best Supporting Actress for *The Poseidon Adventure*, lost to Eileen Heckart. That meant we had a chance, since the papers had chosen Michael Jackson's "Ben" as Best Song over us. My thinking was convoluted, but I reassured myself: *The more upsets, the better our chances.*

The Godfather, another shoo-in, was slighted in category after category, though Marlon Brando did win as Best Actor. When Brando failed to show up, sending an Indian girl named Sacheen Littlefeather in his place to protest the U.S. treatment of Indians, I was momentarily distracted from my tension.

"And now, for Best Song..."

Are you listening, Mom and Dad?

Cher's hesitant voice stumbled through the announcement: "Al K-Kasha and Joel Hirschhorn for 'The Morning After' from *The Poseidon Adventure.*"

I tore down the aisle, past a sea of smiling celebrity faces. It took an eternity to reach the stage. Joel spoke first, giving me time to mentally rehearse the speech I had been working on for so long.

"You've made two people in Brooklyn very happy tonight—Rose and Irving Kasha."

Backstage, reporters assaulted us with questions: "How does it feel?" "Did you expect to win?" "Do you think Michael Jackson's song should have won?"

I thought of my brother, Larry Kasha. What was he thinking? Was he proud? Larry, a Broadway producer, had already won a Tony for Lauren Bacall's *Applause*. He was my mother's favorite, despite the fact that she claimed, "Larry is my right eye, and you're my left eye."

We went to a dinner and dance after the Awards Show—The Governor's Ball—for Academy members at the Beverly Hilton Hotel. I know I smiled and shook the hands of a hundred celebrities—Jack Lemmon, Bob Hope, Angela Lansbury, Liza Minnelli—but I couldn't relax; I couldn't digest my food. Though I tried to savor the glory of the moment, my mind was already sprinting ahead.

What does this mean? Will it bring a lot more work? More fame? More love?

"If nothing else ever happens, this will be enough," Joel exulted.

"What do you mean 'if nothing else ever happens'? This is just the beginning."

Joel called the next day and told me that he and his wife, Jill, had slept with the Oscar. It seemed foolish, childlike. We couldn't dwell on things. We had to go forward.

I didn't understand my depression. I had a wonderful, supportive wife in Ceil and a delightful daughter. The partnership between Joel and me had survived and flourished for seven years.

Then the phone rang. I heard my mother's high, syrupy voice, gushing with excitement.

"L'Alfred, I'm so proud of you!"

"*Alfred*, Mom."

I couldn't help correcting her. Since Larry was always on her mind, she had a tendency to combine our names.

"An Oscar! And someday I'll bet you win a second Oscar!"

A second Oscar! The gold plating on the first was still fresh. The blood drained from my face. I gasped for breath.

My mother's next statement lodged like a bullet in my brain and stayed there for the next ten years. "And someday, L'Alfred darling, you'll really make it, when you win a Tony, like your brother did."

Ceil must have felt my distress, because she grabbed the phone from my hand and coped with the remainder of the conversation.

I had an appointment that afternoon. I was dressed in a corduroy jacket and gray pants, all prepared to pick up Joel in front of his home in Hollywood.

I recall opening the front door and staring at the crowded Beverly Hills intersection. I tried to move, but it was as though my feet had become embedded in cement. Symptoms seemed to attack from right and left—sweaty palms, pounding heart, tightness in my chest.

Senseless, escalating terror.

I couldn't leave the house. I ran back inside and slammed the door, momentarily safe within my sanctuary.

"What's the matter?" Ceil cried.

"I'm not going," was all I said.

Ceil didn't know what to make of it. Neither did I. I didn't yet realize that the jaws of agoraphobia had begun to clamp down on me, ushering in an agonizing period when I would become a helpless prisoner in my own home.

PART I

BATTERED AND ABUSED

1

Broken Bottles

Nobody took the term *phobia* seriously in 1945. Today psychiatrists recognize that phobias represent America's second most common mental health problem behind alcoholism and refer to the 1980s as "the age of anxiety." But when my mother, Rose Kasha, suffered a panic attack on the subway and had to be helped from the train by concerned strangers, her symptoms were dismissed as "nerves." All through my childhood and beyond, she experienced sudden palpitation seizures, provoking her inevitable cry, "I'm having a heart attack, Alfred! I'm dying—help me!"

I was petrified. I didn't want my mother to die; but even at six years old, I felt ambivalent, taken advantage of. Her attacks seemed like one more device to engulf my brother and me, one more attempt to swallow us up.

Larry felt equally frustrated. He was four years older than I was. We had little in common except fear and resentment of our parents.

We shared the same room and same small bed. I remember wishing desperately for one of my own. Larry made his feelings clear by sleeping rigidly on his side, almost tumbling off the edge. Neither of us ever slept soundly. We were too alert to danger, bracing ourselves for the moment when our father, drunk and violent, would come storming in, shouting obscenities. Most of the time he would yank one of us out of bed and beat us mercilessly, for reasons known only to his alcohol-fogged brain. Larry

17

usually made the mistake of arguing back, so his beatings were more prolonged and brutal.

My mother always sobbed and begged him to stop. But when we tried to defend ourselves against his assaults she said, "No, be nice. You'll make it worse."

It was torture to "be nice" to my father. He had once been an amateur wrestler in his native Poland and though only of medium height, he was powerfully built, with a barrel chest and thick, granite arms. When angry and blind drunk, his powder-blue eyes would turn black and his iron knuckles sought flesh to bruise, bones to break. Larry and I were the main victims. From the cradle to the crib and through grammar school, the big, maroon-faced man used us as regularly as a punching bag at the "Y".

Until I was forty years old, I never slipped on a belt without dwelling on the one he wore, the one he used to whip us with. He threw chairs when someone disagreed with him, or overturned the dinner table, watching the food and drink pile messily on the floor with sadistic satisfaction. I saw *A Streetcar Named Desire* at age fifteen and when I observed Marlon Brando smashing dishes, I gasped in recognition. "Tennessee Williams must have met my father!"

My father had a habit that alienated sons and strangers alike, of shaking your hand and crushing it until the pain was unbearable. After arguments, he would say to me in a conciliatory tone, "Let's make up. Shake," and I would extend my hand as he watched. His hands were powerfully developed from opening and closing the scissors he used daily as a barber, and when they folded around my fingers, I bit my tongue, struggling to smother the cries roaring in my throat. He kept staring, measuring me, waiting for me to break.

"Be nice," my mother continued to say, so I suppressed my natural instinct for self-defense. I absorbed her message, "peace at any price," burying my rage while it ate away at me, resulting in headaches and excruciating stomach pains.

I once asked my Aunt Tessie, my father's sister, why he behaved so viciously. "He doesn't mean it, Alfred," she told me. "His father beat him up; it's the only way he knows." But at six years old, I couldn't forgive him.

I also couldn't know that my father was a bitterly frustrated man, married to a woman who had only contempt for him. Often he yelled at her, "Always the sons, always the sons. Never me, always the sons." He pulled me into a corner when I was eight and mumbled, "Look at your mother. *Look* at her!" For a second I saw her through his eyes—short, plump, with small brown eyes and thick lips. "Your mother doesn't know how to please a man. Do you understand what I'm saying?" I didn't understand exactly, but I knew it was something I didn't want to hear. I was too young to grasp the genuine agony behind the confession. I saw that agony more clearly another time when I found him sobbing in the kitchen. He cried for days. My mother explained, "A letter came from his nephew in Warsaw....His father and two brothers were shot and killed by the Nazis."

She was sympathetic for once. But most of the time she grieved about her marriage to "that animal," saying she was deathly afraid of him, that the only thing in life of any importance were her two boys. "You and Larry, you're all I have," was her favorite theme.

The message was obvious: "It's up to you and Larry to rescue me."

I knew my mother had once loved a man. She often spoke of a Mr. Klinger, the pharmacist; and her features softened when she mentioned him. My mother loved to sing around the apartment. Her favorite song was "You'll Never Know Just How Much I Love You," and I sensed she was singing that song especially for him.

"He used to bring me flowers every time he came to the house," she said. "He had no money, but he always found enough for a bouquet. He wanted to marry me, you know, but I was crazy. I married your father." And then her tears would flow. "I married your father because he was so handsome and such a good dancer. What do you know at sixteen, Alfred? You never think a man's gotta make a living."

I was ten years old when my mother and I were stopped on Avenue L by a short, balding gentleman with a mustache.

"Rose," he said.

My mother blushed like a schoolgirl. "Hello, Harvey. Harvey Klinger, this is my son, Alfred."

Harvey bowed his shiny head, then smiled. "You look pretty, Rose." In my mind, I suddenly heard my mother's voice singing "You'll Never Know."

When they shook hands and said goodbye, my mother was, for the only time I knew her, beautiful.

The most embarrassing aspect of our apartment, to me, was its location over a store, a store my parents jointly owned. They ran a business, unimaginatively titled ROSE AND IRVING'S, a combination barber shop and beauty parlor. My mother's iron determination and business acumen kept the business going during the depression years. It certainly wasn't her ability as a manicurist or beautician; her idea of dyeing hair was to make everything as garishly blonde or black as possible. My father was more talented as a barber, with everybody's head but mine. He insisted on cutting off all my hair, making me look perilously close to a monk or a Hare Krishna follower. I vowed I would let my hair grow long, like Samson, when I was old enough.

His mood swings also created crises. Once he got into an argument with a customer and chased him into the street with a pair of scissors, slashing the customer's arm and drawing blood. The customer pressed charges, but they were later dropped.

My father's other problem was even more worrisome: his bigotry. It was always simmering beneath the surface. He served blacks reluctantly, occasionally refusing to cut their hair, and his lifelong hatred of the *goyim*, particularly Catholics, triggered off rudeness when one of the "enemy camp" sat in his chair. As a child in Poland, my father had been beaten viciously by anti-Semites, and the psychic wounds remained fresh and raw throughout his life.

My mother and I would sit at the cash register after the disturbances died down and she would confide: "He beat me today." Or "He embarrassed me before a customer."

Sometimes she would say, "I wish I could leave him. But what then? Tell me. There's no money...and what about the store? If I didn't take care of it, it would fall apart. You know your father, he can't take care of anything."

20

"Don't worry, Mom," I assured her, with the fervent logic of a child. "Someday I'll buy you a mink coat and you'll have a big car and a house."

"I'm depending on you, darling," she would say, hugging the breath out of me. "You're the way out, you and your brother. You're the way out."

My role as rescuer was established then, and every time my father inflicted physical or emotional wounds on my mother, she would remind me, "You're the way out. Remember."

To raise her spirits I wrote little poems for her and she saved them. One said:

> Mom, you're the greatest,
> more than the rest.
> And someday, Mom, you'll have the best.

It was easier, even then, to express myself in rhyme or through melodies than to spell out my feelings.

With each poem, Mom would thank me and emphasize, "I'll leave him when you and Larry make enough money." I thought; *If I do enough, achieve enough, make her dreams come true, she'll have the courage to walk out.* Most kids from troubled homes wanted their parents to patch things up and stay together. I dreamed of the day my folks would get divorced.

If my mother left him, she'd be safe. We'd all be safe.

Part of me hated the barber shop, hated the smell of Vitalis and shaving cream. I had a recurring nightmare of hair down my back, under my shorts, sticking to my skin, making me itch. In the dream, I'd throw myself into scalding hot showers, trying to wash the hair from my skin, but it clung, each follicle a blood-sucking insect.

Life wasn't much better when I was awake. Larry and I had to wash the floors; and my father stood over us, screaming, "You left out a spot there. What's the matter with you *dummies?* Use a little muscle." Larry was an A plus student at Madison High and my teachers at P.S. 99 constantly told my parents how much talent I had in music, but my father measured us by our ability to keep the floors clean. Once, in anger, he stepped on my right hand and broke a finger, because we had accidentally neglected a corner.

The store had a positive aspect, however. Since my parents were hopeless role models, it offered healthier personalities to emulate. I was an attentive listener and a natural mimic and I memorized everything about the parade of customers I met, soaking in their mannerisms, their modes of dress, their speech patterns. They became a huge substitute family. Some were famous—Arthur Miller came to have his hair cut; so did Rocky Graziano. I entertained by singing and doing impersonations of Al Jolson (whom I loved after seeing *The Jolson Story*) and Frank Sinatra. The father of opera star Leonard Warren said, "You could sing in the opera, like my boy."

I treasured that compliment, even though my father howled with laughter afterward, calling Mr. Warren "stupid" for saying it. At nine and ten I was chubby and red-cheeked—the kind of child adults wanted to pinch—and I worked at being lovable. I needed unqualified approval to survive. I don't remember my father ever uttering a word of praise, and my mother viewed my achievements as accomplishments of her own. "You came out of my body," she was fond of saying, patting a protruding stomach. "You're like *me*; you're talented like I am."

Or she would pit me against my brother, stirring up a sibling rivalry that made closeness impossible.

"Be like your brother Larry...he gets such good marks."

"Be like your brother Alfred...he's such a good singer."

"Be like your brother Larry...he's such a wonderful dancer."

"Be like your brother Alfred...he's so good in sports."

Larry's being forced to assume full responsibility for me during the day didn't help. When it counted he was in my corner, protecting me from bullies when they started fights. But he resented bringing me to school and picking me up. He had to help me with my homework, a chore he approached reluctantly. When he met with his friends, my mother automatically insisted, "Now take Alfred along."

Among his peers I saw my brother blossom. He was witty, a

jokester, the life of the party. Years later a columnist called Larry the Brooklyn Noel Coward. Sadly, this sense of fun was stamped out at home.

Both Larry and I dreamed of a show business career someday (he would dance, like Gene Kelly; I would sing, like Frank Sinatra—similar ambitions that would have created competition in the most peaceful of families).

We also dreamed of escaping our tiny, roach-infested apartment, with its mud-brown walls and clanging radiator. Larry was particularly upset by the combined smell of hair dye and alcohol, an aroma that choked healthy air out of the premises.

What upset Larry most, though, was sharing his clothes with me. We were both heavy as children, so his hand-me-downs were a comfortable fit.

Larry was incredibly tidy and meticulous—everything neatly hung and arranged in his closet—and he accused me of dirtying his shirts and pants when I played ball.

I realized the full extent of his animosity when he turned thirteen and lost twenty-five pounds.

"Gee, these pants are too small for me," I said, when my mother asked me to try on a pair of Larry's gray tweed trousers.

Larry was sitting at the kitchen table doing his math homework. He looked up through brown-rimmed glasses, eyes blazing.

"I'm gonna be so skinny," he said, "that you'll never be able to wear my clothes again."

I never felt close to him again either, at least not until we were grown and able to sort out the destructive things our parents had done to us. The bed we shared seemed smaller than ever now, and it was vitally important to maintain a distance. Never to touch again, even accidentally.

Lying on my back at night, staring at the cracks in the ceiling, I talked to God a lot. I always dimly understood that God was dependable, a force that would never fail me the way people did.

"Dear God," I remember whispering, "make my daddy stop drinking." I waited for an answer, as the underground subway rattled and shook our building, as buses raced past my street corner. I prayed with more urgency when I overheard my father smashing a bottle of vodka against the mirror in his bedroom. I thought of all the bottles I had hidden or poured out, all the bottles my mother had diluted with water.

"Dear God," went another prayer, "don't let Daddy hurt Mom." But that prayer went unanswered too. My mother's face was often black and blue in the morning, her face cut, sliced, by the jagged edges of broken bottles, deformed by fists, lamps, any handy object that could wreak damage.

Sometimes I pictured these scenes during the day, when I was away from home and supposedly safe: during a class, in the locker room after gym, having lunch. And the panic would build in me, accompanied by sweaty palms and dizziness. One time I ran out of a hot, crowded classroom. Another time a friend crept up behind me in the hallway and covered my eyes. He meant it as a joke, but I felt so startled and confined by those hands that I leaped at him, punching him and knocking him down. A teacher had to wrench us apart. I remember the stunned look on my friend's freckled face. My violence shocked him because I had always been so mild-mannered.

At times like those, the room would shake, and I had a sense the ground would open up underneath my feet and drag me millions of feet into a black void.

Still, I was stubborn. I felt there was a reason for it all, that God would never abandon me. If I just held on, all this misery and madness would somehow make sense.

2

The Way Out

Much as I despised Brooklyn, I loved the fact that our apartment was across the street from Warner Brothers' Vitagraph Studios. In the late 1930s and 1940s, they were making two-reelers, and my mother managed to get Larry in a few of them as an extra. I even appeared in one.

My parents were frequently hired to cut an actor's hair or do his nails, so I had an ideal excuse to hang around. I remember my father grumbling that Jack Haley (the Tin Man in *The Wizard of Oz*) had no beard, so shaving him was a waste of time. My mother nursed a grudge against lyricist Sammy Cahn because he didn't give her a tip after she found the $500.00 plane ticket he had lost. Fatty Arbuckle was a shining star who worked there before the rape scandal that destroyed his career.

My child's eye blinked away the imperfections. These were all glamorous, successful beings; and someday I would be one of them, singing, acting, doing my impressions on film.

"Show business is for little girls, not men," my father bellowed. "You're not a little girl, are you?"

"No."

"Hey, you're not mad, are you?"

"I'm not mad."

"Sure you are. Okay, I'm sorry. Let's make up. Shake!" He extended his hand and squashed my knuckles until pain shot through my fingers and up my arm.

25

My father objected strongly to any creative pursuits, but my mother gave us dancing and singing lessons anyway. She learned where auditions were from talk around the Vitagraph Studios. Each casting call made my father angrier; he wanted at least one of his sons to become a doctor because his older brother, whom he idolized, had a flourishing medical practice. He screamed, "Shut up," when my mother sang. She usually continued with "You'll Never Know," raising her voice louder in defiance. He would snarl, "You can't *sing*, Rose. You have a lousy voice. You can't sing, and your son can't sing either. I don't want that noise around here!"

"You'll never know just how much I care...."

Those lyrics wounded him, because he knew they were for us, never him. Larry and I watched the same scene unfold daily: her singing, his deafening wrath, her refusal to stop, provoking a slap, if she was lucky, a punch if she wasn't.

"I won't stop," she would sob. "I'll sing around here and so will my sons. You animal, you can't stop me."

Terrified as she was of his violence, my mother, who bent on nearly every issue, wouldn't surrender the few moments of happiness she experienced when singing. Singing was the only way of asserting her dream, letting him know her sons would succeed in show business. Through singing, she made it clear that she, Larry, and I would spring from the ghetto cage one day, leaving him behind.

In my mother's fantasy, she was the pampered focus of her sons' lives, reveling in their triumphs, decked out in furs and jewels on Broadway opening nights. We were her escape route and no girl was good enough for us. Even at nine or ten they were competition. "Boys should be with boys and girls with girls," was one of her familiar statements. Most of the Jewish mothers I knew felt that way about their sons, but my mother's reactions were extreme. She warned us, "Don't let a woman trap you," advice I could have benefited from in the years to follow. Still, whether consciously aware of it or not, her attitude was disturbingly seductive. She walked around the apartment without a blouse, in her bra and sometimes without it. My mother was a heavy woman, with enormous breasts, and the sight of her nudity made me uncomfortable.

Singing in the temple provided a welcome refuge from family pressure. I was eagerly encouraged by a cantor named Alvin Cooper. Cantor Cooper had thick, black, wavy hair and grimly downturned eyebrows; but I knew he admired my voice. I sang for him with all the passion my ten-year-old vocal chords could muster.

"God is applauding you," he said once, and I felt excited and proud. "Someday you'll be a cantor. Just promise me one thing, Alfred. Always sing Yiddish music. Don't go into opera like Jan Peerce and Richard Tucker." Both these great singers had been cantors before making their mark on the opera world. "It would be a *shonda*, Alfred, a shame," he concluded.

My maternal grandfather also thought of me as a future cantor. I allowed both men to believe I would seriously consider it. Religion was important to me during that period. I loved Hebrew school, loved attending temple on the holidays.

Religion, to me, was a promise; to my Russian grandfather it was life itself. He was a formidable figure, even at 5'6", with a reddish goatee, a mustache, and stringy hair. He usually wore a hat with a yarmulke beneath it.

My grandmother was quieter and sweeter; she rarely said a word, and when she did it was only in Yiddish. She looked at her husband with mute adoration while he conducted four-hour seders that occasionally taxed my youthful patience.

She was also a diabetic. My grandfather was more than orthodox. He was a fanatic who refused to administer insulin shots to her on the Sabbath. A man next door, a gentile, did it.

A Saturday came when neither neighbor nor doctor could be reached in time. My grandfather refused to give her the needed shot. A day later she was dead.

When I heard about this I wondered, trembling; "*If this is the Voice of God, why is it so uncaring, so cold? Why is tradition so constricting?*"

After that day my ambition to be a cantor burned less brightly and Cantor Cooper, recognizing my change of attitude, transferred his affections to another boy at the synagogue.

My show business career really began in 1945 when I was seven years old. After auditioning for *Annie Get Your Gun*, producers Rodgers and Hammerstein chose me to play Ethel Merman's baby brother, Jake, replacing Warren Berlinger.

I recall Mr. Rodgers as a cool, formidable person; but Mr. Hammerstein was warm and encouraging. I lived for the times he smiled in my direction. I was always choosing fantasy fathers to replace my own, and he fit the bill perfectly—someone I could respect, someone who would stand behind me and my aspirations. I worked up enough courage to say, "Hi, Mr. Hammerstein," when he was backstage and he waved back. Once he even patted me firmly on the head.

When the time came for *Annie Get Your Gun* to tour, I was asked to stay with it, but my mother couldn't leave Rose and Irving's to travel with me. I begged her to change her mind; I cried. I got down on my knees, like Al Jolson doing "Mammy." (Even at seven, I had a keen theatrical sense.) Nothing worked. I was a modern Dickensian victim, except that my personal prison was a barber shop, not a bottle factory.

My mother continued to do what she could, in addition to slaving away at the shop. She wrote to Warner Brothers in Hollywood on December 2, 1946, asking them to consider me for feature films. Their response was a form letter: Not interested at this time. I still have the letter, and I have to admit it gave me satisfaction in 1975 to win a Best Song Oscar for a Warner Brothers picture, *The Towering Inferno*.

My creative energies focused on school. I wrote shows, organized them, cast them, and gave myself starring parts. Sometimes my casting ideas backfired, particularly when I persuaded my teacher to give me the romantic lead in *The Student Prince*. I was at my heaviest and the audience giggled when I walked on stage.

It quickly hit me that the best route to gain attention was becoming class clown. I answered teachers with wisecracks and made faces behind their backs. "Did you hear the one about..." became my standard phrase.

There was nothing I didn't plan to be at one time or another, as long as it meant maintaining a grip on the limelight: actor, singer, comic, impressionist, writer, producer, director. "I want to please; notice me" were the signals I sent out, and people responded. Most persons who tackle show business have this need for attention, even the ones who express a passion for privacy. Adulthood and increasing security act as tempering influences, but the childlike "Love me, love me" is never totally silenced.

I was anything but silent in those years. But my high pressure, workaholic drive was palatable because I spoke softly. I had a courteous, gentle manner because I loathed my father's loudness.

At eleven I starred in the Seventh Grade Variety Show, playing Curly in *Oklahoma*. The audience cheered, but my father ruined everything by coming to the performance drunk and roaring, "Where's my Alfred?" All heads in the auditorium spun around. I couldn't help saying, later at home, "Daddy, why did you have to talk?"

My reward was the worst beating I'd ever received. My father grabbed me by both shoulders and threw me against a closet door. He hammered those huge fists against my ribs.

"Is that the way you talk to your father?" he shouted, as I fought to struggle free.

"Mom," I screamed. "Make him stop."

"Irving, leave him alone."

"Shut up, Rose," he warned, raising his fist menacingly. She shrank back.

"It's enough," she said, compromising between her instinct for motherhood and her own personal terror.

He clubbed me on the arms, elbows, shoulders.

"That'll teach you, big shot."

Totally out of control, he picked up a half-empty brandy bottle and smashed it over my head. I felt blood spurting from my scalp.

Then he yanked the bedroom closet open and shoved me inside, slamming the door.

"How does that feel, big shot?" he shouted, as I pounded wildly on the closet door. Blood dripped down my cheeks, onto my lips. I swallowed it.

"Please, Daddy, let me out."

29

"Big shot."

I can still smell the shoe leather and the suffocating mothballs in that closet, still feel the suits and shirts dangling like dead bodies.

"Daddy, please, I can't breathe."

He cackled drunkenly, ignoring my pleas. "I'll be good," I swore, not comprehending what good was, willing to promise anything to wrench free of the dark cell he had forced me into. "I'll be good, I'll be good."

"How do you like it now, big shot?"

Then I overheard scuffling. I heard my mother pleading, as usual, and Larry's outraged voice. He had just returned from acting in a local play. My father's brute force had blocked Larry from opening the door, but in the next fifteen minutes there were other voices, footsteps.

The door shot open and I fell out, shaking, and sobbing helplessly. I found myself in the comforting arms of a policeman.

It was the first time the police had been summoned to break up one of our family quarrels. They wanted to lock my father up, but my mother begged them to give him another chance.

"He's still your father," she explained, after the officers left and he was poured into bed.

"He's crazy," Larry shouted. "A stupid, crazy animal."

"He's your father," she repeated. "You don't want him put in jail like some criminal, do you?"

"Yes," Larry screamed. "Before he kills you...or us. Mom, look ...look at your son. Look at his face. Look at the blood. *Look!*"

"Your father's not always like that. If he didn't drink so much..."

"But he does."

"Think of the disgrace, if your father goes to jail. Think of what the neighbors would say."

"Who cares about the neighbors?"

"Darling, don't yell. My pressure."

Larry quieted down.

"It's not like he goes to bars."

"No," said Larry. "It's okay because he gets smashed at home."

"He doesn't go to bars," she repeated. "And besides, what about the business if he goes to jail? Will people still come if they know Irving Kasha's in jail?" She paused. "It's not like he's some common drinker, some *shicka* off the street."

She didn't conclude with her usual words, but I heard them just the same.

"Be nice."

3

Binging

I was grateful to Larry for saving me. I took his intervention as a sign of caring. He did care—I know that now—but he couldn't allow anyone, even me, to sidetrack him emotionally. He felt our environment was evil and would drag him down unless he pulled free of it altogether.

He was never unkind, only quiet. By the time I was bar mitzvahed we barely spoke, and the circumstances were such a disappointment that I finally cut myself off from him emotionally as well.

Four years earlier, my parents had hired a hall for a reception following Larry's bar mitzvah service. Now, in January of 1950, with money a greater problem than ever, they held my reception in our apartment. I was bitterly resentful and jealous. A bar mitzvah reception over a store! I deserved better than that. I had thrown myself into my Hebrew studies with enthusiasm. I had made my mother proud by singing in the temple and at parties and weddings.

Nothing lifted my spirits, not even the loads of presents and checks my relatives handed me. I sang "Thou Swell," accompanied by a piano player my parents had hired. Larry, I thought, had had a three-piece band. I was embarrassed by my haircut—my father had cut it so short I looked prematurely bald.

I remember the haircut vividly. When I protested, my father hissed in my ear, "Shut up...or I'll throw you in the closet."

32

Hours later I was still brooding over the threat, about the sensation of a narrow, airless closet, when a chance remark by my Aunt Helen distracted me. I was eating a chopped liver sandwich when I overheard Aunt Helen, my one skinny relative, comment loudly to my mother, "Rose, what are you feeding Alfred? He's gotten so fat."

"He looks fine," my mother said. I thought of the Boy Scout hike I had participated in a year ago. All my friends' mothers had packed franks; mine had packed three lamb chops with careful cooking instructions. Her idea of roughing it in the woods meant a feast; God forbid her son should starve.

The seams were bursting on my suit—another hand-me-down from Larry. I heard my mother say, "He's a growing boy"; but the trouble was, I was growing in the wrong direction. What was charmingly chubby on a six-year-old looked merely gross on a teenager. I knew it and felt desperately ashamed, but I couldn't stop eating.

Even that day, stung by my aunt's assessment, I hovered around the buffet table, stuffing down sliced turkey, bagels, lox, potato salad, rolls, and pastries. In fact, the remark only doubled my appetite. The sense of deprivation I felt could only be satisfied with food.

I had to have it.

Family mealtimes were never less than a nightmare for me. I ate out of a nervous compulsion to do something with my hands. After jamming mountainous portions of food down my throat, I was inevitably sick afterward. Cramps were a daily occurrence.

To savor eating without the accompaniment of family hysterics, I would rush home from school and sneak in a separate pre-dinner meal of my own. I didn't want to risk provoking my parents, so I ate twice. By thirteen, after years of gobbling down four meals a day, I weighed 220 pounds. My mother would say, as mothers of the 1940s always did, "Think of the poor, starving children in Europe." My appetite was so large by then that I ate not only for Europe, but for Africa, India, and the Far East as well.

"Hey, here comes Kareshape," my friend Barry was fond of saying. The nickname was suggested by a Dick Tracy character named Pearshape, who had bulging, oversized hips. The description fit only too well. Barry was tall and lean, with curly brown hair and the kind of broad shoulders and trim waist that girls favored. From my point of view, he had everything—a loving "buddy" of a father, the kind I wished I had, and a mother who worshiped him and hung on his every word. He was a born actor, a born artist, a born athlete. Nature had showered him with gifts, but I was too in awe of them to be jealous.

Women, from freshmen to seniors at Madison High, all fell in love with Barry. He was captain of the cheerleaders. He was the first of my friends to "go all the way." And he collected As on every exam without studying.

At the time, I wondered why a divinity like Barry would lower himself to befriend roly-poly me. He laughed at my frenzied activity. I was always organizing something—The Sing Show (conceived by my brother four years earlier), the Junior Show, the School Dance. I belonged to the chorus. And most crucially—because I believe it maintained my sanity—I played football.

I wasn't a great football player, like Barry. I didn't have his height or his muscle. But I had one quality that made me valuable to the team—I wanted to win. The same intensity and sublimated anger that made me strive for recognition as an entertainer served me well on the football field. I was hostile, violent, as violent as my father. Every tackle was charged with a fury I couldn't unleash at home.

Off the field I continued to be gentle; I spoke in a whisper. No one could define me, though, because I kept trying new identities. No sooner would someone say "He's so sweet and quiet" than I would mug and burst into a wild Red Skelton or Milton Berle routine. I had a rubber face, a Jerry Lewis face, puffing up my lips, crossing my eyes. Then the class clown would dissolve, and I'd take on the role of muted, silent guru, listening to people's problems with the patience of an analyst. A lifetime of concentrating on my mother's various grievances had trained me to be a willing ear. I "rescued" strangers, the way I kept trying to rescue my mother.

I wavered schizophrenically between adult and infant, slipping into whatever emotional costume would work in a given situation.

"Who are you, Kareshape?" Barry once asked me. I certainly couldn't have told him.

I fell in love for the first time in my sophomore year. The object: a dark, tiny girl named Marlene, with two oversized attributes—singing voice and bust. Both of them mesmerized me, particularly the voice. Marlene wanted to star on Broadway someday, and we shared our dreams of future glory. Our mutual fantasizing was so important to her that she pulled away during lunch from her group of girlfriends, a brave and independent act for a 1950s high school junior.

She gave me hope when she said, "You know, Al, if you went on a diet, you could be very cute." I raced home that day with new resolve; I would starve off the ungainly pounds. I'd cut out my secret meal. If I was slim and handsome, maybe Marlene would go steady with me through high school, even college. And maybe then we'd write shows together, or co-star in a Broadway musical. Even at sixteen I dreamed big, setting my sights on the seemingly impossible.

The diet lasted two days. One clash with my father, one nagging word from my mother and I scrambled to the icebox to stuff satisfaction into myself. Satisfaction usually took the form of ice cream; I was addicted to it, particularly chocolate.

"I lost three pounds," I lied to Marlene during a chorus rehearsal.

"Great. I knew you could do it."

I kept planning to start the diet again...planning to have one sandwich for lunch instead of three, planning to cut out my ice cream after school.

Marlene and I sneaked into the music room whenever it was empty and worked out duets, most of them from shows like *Carousel* and *The King and I*. Sometimes we practiced at her house on Bedford Avenue and 23rd Street, either to Marlene's piano backing or to records. I never brought her to my apartment. My

mother would have found reasons to rip Marlene apart, and I
didn't think I could stand that.

"Barry is awfully nice," Marlene commented offhandedly one
afternoon.

"He's terrific," I agreed. "Not only is he the best student and
the best athlete, it comes *easy* to him."

"I guess he's just lucky. I'll bet someday he'll be the first Jewish
president."

A few weeks later I saw Marlene and Barry huddling together
in the hall. They noticed me coming and jumped apart. Barry
said hello with false heartiness, and Marlene asked me—at this
tactically humiliating time—how my diet was progressing.

"I lost another five pounds." Actually I had gained. My pants
were slicing me around the waist and I found it murderously hard
to tuck my shirts in.

Barry grabbed me at football practice and asked if I minded his
taking Marlene out. "Really, Kareshape, if there's anything between you two, I'll step aside," he volunteered magnanimously.

Stop calling me "Kareshape."

"No, we're just friends," I assured him. I couldn't believe the
tears that were flooding my eyes. "Have to run."

I had never known such pain, not even when my father was
hitting me.

"The hell with you, Barry Smith," I muttered to myself in the
boy's bathroom, after my crying jag had subsided. "Someday *I'll*
be the first Jewish president."

Fat chance. Especially if Barry was my competitor.

Life has given me a few swift kicks, but sometimes it has delivered exciting, unexpected possibilities through the back door.
That year I was asked to run for school president. The kids who
nominated me were the outsiders—the "brains," the nonathletes,
the ones with enough individuality to reject clubs and cliques, or
were too old to be accepted by them. I was one of these. Because
I sang and clowned I had a high profile, but I never quite belonged.

The idea was scary but appealing. Still, I wasn't sure until

Barry informed me he was also planning to try for the honor.

"May the best man win," I said, grinning, surprising myself. I think he expected old Kareshape to automatically drop out and leave the arena clear. I still remember the funny tightening of his eyes, even though he pretended to smile.

Another thought intimidated me—the knowledge that my brother had been vice president of Madison four years earlier. I dreaded losing, of failing to meet Larry's standard.

I won't think that way, I decided. I'll plunge full steam ahead and battle Barry for every vote. From that minute on I was obsessed with the contest. I asked my supporters to write out Kasha for President pamphlets, and I devised a slogan (S.O.S.—Save Our School), which seemed suitably urgent. I had banners made and gave speeches, in the yard, the gym or in front of the water fountain. Inspiring names like Lincoln, Washington, and Roosevelt dominated my thoughts.

I never slept. By sixteen I was a full-fledged insomniac. Usually I crept into the kitchen and continued snacking. When I did briefly sink into sleep, images of myself trapped in a closet woke me up again. I became alert to the danger of that dream, an emotion phobic specialists of the 1980s refer to as "anticipatory anxiety." Sleep represented the terror of confinement; awake I could protect myself.

But I couldn't protect myself against Marlene's lack of belief. She caught up with me after chorus one day and said, "Don't feel bad if you lose, Al."

"I'm not losing," I swore. Her attitude made me push harder.

Barry hardly campaigned. His relaxed attitude infuriated me. He was still friendly, in a patronizing way, although his wisecracks ("Put on a few, didn't you?") were amiably wounding. He indicated that it was bad form to try so hard, vulgar to chase after approval.

Our principal announced the results on a football field. It was a drizzling, windy November day, and I had a cold.

"Treasurer...Barry Freed....Vice President...Richard 'Tiny' Levine...."

I was licked. All the officers belonged to Barry's contingent.

"President..." A momentary hesitation; the principal was clearly startled. "Alfred Jerome Kasha."

The field erupted into applause. I was so shocked and overjoyed that I didn't even mind the use of my hated middle name.

"Yea, Big Al," someone shouted. At first I winced, thinking that *big* meant "fat," but seconds later I recognized it as a compliment, an expression of admiration.

Miracles were possible!

"Thank you, God," I said under my breath.

I thought of Larry; his kid brother had carried the Kasha banner forward. And my parents—they'd have to admit their son had pulled off a remarkable feat.

Barry wandered unsteadily over to shake my hand. He looked bewildered, a damp and defeated Golden Boy who had aged before my eyes.

"Hey, you did it, Kare—" He stopped. "Kasha." His taut lips appeared to be framing the question: *Why?*

I understood then that rewards—a class presidency, any kind of success—only come about by relentless effort, sheer tenacity and struggle. Natural ability is just the first step.

I was transformed, for a few hours, into a Golden Boy myself. It was a short victory. Marlene, after bestowing a dry, congratulatory kiss on my cheek, walked off with Barry. I watched them disappear, arm in arm, leaving me alone on the now-empty football field.

4

The Brooklyn Beat

The royal rug of the presidency was pulled out from under me at the end of my junior year. In July, president Kasha became a busboy at the Karmel Hotel for the summer. Located in the Catskill Mountains, this Borscht Belt prison was owned by my Uncle Perry, my mother's youngest brother. Understaffed by any standard, the Karmel employed five busboys to service three hundred people. The pay amounted to slightly less than slave labor. Uncle Perry used to whip me into line by saying, "Working hard builds character."

I began the depressing process of building character every morning at 6:30. The five busboys shared one bunk. Standing under the shower was like being rained on by cubes of falling ice. From there the day slid downhill. My first responsibility was to cut up grapefruits; there were a minimum of two hundred to handle daily and I was less than graceful about it. My fingers would slip from the center of the grapefruit and I always wondered what the guests would say if they knew they were eating grapefruit covered all over by Al Kasha's finger.

Larry worked at the Karmel too. He held a higher position—waiter—and also staged a couple of amateur shows. He still enjoyed acting, but his ambition to become a director and producer had already flowered. The brilliance that later earned him a Tony was already in evidence.

Along with the other busboys, I was instructed to dance with the guests. These were usually older women, and it was unspoken but understood that they needed sexual attention during the week while their husbands worked in the hot city.

Many of the young Karmel employees were happy to oblige. I felt the same hammering lust they did, but I wanted something more: romance, love, a feeling of exclusivity. I still pined after Marlene. I even wrote her a letter but she never answered. The ultimate heartbreak occurred when her parents came up to spend three weeks at the Karmel and she didn't join them. "Marlene was supposed to come," her mother rattled on thoughtlessly, "but she didn't want to leave Barry. You know Barry, don't you Al?"

"Yes, I know Barry."

Rescue finally arrived in the form of a girl named Sarah, the baker's daughter. Sarah had heavy thighs and arms, but her generous breasts always appeared to be tipped in my direction and she had dazzling white teeth against a dark complexion. We blundered through sex and all I could think of was, "Well, I *did* it." Another milestone reached and not very exciting.

Still, women were willing to sleep with me even if I was chubby. Sarah and I had eating in common, of course (we gorged ourselves at every opportunity) and she shared my love of theater. On nights off we would roam from hotel to hotel, watching their shows and comparing them to what Larry was doing for the Karmel. I saw more bad musicians, klutzy comedians, tone-deaf singers, and wooden actors than I would have thought possible. I caught old-timers like Harry Richmond. Occasionally I was fortunate enough to catch great comedians like Red Buttons and Dick Van Dyke.

Sarah and I lasted four weeks into the summer. Love, or my frantic efforts to see it that way, ended when I passed a mirror in the hotel lobby. Sarah and I were both in bathing suits and we looked like twins: walking blobs of flesh holding hands. My curly hair and boyish grin looked as though they were welded to the body of a middle-aged man. Sarah's posture was bent, making her seem ten years older than her actual age, fifteen.

In typical extreme fashion (I never did anything halfway) I gave up eating. Grapefruit and coffee sustained me through the gruel-

40

ing hours, but I was determined to pass that lobby mirror on Labor Day and see a human being of normal proportions. Sarah
refused to diet. "I only need to lose five pounds," she protested. I
knew our togetherness would kill my discipline and tempt me
into old patterns.

Reluctantly I said goodbye to her.

That summer I also met a brash, energetic pianist named Jack
Keller. Jack was so hyperactive he made me look catatonic; his
mouth was always moving, his feet and hands competed for a
Nervous Tic award. He was a dreamer, like me, and we decided to
work together when the summer ended. Jack would be my accompanist and we'd "make some decent bread" (Jack's words)
doing weddings and dances until he got on his feet as a songwriter.

I didn't realize it then, but Jack was one of a group of Brooklyn
natives destined to make rock-and-roll history in the late 1950s
and early 1960s. All of them attended Madison or Lincoln High
and all lived within twenty blocks of each other. They included
Neil Sedaka, his partner Howie Greenfield, Barry Mann ("You
Lost That Lovin' Feelin' "), Mort Schuman ("Save the Last
Dance for Me," "Teenager in Love"), Neil Diamond, and Carole
King. In 1970, a trade paper claimed that the combination of
these Brooklyn-born composers (including me) accounted for the
sale of over 700 million records.

I still couldn't identify completely with Jack's passion for writing. Writing was the work of anonymous contributors, and I was
no shadow; I wanted to be seen and applauded because applause
was proof I existed. Direct acknowledgment and praise were necessities since I got neither at home.

By Labor Day I was thinner, thin enough to face the lobby mirror without flinching, but the pounds I had starved off slowly re-
appeared in October. By November they were all back. I was
ashamed of my nonexistent willpower, and when I spotted
Marlene on a street corner, I turned and walked the other way.

I had been a member of the Madison Chorus for three years
when I graduated in 1954. It was a school tradition to award
medals to its most outstanding members. Marlene got one. So

did a few other people whom I felt had average, even mediocre, voices. Yet Miss Stein, the grayish, spinsterish chorus teacher, saw fit to deny me the honor.

It was the day before graduation when I confronted her with the subject.

"I'm sorry, Al," she said, in a clipped voice. She had a thick Brooklyn accent and she affected a ludicrous, pseudo-British tone to disguise it. "I didn't feel your work merited an award."

"I sing better than anyone here." Shock had stripped away my usual modesty.

"You have a better *voice*," Miss Stein said. "But you've been fooling around too much. You've disrupted the class on *far* too many occasions."

"What does that have to do with my ability to sing?"

"Singing isn't everything."

"It is in a chorus. It's not fair."

I don't know why the medal meant so much. Maybe because my father had said, "I'll eat my hat if you ever make it. You're no singer."

"You have to learn to be part of an ensemble," Miss Stein continued. "And unfortunately, you're a show-off. You can't be better than a group if you're part of it. You have to blend in."

"How will I ever be noticed if I blend in?"

She shrugged, as if talking to an idiot.

Careful. Keep a lid on the anger.

My hands were sweating. The palpitations I dreaded were already galloping in my chest.

Be nice!

"I deserve that medal. And you know something else? In five years I'm going to be famous, more famous than anybody in this rotten chorus."

"Perhaps. If you learn discipline."

"I deserve that medal," I repeated.

In my frustration, I somehow hoped she would see the error of her ways and relent. She didn't. Shaken as she was, she stood her ground while I muttered "It's not fair" over and over again.

5

Forced to Leave Home

It was November, 1958, and my bed was shaking. I felt fear even through the smothering curtain of sleep. Sounds tore at my ears: the clanging radiator, my father's roaring voice through the paper-thin walls, my mother's whining pleas, "Irving, leave him alone."

"Get up, damn it," my father raged. "Get out of bed, you bum!"

I couldn't seem to rouse myself. The alarm clock on the table read 6:30.

"You think you can stay out all night," my father demanded, "drinking and whoring with your no-good friends?"

"I was working. Singing."

"Singing? That's what you call it, singing?"

Yes, I thought. Singing for pennies at the Harbor Club in Staten Island, sailing back and forth on a ferry with Jack and our drummer and guitarist, pounding out standards for disinterested customers who had come to see Desiree, the club's featured stripper.

I had gotten home after four, famished for sleep. Even the deafening sound of my father's snoring in the next room hadn't kept me up, as it usually did.

"You gonna wash the floors of the shop, big shot? Like you promised? *Big shot!*"

I buried my head in my pillow, unprepared for the bearded face,

43

the bloodshot eyes, the sickening breath that smelled, more than ever, like sweet and sour vomit.

"I'll come downstairs when I'm ready," I said. "Please..." always polite, even in jeopardy... "Please get out of my room for a minute."

"Your room? Who the hell pays for this room? For the food you eat? So you can waste time screwing around with your friends?"

I wanted to say: *I pay for this room. I pay for my food. I've been working since I was seven years old. As a delivery boy, a busboy. At eight I had a paper route. At ten...*

Be nice.

"I said *get out of bed!*"

My vision was still foggy, but I looked up in time to see a mop handle bearing down on me. My father had torn the mop portion off.

I jumped out of the way and the wood crashed into my yellow Emerson radio on the night table, cracking it in half.

It would have been my head.

He rushed toward the table that contained my records—a collection I treasured, with 78s by Perry Como, Frank Sinatra, Bing Crosby, Al Jolson, and some of the new songs that were beginning to gain popularity—songs from the rock-and-roll wave my parents and brother denounced as trash: "Don't Be Cruel" by Elvis Presley, whom I had added to my list of imitations; "Whole Lotta Shakin' Goin' On" by Jerry Lee Lewis.

He was picking them up, bending them in half like a circus strong man, shattering the 78s to bits.

It was, finally, enough.

The rage I reserved for the football field exploded. I slammed my father against the wall. More surprise than pain showed on his face.

"Alfred," my mother cried, "don't hit your father." Her voice was dim. My brain, in self-defense, had blotted out the incapacitating phrase, *Be nice.* I couldn't let him kill me.

But her cry had distracted me long enough to allow him to race to the kitchen and scoop a knife from the silverware drawer. He

44

came at me, grinning, chopping the air. The blade grazed my forehead.

I lunged, shoving him to the floor. The knife flew from his hand. We rolled around, pummeling each other. My youth, the years of suppressing hate for peace overwhelmed him. The wrestler from Poland was no match for twenty years of hate.

Blood squirted from his nose, and my fist kept hammering away. I felt something break. I wanted all his features to disintegrate in a sticky red pool. This time the police wouldn't have to come to protect me, to extricate me from an imprisoning closet. I could take care of myself.

He was stretched out on the floor, moaning, semi-conscious, when I fled. My mother called, "Alfred, stop, where are you going? Don't leave me here with him," but nothing could have stopped me. It was a bizarre scene; me racing down a Brooklyn street on a quiet Sunday morning, my mother running behind, sobbing, imploring. She must have known that unless she calmed me down, I would be gone forever.

The distance between us grew wider. Her words were swallowed up in the sound of cabs and buses. Soon I was on a subway, shaking as violently as the train itself as it bounced along aging tracks on the way to Manhattan.

I showed up at Larry's apartment an hour later. I couldn't think of anywhere else to go.

Two years before, Larry had finally taken his own place on West 58th Street. In that time he had gained a good reputation as a stage manager, and was currently stage managing the hit Johnny Mercer musical, *L'il Abner.*

When Larry answered and saw his bloodied brother in the hall, he turned white. I had no suitcases, but he knew instantly that his privacy was about to be invaded. A part of the Brooklyn nightmare he had struggled to escape was crashing in on his hard-won turf.

Because my brother was, and is, a sensitive, compassionate person, he disguised his shock and hugged me. But he was un-

45

changed in one respect: ever neat and meticulous, he made me shower before listening to my story.

The hot water soothed my cuts and bruises, and I explained everything rationally after putting on fresh clothes that Larry lent me.

Just like the old days, I thought, and Larry must have felt the same.

"It was just one of Daddy's drunken fits," said Larry. "He's probably forgotten all about it."

"Well, I haven't," I said. It struck me funny that Larry used the word *Daddy*.

"Where will you stay?"

"I thought..." *Okay, I'll ask...I'll swallow my pride.* "Here ...until I find a place to live."

I ached for a gesture from him. I wished he would welcome my presence.

"All right. For now."

In the next few days, my mother called repeatedly. She begged me to come back. "Your father is sorry," she said. "He loves you."

"No, Mom."

"L'Alfred, please!"

"*Alfred,* Mom." I held my ground, to the accompaniment of palpitations, rubbing my sweaty palms against the jeans I'd borrowed from my brother.

I wound up staying at West 58th Street for six months and then shuttled from one friend's apartment to the next. Couches became more familiar to me than beds. I dreamed of comfort and security but lived like a gypsy, finishing up at New York University, performing on weekends, trying to get a deal with a record company.

I also let my hair grow; I loved the curly feel of it against my neck. Never again, I vowed, would I let my father's razor come within a mile of me.

Armed with the optimism and innocence of nineteen, I set out to conquer the world of music. Life on 49th and Broadway had to be easier than the tension and tyranny of Avenue M.

My first rude awakening took place in front of the Brill Building, 1619 Broadway. The Brill Building housed the majority of important New York publishers and songwriters. When I first approached the entrance, I was assaulted by hostile, repeated screaming. Startled, I turned to face an unshaved hobo who continued to shout, "Drop dead....go to hell," amid obscene noises and gestures. Trembling, I escaped into the building.

Later on I learned that the middle-aged tramp with the empty shopping bag was known as Broadway Larry, and everyone had to duck past his hostile ravings whenever they entered the Brill.

I soon learned that Elvis Presley's music publishers, Hill and Range, were based in the Brill Building. Blues singers such as Chuck Berry and Muddy Waters were signed to a Brill Building publisher, Merrimac Music.

Shortly afterward I became familiar with the other half of the publishing/songwriting world across the street at 1650 Broadway. This building was the home of Don Kirshner, a boy genius who had already signed several of my Brooklyn classmates: Barry Mann, Neil Sedaka, Howie Greenfield, and Carole King.

Unfortunately he didn't sign me. He did, however, ask me to sit down and write a song for Connie Francis, then at her hottest. I felt encouraged, till I realized that every one of his writers was competing for the same session. That was Kirshner's method, to give all his staff writers an assignment, stir up fierce competition. A smash hit inevitably emerged.

Everyone remembers those days through a rosy, romantic haze. It's true we were all young, feverishly committed, and full of dreams; but the battles were emotionally wrenching. Jack Keller admitted, after the Brill Building days were over, that he suffered nightmares all the time, hearing the voice of Kirshner, the benevolent but driving father, pushing him to *produce*. And then the sense of loss, when "father" withdrew, and the singer-songwriter changed the course of the industry.

Meanwhile my masterpiece for Connie Francis, "Blue Tears," got lost in the shuffle.

The demonstration record I made didn't help either. I had recorded a piano-voice rendition that sounded empty next to the fully produced and orchestrated demos my rivals were making.

My brother lent me some money, following my guarantee that "Blue Tears" was perfect for Connie Francis and would be Number One. I guess my youthful fervor convinced him, or he was just being kind.

A year later, when I listened to "Blue Tears" again, I knew just how kind he had been.

By then my naiveté had faded, but not my optimism. I knew the joy of getting an "A" side, only to be told by the producer that the record "didn't turn out well; we're putting it in the can." Which meant permanently shelved.

I knew that forcing my way through a few doors and getting songs published was simply the first step in a long road toward making the charts.

Worst of all, I knew the feeling of getting on Billboard's Hot 100 (at number 99), staying there a second week, and falling off.

The publishers were a varied bunch. Some were heavy, with dark, intimidating cigars. Others wore custom-made suits and slicked their hair straight back. Some, or so went the whispers, were "mafioso"; others were gay. But they all, in the 1960s, had one thing in common: a sharp, nearly infallible song sense. They went out there and courted artists, wined and dined producers, did *anything* to get the record.

They also gave advances—usually $50.00—to free-lance writers when they liked a song. The advances were never enough to cover expenses but they kept me going.

I continued to move from one friend's place to another, intermittently returning to Larry. The money struggles were frustrating, but not as frustrating as the awareness of my contemporaries securing a firm hold on the charts. Barry Mann (who became my roommate for six months before marrying Cynthia Weil) already had "Who Put the Bomp," and Neil Sedaka was a success with "My Diary." Carole King and Gerry Goffin had electrified the industry with "Will You Love Me Tomorrow?"

The other side of the coin was equally disconcerting: observing those who tried and failed, who became waiters, clerks, bellhops, anything to stay in, to realize their dreams. Some were just a few years older than I, others were middle-aged, discouraged but persistent. They were the group who had had some success, but had been cheated of royalties. Or they were the "one-hit wonders," who never followed up after a chart bullseye. The ones who had had that taste, that isolated charge, that had sentenced them to a lifetime of effort and false hope.

As I plugged along, I was also unjustly deprived of royalties. On one occasion, I learned this through a secretary; but when I pressed a day later for more information, she turned white and said it was a "mistake." Her boss had obviously gotten to her.

I was too poor to involve a lawyer and incur legal fees, fees that would sap the royalties in question if I ever collected them.

In my lowest moments, I had nightmares that I would have to move back to Brooklyn or turn to my parents for money. I heard my father's voice, "You'll never make it," and wondered if he was right. Songs poured out, songs I rewrote endlessly and put on demos. With each one I thought, *This is it,* until the turndown a few weeks later.

"Not right for Connie."

"Dion's going in a different direction."

"The Shirelles don't want ballads, they want up-tempo songs."

I wrote with a dozen collaborators during this period, searching for that strange, indefinable chemistry that Goffin and King had, or Sedaka and Greenfield. It never seemed to happen.

Still, the occasional record was exciting, and the heated competition stirred up my creative juices. I learned to make polished demos, the kind Kirshner demanded from Barry, Neil, and the rest of his staff people. I would often sing lead and all the harmony parts; anything to save money, yet make a demo sound full on a miniscule budget. My skills as an impressionist helped too. I imitated artists such as Bobby Darin and Jackie Wilson, and they did the songs because they were so flattered by my imitations. Jackie Wilson's publisher, Arc-Merrimac, kept me busy writing for Jackie's dates.

Good fortune smiled when Roulette Records volunteered to produce four sides with me. The "A" side was a deathless item entitled "49 Jukeboxes," co-authored by Lee Morris of "Blue Velvet" fame.

"49 Jukeboxes" failed to enhance Morris's career or mine,

though it was picked by *Cashbox* and *Billboard*. Discriminating disc jockeys and record buyers were less impressed, and my name, Alfy Weatherbee, didn't help. It was the era of Buddys, Bobbys, and Frankies. Alfy seemed appropriate.

Personal appearances included Dick Clark's *American Bandstand*, and Roulette sent me on a tour with Jimmy Bowen (who had the hit, "I'm Stickin' With You"), Buddy Knox ("Party Doll"), and other lesser-known names like myself. The performing was fun, the interludes between shows boring. Some performers plugged up the gaps with gambling, drinking, drugs. Even then hotel rooms were being wrecked, vicious arguments would erupt among group members due to tension and lack of sleep.

I never drank; I think I feared the loss of control. I did, however, fall into my familiar role of listening to the problems of other singers and musicians. Listening to others' problems eased the isolation, made me feel useful and made me more comfortable about refusing the sensual temptations constantly being tossed my way.

I tried to help junkies and alcoholics, sometimes holding their hands for hours. Often I dried their tears. I had no formal speeches or advice to give them; but even "winging it," I instinctively knew what to say to bring temporary comfort. Occasionally their anger would spill out, even at me; and I would do what I could to give them a sense of worth, a sense that life still held good things if they kept trying.

Extending to people what I had always yearned for—a loving and supportive parent—bolstered my own sense of self-worth. By becoming a parent to those in need I became, in a sense, my own parent—what the organization for recovered alcoholics and their families, Al-Anon, refers to as "parenting yourself."

Dealing with alcoholics presented a challenge. I thought of my father, especially when a twenty-year-old bass player admitted that he often got drunk and beat his wife. My first impulse was to lash out, to scream: "Do you know what you're doing? Do you know the pain you're inflicting on your family?" I sat rigid, bit my tongue, and held my temper in. It was important to understand the bass player's suffering, important to project into his troubled soul and glimpse the self-hatred and guilt.

A drummer with a group called "The Hollywood Flames" dubbed me Preacher. A black background singer tagged me Father Al and the name stuck.

Father Al and only twenty-one years old!

Somehow I earned enough money to keep going. I worked on weekends as an impressionist when the "49 Jukeboxes" tour ended. Jack Keller and I continued to entertain at Jewish community affairs, and I was paid minimal wages to cut demos of songs Barton Music published, written by other people.

A follow-up record was released, "String Along with Pearl". No one strung along with Alfy on that one either.

When I met Jean O'Hara she was thirty-two, ten years older than I was. She worked as a secretary at Warner Brothers and was sympathetic to my struggles. Her eyes were pale blue with premature lines underneath them, the result of too many late nights. Jean lived on Central Park West with her sister Harriett.

This was during a period when I had run out of couches and was back with Larry. I confided my frustration that I had no place to live.

"Why not move in with me for a while?" Jean offered. She said it casually, making it simple for me to accept or reject the invitation.

I didn't know what I felt about Jean, beyond a strong physical attraction; but I said yes.

The situation made me feel daring and excitingly grown-up. I was sleeping with a much-older woman. Not only that, but her sister had a fondness for black musicians, and she lived, on and off, with two—Joe Jones, a drummer with Count Basie's band, and Howard McGee, a jazz trumpet player. (I never met their other sister, a nun.)

Howard quickly became my friend. He had faced a lifetime of hard knocks, including an addiction to heroin, and evolved a philosophy that helped him to cope.

"You know, Al," he once said, as we stood in front of our fifth-floor window overlooking the park. "I'm a black man. I've been on heroin. I've been higher than a bird, lower than any gutter. But see those buildings?" His long, dark finger indicated a high-rise in the distance. "A lot of buildings are being torn down, sure, but remember, a lot of new ones keep going up."

The optimistic truth of that statement, its positiveness in the face of Howard's misspent life, gave me a fresh charge of hope. So what if I'd had a couple of bomb records? I was only twenty-one; I had no right to feel discouraged.

I also identified with Howard's other statement: "You know why black people sing so loud in church? 'Cause they're afraid the Lord ain't hearin' them."

Except that Howard believed the Lord *was* hearing him. "Jesus is always there," he said, and when he spoke a light seemed to erase the lines of pain and hard living that creased his face.

Howard's belief in Jesus, in view of his troubles, amazed me. He made God sound like his best friend, someone loving and ever-present. I had always thought of God as caring, but far out of reach, not someone I could touch.

My friendship with Howard reinforced a feeling I'd always had, of being completely at ease with black people. I had none of my father's bigotry. Black people possessed a marvelous freedom, an unself-conscious, pulsating energy and passion that was appealing to a Jewish boy whose stomach had been tied up in knots all his life. They laughed easily; expressed emotions with spontaneity. They appeared to be more comfortable with sex than any of my Jewish friends.

Including me. I felt guilty every time Jean and I made love. I knew I didn't really want to. A stubborn romantic streak in me rebelled at the looseness, the lack of commitment. The lack, fundamentally, of real caring.

But I thought: *I should* find this exciting. *I want to be "in," "cool," "with it."* My friends would have laughed at me for the old-fashioned thoughts I was having. They already laughed at me when I didn't get drunk or try the numerous drugs that were always being passed around.

Jean laughed too at the discomfort I occasionally showed about our living arrangement. "Forget what you see in Disney movies," she said. "This is real life."

52

I went along, uneasily. The best part of the whole setup continued to be my talks with Howard. He opened my eyes to great black entertainers: the silky magic of Sam Cooke, the wit of Chuck Berry, the pounding piano of Fats Domino. I still played soundtracks of *My Fair Lady* and *West Side Story*, still worshiped Rodgers and Hammerstein (quietly). Jean hated their squeaky-clean *shmaltz*, but I was learning that an affection for one kind of music didn't preclude appreciating another.

I was embarking, at last, on the one, consistent, never-ending love affair of my life: writing. I still clung to dreams of singing stardom, but they were beginning to recede. I was overcome with a need to convey everything I felt and saw—the beauty and ugliness, the loneliness and hope, all shadings of human feeling. My own emotions followed a roller-coaster course, up and down, unable to settle on anything; but the ride was exhilarating and I yearned to give it creative shape.

Howard introduced me to a highly respected black writer, Luther Dixon. Luther had written "Sixteen Candles" and "Why Baby Why" and had a golden commercial touch. A few of our songs got recorded immediately. None were hits, but I felt sure I was on the verge of a breakthrough.

Luther took me to Adam Clayton Powell's Abyssinian Church in Harlem. It was my first exposure to a church that seemed to rock with a passion for God, a passion that rose from stamping feet, clapping hands, and voices raised straight to heaven. The pianist wasn't reproducing hymns, he was making an urgent personal statement, a statement taken up by the men, women, and children who sang their souls out. "Thank You, Jesus, thank You, Father, thank You," the voices cried in frenzied unison. I felt, for that moment, part of something much bigger than I had ever known.

They sang a hymn "Standing in the Need of a Prayer." I was so mesmerized by the melody that I put my own lyrics to it, "Sing and Tell the Blues So Long." When Jackie Wilson later recorded it, I felt no guilt about the secular rewrite. It was a joyous tune that could move people, make them feel good, and give them a sense of belief in the future.

Luther and the promise of songwriting success carried me

through my next personal crisis. Jean and I met, at her insistence, in front of Jack Dempsey's Restaurant on 49th Street, and she told me I would have to move out. "I'm older than you," she said, her lined, blue-gray eyes apologetic. But I knew better; Howard had tipped me off that Jean was now involved with a black bass player.

I didn't see Howard for a year. When I ran into him, he admitted that he had gone back on heroin, then kicked it again. "Remember the new buildings," he reminded me, hugging me with gruff, reassuring warmth.

I worked feverishly. Luther was hard to pin down; he was an undisciplined genius and only wrote when he got "the mood," usually at two or three in the morning. I kept after him, more aware than ever that my Brooklyn friends had the charts almost sewn up. Neil and Barry were now taking turns at Number One. Even my old Catskills buddy, Jack Keller, had a hit, "Just Between You and Me," by the Chordettes.

I couldn't fall behind.

PART II

"ACHIEVE! ACHIEVE!"

6

Negative Voices

Happiness is a mystery, a kind of optimistic, untroubled state that springs from a healthy self-image. If you feel you *deserve* happiness, you'll stand a much better chance of being happy. Otherwise you'll twist even good things into negatives so you can suffer.

If someone had said to me in 1960 that I wanted to suffer, I'd have stared at them uncomprehendingly. Hadn't I suffered enough? I'd paid my dues with an unstable childhood. I'd grown up in poverty. From now on, all I wanted was harmony and peace.

For all my self-analyzing, it didn't occur to me that I felt unworthy, that I deliberately set out to wreck any harmony and peace that came my way. In work I suffered because I never felt I was doing enough, even when I hit a lucky streak. In relationships I zeroed in on the most unsuitable, unavailable women, women who could be relied upon to disrupt my life.

My tendency in that direction reached its height when I met my first wife, Felicia.

Felicia was eighteen at the time; I was twenty-two. Attractive, blonde, a cross between actresses Nina Foch and Susan Oliver, she was bright and opinionated. She was also dating my friend Noel Goldstein.

Noel was, like Barry, slim and handsome, another Boy-Most-Likely-to-Succeed. I was flattered that Felicia seemed to prefer me. Unlike Marlene, she was choosing the underdog. I was still chubby, still alternating between crash diets (accompanied by excessive pill taking) and middle-of-the-night ice cream snacks.

On our second date, we went to the Avalon Theater in Brooklyn to see Rita Hayworth's *The Story on Page One*. A song of Luther's and mine, "Irresistible You," was climbing the charts with Bobby Darin, and we talked a great deal about my musical ambitions. A top publisher, Merrimac Music (managers of Jackie Wilson) wanted to sign me to a writer's contract. I was gratified that Felicia seemed to take joy in my success.

We became lovers that night.

Maybe the relationship could have developed into something meaningful and lasting. As it turned out, her mother called only weeks later. When I said hello, there was a silence, followed by three angry words:

"Felicia is pregnant."

It's strange; I didn't lash out, didn't fight back. I accepted the situation as my due. It didn't matter that Felicia was little more than a stranger. It didn't matter that the freedom I had finally tasted, away from the constricting controls of my parents, was about to be stolen. I experienced the calmness of a man on his way to the electric chair.

The calm lasted about a day, then yielded to panic. How could I saddle myself with a wife, a woman I barely knew, and a child? I was almost broke; record royalties for "Irresistible You" wouldn't be coming in for another nine months to a year. The Merrimac contract might mean future security, but I had no guarantee my option would be picked up after the first year. I was twenty-two years old, in a notoriously insecure business.

But there it was: I wanted to do the right thing.

We decided to be married secretly, so my parents would have adequate time to accept the decision. In February we would dance through the ritual of a large wedding at the New York Hotel on 34th Street. Despite everything they had done, I was afraid of displeasing my parents. Getting married young was bad enough, from my mother's point of view: doing it without any interval of preparation, without a formal wedding, would have been a heinous crime.

Ironically a month after our secret wedding, Felicia suffered a miscarriage.

Plans moved ahead for our second ceremony, even though my mother received an anonymous note, informing her that Felicia and I were already married. She was enraged and hurt. And for once my parents were united in an emotion: their anger toward me.

I never found out who sent the note. It was pieced together with letters from a newspaper. When bitterness began to overwhelm our marriage, I speculated that Felicia might have done it.

In any case, it was a bad start. The wedding was a disaster. My mother wore a heartbroken expression throughout (clearly shown in the family snapshots). She later admitted that the marriage "nearly killed her." Felicia's parents regarded me as a villain for what I had done to their daughter.

Pictures of me reveal an unsmiling, heavyset groom. They don't reveal panic symptoms that were now becoming familiar; shortness of breath, drenched palms, and an overwhelming urge to hide. The previous night, after lying dormant for years, my closet nightmare had returned. But this time I was bigger, and my body had become wedged between the walls of the closet. Movement became impossible, until the only recourse was to beat my head against the door, smashing my skull.

My father's insistence on cutting my hair for the wedding was another bad omen; it brought back the bar mitzvah. "Promise you won't make it too short," I had said, but he scalped me, probably in revenge for growing long hair as soon as I was free of him. "See, Rose?" he said, pointing with pride to my shorn skull, as if to announce, "They're *my* sons too!"

The only saving grace was Jackie Wilson, whom I had come to know as a friend. Jackie volunteered to sing, and his touching rendition of "Danny Boy" moved nearly everyone to tears. Everyone, of course, except my father, who wondered loudly, "What's that *schvartze* doing here?"

"Daddy, that's a famous star. That's Jackie Wilson," I said, trying desperately to shut him up.

"He's still a black man."

"Daddy!"

"He's a *schvartze.*"

When they were introduced, he crushed Jackie's knuckles. Jackie didn't flinch; his expression remained polite, but he squeezed my father's fingers with answering tightness. I saw those drink-reddened eyes widen with shock.

I held my breath. My father was competing, applying more pressure. Jackie grinned. What my father didn't know was that Jackie had once been a Golden Gloves champ and his grip was still powerful.

"You're wearing a Jewish star. Why?"

"Because I'm Jewish," said Jackie.

"You're Jewish? A *schvartze?* Jewish?"

"My dad's a rabbi."

"*Ha!*"

"Irving," my mother said, pulling him away. I noticed him moving his fingers and wincing; Jackie had hurt him.

"I'm sorry," I said to Jackie. "When he gets drunk..."

"It's okay, man. I understand."

I wished *I* did.

The pattern of my married life can best be expressed by mentioning the movie Felicia and I went to see on our wedding night.

Psycho.

Felicia and I tried to make a go of a difficult situation. We found an apartment on Central Park West and her parents, reconciled now to our marriage, helped with the down payment. I had a record in the Top 10 with Jackie, "My Empty Arms," co-written with Hank Hunter.

I was still trying to be a singer, so when Jackie went on tour and asked me to be part of the performing package, I jumped at the chance. I hadn't forgotten my distaste for the road, but it meant freedom, a chance to think about my marriage, to sort it out.

I enjoyed touring more this time, principally because Jackie was the headliner. I was his greatest fan; I worshiped his talent. In my opinion, no one has ever had the charisma, the energy, the sheer, unrestrained magnetism that Jackie had on stage. (Michael Jackson today credits Wilson as his greatest influence.) Women went into hysterics. His teenage experience as a boxer accounted for his aggressive grace and body language and breathtaking agility while dancing. He projected raw sex and high spirits.

Most of all, though, he had a fantastic vocal instrument, a voice that encompassed operatic notes and rhythmic curls with equal ease. I felt an incredible pride that this rock-and-roll great was doing my songs. Until then his hits had been penned by Berry Gordy ("Lonely Teardrops", "That's Why"); but Gordy, following a run-in with Jackie's manager, had left the office. Shortly after, Gordy established Motown Records. Jackie always spoke of Gordy's songwriting talent with awe, and I felt privileged to follow in his footsteps.

Jackie's Judaism gave us a basic bond. We spent endless hours talking about faith, about the need for a spiritual anchor. We agreed that God provided a balance against the shabby underside of show business: disloyal co-workers, thieving managers and publishers, hangers-on, record company prejudice. Prayer was a vital protection, and whenever we could, we'd pray or go to a synagogue. We also went to movies, concerts, and prizefights; we met after shows and took walks to unwind. Jackie was warm, considerate, and loving; but his personal excesses warred with the spiritual side of his nature.

In February, 1961, his womanizing backfired when a twenty-eight-year-old black woman showed up at his 57th Street apartment and tried to persuade him to make love to her. He refused and she pulled out a gun. In the ensuing struggle, Jackie was shot and seriously wounded. Luckily, since he was bleeding profusely, his apartment was only a block from Roosevelt Hospital. The quick availability of medical help saved his life.

I went to the hospital and tried to offer words of encouragement. I even prayed for him, though I was still self-conscious about it, still searching for rules, for the proper "exact" mode of expression. I didn't know, yet, that prayer has no rules—except that you say what you truly feel, what is in your heart. But Jackie thanked me and said it helped.

Gene Goodman was also at his bedside, and in typical publisher fashion, he said, "Okay, we need a song to bring Jackie back. Got any ideas?"

I went home and wrote "I'm Comin' on Back to You," which Jackie cut as soon as he was out of the hospital. It became a Top 10 record, and he was bigger than ever.

I doubt if Jackie ever found personal peace. At that time, the early 1960s, I didn't think I ever would either. I worried incessantly: Would the hit records stop? Would I ever have a hit as a singer? Would my parents and brother approve? Would I ever make a success of my marriage?

Keep trying. Run faster. Outrace the negative voices.

In early 1962, I became friendly with a gregarious, outgoing music publisher I'll call Carl. I knew Carl was married, but few people had ever met his wife and no one mentioned her. There seemed to be an unspoken agreement to omit her name from any conversation.

My curiosity prompted me to ask around. I learned that the missing wife never left her home. She had, in fact, existed in self-imposed isolation for twelve years. Nothing could wrench her from the safety of her three-room harbor.

"I've heard of *house*wives," one friend of mine joked, "but this is carrying it too far." The attitudes varied from "she must be crazy" and "maybe she's a phantom" to "I'll bet old Carl keeps her tied up." Nobody demonstrated any compassion for a human being so troubled that she lacked the courage to walk in the street.

I remember feeling a shiver of empathy. I had no idea why at the time. It was my first brush with agoraphobia, and I experienced a wave of fear and a desire to shut the situation out of my mind.

To combat my mysterious, unaccountable reaction, I decided to drop in on Carl one Saturday. I located his apartment on West End Avenue and pushed the downstairs buzzer.

"Hello?" A high-pitched, tremulous voice fluttered through the intercom. "Who is it?"

"Al Kasha. Is Carl there?"

"No." She sounded frightened.

"Could I..." But before I finished, she cut off. I was reluctant to leave. Just then, a tenant came down and the door swung open. I hurried inside and climbed three flights of stairs to Carl's apartment.

I rang the bell. The same muffled, bird-like voice greeted me from behind a thick, discolored door.

"This is Al Kasha," I said. "I'm a friend of Carl's."

"Please go away," the woman begged. "Carl will be home later. *Please.*"

"I'd like to talk to you." The compulsion to help pushed me on, even though I felt guilty about alarming her and invading her territory.

"I'll call the police." Her words were bold, but the pitiful tone stayed the same. "I'll call the police right now." She began to dial.

I had no choice but to leave.

Instinctively I understood her dread of leaving the apartment. I was already beginning to suffer similar feelings. Even then, I picked places where I could be comfortable, and nothing could pry me from them. When I met with writing collaborators, I fought to arrange the sessions on my turf. Once I'd chosen a re-laxed place I conducted business there, ate there, stayed there un-til late at night. The New York streets were suddenly threatening, and sometimes I took cabs to avoid walking a few blocks to my house.

Impatience—anxiety—in restaurants began to surface and I hurried through meals, or asked for the check before my main course was half finished. I claimed to hate dessert (although I ate compulsively at home) so I could leave quickly.

These phobic feelings were inconsistent in my twenties. Some-times they would loom up with terrifying power, other times they diminished and disappeared. The same syndrome that made it impossible for me to sleep (anticipatory anxiety) now ruled my waking life. I avoided situations that *might* prove threatening: ele-vators, crowded supermarkets. I could control what happened to me on my own ground, nowhere else.

Felicia's possessiveness aggravated the tension. The more I

clung to the life raft of workaholism, the harder she held on. Looking back, I can't blame her. I was an inattentive husband, verbally and physically. We never touched. I retreated into my private thoughts, and she criticized and needled me to make contact.

Under happier circumstances, she might have been an invaluable help in my struggle, if I had only let her in. But I couldn't.

I followed trends, seeking to learn, to find a "handle," a permanent answer that would guarantee continued success. I saw Bob Dylan in his early days at Gerde's Folk City in Greenwich Village. His voice and appearance were odd, but I recognized something brilliant and innovative in his music. I had an open mind to folk (as symbolized by the Kingston Trio), tearful Connie Francis rock ("My Heart Has a Mind of Its Own", written by Jack Keller and Howie Greenfield), and of course, the R & B represented by Jackie, Brook Benton, Hank Ballard, and Jerry Butler.

Records were also an effective way of maintaining marital peace. The constant blast of music in our apartment prevented hostile confrontations. In its absence, TV took over.

7

Up the CBS Ladder

My career continued on an upward curve. Columbia Records (influenced by a recommendation from my friend George Alpert, owner of *Cashbox* magazine) asked me to sign as a staff producer. They had heard, and been impressed, by demos I'd produced for Merrimac, as well as my hit recordings. It was an incredible plum for an inexperienced twenty-three-year-old.

"Don't do it!"

The lone, dissenting voice came from Phil Spector, a musical legend as writer and producer, later to be dubbed by Thomas Wolfe as "the tycoon of teen."

"It'll ruin you. *Rock-and-roll is rhythm and blues*. It's what you've been doing with Jackie Wilson. Not 'Sing Along with Mitch' and all that junk. CBS is white man's land. That's not rock music."

I didn't take him seriously for a minute, not even when Mitch Miller himself said, "These rock-and-roll kids are the worst. If I have to record people who sing no better than the kid next door, I don't want to record *anybody*. Vic Damone and Tony Bennett—now *they* can sing."

CBS, whatever the drawbacks, was power, prestige, a lucrative salary. And I couldn't help thinking: Larry would approve of this. He would be proud of me.

My father said, "Are you sure they mean it?" and my mother cautioned me not to "upset anybody. Just be nice, do your work and stay out of people's way."

I was given Steve Lawrence and Eydie Gorme to produce. Both were initially reluctant to work with "that kid" but they finally consented. I turned to old friends Carole King and Gerry Goffin, and they came through with "Go Away, Little Girl" for Steve. Barry Mann and Cynthia Weil submitted another smash, "Blame It on the Bossa Nova," for Eydie.

During this period I socialized constantly with both couples. We all had an overriding drive in common. I filled them in on my daily activities, letting them know which artists were available.

Sometimes, though not often in those pre-singer/songwriter days, an artist wrote for himself. Neil Diamond was an example. I produced Neil's first record, "Clown Town." His voice was a strikingly individual instrument; it had a highly charged, compelling timbre that conveyed both sexuality and emotion.

Neil and Columbia parted shortly afterward, but years later, in one of the typical ironies of show business, they re-signed him for six million dollars.

I also became a big fan of another Columbia artist, Bob Dylan. The company wanted to drop Dylan. His first album had sold a paltry four thousand copies.

"He doesn't have a great voice," said one executive.

"Forget his voice," I said. "Listen to those *songs*. He's going to be the biggest writer in the country someday." I later learned my intervention was a factor in their decision to keep Dylan on the Columbia roster.

The label *did* believe in Aretha Franklin, but they saw her as an elegant, sophisticated Nancy Wilson type. When Aretha's producer and discoverer, John Hammond, fell ill, she was placed in my hands.

I thought of Phil Spector's warning: *"It's white man's land."* Funky rhythm and blues material was out of the question. Yet the songs had to be exciting, they had to showcase her animal energy and strength.

The answer presented itself when I saw her perform "Rock a Bye Your Baby" at the Village Vanguard in Greenwich Village. Her father, Reverend C. L. Franklin, a giant on the gospel circuit and later a Chess recording star, had always encouraged Aretha's ambitions; and he involved himself strongly in the selection of her material. I found myself sweating when he stared piercingly in my direction and asked, "What do you think of that?"

The song was an oddball by commercial standards. I felt the Reverend's eyes measuring me, but I said, "I think it ought to be her next record."

The man whose powerful voice could explode a church shook my hand heartily and said, "Good for you."

My boss, Dave Kapralik, didn't see it the Reverend's way. He was apoplectic. "A *black* singer, and you cut her on an Al Jolson song!"

Trembling inside, I stuck to my guns. "I think it's a hit."

"It had better be—or it's your job."

"Rock a Bye Your Baby" was the first major success of Aretha Franklin's recording career, and the only Top 40 single she had with Columbia before her string of successes on Atlantic. The song had a basic power, enabling her to release the drive that had been hidden under ornate arrangements and timid, bland melodies.

Aretha also cut a song of mine that became a Number One R & B hit, "Operation Heartbreak." The song reflected my personal tensions at the time, and Aretha captured all the pain I had felt while writing it.

What I observed in Aretha was the split that can exist in a performer's personality. Offstage she was, by her own admission, "shy"; but a wild, unrestrained quality surfaced in front of audiences. Any fears she had melted away.

Watching Aretha made me long for the release I had experienced while touring with Jackie. Without the outlet of performing, all my tensions went unreleased, turning back inside myself.

I tried to learn from everyone. The journey took me from the hard-hitting world of Aretha and Reverend Franklin to the studied elegance of CBS Records president Goddard Lieberson. I took note of his polished, sophisticated style, his custom-made suits, the fine wines he drank.

I never found him alone in his office; a tailor would be constantly in attendance, altering a jacket or a pair of pants. Lieberson had a satiric way of making his importance known: "All great men are dead, and I'm feeling a little sickly myself" was a typical remark.

Lieberson defined rock as "pre-puberty singers singing about post-puberty problems." But he was a man of artistic taste and vision. He signed Barbra Streisand against the advice of those who thought her uncommercial.

I knew Barbra slightly because my brother was the associate director of *Funny Girl*. I had attended some *Funny Girl* rehearsals, and I knew her relentless quest for perfection. I dropped by one of her recording dates and saw the same quality emerge.

"It's not *there*," she repeated. The arranger kept changing notes, switching unisons to harmonies and back again.

"What do you think, Al?" she asked suddenly. "Which take was better, the last one or the one before?"

I volunteered an opinion. "Maybe," was her reply. "But I want to play them back one more time."

Some of the musicians were intimidated, obviously impatient. I knew how grueling her perfectionist tendencies were, but I couldn't fault her. In the end the albums she did were brilliant, and that was all that counted.

I cut a Number One album, "Winners," with Steve. Driven on by my own standards, and further influenced by Barbra's unwavering intensity, I worked all night and returned to the studio at eight in the morning. Felicia complained bitterly that she never saw me.

Overdubbing, mixing, listening again and again—I don't know how I found the energy. I heard my mother's voice, "Remember, Alfred, a man is nothing if he's not a success." The phrase, *You're nothing, You're nothing*, beat like a drum in my head.

It wasn't enough to have a hit. As Lionel Richie put it, years later: "Say I've come off a big album; the new one I'm cutting now has to be just as good. And I have to write the next one and make sure that's as strong as the first two."

Engineer Roy Hallee (later producer of Simon and Garfunkel) would listen as I muttered: "Not enough bass, not enough drum, too much piano." Finally, at five in the morning, he would comment, "I thought I was bad, but you're insane."

Gratification came when "Go Away, Little Girl" hit Number One and "Blame It on the Bossa Nova" was Number Five the same week. A call from Quincy Jones also buoyed my spirits. Quincy, a superb arranger and producer, had a fantastic ear; and when he had difficulty identifying the instrumental sound used on "Go Away, Little Girl," I felt I had accomplished something innovative and unusual. The instrument was actually Steve's whistle, speeded up.

My brother took my parents and me to Sardi's for a celebration. I was rattling on, permitting my elation to pour over. For once my psychological boxing gloves weren't on, so I was unprotected when my mother asked, "I know you have all these hits, but do they like you? Do they really like you, L'Alfred?"

"*Alfred*, Mom."

In retrospect the question seems silly, too silly to dwell upon, but it filled me with fear.

BE NICE.

"Of course they like me," I said. But I wasn't sure they really did—as if it mattered. The chain reaction of doubts began: Do they respect me? Do they know how much I contributed? Would they want to work with me again?

I coped with the dinner by having four portions of ice cream. When I got home, I spent the whole night throwing up.

In late 1962, I spent an evening with a woman who was to alter the course of my life. The evening was a brief, memorable ray of sunshine in the growing darkness of those anxious days.

Her name was Ceil, and she worked for a publishing firm called Shapiro Bernstein. Ceil was officially a secretary, but her boss (Leon Brettler, who ran the company) relied on her opinions about music and people. She possessed a rare, instinctive understanding of both. Her musical taste ran toward exciting, dance-oriented tunes, especially with a Latin flavor; she was a regular at the Palladium during the Tito Puente era. But she knew what was commercially strong, whether it came in the shape of "Twist

69

and Shout" by the Isley Brothers, or "Roses Are Red" by Bobby Vinton.

Ceil always made me think of Gittel in *Two for the Seesaw*. She was small, with dark, beautiful eyes and a sparkling smile. Her slender, dancer-type body was always in motion, and even though she parted her dark hair conservatively in the middle, her fiery, expansive gestures and lusty laughter suggested a free spirit.

I had talked to her on the phone many times, asking her to send Shapiro Bernstein material over to CBS for Steve and Eydie. I found myself calling more often than professionally necessary, and somehow I managed to invite her out to dinner.

We talked and talked, our conversation broken only once when Ceil stared in horror as I poured ketchup on my steak. In those years I poured ketchup on everything but ice cream.

Manhattan seemed intensely alive that night. The crowds, the lights, the towering buildings, briefly became visions of promise, beautiful and beckoning and safe. I didn't think about running home, hiding, sneaking back into the cocoon of my office at CBS. I remember noticing a theater where *The Days of Wine and Roses* was playing. I had suggested a movie earlier, and that was one I wanted to see (I was drawn to all movies about alcoholics) but I steered us past it. Our togetherness was too precious to be interrupted.

And I talked about myself, my home life, my marriage, my frustrations. I didn't feel the need, for once, to come on as a confident, all-knowing parental figure. I opened up, fearlessly, astonished that I was doing it.

We were walking by the East River when I said suddenly, "I wonder how God makes sense of it all."

"But he does," Ceil responded with conviction. She took my hand. It was a gesture of warm, basic connection, the touch of a friend. But it was more. Her firm, spontaneous touch triggered off a hope I had hidden under my fanatic work drive. Her gesture suggested what was possible, the kind of love between a man and a woman I had yet to experience.

The water looked cold and black in the November night.

"I pray and He always hears me," Ceil said simply.

Did he, I wondered? Ceil had suffered through a disastrous automobile accident earlier in the year, followed by a six-month hospitalization. Yet her attitude remained positive.

When I mentioned the accident, she said, "I lived, didn't I?"

As always, her thinking was clear and honest. "God was watching over me. By all rights I should have died. But here I am."

"I'm glad," I told her. I was filled with happiness as we stood together, the wind from the river blowing away all confusion within.

We both knew something special had happened, some line had been crossed; but Ceil finally said, "I can't see you anymore, you know. You're a married man."

Not really.

"I wouldn't feel right, seeing a married man."

"Okay, then." I squeezed her hand. "But let's not leave here for another few minutes."

She nodded, smiled, and kissed me.

The hits continued: "Poor Little Rich Girl" for Steve, "Don't Try to Fight It, Baby," for Eydie, a duet for both of them, "I Can't Stop Talking About You."

With so much chart action, it was a perfect time to strike out on my own and start a production company. It was also time to embark on a new and separate life. Felicia and I tried our best to move closer, without success.

I packed and drove away in the spring of 1963.

Our final clash took place at Associated Studios on West Seventh Avenue. I was doing a few sides with myself as the artist, songs written by Bacharach and David; I still wanted that elusive hit as a singer.

Charlie Calello, responsible for orchestrating the Four Seasons' records, was doing my arrangements.

I was in the middle of a take when I noticed Felicia walk into the control booth. I flubbed a note and did it again. No luck. The next take was even worse.

Felicia waved at me. I couldn't go on until I found out what she wanted.

What she wanted was a reconciliation. "You've got to come

71

back," she insisted. "You've got to. You don't answer your phone…you won't take my calls. You can't treat me this way."

Why, I wondered, was she so anxious to hang on to something we both knew was a terrible mistake? Pride? A sense of failure?

8

Please, God, Let Me Sleep

We don't love each other, I wanted to say. *We never did.*

I pulled her into a small office packed with crates and boxes of tape.

"I demand that you come back," Felicia said.

The word *demand* gave me the strength to stand firm. "No."

Suddenly she slapped me.

I stumbled backward, upsetting a row of cartons. Several of them flew off the shelves. Boxes opened and tape unraveled at our feet. Charlie dashed in, followed by one of the secretaries.

"Everything okay?" the secretary asked.

Neither of us spoke. Felicia stared at me, as if to say: *All right, it's enough. Now come home with me.*

She knew how much I wanted peace, how much I strained to "be nice."

I didn't move.

"Hey, man, we'd better get back inside," Charlie said. "I've got to let the band go in twenty minutes."

Felicia stared rigidly as I began to follow him.

"You haven't heard the last of this," she threatened, edging toward the exit. "You'll be sorry. I'll make you sorry. I swear it."

I felt sweat trickling from under my arms, even though the studio was ice cold from air conditioning.

"Man, you should have let her have it," said Gary, the engineer. "If it was me, I'd have killed her."

73

I knew Gary was all talk, but I had my father's crazy Polish temper. It was a part of me I rejected, a part I associated with everything animal and low-class. But it was there.

I managed a feeble, "It doesn't matter," till my throat closed, strangling off the words. I mumbled an excuse and headed for the men's room. It was empty. I turned on the cold water and splashed it against my face. The water spurted loudly from the tap, but it was drowned out by my crashing heartbeat. The walls of the bathroom began to contract; my vision blurred. The echo of my screams nearly exploded my skull, caged and desperate, though I knew no sound was coming from my lips. I had to control the panic, control the senseless, hammering demons that were taking possession of my body and brain.

Finally the shattering heartbeats calmed, and there was an eerie, unnatural quiet, broken only by running water. I groped for the sink and turned the faucet off, grateful to be alive.

During 1964 my dependence on diet pills increased. My weight continued to fluctuate, dropping dramatically, then bursting back up. At night I relied on Valium to soothe the hyperactivity the diet pills caused. Insomnia, always bad, continued to plague me. My mind chugged through the long hours between midnight and morning:

> *I've got to make it big.*
> *I've got to get over the top.*
> *If I just make it, I can sleep.*
> *Please, God, let me sleep.*

I increased the dosage from thirty to forty milligrams, and soon that wasn't enough.

I *had* to sleep, because if I didn't, I couldn't maintain my non-stop working regimen. I couldn't satisfy the never-ending, now-internalized demands of Rose Kasha.

Don't worry, I reassured myself. *Everybody I know is on diet pills. Everyone I know takes Valium. They're harmless.*

An actor I knew observed, "Look, it's practically a status symbol. What red-blooded guy doesn't take *something*!"

74

My most creative experience during this time centered around Rodney Dangerfield. I first became aware of Rodney through my friend Herb Gluck. Herb had seen Rodney in the Catskill Mountains and felt he had untapped ability.

I respected Herb's judgment. As proved later by his best-selling biography, *The Mick*, Herb had an innate understanding of talent. He urged me to come to the mountains and check Rodney out.

When Rodney and I met, he admitted, "I've worked in clubs so bad you took two steps down, socially and economically." But I saw the unmined abilities Herb had referred to and suggested he concentrate on his loser image, rather than bombarding audiences with unrelated jokes. I persuaded a good friend, Irving Mansfield, to put Rodney on TV. Irving was the producer of a popular variety show, "On Broadway Tonight," and he agreed with me about Rodney's potential.

I produced Rodney's first album, "The Loser," which became a cult item and started him toward his No Respect image. I was delighted when the world recognized his genius and made him a superstar.

Irving remained a key figure in my life. He became my adviser, my guide, my father, in a way my real father had never been. I liked his dapper, Goddard Lieberson style, his blue cashmere jackets and red silk handkerchiefs. And I liked his personal style too: kind and gentle, yet intense and high-powered. After years of success as press agent for Milton Berle, Eddie Cantor, and Billy Rose, then as producer of the "Arthur Godfrey Show," Irving was devoting all his considerable energy to the promotion of his wife, Jacqueline Susann's, literary career.

Their mutual affection and teamwork were an inspiration. Growing up, I had only witnessed two people pulling apart, clashing on all major issues. My brief and painful marriage to Felicia was over by 1964; we were divorced. Irving and Jackie, on the other hand, fulfilled their dreams through each other. Jackie's first book, *Every Night Josephine* (about her pet poodle), was gaining popularity. I liked the title and suggested a song be written around it. Irving was enthusiastic. The record was released

75

soon after and helped accelerate the book's sales.

Every Night Josephine eventually hit the Top 10 nonfiction list in *Time* magazine, a tribute to Jackie's talent and Irving's tenacity. *Valley of the Dolls* followed shortly after.

Irving and Jackie were generous and caring; they adopted me, treated me like a son. Most accounts of Irving and Jackie stress their genius at promotion, but these anecdotes leave out their dedication and hard work. Jackie took her writing seriously; she knew the world of entertainment from the inside, as model and actress, and wanted the Hollywood scene portrayed with honesty. She hated the way Hollywood was caricatured in second-rate novels.

"These people have been through the mill," she told me. "It's not all glamour. They hurt, they have fears, they live with constant insecurity. It's that side of the famous that I want to put into print."

When she talked about the secret agonies of celebrities, she was talking about her own private battle with cancer, although I didn't know it then.

Irving treated me to lunch at least twice a week at the Oak Room in the Plaza, filling my ears with show business vignettes and sound advice. One of his lessons was: "There isn't *anyone* you can't meet. Don't take the direct route, like asking for a job. You'll never get one that way. Think to yourself, who is this man's barber, his dentist? Barbers and dentists talk a lot. Surround the troops!"

These statements were similar to the suggestions Mickey Rooney offered when I worked with him on *Pete's Dragon* in 1976: "If you can't get in through the front door, try the back door. If that's locked, climb in through the window. If you can't squeeze through the window, try the roof."

In 1964 Harriet Wasser, the publicity agent who had helped promote Bobby Darin to success, introduced me to a tall, lanky songwriter with a crew cut named Joel Hirschhorn. Joel had been a record artist named Hathaway and a writer whose song "All About Love" had been recorded by rhythm and blues great Clyde McPhatter. To support himself, he had become a court stenographer.

I knew we were born partners when Joel told me of an incident during his shorthand reporting career. In the midst of a heated case, a lawyer started cursing furiously, and Joel had automatically edited out the curse words. The attorney exploded when he studied the transcript and saw how Joel had rewritten his language.

"I guess you like peace as much as I do," I told him.

We had a natural chemistry, an interlocking of needs and ambitions. Though we were two boys from the Bronx and Brooklyn, our collaboration quickly evolved into a Manhattan rewrite of *Pygmalion*.

I had a burning desire to teach, to shape someone's vision to my own. Joel wanted to soak up my experience, my dreams, because they were fundamentally the same as his. We both had a need to try everything—records, theater, movies, TV—and we both had the versatility to accomplish it. The only difference was, my dreams encompassed a lifetime and Joel's were rooted in the present.

I remember talking over a cup of coffee at the Pink Cloud, a diner on Columbus Avenue. I liked the Pink Cloud because it had the greasy, comfortably chaotic feel of a neighborhood hangout; only the bowling alley was missing. Joel felt at home there too.

He listened, blue eyes thoughtful and attentive behind dark glasses, as I babbled wildly on: "We can write musical movies, shows, we can be Richard Rodgers, we can be Gershwin, we can be *more famous* than they are."

"Well," Joel ventured, "first I'd like a hit record."

"What's one hit record?"

"More than I've had so far."

"You can't think of one hit record," I said. "It takes you nowhere."

I could hear his mind ticking: What does this madman mean? A hit record pays the rent. It buys clothes. It helps you eat.

I voiced what Joel hesitated to admit; he wanted to achieve as strongly as I did. Behind his good-humored reserve lurked a powerful current of ambition. I recognized it.

I welcomed the role of mentor. I had been in the business longer than Joel, had a more intimate and thorough knowledge of the music industry and how it worked. Joel, despite a history as piano prodigy and student at the High School of Performing Arts, still lived at home with his parents in the Bronx. But he was ready to make his move, ready to take the world head-on.

I would help him, direct him. He wanted my direction. I would chart our career because Joel trusted me. His trust gave me fresh confidence.

Most gratifying of all, we were friends, best friends. I would start a sentence, Joel would finish it. If I had an idea for a tune, he would sing the following line, and it would be exactly what I had heard. We were, literally, one mind.

We were also alike in our need for harmony. In working together, if Joel said, "I think your melody is *pretty* good," it meant he hated it. If I asked him to "file something away for a future time" it meant that the lyric or tune in question should be immediately discarded. We instinctively grasped this language, the language of let's-never-argue, let's-not-hurt-the-other's-feelings.

Joel typed 120 words a minute, a skill acquired from his court stenography days. Sometimes I would come up with a lyric line, then turn and start to repeat it. "I've already gotten it down" was his invariable answer. I used to wonder how the typewriter didn't start smoking or simply explode.

This spectacular ability helped our writing pace and rhythm. Occasionally stenography proved a drawback. In Joel's dedication to speed, he would write down a lyric we had just completed—in shorthand. If I wanted to examine the lyric alone at the end of the day, I'd pick it up and find our afternoon's work in code. Part of our work procedure was to assemble a list of possible titles. They, too, were frequently a mass of lines and curliques when I wanted to go over them.

"*Please* stick to English," I begged. With a grin he promised to comply. Most of the time he did.

Joel's home life was as much a revelation as his stenography. His parents had a warm, giving relationship. They laughed easily and applauded each other's stories. They urged us to perform our songs (Joel's sister, Madeleine, a CBS recording artist, often joined in), and they listened. Sometimes, when the Hirschhorns were sitting silently and appreciating a new piece of material, I recalled my mother's tendency to chatter through any song I presented to her. "It's wonderful, L'Alfred," she would say automatically, over and over, without hearing one word of a lyric or a shred of a tune.

The Kasha-Hirschhorn partnership bore fruit almost immediately. After a recording by Anthony Newley entitled "Is There a Way Back to Your Arms?" we had our first chart success by Jay and the Americans, a Latin-flavored, "La Bamba" kind of dance record, "Why Can't You Bring Me Home?" The lyric told of a woman's reluctance to bring her lover home because she felt self-conscious about her poverty.

Our follow-up, "Let's Start All Over Again" by Ronnie Dove, did even better, placing Number Ten on the charts. Joel finally understood the frustration I felt about my mother when she heard the news and said, in an alarmed manner, "Number Ten? But will it be Number *One?*"

"Number Ten is great," Joel chimed in; but she didn't hear him.

"Achieve, achieve. For me!"

I continued producing artists. Peter Allen (co-writer of "I Honestly Love You" and "Arthur") was one of them. In 1968 he was married to Liza Minnelli and was one half of a brother singing act (Chris and Peter Allen, though they weren't actually related). I felt, even then, that Peter had exceptional magnetism and talent, talent that would someday gain national attention. He was easy to work with, and he and Liza struck Joel and me as a happy, compatible couple. I was startled to hear of their divorce years later.

My concentration mainly focused on my new writing partnership, however. When Joel found a place on 68th and Columbus, near Lincoln Center, our working hours tripled. We were only five blocks from each other, and the songs poured out at an astonishing rate. We wrote compulsively, day and night, gathering titles, scribbling bits of tunes on napkins, shopping bags, stationery, whatever was handy. I carried a title book everywhere. We combed the music trades, *Billboard*, *Cashbox*, and *Record World*, to see who was popular, who needed material. No piano was safe, whether it turned up in a hotel lobby, a restaurant, or a music store. Joel's piano bench bulged with lead sheets, and our file of demo records grew till it threatened to take over the room.

We sat in movie theaters writing lyrics on our laps, undeterred by the dark. Patrons ordered us to shut up, distracted by our steady stream of dialogue...."How about this bridge?"...."Let's change the first line to..." "Say, the tune should go mmmm mmmm mmmm...."

Cars shrieked to a stop when we crossed 8th Avenue or Columbus; we were too immersed in the creative process to see them. And we never slept. If either of us got an idea at four in the morning, we'd reach for the phone.

Whenever an opening presented itself, we aimed for it. We lived in studios—Associated, Dick Charles, Variety Arts—making more and more demos. Three, four, five tunes a week weren't unusual. A $100.00 advance from publishers such as Screen Gems, Duchess, and Pincus kept us going.

I learned a valuable lesson. The brain rises to meet any challenge if pushed. Logic told us that five, six songs a week was an unrealistic, absurd goal. But need, ambition, obsession, youthful *hunger* made these five songs possible. We were too naive, too ignorant, to recognize it couldn't be done—so we did it.

"Let's try for Elvis Presley," I suggested one morning at the Pink Cloud.

"Elvis? That's crazy. Lieber and Stoller write all his things."

"Not anymore. We can get him."

Half believing me, Joel went along with the plan. We submitted a dozen songs to his publishing representative, Freddie Bienstock, of Hill and Range Music. Freddie subsidized demo after demo.

Nothing happened.

"We have to keep trying," I told Joel. "It's a way to get into movies if we're ever going to win an Oscar."

The word *Oscar* had a profound effect. Any mention of movies sparked Joel, who loved films with a passion. He was one of those buffs who could recite the script of *Casablanca* verbatim ("I remember every detail—the Germans wore gray, you wore blue"), or sing obscure numbers like "Spring Came Back to Vienna" from *Luxury Liner.* When we weren't together, he lived in movie theaters. One of his dreams was to be a film critic, and he often wrote movie reviews for relaxation.

Joel had a few odd quirks: as a former court stenographer, he was accustomed to writing down speech; and he would scribble conversations in the air or under the table as they flowed. After taking imaginary notes, he would erase them with the flick of his palm.

Joel's love of movies was exceeded only by my worship of songwriters. I concocted pet theories:

(a) Irving Berlin writes like a Jewish grandmother: he asks and answers a question. *Maybe It's Because I Love You Too Much— Maybe That's Why You Love Me So Little; They Say That Falling in Love Is Wonderful, It's Wonderful, So They Say; How Much Do I Love You, I'll Tell You No Lie, How Deep Is the Ocean, How High Is the Sky?*

(b) Oscar Hammerstein is always indirect: he can't come out and say "I love you." *"If* I Loved You"; *"People* Will Say We're in Love"; "Do I Love You Because You're Beautiful, Or Are You Beautiful Because I Love You?"

As a result, I was able to project into the minds and feelings of artists. Joel had the same facility, and the artists who did our material ranged from Peggy Lee to Anthony Newley, Jackie Wilson to Fred Astaire.

"Oh, my God, look at this!" Joel shouted.

We were once again in the Pink Cloud—we practically lived there during the 1960s. The Pink Cloud, with its underdone omelets, watery orange juice, and bitter coffee, had evolved into a symbol of all our struggles. Its shoddiness was romantic.

"What's the matter?"

Joel thrust a copy of the current *Cashbox* into my hands, and I stared at a full-page ad. Page 28. I never forgot the page number. "Your Time Hasn't Come Yet Baby"—Elvis's new single, by Kasha and Hirschhorn.

"I can't believe it," Joel gasped.

"I told you." But I was overcome too. It's one thing to take a confident approach; another to see a dream realized.

9

Starting Over

Run faster. You've made some inroads. Press on and make the most of them.

In 1968, I flew to Hollywood to consult with Liberty Records about producing Nancy Ames. While there, I went to the *Speedway* set for the last days of shooting and met Elvis. He only reinforced what Jacqueline Susann had said about the insecurities of celebrities. At first he appeared relaxed, joking with people. When I got him alone for a few minutes, though, he was quiet and withdrawn; he seemed frightened, totally opposite from the King image I had read about so often.

"It's not a great picture," he remarked, almost apologetically. That line offered me a clue: Elvis wanted to do better things than the mediocre Hollywood vehicles he had committed himself to. But by 1968, he had become too much a victim of big money and merchandising to dig his way out.

My own panic was increasing. Palpitations, butterflies in my stomach, a sense of jeopardy—all became daily companions, even though I was still able to conceal them from Joel.

I started watching for similar symptoms in other people. Soon I developed an intuitive awareness of phobics around me. I'd catch a pair of frightened eyes in an elevator, or notice an elderly woman tremble when requested to sign a check at the bank. Nervous illness was everywhere.

On a PSA flight to San Francisco, I sat next to a redheaded

woman in her thirties who kept fastening and unfastening her seat belt. She grasped my arm more and more tightly as we talked.

"Somebody's got to let me off this plane," she whispered. At the time we were thirty-one thousand feet above San Jose.

"You'll be all right," I assured her; but she wasn't. She repeated "Get me off this plane," spreading concern and fear with brushfire rapidity throughout the aircraft. Stewardesses rushed over and led her to the rear of the plane, unsuccessfully attempting to soothe her mounting hysteria.

I never released my terrors publicly, the way this woman did. I had to appear brave. But self-imposed isolation left me desperately lonely. Fellowship with other people is vital if you're to become desensitized, freed of phobic symptoms; and I held all my emotions in. I felt increasingly adrift, without a sense of belonging.

The times didn't help either. Nineteen sixty-seven was an alarming period for all free-lance composers. I watched helplessly as the Brill Building era died. With the arrival of the Beatles (already hailed by the London *Times* as "the greatest composers since Beethoven"), singer-songwriters seized power; and the charts bulged with groups from England as well as America: The Rolling Stones, The Kinks, The Animals, Simon and Garfunkel, The Beach Boys. None of them considered doing "outside" songs, and before long *Billboard*'s Top 100 listed fewer than fifteen artists who welcomed tunes from a free-lancer.

It was a period of panic. Neil Sedaka was suddenly derailed. There was a pained, what-can-I-do-now expression on the faces of Gerry Goffin and Carole King. For Carole the late 1960s was a period of searching, of struggling to become an artist, a struggle brilliantly consummated with the popularity of "Tapestry."

Morty Schuman (co-writer, with Doc Pomus, of many Elvis Presley hits as well as "Save the Last Dance for Me") went abroad and became a cabaret star in *Jacques Brel Is Alive and Well and Living in Paris*. Burt Bacharach left for Hollywood and continued his string of hits with Hal David by writing movie themes.

I chose the Bacharach route. Burt and I were friends, and he made the motion picture world seem excitingly attainable. Joel and I scored a film about ghetto life, *The Unemployables.* We also supplied a rock score for an excruciating, low-budget venture entitled *The Fat Spy,* starring Jayne Mansfield.

Jayne had climbed to success on her curves, but she took herself seriously as an "actress." We wrote a few, far-from-immortal lyrics for her:

I'd like to be a rose in your garden
But I'm just a thorn in your side.

Jayne rehearsed the words hundreds of times, straining to extract their "deeper" meanings. Joel and I holed up in the record booth with her when she did the session, watching her grimace dramatically, as though every word was being torn from her soul.

Life was no rose garden, but it had its humorous aspects, even concerning my family. I was living with a Catholic girl named Emily. I knew my parents would disapprove, so I told them Joel and I were rooming together. When my mother called Joel's apartment, which she did frequently, I was never there. Joel had an automatic response: "Al's shopping, Mrs. Kasha."

"You're always shopping," she told me indignantly. "What's wrong with Joel's feet? Doesn't *he* ever go to the store?"

"Shopping's my job," I explained. "Joel does the dishes."

The situation reached its ludicrous height in 1967 when the New York blackout spread darkness all over Manhattan. My mother called and Joel, disoriented by the circumstances, answered in robot fashion: "He's out shopping."

"Shopping? During the blackout? I don't believe it."

"We...needed a few groceries."

"He must be there. Put him on the phone."

"I swear, he's at the market. He'll be back soon."

Joel contacted me and I called her back. She told me I was being used, that Joel was a selfish monster, that I should get another roommate and partner willing to carry his share of the load.

Then the guilt was poured on: "Larry calls me. Why don't you?"

"I called you on Wednesday."

"So? This is Friday. And I thought you were calling me at eight Wednesday. You didn't call till ten."

Her intervention on my behalf was sometimes embarrassing. In 1967, Larry directed a revival of *Showboat* at Lincoln Center, an occasion that re-introduced me to my childhood idol, Richard Rodgers. Rodgers was co-producer of the revival. My mother noticed him in the lobby and said, "Now *there's* a success. That's what you have to be." Then she raced to his side and reminded him who I was. "The boy who played Little Jake in *Annie Get Your Gun,*" she said, as he smiled politely.

"You write for the theater, don't you, darling?"

He nodded.

"Well," my mother burst out, thinking of my song in *Speedway,* "my son Alfred is a songwriter too. Only he writes for *movies.*"

I cringed. Here was the greatest show writer of his time, perhaps in history, linked as an equal with the man who had written a tune for Elvis Presley's *Speedway.*

Rodgers had also written for "movies"; that year his *Sound of Music* had become the biggest box office film of all time.

"You could team up with Alfred...now that Oscar is dead," my mother suggested.

"Mom, *please.*"

"Why not? Maybe Mr. Rodgers needs a new partner."

Needless to say, the team of Rodgers and Kasha never materialized.

Those Broadway opening nights my mother had dreamed about were now realities, and she relished every minute of them. When photographers took pictures backstage, her mink stole was more prominent than the images of the stars. Only on these occasions did she wear her mink, and acquaintances on Avenue M never saw it. Convinced that the neighbors would wish her ill and give her the evil eye, she wrapped the mink in a white sheet and stuffed it into a suitcase. Then, on a dark street several miles away, she would switch outfits and prepare herself for the big evening ahead.

Larry earned most of her approval as the years passed. He was more attentive. Despite my childhood promise to give her a mink, Larry had beaten me to it. He took her out with his friends and saw to it that she occupied front row center when she attended a show, his or anyone else's. He remained a bachelor, while I committed the cardinal sin of getting married. Even though she still claimed, "Larry is my right eye and you're my left eye," even though she still sang "You'll Never Know Just How Much I Love You" when she hugged me, her Lawrence was Number One man in her heart.

My father knew, and increasingly resented, his position as Number Three. The calls from my mother about him became more frequent: "He beat me last night....he's ruining my life....I need my sons."

"Mom, you've got to move out. Get your own place. I'll pay for it."

"No, darling. When you make it...when you can afford it ...then..."

"I'm doing fine. I can afford it."

"Not yet, darling. Soon. When it's time." There was a pause. "Maybe I could live with you or Larry."

"That's not a good idea, ma."

"I wouldn't be in the way. I promise."

I ignored her plea. I think she knew I would refuse. She wasn't quite ready to make the final break from Avenue M.

Joel and I kept writing. Nineteen sixty-eight melted into 1969. Hippies with beads, reeking of marijuana, filled the streets and I grew more and more restless with New York. I dreamed of living in California or Nashville or even London—anywhere but Manhattan where my parents could, if they chose, jump on a subway and reach me within half an hour.

My moods became more erratic, owing to the diet pills I took to suppress my appetite and the downers I took to mellow me out. Joel bore the brunt of my unpredictable personality swings.

At that crucial moment, February, 1968, I received a call from the publishing wing of CBS, April Blackwood. Would I consider running the firm in Los Angeles?

The answer was yes, before I heard any talk of salary. Working in L.A. would place me in the thick of the motion picture industry.

Events sped forward, like film being wound ahead at twice the normal speed. Ceil called. It had been four years since my divorce. We met again and I knew, intuitively, that this was it. If any woman could share my life, understand my workaholism, lend support, Ceil was the one. She understood the music profession, knew its pressures and demands.

I thought of that night by the East River, the warming sound of her laugh, the playfulness of her humor, the beauty of her spirit. I thought of those hours when, briefly, I had felt calm and unafraid.

Ceil decided to convert to Judaism. She wanted a united feeling in our home, a sharing of roots and faith. She wanted our children to grow up without confusion and conflicting loyalties.

As I had expected, my parents were passionately opposed to my marriage, opposed to Ceil on principle as a *shiksa* (her conversion didn't count), and opposed to my planned move to California. When Ceil and I went to Avenue M for dinner, my mother would talk *about* her, never to her: "See what *she* wants....Give her more potatoes....Pass her the roast."

"My name isn't *her*," Ceil said, hurt by the rejection. "Maybe if you were marrying a Jewish girl..."

"I did marry one," I reminded her.

After the conversion, Ceil, my mother, and I went for breakfast, and Ceil unwittingly ordered bacon and eggs. My mother straightened up, squared her mink-padded shoulders and said, "She'll never be a Jew."

The incident made me recall Larry's brief engagement. I had liked his prospective fiancée, a tall, attractive brunette named Peggy.

"She says she's thirty," my mother remarked. "I think closer to thirty-five. Look around the eyes. And why hasn't she ever been married? There's something wrong."

Or: "Maybe she has been married, and she's hiding it. I don't trust her."

Or: "Did she go to college? I don't think she went to college. She's not smart enough for Larry."

Then, running out of reasons: "I know...my *heart* tells me ...that it's wrong, wrong, wrong."

A few weeks later, Larry broke his engagement.

Now it was my turn, and I had no intention of letting her destroy a relationship that meant so much to me.

Ceil's parents, by contrast, welcomed me immediately as a son. Her mother called me a "prince," and told Ceil, "Be good to him." Her father said something even more meaningful: "You're my son. I know you're Jewish; but listen, after all...Jesus was a Jew."

10

Hollywood Lifeline

California was perfect through the fall of 1968. Ceil and I rented a beautiful home in North Hollywood, complete with garden, spacious backyard, and pool—a far cry from living over a store. We loved the weather and the natural beauty of the countryside. Talk of a giant earthquake that would sweep California into the sea was rampant that year, but we laughed it off.

Joel decided to share a house on Laurel Canyon with our mutual friend, songwriter Gerry Robinson. We were set to write lyrics to Marvin Hamlisch's melodies for *The April Fools,* a film starring Jack Lemmon. And Ceil was pregnant.

I have it all, I thought, as the American Airlines jumbo jet roared through the clouds from L.A. to New York. Seated to the right and left of me were two top CBS executives, one president of the picture division. Joel and I had three records on the charts simultaneously: "Will You Be Staying After Sunday?" and "Don't Wake Me Up in the Morning, Michael" (both by the Peppermint Rainbow) and "Stay and Love Me All Summer" by Brian Hyland.

"Thank you, God, for all these blessings," I whispered, just before the terror began.

"You all right?" one of my companions asked. I nodded, sweat streaming down my forehead. I excused myself and stumbled to the bathroom.

This time it wasn't only palpitations. I felt trapped. The walls of the tiny bathroom intensified my fear. I was sealed inside my father's closet again, and this time the closet was suspended in midair. The prospect of walking back to my seat, negotiating the narrow aisle, was worse.

I felt faint; my head was whirling. All sense of time and place deserted me. Voices faded in and out.

You're an important executive, I reminded myself. *The head of a major publishing operation. Yesterday you spoke to CBS record company president Clive Davis. This morning you met with Jack Lemmon. Get hold of yourself.*

Somehow I did, after dousing my face with cold water and holding my breath for half a minute. The panic subsided, and I returned to my seat, falling normally into a discussion about the state of the record business and what influence San Francisco and the psychedelic scene would exert on the industry in years to come.

I flew many other times in 1968 and 1969, without fear. Eventually I persuaded myself that the attack was an isolated incident. Yet a part of my brain kept waiting, like an animal in the jungle, every nerve sensitized to a future threat.

Creatively, the late 1960s were an exciting, fruitful period. Joel, Marvin, and I wrote "Wake Up" for *The April Fools.* The Chambers Brothers cut it and a hit single emerged. We had an opportunity to collaborate with that master of urban blues, Taj Mahal. Our song "Give Your Woman What She Wants" also appeared in the movie.

In 1970, I heard through the executive grapevine that Sal Ianucci of National General was searching for someone to head the company's new record division. The announcement had little effect, until they contacted me and asked if I would consider the job.

Two thoughts assailed me at the same time: *What an honor* and *Don't take it!*

I was a songwriter first. Would this deeper immersion into the executive world pull me further away from my first love? Could I be executive by day and songwriter by night?

Ceil was doubtful. "You know what a workaholic you are," she said. "You always give everything 100 percent. If you carry two separate careers at once, you'll crack up."

"Not if I divide my time properly."

"The two jobs will overlap. They have to. You know this business. And when will you have time to sleep?"

It doesn't matter. I never sleep anyway.

"I love you," Ceil said, burying her head in my shoulder. "I want you alive and healthy at forty."

The birth of our daughter Dana decided me. Golden-haired, blue-eyed, Dana was the greatest gift in a life already showered with blessings. From birth she displayed the sweetest disposition, the brightest smile, the most giving nature of anyone, child or adult, that I had ever known.

She would have the best, no matter what I had to do to get it for her. So would Ceil, who had been born on Gunhill Road in the Bronx and had experienced the same economic deprivation I had. I wanted their lot to be an easy one.

Becoming president of a record company added more to my prestige than to my peace of mind. The corporate game, even under the best of circumstances, requires a certain paranoia. Executives must protect themselves from the competitive danger of rivals who need to discredit the next man to build up their own positions.

Another emotional split occurred. Not only did I have to divide myself between songwriter and executive, I was compulsively driven to maintain two mind-sets within the executive framework: the get-them-or-they'll-get-me mentality and the "be nice" syndrome—directly contradictory goals. Powerful executives are rarely concerned with being "nice," nor do they care about satisfying Rose Kasha's requirement, "Do they like you?" Fair means or foul, they aim to get ahead.

Work wasn't enough; giving parties for the "right" people was stressed to me by manager Ray Katz (who handled Dolly Parton) and by top real estate broker Elaine Young (ex-wife of Gig Young). Ray advised, "This is a town built on publicity. Hire a press agent. Buy a home in Beverly Hills. And get yourself invited to as many important functions as you can."

Ceil was a natural hostess; she was gregarious and loved people. So we threw a surprise birthday party for Lionel Newman, head of music at Twentieth Century Fox, and did the same shortly after for E. Y. (Yip) Harburg, lyricist for *The Wizard of Oz* and *Finian's Rainbow*. Yip was particularly important to us, as friend and teacher. He had encouraged our theatrical ambitions in New York, analyzing our work and helping us polish our writing skills.

For Yip's party we invited composer Jerry Herman, a boyhood friend of mine, Alexis Smith, Craig Stevens, Gary Collins and Mary Ann Mobley, Michele Lee and James Farentino, just a few of the talented guests who admired his work. A high spot of the night was Yip singing his own classic "Brother, Can You Spare a Dime?"

These events were always lively and tuneful. But there was pressure too. I was nervous beforehand, wondering how to please the stars that attended. I geared myself up, along with Joel, to perform our songs, hoping for a favorable response, breathing a sigh of relief when I got one. And the conversations that emphasized "What are you doing?" rather than "Who are you?" wore me down.

After a long time I discovered that parties weren't what counted, only the quality of your work.

It was enjoyable and challenging to strive for quality on our next project, *The Cheyenne Social Club*. Gene Kelly, the director, provided creative stimulus; and the stars we were to compose a duet for, James Stewart and Henry Fonda, were legends and personal favorites.

Joel and I felt awe in the presence of Kelly, Stewart, and Fonda. What impressed us most, beyond the individuality they projected, was their truth. They knew who they were, and never tampered with their natural personalities.

I observed Fonda's professionalism when National General, producers of *The Cheyenne Social Club*, asked me to cut three hundred spots of Fonda plugging our song "Rolling Stone." He was on location in Oregon, filming *Sometimes a Great Notion* with Paul Newman, and I found him in a small motel.

Fonda was less intimidating in jeans and red plaid shirt. My engineer and I set up. With complete ease, Fonda lay in bed and repeated phrases such as: "Hello, Kansas, my friend Jimmy Stewart and I have a new record, 'Rolling Stone.' Hope you'll put us on your playlist....Hello, Akron....Hello, San Diego...."

After 150 were done, I was hesitant about asking for more. Fonda spotted a stack of papers in my briefcase, listing the stations that wanted spots. "How many more do you need?" he asked.

"Uh...about 150."

Without missing a beat he said, "Well, let's do 'em then. Wanna give the song all the promotion we can."

Fonda's handling of the situation was the most impressive definition of "being a pro" that I had ever witnessed. No fuss, no temperament, no patronizing airs—just do the job, help the picture, play on the team.

Gene gave me more than a lesson on professionalism; he heightened my desire to do large-scale, ambitious things—a full film musical, like *Singing in the Rain,* or a Broadway show. He was warm and likeable and encouraged my dreams.

He also taught me a valuable, if painful, lesson. Until 1970, I had always been chronically late—a childish gambit to get attention. One night I had an appointment with Gene at his home on Rodeo Drive. I don't recall what delayed me, but I presented myself on his doorstep at nine for an eight-o'clock get-together.

Gene's normally amiable, grinning face was purple with rage when I arrived. "I've never been treated so rudely," he said. "There's no excuse for keeping someone waiting this long." With that he marched up the stairs and left me alone, completely humiliated.

He was right, of course. And from that day forward I was never late again.

When I saw Gene next, he made no reference to the incident; he was as sweet and caring as ever. Joel and I loved to listen to him talk. He brought the MGM days glitteringly alive, referring to that constant state of anticipation and joy that he, Judy Garland, Fred Astaire, and all the writers and musicians felt when doing a movie. "It was never work," he said. "We beat our brains out but somehow it was fun." He also told us how the studio had said, "You'll never make it with the name Gene Kelly. Change it to Gene Black because you have black hair." He chuckled: "Can you imagine Garland and Black? What a disaster!"

Most of all, Gene projected a love of work, the kind of love that once prompted Picasso to remark, "Always you put more of yourself into your work, until one day—you never know exactly which day—you *are* your work. Your work in life is the ultimate seduction."

Writing had become, by then, my ultimate seduction, and I felt increasingly torn by the executive responsibilities that wrenched me from it. As Ceil had predicted, Joel and I worked late into the night. I had to triple and quadruple my Valium dosages to calm down and grab any sleep at all. I was in a stupor through breakfast; rarely could I string together a cohesive sentence.

Gene adored every aspect of his career, but he didn't suffer as I did. He wanted to do his best, but not to say, *See, I did it.* A job well done appeared to be sufficient reward.

He wanted to achieve, not for mom and dad, not for old school teachers who had slighted him, but for himself!

Joel got married in April, 1969. On the surface it seemed as though he and his wife Jill belonged in two separate worlds. Joel was the cerebral New York Jewish boy who identified, during *Annie Hall*, with Woody Allen's reluctance to kill a spider until he was thirty. Jill was the daredevil West Hartford WASP, who had made the perilous 136-foot dive from the Acapulco cliffs.

I saw what attracted them to each other. Joel found Jill's recklessness exciting. She found his comedic "I-can't-even-fix-a-flat-tire" fumbling a welcome change from the humorlessly macho men she had known in her West Hartford world. In addition they had music in common. Jill was a gifted songwriter, intensely driven, determined to show the world she could make an important mark in her profession.

It was a loving relationship, but the competitive element

caused problems. Both kept busy—Jill with an album on RCA Victor, for which she sang and wrote all the material, Joel with our joint films and hit records.

The competition was sticky but manageable. More seriously, Jill felt Joel was putting too much time and effort into our work, rather than spending weekends and evenings home with her.

"She doesn't want me to be a workaholic," Joel would explain. Intellectually I understood. Jill was the child of an alcoholic herself; her mother had died of the disease and like all adult children of alcoholics, she needed tremendous amounts of love and reassurance. The only trouble was, her needs clashed with my goals, my timetable. I had my own race to run, my mother to please, my peers to impress. Joel and I, as partners, had to work toward those objectives. He had to be available night and day when key assignments came in, and I felt that Jill, as a fellow songwriter, should understand the erratic, unpredictable deadlines of show business.

Joel and Jill solved—or at least handled—their conflicts in a strange fashion. Jill was a borderline anorectic. She ate only one meal a day and lived in a constant state of semi-starvation. Joel loved chocolate and all sweets. He began to overeat, to consume huge portions of cake, ice cream, and candy. It was a game at first. They would laugh as he finished off boxes of Oreo cookies. They joked about his Jewish appetite, his love of delicatessens. But the pounds piled on. His sweet tooth vicariously satisfied her unfulfilled longings for meals of her own.

It was almost as though he were saying, "I'll eat for you if you'll let me have the time I want to work."

This unspoken deal between them preserved the balance enough to keep our partnership functioning. Joel's weight, meanwhile, continued to rise.

He was caught in the middle of two powerful forces. Jill pulled one way, I pulled the other; and he, as a lifelong peacemaker, sought to satisfy both of us. His attempt to be the perfect partner and the perfect husband resulted in high blood pressure.

He ignored the doctor's warnings, as their game slipped slowly out of control.

*My parents, Rose and Irving,
on their wedding day,
January 5, 1930.*

*My parents were a handsome
young couple in this 1930 picture.*

My mother with Larry and me at the Karmel Hotel in the Catskills in 1938. Larry was about 5, and I was 1.

Larry at age 15, also at the Carmel Hotel

My high school graduation picture. I was the proud president of the class of '54 at Brooklyn's Madison High School.

*Singing at age 22 with the Johnny Otis
Band at the United Artists Theatre,
Los Angeles.*

*For a brief time in my singing
career, I used the name Alfy Weatherbee on
Roulette Records. This picture was taken when I was 20.*

With the Olympics in the United Artists Theatre, Los Angeles.

Backstage with Jackie Wilson at the Apollo Theatre in 1960.

SHEEDY AND LONG   COURTESY OF THE ACADEMY OF MOTION PICTURE ARTS AND SCIENCES

Receiving our first Oscar from Sonny and Cher in 1973. I'm on the left; Joel is on the right.

PHOTO COURTESY OF THE ACADEMY OF MOTION PICTURE ARTS AND SCIENCES.

Our second Oscar, in 1975, was presented by the great Gene Kelly.

The two of us at the Walt Disney Studios during the making of the musical "Pete's Dragon."

JILL WILLIAMS

Teaching a class songwriting UCLA in 19

SAUL KAHAN

Backstage at the opening of "Seven Brides for Seven Brothers" in the Fox Theatre, San Diego. From left to right are Larry Kasha, me, Joel, Debby Boone, David Landay, Shirley Boone, and Pat Boone.

Receiving 1975 People's Choice Award from Ann Miller and Ricardo Montalban for the theme from "The Towering Inferno."

With my beloved wife, Ceil.

DIANE SEAY

Our work, miraculously, got done. All this juggling resulted in a steady flow of successful songs.

My executive juggling resulted in a four-million-dollar tape deal for National General with Ampex, to be distributed through Buddah Records. It was the largest tape deal ever made up to that time, 1970, and a strong way to establish my effectiveness. For the moment, I enjoyed the privileges heaped on a division president: limousines, private jets, a floor-long suite at the Waldorf Astoria where Cole Porter had once lived, trips to Cannes, Spain, London. No longer was I trapped over a store in Brooklyn.

Except inside: my emotions lingered back there. I struggled to escape that prison, not knowing my sentence had been commuted. I felt like a rejected ten-year-old when the National General bigwigs didn't acknowledge my achievement. What I didn't realize was the major trouble National General's motion picture division was in. They needed much more than four million dollars to offset a series of box office disappointments.

I encountered heavy anti-rock-and-roll sentiment. One of my primary jobs was to recommend writers for National General films. After suggesting Brill Building great Gerry Goffin (ex-husband of Carole King, a gigantic record seller and a superlative lyricist), a director stared coldly and said, "We don't want rock-and-roll writers. That music is for kids. It's garbage."

It was bewildering. The Beatles had already made legendary contributions to music, including praise from establishment heroes like Leonard Bernstein. Songs about protest and civil rights and flower power had shaken the world. Dylan had denounced "The Masters of War;" Barry McGuire had warned about "The Eve of Destruction;" Joni Mitchell had evoked the beauty and significance of "Woodstock."

And here was a director saying, "Rock-and-roll is for kids."

I knew it was only a matter of time before movies caught up, embraced rock, responded to its creative and financial implications. But the era of sound track fever was still years away. The 1985 Oscars, which included five rock hits in its Best Song category, was in the undreamed-of future.

PART III

BREAKING DOWN—
WORKAHOLISM

11

Panic

Maintaining a full-time writing and executive schedule was becoming unbearable. I walked around with a permanent headache. My insomnia was worse than ever, and I piled another crushing pressure on top of all the others. In addition to pop songwriting and executive responsibility, I now plunged into the task of creating a Broadway show.

My longing for Broadway was stronger than ever, due to a recent collaboration with Charles Aznavour. Joel and I had written English lyrics to several of Charles's songs, including "The Old Fashioned Way," "I Have Lived," "Like Roses,"and "Little Fool, I Love You," and Charles had performed them all in his Broadway one-man show. After that, we were determined to write a full-fledged theater vehicle of our own. The project we selected—because it was family-oriented and in the public domain—was Charles Dickens's *David Copperfield.*

We read the book aloud and picked spots we felt were appropriate for songs. After completing five, we contacted Gene Kelly about the possibility of directing.

"Sounds like a great idea," said Gene. "Come over tonight and play the stuff for me."

When I hung up the phone I was trembling. Presenting our material to Gene meant everything to me. I had always considered myself a show writer, deep down. Rodgers and Hammerstein were still the two men I wanted Joel and me to emulate. If Gene, a man of vast theatrical experience, an actor who had worked with Rodgers and Hart on *Pal Joey* and Cole Porter on *The Pirate*—if *he* liked it, it meant we were fit to function in that rarefied world.

By sheer coincidence, a leading London producer, Sir Bernard Delfont, was staying at the Beverly Hills Hotel, and Gene invited him to hear the music.

Joel and I each took a pep pill beforehand (Ritalin) to ensure an energetic, show-stopping performance. Ritalin was the latest of my uppers; I found it cleared the brain and enabled us to get more work done. Ritalin seemed harmless. It wasn't really a powerful stimulant, I told myself. After all, doctors gave it to hyperactive children to slow them down, though it had the reverse effect on adults. If a five-year-old could take it without harm, surely it couldn't threaten two healthy men in their thirties.

I also felt, as many drug-dependent people do, that I had a high tolerance for pills. Valium and Eskatrol hardly affected me. I only turned to Ritalin under special, stressful conditions.

Joel and I didn't simply perform the score that night—we lived it. I was David Copperfield, Aunt Betsy Trotwood, Mr. Murdstone rolled into one; Joel was Uriah Heep, Mr. Micawber, Mr. Dick. I became, once again, the kid from Rose and Irving's barber shop, singing myself hoarse for approval. Joel pounded the piano until the keys nearly collapsed. Gene grinned more and more at the conclusion of each number, particularly "Something Will Turn Up," an ode to optimism sung by Wilkins Micawber.

"I love it," Gene said, when the last big note had been sounded. My hands were clammy-cold, a side effect of the Ritalin, and my heart was pounding. Then he said the words I had prayed for: "Bernie, if you want to open it in the West End, I'll be glad to direct."

Larry will be so proud of me.

Driving home we were hysterical with joy. We saw the standing ovation on opening night, the rave reviews, the headlines that read: *Kasha and Hirschhorn, Heirs Apparent to the Rodgers and Hammerstein Throne.*

I didn't know then that *Copperfield* would be the single most crippling force in our lives, emotionally and creatively, for the next ten years. I certainly didn't know it when I raced across the lawn and woke Ceil up to share the incredible details of our evening at Gene's house. Joel and Jill were awake half the night dwelling on the future glory and recognition about to come our way.

I was a dedicated writer and an executive who dreaded his job. Tension headaches became routine and I would often cry out from the pain.

During this time I had dinner with Janis Joplin, her manager Albert Grossman, and the president of Kama Sutra Records, Artie Ripp. The selection of a rundown Chinese joint on Hollywood Boulevard was odd, but it was Janis' favorite. She pulled up in a limousine, and I was surprised to see how small she was. The huge feather hat and the heavy shawl seemed to overwhelm her.

Throughout dinner she drank vodka, straight up, and talked vaguely about getting into movies. "Can you get me a part?" she asked, her eyes protected by dark sunglasses.

I said I would try. I was a tremendous fan of her talent, and felt she would be electrifying on film if a director could be found who would tone her down for the camera.

Though she appeared shaky and distracted, I was totally unprepared to hear of her heroin overdose, only a day later.

Her death hit me hard. I had barely known her, but I identified with the pressures that had driven her to destruction. I kept picturing her sad face under the huge hat and her unexpectedly small, vulnerable body.

One night in desperation, riddled with pills, dead tired and dizzy, I took a long walk past Moorpark Street, up to Laurel Canyon. I felt hypnotically drawn toward Mulholland Drive, an area that overlooked the entire city. When I arrived there, the splash of colored Los Angeles lights glittered below. Above, the night sky was overcrowded with stars. I felt I was watching a light show especially designed by God.

I hadn't realized the depths of my despair until I stood over the edge of the canyon. How easy, I thought, to jump, to vanish into the blazingly impersonal lights, disappear.

"Hey, fella, are you all right?"

I couldn't make out the driver's face, but his voice sounded reassuring.

"I'm fine, thanks."

"Sure now?"

"I'm sure."

He drove off.

I stepped back. God was looking out for me, after all, even if I had momentarily lost grip of myself.

I prayed for guidance, then spoke into the solitary darkness: "If I return to being solely a free-lance writer, my income will be erratic, changeable. I can't guarantee Ceil and Dana the paycheck-every-Friday protection they deserve."

I rubbed my eyes. The flickering lights were too bright. My fingers dug through empty pockets, nervous agents searching for a pill to calm me.

Ceil was watching "The Tonight Show" when I returned at twelve-thirty.

"Where were you?" she asked anxiously. I seldom took long, nocturnal strolls.

"Mulholland Drive. Honey, I wonder—if I never took another executive position, how would you feel?"

"I wouldn't care."

"The going could get rough. But if Joel and I just concentrated on writing, on *Copperfield*, if we gave it all we had, I *know*..."

"I know too," Ceil said, putting a finger to my lips. "You're a writer. That's all you want to do, isn't it?"

"Yes. But the life of a writer..."

"Is what?" She laughed, as if talking to a child. "Hey, this is Ceil you're talking to, remember? I worked for a publisher. I know all about writers and what they go through. And what's a little struggle anyway? Nothing at all for Ceil Batista from Gunhill Road and the Bronx."

We heard a squeal from Dana's bedroom.

"Is she crying?" I asked.

"That's not crying," said Ceil, embracing me before running off to attend to our daughter. "That's a cheer. She's telling her daddy to go for it!"

12

Addicted

I was half-convinced, but the blaring static of my thoughts kept me awake most of the night. Then at six-thirty I heard Ceil's gasp.

The room was shaking.

For a few seconds I couldn't comprehend what was happening, until I heard Ceil wail, "Oh, God, the baby." She raced to Dana's room as the house trembled in the grip of a powerful epileptic seizure. Dishes fell from shelves, smashing to bits; doors flew open. A window cracked. And the rumbling went on. I felt as though I had been catapulted back to Brooklyn, to my room above the subway. For an instant I was lying next to Larry, listening to my parents crucify each other.

My bed rolled and bashed against a wall. Plaster rained on the rug.

I remembered what I had read: stand between the door frames. I beckoned to Ceil, who was carrying our sobbing daughter in her arms, and we huddled together by the front door, waiting for the earth to stop dancing.

It was February 9, 1971.

The shaking stopped, only to be followed minutes later by an aftershock as powerful as the initial tremor. More dishes broke. Down the road I heard a woman's cry.

When the quake was over, when we heard about the deaths in Sylmar, about the collapsing bridges and shattered roads, the billion dollars worth of damage, Ceil and I stared at each other. It could have been all over. One of us, all of us, could have died. Just like that.

There were no guarantees, yet I had fallen into the trap of playing it safe, hanging on to a dream of security.

"I'll never stick with something I don't want, ever again," I swore to myself. I was a writer and it was wrong, a death to the spirit, for me to be anything else.

I gathered enough courage to shake off a lifetime fear of driving and took the test. I passed it, but the uneasiness remained. I tended to clutch the steering wheel so hard that my knuckles ached. I couldn't shake my premonition of disaster.

Disaster came, on July 1, 1971.

The setting was an empty side street two blocks from my home, deceptively calm and safe. I remember I was mentally reworking one of the *Copperfield* lyrics when I drew up to a stop sign. After pausing I crossed the intersection and a Ford station wagon plowed into my Toyota.

Police were on the scene in minutes. The woman who hit me, a middle-aged, overweight blonde, kept muttering, "Are we through now? My ice cream is melting." I thought at first that she was in shock, but it turned out the melting ice cream *was* her prime concern.

I kept hearing her shrill voice, repeating: "My ice cream is melting, my ice cream is melting," and the absurdity of it made me laugh—an excruciating process, since laughter aggravated the shooting pains in my chest.

The final results for me were whiplash, hairline fracture, and dislocated back. My car was totaled, and I realized later what a miracle it was that I hadn't been killed.

God, graciously, had come through again.

But all I could think of, beyond the heavy sedation administered by my prescription-happy doctor, was: *I'm losing work time. Copperfield has to be rewritten. There are artists out there who need songs. I can't afford to be idle.*

I remembered a quote I had once read by Brian Epstein: "My

idea of heaven is to have ten hits in a row on the charts." *I know what you mean,* I thought, forgetting subsequent revelations about Epstein's life: the tortured ambition, the drinking and pill taking. The insatiable need for more and more acclaim.

Pills were also becoming my refuge. Sleeping pills—Valium, Tuinal; Percodan and Darvon to obliterate the pain that plagued me from the accident, pain resulting from not allowing myself a proper recuperative period. Fanaticism about weight made me gobble diet pills to suppress my appetite. I couldn't manage a single day without one crutch or the other, and my dependence deepened.

"Just rest a *few* days," Ceil begged; but I ignored her advice. Joel and I met daily and stepped up our work pace. I was thirty-four, one year from thirty-five, six years from forty. Time hovered more threateningly than ever. How could I catch up to Rodgers and Hammerstein, Bacharach and David, Goffin and King, if I lost an hour here, an hour there?

We received a letter from Delfont, agreeing to produce *Copperfield* with Gene Kelly directing. He began to scout around for available West End theaters when Gene suddenly became unavailable. "There's a personal problem" was the most specific line we could elicit from his secretary Lois.

Not long after, Gene's wife, Jeannie, was dead of leukemia. It was a heartbreaking blow.

We had observed, at close range, the genuine feeling and affection between them, the sort of unostentatious love and warmth that filled onlookers with vicarious pleasure. The tenderness they shared had been one reason why visiting the red house on Rodeo Drive had been so pleasant and memorable.

They had two young children, a boy, Timothy, and a girl, Bridget. Gene would have to raise them alone.

London, of course, was out of the question now.

Around this time, Larry directed a Broadway musical, *Lovely Ladies and Kind Gentlemen,* based on *Teahouse of the August Moon.* It closed after a short run. I felt badly for Larry and rationalized: *The theater's a murderous racket, who wants to go to New York anyway?* and *Why bother with* Copperfield? I was lying to myself. The theater bug, sparked at seven years old, still burned in me.

In the meantime, while searching for a new producer and director, Joel and I used *Copperfield* as our audition piece. One of the impressed listeners was a man named Happy Goday. Wiry, dynamic, always in motion, Happy ranked among the industry's top five publishers. I had known him since my CBS days and had cut many songs in his catalog, notably "As Long as He Needs Me," "Cotton Fields," and "Who Can I Turn To?"

Now based primarily in Hollywood, Happy heard that Twentieth Century Fox wanted a theme song for their blockbuster production of the year, *The Poseidon Adventure*. Every writer in town, apparently, had submitted something and had been turned down. The producers were in a panic.

A long shot, but we met with the record company president Russ Regan, studio music head Lionel Newman, director Ronald Neame, and producer Irwin Allen. They handed us a script and told us to "go home and bring something in by nine in the morning."

Not having seen the picture presented a handicap, so we tested a thousand different alternatives, recalling director Ronald Neame's request that "the lyric content must be positive." This task was not easy when an ocean liner is about to be demolished and most of the cast members drowned in photogenically ghoulish ways.

"Make it a love song," said producer Irwin Allen, a further challenge in the face of so much disaster.

At four in the morning, Joel started writing shorthand ideas in the air. My patience was gone by then and I yelled, "If you have a line, write it on *paper.*"

Joel nodded, erased the midair thought with a swift jerk of his palm, and made note of it on a pad.

By five-thirty our nerves were frayed, and we were snapping at each other—one of the few displays of outward temper in our career.

"I *still* think the last verse could be stronger," I insisted.

"It's fine," said Joel.

"One note change, just *one* note."

108

"I think the note makes it hard to remember. It's illogical."

"It's too obvious the other way."

Our differences of opinion subsided by seven-thirty, and "The Morning After" emerged. Joel never made it home. We had a quick breakfast with Jill and Ceil before driving, in a sleepless haze, to the Twentieth Century Fox lot.

All the way to Century City we sang the song, analyzing to make sure it was the best we could do. We were anxious but satisfied. The writing of the lyric had been tremendously helped by some advice I'd once received from Johnny Mercer in New York: "Don't tell the story—tell the feelings *behind* the action." Every line we wrote related to the plot, without spelling it out:

> There's got to be a morning after,
> If we can hold on through the night.
> We have a chance to find the sunshine;
> Let's keep on looking for the light.

Our imagery—bridges, lights, darkness—had some connection to plot events, but we made no reference to the actual shipwreck, or to a cast of characters forced to climb through an upside-down ocean liner.

I also felt, without knowing quite why, that the song should have a sense of hope, a spiritual undercurrent. My past had been so negative that I automatically projected Hammerstein "cock-eyed optimist" flavor into lyrics.

We staggered into Lionel Newman's office at eight-thirty the next morning. Joel had barely learned the melody and hit a few clinkers; I was asleep on my feet, and my voice croaked on the high notes. At the conclusion there was deafening silence.

"Want us to play it again?" I asked.

They nodded. This time I sang with more authority, and Joel supplied a background voice to add power.

"Hmmm," Ronald Neame said, turning to Irwin Allen, "I believe it has something. What do you think?"

After a long pause, Irwin Allen smiled and said, "Let's go with it."

As filming commenced I thought, *We've come a long way from the Pink Cloud.*

"Maybe we'll even be nominated for an Oscar," I said to Joel.

He smiled, that familiar I'll-let-him-fantasize smile, but I could tell he was hoping too.

The spiritual quality of "The Morning After" was picked up by a lighting man on the *Poseidon* set, a man named Mark, who walked up to me and said, "You know you've written a Christian song. That lyric could have been written for God."

And he quoted:

> It's not too late—we should be giving.
> Only with love can we climb.
> It's not too late—not while we're living.
> Let's put our hands out in time.

I thought of the lighting man, Mark, and the peace he radiated. He was young, with wheat-colored hair and green eyes. What struck me most was the relaxed air he projected; he seemed totally in tune with himself. I envied that peace.

I ran into Mark again at the Twentieth Century Fox commissary, and he invited me to join him for lunch. When our sandwiches arrived, I reached for mine; but the look in Mark's eyes made me hesitate.

"Do you mind if we pray first?" he asked. I said no and Mark whispered thanks for the food, for the day, for all the blessings in his life.

"You know, Mark," I said, after a few minutes. "You always seem so together. What's your secret?"

"My faith," he said simply. The gentle conviction of his tone rose above commissary clamor. "You know, I have Bible classes in my home every Tuesday. Why don't you come to one?"

"I'm Jewish."

"I know."

"It's not that I don't think Jesus was a great man...a great rabbi....a great force for good." I found myself stuttering, trying to explain.

110

"He's more than that."

"What do you mean?"

Mark put his hand on my sleeve. His grip was strong, full of pressure. "I can only tell you that Jesus changed my life. You can't believe what I was like five years ago...strung out on drugs all the time, missing work, never sleeping. And always bitter. Man, all that hate can eat you up alive." He hesitated. "You think I'm crazy."

"No, I don't."

"It's just that you wrote that spiritual song and I felt...a searching. A need."

Mark's serene and tranquil image remained with me in the days ahead. I mentioned him to a drummer I knew. "I'll bet he doesn't have a trouble in the world," I said.

"Are you kidding? Mark lost his three-year-old son last year. The baby was born with a defective heart, and they gave him all kinds of operations; but he died anyway. I don't know what my wife and I would have done if it had been us."

I recalled Mark saying, "My Father is with me all the time." Could his faith really have eased the pain of such a tragedy?

I decided to go to one of Mark's Bible classes. But Joel and I got busy on *Copperfield* and I couldn't find the time.

13

Oscar

After *The Poseidon Adventure,* Ceil and I felt secure enough to buy a home in Beverly Hills. For all its rustic charm, however (aptly conveyed by our address "Shirley Lane"), I felt the house was slightly small. But Ceil said, "Just leave it to me. When I finish adding on, we'll have a showplace."

Ceil had a decorator's eye (she had already expressed an interest in pursuing home design professionally) and I decided to trust her instincts. She ripped up carpeting, steamed down wallpaper, and slowly turned Shirley Lane into a hilltop paradise. In 1975, Los Angeles's *Home Magazine* did a piece on her work, with a picture of "the 40-foot garden which she floored with Italian tile and bedecked with white wicker furniture and scores of plants."

Her sense of decor and color was soothing—and I needed the soothing solitude it provided, because my emotional world was growing more chaotic. Every phone call from my parents tied me tighter to the bonds of achievement. My mother only had to say, "How are you, L'Alfred?" and I felt compelled to issue a full report, embellishing the truth until she was satisfied.

"I'm doing a new picture, Mom."

"I have three records on the charts, Mom."

"Joel and I are doing a show, Mom."

"How's that, Mom?"

I sensed a dangerous desperation growing and it related directly to *Copperfield.* The project had begun to represent my overall

112

worth, a yardstick to measure success or failure. Common sense warned me about the perils of investing so much juice in one show, but I couldn't help it. Prestige, fame, wealth, Larry's respect, enthusiasm from my parents—all, I felt, would be mine if this *one* production got off the ground.

I would be my brother's equal. The left eye would attain the stature of the right eye.

Sir Delfont fed the anxiety by wiring us: "Still interested in *Copperfield* for West End next year, if proper director can be found to replace Gene Kelly." I compiled a list of possibilities and sent them to London.

A month dragged by with no response. We were told that Delfont had gone on vacation, then a business trip in France, then to visit a sick member of his family.

Other symptoms of emotional breakdown appeared and intensified. I found I couldn't enjoy a movie unless it related to my work. There had to be a "reason" to see it. Could I learn from it? I sat in darkened theaters as a pupil, tearing apart the lighting, editing, scoring, and performances.

There's nothing wrong with this kind of self-education; creative people are perpetually hungry for knowledge. But when you cross a line, as I did, and find yourself unable to respond purely as a spectator, the whole process becomes a chore—like cramming for finals in school on subjects you hate.

The *Copperfield* saga continued. Our friend, Irwin Kostal, arranger of *West Side Story*, *The Sound of Music*, and *Mary Poppins*, offered inspiration and encouragement.

With Irwin in our corner, I redoubled my efforts on behalf of *Copperfield*. Happy introduced us to producer Arthur Jacobs. Slim, hyperactive, dapper, Arthur was a former press agent for Gary Cooper and Marilyn Monroe; a man who adored show business. He also adored musicals, and had done three by the time we met him: *Dr. Doolittle*, *Tom Sawyer* and *Goodbye, Mr. Chips*.

"Play him *Copperfield*," Happy suggested.

We did, and his first response was, "Can I produce it?"

I pointed out that Sir Delfont owned the rights. Arthur wasted no time—what was Delfont's number, when could we finish the script, where did we feel it should be shot? "Ireland," he went on, without waiting for a reply. "In the summer. And I know the perfect guy to do the sets—Tony Walton."

He meant it. A day later he reached Delfont, and a week later he had purchased the rights from Delfont for thirty-five thousand dollars—thirty thousand more than Delfont had paid for them in the first place.

"Just think, Ireland," I told Joel. "A movie musical of our own—book, words, and music. Think of what this will do for us in the industry."

A minor stumbling block slowed us down. Joel's wife Jill had written an original show, *Rainbow Jones*, and needed an accompanist for the first two weeks of local performances. Jill didn't want to hire anyone—felt Joel had the right pianistic touch—and he agreed to help out.

The show's cast members included Richard Dreyfuss, Lee Merriwether, and Betty Garrett and had strong potential. Only trouble was, rehearsals ate into our writing time.

"Arthur needs these rewrites in a week," I told Joel. "We'll lose this chance. *I'll* pay for an accompanist."

"It's the least I can do, as her husband," Joel said. "We'll be able to get the work done."

I might have overreacted to the situation from my own vantage point. I had a problem with the idea of wives with careers, whether they held secretarial jobs or wrote Broadway musicals. My mother had been a working wife, had devoted her main energy to the store, and I blamed that for her lack as a homemaker.

I wanted my wife to be home when I got there.

"Al," Ceil said one evening. "I'd like to go back to work."

She said it casually, but I felt myself stiffen.

"Matter of fact, I'd like to open a shop with my friend Barbara." Mistaking my silence for agreement, Ceil rushed on: "And we thought we'd call it Setting Up House. How do you like the name?"

I don't like the name. I don't like the whole idea. I'm not on Avenue M anymore!

"Honey, why do you have to work?"

"Well, I had a job before we got married. And you're busy with Joel. I can't just sit around with a four-year-old all day. And I'll be home in the morning and evening." She was talking too fast, running her words together. "If I don't like it, if it interferes with us, I'll give up the whole thing. I just want to try."

"My mother worked in a store."

"I'm not your mother."

"It's Rose and Irving's all over again."

"That's not fair."

"All over again."

"Your mother was a selfish woman. I'm not like her."

"You'll *become* like her!"

I saw that Ceil was hurt.

"I love you," she said quietly. "I'd never do anything to jeopardize our marriage."

"A store can take over your life."

"It won't."

"Okay," I said, though every bone in my body ached with opposition. "Try it for a couple of months. But if it gets in the way, you'll quit, won't you?"

"Yes."

I kept pace with my Brill Building friends. Carole King was a recording star, Neil Sedaka was in the midst of a comeback on Elton John's Rocket records. But Gerry Goffin (now divorced from Carole) was relatively inactive. Mann and Weil were burned out from the nonstop, night-and-day work regimen, and Jack Keller was struggling. We had maintained a relentless pace since our teens and now, in our mid-thirties, were physically and emotionally exhausted.

I wondered what kept us all going, and which of us would crack first.

"The Morning After" was nominated for an Oscar. No one thought it had a chance against "Ben," a Number One hit for Michael Jackson, written by veterans Walter Scharf and Don Black.

115

My old friend Jackie Wilson called after reading the news. Jackie had been through many professional ups and downs. His hits stopped in the late 1960s, after the artistic and commercial high of his smash, "Your Love Keeps Lifting Me (Higher and Higher)," but he sounded as positive and powerful as ever.

"Man, I *know* you're gonna take it," he said, and his conviction made it easier to dismiss the majority viewpoint.

My mother's good wishes were, as always, couched in anxiety.

"Oh, darling, I'll die if you don't win," she moaned. "I'm going to temple tonight to pray, and I'll go there every day until the Oscar show."

Arthur Jacobs unwittingly added further pressure on us when he said, "If you win, it'll give *Copperfield* a much better chance for success."

Coincidentally, Larry was opening his new musical, *Seesaw*, on Broadway at the same time. My mother spoke proudly of "both my sons."

"Both my sons are going to be famous," she repeated, over and over, and I thought of all the times Larry and I had shared things: a room, a bed, credit.

I won.

And Larry's show opened to good reviews.

It's a tie!

Why am I fighting? I asked myself, when I got home. *I know it's an incredible victory. I know it will help me with my peers. I know Irwin Allen and Lionel Newman are delighted.*

I wanted to cry.

I felt old, prematurely old. I would have given anything to be a child. I felt as though I were scaling a hill that kept growing steeper with every step I took. I thought of Gypsy Rose Lee's mother singing "Rose's Turn," and her plaintive question: "What Did I Do It For?"

I didn't know the answer, yet the image of *David Copperfield* hung over me—a crazy quilt of Dickensian characters, taunting me in shrill, ridiculing tones: the irresponsible Micawber, stern Aunt Betsey, harsh Mr. Murdstone hitting David.

He had my head in a vise, but I twined round him somehow, and

116

stopped him for a moment, entreating him not to beat me....
He beat me then, as if he would have beaten me to death....
I was lying, feverish and hot, and torn, and sore, and raging in my
puny way, upon the floor.
Dickens knew. He understood.

"The Morning After" became Number One around the world
with Maureen McGovern. Maureen had been a secretary from
Cleveland, Ohio, with no recordings to her credit. This debut record made her an instant star.

Timing helped too. The nation was still euphoric, coasting on
a wave of hope following President Nixon's January 27 announcement that the war in Vietnam was over. "The Morning
After" spoke optimistically of the future, underlining the national mood. Watergate had begun, but no one fully realized its
seriousness yet.

"Your Oscar is nothing," Arthur Jacobs assured Joel and me.
"*Copperfield* will make 'The Morning After' look like chopped
liver." He outlined plans to hire Herb Ross as director. His production man, he said, had even found the site of the 1851 London Exhibition; most of the exhibits from that fair had been
preserved.

"We can shoot the whole thing for three million," he announced exultantly.

Ceil and I were already making preparations for a stay in Ireland. Gene Kelly's descriptions of the beautiful countryside had
whetted my appetite, and I was reading a *Hollywood Reporter* announcement about *Copperfield* when my phone rang. It was
Lionel Newman.

"Hey, I'm sorry to tell you this, buddy, but Arthur's dead."

The *Reporter* fell from my hand.

"Middle of the night...massive coronary...a shame, only fifty-
two years old." Lionel kept talking, though I only heard him in
bits and pieces.

Arthur had been a popular man, and hundreds of friends clus-
tered together for his funeral at the Hillside Chapel in Culver
City. With morbid, uncharacteristic ESP, Joel had dreamed the

night before we heard the news of Arthur's demise in a car crash. He had been wrong about the particulars, but the dream's accuracy was chilling.

Joel and I began to feel threatened—there's no other word for it—when we read in *Variety* a few days later that Sean Kenny, the designer Gene had chosen to do *Copperfield*, had died in his sleep.

"Is this project jinxed?" Joel wondered aloud.

We can beat the odds, I thought. As always when confronted with challenge, my determination grew.

14

The Towering Inferno

Copperfield continued on its brutally bumpy course. United Artists president David Picker optioned it, then left the company. Director Peter Medak (who had done a critically acclaimed film, *The Ruling Class*) was eager to tackle it, until United Artists ruled him out.

Lightning struck twice when *Poseidon* producer Irwin Allen called on a Monday and asked Joel and me to write a love song for another disaster film, *The Towering Inferno*. Only catch: He wanted it on Tuesday.

We went to work, reading the script, living through the same pressure we had experienced on "The Morning After."

"Black coffee coming up," said Ceil, as we struggled to finish "We May Never Love Like This Again."

Allen liked the song. It came down to a competition between our tune and a song Fred Astaire (one of the film's cast members) had written. To our great relief, we were the final choice.

"We May Never Love Like This Again" was nominated for an Oscar. The ceremonies were as nerve-wracking as before, but there was great personal pleasure in being presented our *Towering Inferno* awards by Shirley MacLaine and Gene Kelly. Gene had specifically requested our category, feeling we had the best chance to win. Another friend from my Columbia days, Aretha Franklin, sang the song.

Aretha and I spoke at the Academy Award banquet afterward,

and she seemed glowing and full of optimism. Before we parted, she was gracious enough to say, "Best of luck, honey. You deserved that award."

My mother's words were less palatable, more anxiety-provoking. "I prayed for you to win," she said. "I stayed all night in temple. How I prayed, let my Alfred make it. I know someday he'll make it. Someday he'll be famous."

What do you mean, someday? What do you mean, you're praying I'll make it? I won a second Oscar last night!

Domestic clouds began to build up. I had never gotten over wishing Ceil would abandon her business and stay home, and when Setting Up House proved a disappointment, I expected her to give full concentration to our joint goals.

Instead she told me, "I had lunch with Jackie Mazur. We talked about going into a partnership."

Jackie was a good friend, wife of Billy Joel's manager Irwin Mazur, a busy interior decorator on her own.

"Why work?" I asked her. "Don't I make enough money? You don't *need* to work."

"I told you, I have to keep busy. But it won't be a store. I'll make my own hours. I'll work out of the house. You won't even know I'm working."

I'll know, I thought. But I acquiesced.

Joel was under tension too. Jill's musical, *Rainbow Jones* (for which she had written book, words, and music) was set to open on Broadway at the Music Box Theater. It had gotten superb reviews in Boston and Washington, but I felt its fanciful Charlie Brown charm would be out of place in a large Broadway house. Even though Peter Kastner was brash and appealing in the Richard Dreyfuss part, the critics decided it wasn't Broadway-type material. The difficulty was best expressed by a woman in the audience, who whispered to her companion, "Where are the dancing girls?"

Jill's work as lyricist, librettist, and tune writer was outstanding. Since merit wasn't the issue, I had to look elsewhere, and *Rainbow Jones* taught me that every genre has its rules: rock-and-roll was aggressive; movies were a visual, rather than a dialogue,

120

medium; Broadway musicals emphasized opulence and production values over subtlety. We had to make sure that, when *Copperfield* arrived in New York, it had the right "look"; eyefilling costumes, imaginative lighting, expansive choreography.

I tried to hide my growing despair by socializing. Ceil arranged a joint birthday party for Ernest Borgnine and me at Ernie's house. He and I had been friends since *The Poseidon Adventure*, and I enjoyed his genial charm and urbane wit, qualities far removed from either the vicious Fatso of *From Here to Eternity* or the inarticulate butcher of *Marty*. Ceil and I also liked his wife, Tove. The two of them reminded me of Irving Mansfield and Jacqueline Susann. Tove had gone into the cosmetics business, with Ernie's full approval and backing, and had succeeded at it. They were mutually supportive of each other. At the party Ernie confided, "I found the right woman. She's for me, I'm for her. When you've got that, you've got everything."

During this period Joel and I acquired an "image." Immediately following *The Towering Inferno*, Frank Capra, Jr. hired us, on the recommendation of scorer David Shire, to supply the music for a two-hour TV movie *Trapped Beneath the Sea*. The papers later announced: "Masters of Disaster Al Kasha and Joel Hirschhorn to Score Telemovie." Columnist Dianne Bennett picked up the phrase and referred to the "Masters of Disaster" in her column, and from then on we were branded with that name.

The phrase also seemed an apt description of my private life when I learned that my parents were planning to fly to California to stay with us for a month.

I was in my mid thirties, but my father's animal physicality still made me uneasy. After crushing my hand, he pounded my back. "Stop that," I said, too sharply, and he grinned. My quick response let him know he was still a threatening presence. His grin also announced *I'm stronger than you are. I can whip you anytime.*

His strength amazed me. Nothing slowed him down, not the diabetes he had developed, nor the morning vodka he combined with herring.

"He's worse than ever," my mother confided, clutching my arm possessively to underscore the point. She indicated a scar on her forehead, a scar that stood out clearly above the pancake makeup. "Mr. Weinberger next door had to come and stop him from killing me," she said. "He would have killed me, Alfred. What can I do?"

I had heard this so many times. Her pleas for help, for rescue, before forgiving him and lapsing into the old pattern. I thought of all our conversations by the cash register, the promises I had made to give her a better life.

"Ma," I said. It seemed so clear, suddenly. "Why not move here?"

"Your father doesn't like it. He wants to stay in Brooklyn."

"Not with Daddy. Just you."

"I can't do that."

"Why can't you? Don't worry about the money. I have money. I can find you a nice apartment, and you'll be free of him. He won't hurt you anymore."

"So quick....just leave?"

"What do you mean, so quick? Yes, leave. Leave it all behind. You hate him. He's made your life a misery for forty-six years. Do it."

"I have to see."

"You keep saying that. What's to stop you?"

"L'Alfred..."

"Alfred!"

"Alfred, he's still my husband."

"He beats you. He drinks. He's crazy. He's made life miserable for all of us, you and me and Larry. You've always talked about the way out. This is it."

"Someday, when the time is right."

"Ma, you're sixty-eight years old."

I couldn't understand her reluctance. She had been delaying this decision since my childhood, waiting for the "right time"...when she could afford it...when we were successful...when they retired.

"Alfred, save me."

"Ma, I'm trying to save you, but you won't let me. If you don't leave him now, you never will. And you'll hate yourself for not taking the chance. For never having lived."

She said she would think about it, and nothing more was said.

Ceil and I did our best to entertain my parents. By this time Ceil's decorating career with Jackie had taken off, a partnership that would eventually bring in such clients as Ernie Borgnine, Nell Carter, Harry Sloane (head of New World Pictures), Dom DeLuise and Stephanie Powers. She put aside her growing business obligations and took them to movies, to Disneyland and Universal, to department stores for new clothes. But they *kvetched*: the movies were smutty; Disney and Universal tired them out, made them walk too much; clothes at Saks were too expensive; the dresses at Bullocks were ugly.

Our friends, producer Jack Wohl and his wife Micki, invited us to dinner and we brought them along. Micki thoughtfully prepared a Jewish meal, and in the familiar atmosphere of matzo, potato pancakes, and chicken my father denounced "those lousy *goyim*...do you know how they used to beat me up when I was a boy in Poland?" Ceil held her tongue. Later on my mother called Micki, "the perfect daughter-in-law to have, a wonderful cook, a nice Jewish girl"; and the old rage sprang up again.

They refused to give Ceil her due—or Dana either, beyond my mother's observation, "She's gorgeous, L'Alfred. She looks just like me."

My brother called and announced he was moving to Los Angeles. "I've got to get away from the theater for a while," he told me. "I want to produce movies."

Flying from Avenue M was pointless; Avenue M was flying to meet me.

The temperature was 102 degrees, with smog so chokingly thick I couldn't breathe. My mother complained, "You call this weather wonderful? It's worse than New York."

We were lounging by the pool; Dana toyed with a mop handle. I stared at the mop handle, vaguely preoccupied with it, not making any specific connections.

My father sat back on his beach chair, shirt off to reveal a still-muscular chest.

"Grandpa," Dana said. "Play with me."

"Go to your grandmother," he answered, still facing the sun.

"Grandpa, I want to play with *you*."

"Come over here, Dana," Ceil ordered. Dana didn't move. There was a moment of dead silence—the kind of unnatural silence that precedes an explosion—then Dana, swinging the mop handle, accidentally hit my father in the leg with it.

He leaped up wordlessly, a puppet programmed to do one thing—strike out. I watched in horror as that hated hand smashed my daughter's face. She fell to the ground screaming.

In a split second I was on my feet, grabbing him, punching him with insane force. I couldn't believe that old, brutal Avenue M scenes had spilled into the second generation.

Okay, big shot. How do you like that, big shot?

Dana was inconsolable; Ceil fought to placate her.

"You're never, *never*, to lay a hand on my daughter again, or I'll kill you," I shouted. "Never touch her again."

"She...was...hitting...me," he protested.

"She's five years old. *Five years old*."

"I didn't hit her hard," he said, as though he and Dana were physical equals and contemporaries.

"Five years old," I repeated. My voice was weird, inhuman, an unearthly sound echoing through the neat, manicured Beverly Hills backyard. "Five years old."

"Al, it's all right," Ceil said, frightened now. I was out of control. I could only utter those words again and again, while my father insisted, "I had to teach her a lesson," my mother sobbed, and Ceil held on to me in the dimming afternoon light.

My parents left in the morning, but I didn't calm down. Phobic symptoms returned and multiplied. My pill dependence was reaching crisis proportions. Nightmares of being tossed into a closet returned. I woke up, chilled and soaked simultaneously, after terrifying visions of being beaten and bloodied. Sometimes I screamed myself awake, and Ceil had to hold me for an hour before I regained control. Later she would describe to me the gasping, moaning sounds I made while in the grip of panic.

Often I'd tiptoe into Dana's room and watch her sleep, study-

124

ing her peaceful expression, reassuring myself desperately that she was safe.

Please, don't let her be scarred by that experience, I said to myself. *Don't let the sight of my father's violent hand burn a permanent scar on her memory.*

Sometimes I sang "The Morning After" to her quietly in the darkness:

> Oh, can't you see the morning after?
> It's waiting right outside the storm.
> Why don't we cross the bridge together
> And find a place that's safe and warm.

I would seize the rim of the bed and swear, "My father's father beat him up, my father beat me up, and now he has hit my daughter. I swear, the chain stops here. No one will lay a hand on my daughter again."

Once Dana woke up and saw me standing over her.

"What's wrong, Daddy?"

"I'm just checking up on you, darling. Are you all right?"

Her sleepy eyes met mine and she said, "I'm fine."

I kissed her and went back to bed, praying she really was.

I had always dreaded driving, avoiding it whenever possible. Now I found I would begin to choke on the road, hyperventilate and have to pull over. I had never been entirely comfortable in restaurants; now I refused to enter one unless a business meeting demanded it.

These attacks of fear infuriated me. I thought of myself as strong, a leader, and I was dominated by terrors that pounced on me unexpectedly and made each day a new nightmare. The palpitations, which had ceased for a few months, assaulted me with heart attack fury.

"Let's go to a movie," Ceil would suggest. "It'll do you good." I pleaded exhaustion.

"I can't get over what my father did," I said.

There was a long pause.

"It didn't only happen to you, Al," she said. "It happened to me too. And most of all, it happened to Dana."

I felt defensive. They were my parents; it was my history. I was the only one they had destroyed with their cruelty.

She began to sob bitterly.

"It'll be all right," I said, putting out my arms.

She avoided the embrace. "It won't be all right unless you give up the past. You have to let go of your old family. Dana and I are your family now."

"I know that."

"You *don't* know it," Ceil cried. "You hang on, you keep hoping they'll change. They won't change. And as long as you make them the center of everything, we can't live a decent life."

She began to pace. "Forget me. What about your daughter? Do you *see* her? Do you know what she's doing in school? What her grades are? Do you know her friends? Do you even know that she's been sick with the flu all week?"

"She had a cold."

"A *flu*. And that's another thing. You're not the only person in this house who gets sick."

She was on the verge of hysteria now. "I love you, but I can't stand to see what's happening to you...what you're *letting* happen."

"I'm sick."

"You're not trying to get well."

"I love you," I whispered. But I felt more alone than ever.

Temporary distraction arrived in the form of Bette Davis. She had contacted our agent, expressing a desire to play Aunt Betsey Trotwood when *Copperfield* became a film.

We arranged to play our score for her in the dining room of the Bel Air Hotel. Ms. Davis met us in the lobby. She was surprisingly small, less imposing in person than on the screen, but we recognized her authority when I mentioned my friendship with Ernest Borgnine. "You know," I said, "he starred in the *Catered Affair* with you." She stared imperiously, puffed her cigarette and replied, "I remember the picture, dear. I'm not *that* old."

"She sounds just like she did in *The Great Lie*," Joel mumbled, then proceeded to turn movie fan again. He brought up a Davis double feature he'd recently seen at a nostalgia festival: *Three on a Match* and *Cabin in the Cotton*, which pleased her. Did she think he wondered, that *Of Human Bondage* had stood the test of time? What was it like working with George Arliss? ("A *dear* man. I owe him so much.") Leslie Howard?

I kicked him under the table, to remind him that *The Great Lie* was yesterday's news and *Copperfield* was the issue.

Davis's reactions were gratifying. "Your script is brilliant," she said. When we modestly pointed out that Dickens had been a great help, she answered vehemently, "But look what you *did* with him." She applauded after every number we did.

"You can count on me for this role," she said. I felt fresh hope. How fantastic to have Bette Davis play a role written by us! And someone would be bound to fork up full financing if they knew she was a definite part of the package.

That night I dreamed about *Copperfield*. The characters, sometimes enemies, sometimes friends, had become so real that I carried them inside me all the time. I imagined Bette Davis as the seemingly severe but warmhearted Aunt Betsey. If the picture was made, she would have its strongest moment: the moment when abused, tormented young David is adopted and permanently rescued from the tyranny of his stepfather:

> ...Her face gradually relaxed and became so pleasant that I was emboldened to kiss and thank her, which I did with great heartiness, and with both my arms clasped 'round her neck....
> ...Thus I began my new life, in a new name and with everything new about me. Now that the state of doubt was over, I felt, for many days, like one in a dream.

It was a scene I never tired of reading. I felt rescued, temporarily, when I played the words over in my head.

I dreaded leaving home more and more. Agoraphobia, once held at a manageable distance, was assuming full control. Strange symptoms began to appear: a spastic colon, which caused me to double up in pain; headaches; rashes all over my body. I checked into Cedars Sinai Hospital in October, 1975, and spent the week undergoing tests.

One of the doctors was a dark, burly man with thick arms. He reminded me of my father, triggering off visions of abuse. I asked for another doctor, without explaining why.

"Doctor Baker is supposed to be the best," said Ceil.

"You've got to get me somebody else."

While there I brooded that my mother hadn't called. It took a TV report about Jackie Wilson to divert my attention. Jackie had suffered a serious stroke during a performance at the Latin Casino in New Jersey. When I checked and discovered how serious the attack was, my depression grew worse.

"He's going to die," I said to Ceil. "We're all dying." Images of the Brill Building swam in front of me. Jackie's rehearsing "My Empty Arms" in a tacky, airless cubicle. Burt Bacharach and Hal David's singing and playing in the next room. Lieber and Stoller down the hall.

We're all middle-aged, I thought. *Where did the time go? And what have I done in the meantime?*

"There's nothing wrong with you," the doctors said. "It's just nerves." And Ceil added, "Isn't that great? You're healthy."

"There *is* something wrong," I protested. "They're just not finding it."

I hated to leave the hospital, hated to leave the cocoon of sympathetic doctors and nurses.

Copperfield reclaimed my attention. A Canadian producer, Harold Greenberg, loved our script and score and wanted us to fly to Toronto to perform the music for some backer friends.

I went, heavily sedated. Larry joined Joel and me. He was enthusiastic. "This is first-rate," he raved. Those words meant everything. All my life I had waited for my brother to admire my work.

"I'd like to co-produce," he continued. "I'll help you get the script in shape and bring in any money people Harold doesn't come up with."

Toronto was encouraging. Harold claimed he had all the financing, and I once again told Joel, "*This* time it feels right." He agreed.

I returned to the hotel, fired with excitement, and noticed the red light flickering: a message from Ceil.

128

"Your father is sick, Al," she said. "I just heard from your mother, and she's falling apart. The doctors told her he'll be dead in six months."

Larry and I flew to New York to see him. I thought I'd be prepared; I'd seen shriveled, wasted cancer victims during my stay at Cedars. But it's different when the frail, emaciated near-corpse is your own father. Overnight his strength had deserted him and his handshake, so repellently powerful in the past, was feeble, limp.

"Alfred," he said. "My son. My son."

He was frightened. It was odd to feel his childlike panic, odd to see him clutching me for support.

"I'm here," I whispered. "And I'll take care of you." I phoned Ceil and asked her if she would mind my bringing my parents to California to live with us, until...

There was the briefest hesitation on the phone. Ceil was wiser than I; she knew what trouble I was courting.

"It's the least I can do for him," I told her.

"All right. If you think it's best."

The moment of tender self-sacrifice passed, and I realized the enormity of what I had undertaken. I remained at Avenue M for three days. All the years on my own—years that had brought me awards, acknowledgment from famous people, a shaky but growing sense of self—vanished everytime I stretched out on my old bed. Valiums could have been peppermints for all the power they exerted on my hotly active brain.

The underground subway still rattled and shook our building. Buses still stopped on the corner and squealed back into gear. My mother's voice droned over the noise with "You'll Never Know." Each note, in my tortured mind, was stretched twice or three times its proper length.

"And...if...I...tried...I...still...couldn't...hide...my...love ...for...you...."

Roaches had extended their previous territory beyond the kitchen and bathroom. I found one racing across my pillow.

My father's doctor cautioned me: "He really shouldn't fly. There's arteriosclerosis as well as cancer. I *think* he can survive the trip, but I'm not sure."

129

"At least he'll be in California with his sons."

The morning of the flight, my father complained bitterly: "I don't want to go to L.A." Helping him dress was difficult; he couldn't decide what to wear, and he maintained a running argument with my mother. Even in his broken, terminal state, his hostility for her remained strong; the strongest part of him, as it had always been.

"Let me shave you, Daddy," I suggested, when I noticed the razor trembling in his hand.

"No," he snapped. "I shaved myself all my life, I can shave myself now."

I jumped back at the jerky motion of his arm, till I remembered his condition. He couldn't hurt me. His power was gone.

"You're cutting your chin."

"What's some blood? Am I a little girl, that I'm afraid of blood?"

"I didn't say that."

He nicked himself again. More blood mixed with the white lather.

"Keep in mind...*nobody* shaves Irving Kasha, nobody."

The limousine came to pick us up. "I'd rather die in Brooklyn," my father said, as we drove to JFK.

"You're not dying," I told him, repeating my assurances as we boarded the plane.

My palpitations had already begun by the time the doors of the DC 10 closed. Turning to the stewardess I said anxiously, "Maybe we can take a later flight."

She looked bewildered. "Sir, the pilot's been given the signal for takeoff."

Trapped.

"I'm cold," my father cried. "I'm freezing cold."

The stewardess brought him a blanket.

"This tea isn't good." And then, five minutes later: "This coffee isn't good."

"Look how red your father's face is," my mother said, grasping my arm.

"Rose," he screamed. "I have a pain in my chest. A terrible pain."

I clung to my composure as the stewardess slipped an oxygen mask over my father's face.

"He's going to die. My husband's going to die. Oh, God, help me, my pressure, my pressure!"

As always in an emergency, my mother made things worse by bearing down on the tragic aspects of the situation. Milking it, turning it into hysteria.

"Irving, Irving. My Irving!"

Again, as I had done before when in the throes of a panic attack on a plane, I took refuge in the men's room. The claustrophobic walls, the miniature sink and toilet, seemed smaller than ever now.

When I returned, I saw they were still driving the stewardess crazy with their histrionics, their demands. My father's illness was pathetically genuine. Yet I knew his querulous, childish behavior would have been the same no matter what state of health he was in.

I'm going to die before he does, I thought, returning to the men's room. My presence of mind was fading. This fear wasn't normal; it was a paralyzing, all-consuming terror. Every symptom of the past—headaches, lump in the throat, heart skipping beats—descended with crushing impact.

I'm having a nervous breakdown, I realized. *And I didn't know it. I wouldn't face it.*

The DC 10 hit an air pocket and dropped hundreds of feet.

He's going to die, he's going to die. My mother's words hammered at my eardrums, and then I saw it was someone knocking on the bathroom door. I had been closeted there for fifteen minutes.

Always locked away, in one closet or another.

Maybe I can die first.

It seemed simpler to die than to face the months that lay ahead.

Miraculously, I kept working. Joel and I composed a theme song for Ronald Reagan's 1976 presidential campaign, at the request of record executive Mike Curb. Mike later became lieutenant governor of California. He was brilliant, imaginative and—most crucially, since it gave us a basic characteristic in common—a tireless worker.

Record producer and writer Michael Lloyd, who worked with Curb, was another non-stop perfectionist who became a friend and collaborator. Michael, Joel, and I launched a productive, consistent partnership in the mid-1970s. A country hit, "Charlie, I Love Your Wife," resulted immediately from our teamwork.

I was grateful to Curb and Michael Lloyd for their belief in me and their friendship, especially during the months of my father's final deterioration. Meeting Governor Reagan the night our song was performed and introducing him before a black-tie audience at the Cocoanut Grove offered a temporary feeling of optimism.

This optimism was reinforced when he said, "Thank you for your music," and commented specifically on the lyrics; he had really listened to every word. He shook my hand with genuine warmth.

I thought of that handshake and the hope it conveyed when listening to my father complain, "What kind of doctors are those? Why can't they give me something for the pain?"

Be sympathetic. He's suffering.

"Let Ceil cook for me...don't let your mother cook," he said once. "Always hated her lousy cooking anyway."

My father didn't let up:

"Your brother doesn't even call."

"Your mother wishes I would die."

"You all want me to die."

"You're not dying," I said automatically, as he lost weight and his skin turned a sallow, yellowish color.

My mother flew back to Brooklyn to collect the rest of her belongings, close all bank accounts, and sell the store. On the day of her return, Joel and I were well into a book on songwriting, *If They Ask You, You Can Write a Song,* and Ceil volunteered to pick her up at the airport.

After Ceil left the room, my father said, "You go and pick up your mother."

"But Ceil's going."

"Alfred, it's not right. You can't let the *shiksa* go."

"What do you mean?"

"I mean, she's not family. She shouldn't go to the airport. *You* should go."

I couldn't believe it. He was living in my house, receiving care and attention that amounted to professional nursing from my wife, and he was still saying the *shiksa*.

I didn't argue; he was clearly dying.

Without explaining the reason to Ceil, I told her I would get my mother.

She was waiting, suitcases on either side of her. In her chubby hand was a large blue bag. I reached for it.

"No, I'll carry the bag myself."

"What's in it?"

"Nothing. Papers."

"What kind of papers?"

"Papers. Does it matter?"

"I just wondered. Is it a secret?"

"No." But she clutched the bag tighter.

"You know, Ceil was going to come and pick you up. And Daddy said, don't let the *shiksa* go; *you* pick Mother up."

Without the slightest pause, she answered, "He's right. You're my son, you should be the one to come."

"Not the *shiksa*."

"That's right."

"She's not family, right?"

"Look, Ceil is a nice girl."

"A nice girl."

"But you're my son."

I reached again for the blue bag. "That's heavy. Let me carry it."

"No."

I grabbed the bag from her hands.

"I want to carry it."

"Give it back."

Alarm creased her features. Animal fear.

"What's in it?"

133

"Give it back or I'll call the police."

"Call the police? You'd call the police on your son?"

She lunged for the bag. I held it out of her grasp.

"Police, police!"

Horrified, I let her have the blue bag back. We fought all the way home; freeway traffic doubled the normal length of the drive.

We arrived at the house, and my mother leapt from the car and ran inside. I followed her, not unloading the valises.

"I want to see what's in that bag," I demanded.

"It's mine."

It occurred to me, for the first time, that my mother had never backed down from anything, never admitted she was wrong, never yielded one point in an argument. Though round and fleshy, her jaw had a tight, determined quality. Her eyes never smiled, even when her lips did.

"Rose, what's happening?" My father's breath-starved voice distracted her. In that instant, I took the blue bag and ran into my room, slamming the door behind me and locking it. Something told me I had to know, that the key to comprehending my life lay in that bag. I hardly heard the pounding on the door. Hypnotized, I unzipped the bag and stared at its contents as they poured onto my bed.

Wealth—stocks, bonds, cash, checkbooks from a dozen different banks—tumbled out. One hundred, two hundred thousand dollars, and then I stopped counting. How could I reconcile this hidden wealth with the sordid circumstances of my early life? My mother's phrase, "We can't afford it," sang discordantly in my mind.

"We can't afford a bed for you *and* Larry."

"We can't afford clothes for you *and* Larry."

"We can't afford a vacation."

"We can't afford to give you money for the movies."

And all the time, she was piling up a hidden fortune—money pocketed from the cash register, when my father was too drunk to notice.

I opened the door and she fell upon the bed, gathering up her

134

treasure, incoherently screeching and cursing, a wild-eyed female Scrooge. Totally exposed. The worst of it was my realization that she felt no embarrassment or guilt, only rage that she had been found out, that her treasure might now be torn away.

"Did you think I'd steal it if I knew?" I asked her. "Do you think Ceil and I need your filthy money? I can make my own money...." and I rattled on and on, trying to whip my outrage under control by shouting it into submission.

"It's mine," my mother sobbed. "Mine and your father's, for our old age. Our old age."

Enraged as I was, I couldn't say the cruelest words of all: *Your old age. What old age? Your husband is a dead man. He can hardly move. Your old age alone, you mean. Your old age. Only yours.*

In the days ahead, my mother struggled to smooth over the disagreement.

"I was saving it for you—for you and Larry."

"I was saving it for Dana, for my granddaughter, so she should have the best. For Dana, darling, for Dana."

As my father disintegrated, Joel and I were exposed, by contrast, to a lighter, more fanciful world—the world of Disney.

For five years we had had meetings with story editor Frank Paris. Frank had repeatedly told us: "Disney will do a musical but only if it's a classic. It has to be a classic."

We were finally given the go-ahead on a project, an original, called *Pete's Dragon*, conceived in the 1920s by Walt Disney himself. My dream of a full movie musical had come true. We were told to write twelve songs for the picture, which would combine live action and animation.

The sense of cheerful unreality was heightened by our surroundings: Mickey Avenue, Dopey Drive. Our little office had posters of Donald Duck, the Love Bug, and Snow White. Everyone on the lot was friendly; it was a shiny world of Doris Day smiles and spontaneous handshakes. A world that said, "You can have problems, but don't bring them to the studio."

Our old friend Irwin Kostal did the arrangements, and the casting of *The Poseidon Adventure* friends Red Buttons and Shelley

135

Winters made for a family-type atmosphere. Mickey Rooney and Jim Dale were cast quickly. All we lacked was a leading lady.

Helen Reddy wanted the part. The company's first choice was Olivia Newton-John but she was unavailable. Joel and I recommended Helen to head of production Ron Miller.

"Put in a good word for me," Helen urged, whenever we saw her. She won the role after a natural and assured screen test.

Red, Jim, and Helen displayed consistent good humor. Shelley was outstanding as Pete's wicked stepmother, though she created as much drama off set as on. She called me at two in the morning, requesting lyric changes for a nine-o'clock recording session. She came on the set in a wheelchair to protest choreography she considered too acrobatic.

I remembered a Bette Davis quote, in which she claimed that people had to fight for perfection, even if it created temporary turmoil. In the end, Shelley was brilliant, and I understood the integrity that had directed her behavior.

I thought of Henry Fonda, in that small Oregon motel, doing three hundred spots, investing heart and soul in a tedious but necessary job. That memory helped. It reminded me of the essential quality pros need, a willingness to stretch, to test new things, to think of the whole picture.

Love can flow from creative interaction, but it isn't the main point, only a happy by-product in certain instances. One instance where it did happen was when I became friendly with an actor in the film named Gary Morgan.

Gary played Shelley Winters's son, the younger of two evil brothers (Jeff Conaway of "Taxi" was the other). Gary was an acrobat, slim and muscular, with a leprechaun smile. He was also a Jew who believed in Christ.

I couldn't help noticing the parallels. On *The Poseidon Adventure* set, I had met Mark, the first man to share his spiritual feelings with me. Shelley Winters and Red Buttons had both been in that film. Now Shelley and Red were working with me again, and another young man, similar in size and build to Mark, was talking about his faith.

"I've never been happier," Gary said, executing a cartwheel.

"You don't seem religious."

"Why? What's religious supposed to be?" He pulled a long face. "Serious...grim...full of authority? Bunk! I have fun. I love my wife and two kids and my ten animals" (among them four monkeys and two snakes). "But I love God too."

I remembered my grandfather, and my own question: *If this is the voice of God, why is it so uncaring, so cold? Why is tradition so constricting?*

"God is my friend," Gary said. "Not some big shadow on a mountaintop." Stern visions of my grandfather swept my thoughts. Then Gary hugged me before going back to work on a scene. "You'll find out one of these days."

"Maybe."

He winked. "You think I'm a little *meshugenah* for a Christian? Hey, I'm Jewish. I'm a Jew who believes in Jesus."

"When was the last time you had a salami sandwich and cream soda?"

"Last night. At Cantors. Just before I went to church."

"Gary, you're putting me on."

"I'm not," he said, with unexpected intensity. "You'll find out."

137

15

Escaping the Darkness

The movie was into its final days of shooting when my parents announced they were returning to New York.

"I said I'll die in Brooklyn, and I will," my father insisted.

The morning he left I watched him shaving. The razor hung loosely in his fingers; he was so weak that even a razor qualified as a heavy object.

"Alfred," he whispered. "Shave me."

Those were words I had never expected to hear. I had to hear him say the phrase twice before I could act on it.

"Shave me, Alfred. Shave me, son."

I took the razor—a straight razor, the one he had used when he was active as a barber—and carefully grazed his face. The skin seemed like paper; I had a feeling it would strip off, layer by layer, when confronted with a blade. But I went on, watching the tears he had at last allowed to fall.

"Thank you, son." His gnarled right hand touched my cheek. "I love you, son."

"I love you too."

A month later he died, on Avenue M. Right above the store, where he had been a barber for forty-five years.

I didn't fly back East. By now my agoraphobia was totally paralyzing. I didn't drive, or take a train, or go near an airport. Even traveling to Disney was accomplished through the aid of tranquilizers, and Joel always drove.

Ceil and Larry flew to the funeral without me. Later on, Ceil called and described a macabre moment when my mother threw herself on the casket and cried, "Irving, Irving, how could you leave me in the prime of our lives?"

Was any shred of her grief genuine, or was she simply surrendering to her tendency for self-dramatization? According to Ceil, onlookers blanched at this display, knowing how much my mother had hated her husband for over forty-five years. Hated him enough to corner Joel at a party and say, "Your wife is a lucky woman to have such a nice man. I wasn't so lucky. But there was a man, a Mr. Klinger. He was a pharmacist...."

Nevertheless, the simple act of *sharing*, of close proximity, creates bonds, no matter how neurotic these bonds may appear to other people. Part of her must have suffered, part of her must have felt abandoned. The known, even if painful, is preferable to the unknown when human beings are basically fearful. And my mother, for all her talk, was a frightened person.

I only had to ask myself the question: *Larry and I could have supported her. She could, in fact, have supported herself. Why hadn't she ever left him?*

Someday I prayed I'd find the answer.

Tragedy replaced tragedy, making it impossible for Ceil and me to recover from the pressure of living with my parents and the shock of my father's death. Ceil's mother and father—both ill, respectively, with cancer and the aftermath of a stroke—died within three months of each other in 1977. The horror of visiting gravesites became an almost routine occurrence.

Suddenly Ceil felt lost, cut loose from childhood securities. She needed my strength, and I was psychologically unable to supply it.

There's a point, experts now recognize, when the nerve endings in certain people are physically burnt down—like defective wires. I was one of those people. It was nearly impossible for me to get up in the morning. I had no energy. Eating was a chore. Working, once the prime passion of my life, was back-breaking effort that yielded no satisfaction.

Joel and I continued to write music for Disney, *Freaky Friday*, *Hot Lead and Cold Feet*, and *The North Avenue Irregulars*. But we did all the writing in my home, even though I had once loved our Disney office. If our presence had been required daily on the lot, I would have given up these jobs.

I turned forty on January 22, 1977.

"It doesn't really bother me," I told friends. "I don't feel any different." A burst of youthful energy carried me through the first few months. I played basketball in my back yard, swam vigorously at eight every morning, did push-ups, read a whole stack of books I had been meaning to get to. And collapsed.

Dying became an obsession. The idea that I hadn't gone far enough, that my goals were still unachieved, haunted me. I read an article in the L. A. *Times* about "boy geniuses" and decided I was over the hill; it was too late to write all the books, shows, and songs I wanted to write.

Leaving the house, even to walk around the corner, became virtually impossible. Nor did I welcome the presence of people. One Saturday night Ceil invited a group of fourteen for dinner, and I ordered her to cancel it—an hour before guests were scheduled to arrive.

In a panic, intimidated by my hostility, she rushed to the phone and managed to stop guests who were halfway through the front doors of their homes.

Ceil formed a habit of covering up for me. "He's not feeling well....Dana's sick....We're too tired...." became automatic responses. She erected a life pattern around my neuroses and fears.

Suppressing rage—not an easy thing for Ceil, who is direct and spontaneously emotional—resulted in headaches and fits of crying. Little irritations, like a misplaced bill or an unreturned phone call, provoked a flood of tears. Through it all, she fought to be strong and supportive, to reassure me that everything would be all right.

She tried to treat my illness as though it were just a phase, a period of temporary insanity. Canceled plans, delayed meals were "no big deal."

"Is it my fault?" she would ask me. "Is it something I've done?"

140

I guaranteed her it wasn't.

Only after I hid from guests we had invited over, when I refused to come downstairs to greet them, did Ceil acknowledge the severity of my condition.

"Al, what's wrong?" she asked, with undisguised horror in her eyes.

"I don't know," I told her. "I just…couldn't face having them here."

It was inevitable, given the accumulation of differences, that our marriage would suffer. We clashed when Joel and I were offered a movie in England and I turned it down.

"It's a terrific script," Ceil said. (I always gave her my scripts to read for her opinion.) "It has a good cast. They're spending a lot of money to plug it."

"We have plenty to do right here in California," I answered feebly.

"What are you doing? You've worked twenty-five years to build up a reputation in this business. Are you going to throw it away now?"

"It's too far.…Dana needs me.…The money's not good enough.…" I made every conceivable excuse.

"You can't just hang around the house," Ceil said.

And then: "Maybe you should see a doctor again."

"By doctor you mean analyst?"

"Yes."

"I don't need an analyst. I just need to rest for a while…stay home and rest."

I pursued projects when the meetings could be held at my house. Elia Kazan and Budd Schulberg came to talk about a musicalization of *A Face in the Crowd*. They agreed to work with us if money could be raised.

Larry volunteered to raise the needed capital. He didn't get financing for *A Face in the Crowd*, but he did find backers for a stage version of the old MGM classic, *Seven Brides for Seven Brothers*. He asked us to write eight songs for the new Broadway-bound version, and signed Jane Powell and Howard Keel to repeat their original film parts. My anxieties descended: *How could*

141

*I go to a theater every day for rehearsals...fly to out-of-town openings
...meet at the homes of writers, choreographers?*

My brother persuaded me to get involved. Our relationship was
on a smoother, friendlier course. He sensed my emotional difficulties and told me to relax, not to worry; he offered tactful criticism and generous praise.

Age and experience helped. So did the passing of my father.
My parents had always been a dividing force and even the absence of one made our communication more comfortable. My
mother still resorted to old tactics: "Larry called me today and
you didn't," or "Alfred got me a birthday present. Why didn't
you?" But her efforts had less impact. An artistic barrier had also
been knocked down. Larry had been impressed with *Pete's Dragon*, and felt that the song, "Candle on the Water," and score
(which were both nominated for Oscars) indicated a flair for
Broadway writing.

Seven Brides opened in Dallas, to triumphant reviews and the
best box office that city had ever seen.

"You should be happy," said Ceil.

"I am."

"Can we fly to Dallas to see it?"

"No."

At last I acknowledged that the problems were too deep-seated
to handle alone. Battles between Ceil and me were increasing; I
was neglecting our daughter.

Symptoms ran my life: Palpitations before every professional
meeting. Hyperventilating the few times I stepped into a car.
Headaches.

I refused to enter department stores, even when Ceil was with
me. I couldn't finish a meal in a restaurant; I had to dash out
abruptly, sometimes after the first few minutes, sometimes in the
middle of the meal.

Vacations were out.

Flying was out.

An attempt to defeat the flying phobia was disastrous. Ceil and
I had planned a trip to New York. We made it to Los Angeles In-

ternational Airport and gave the skycap our luggage. So far, so good.

"It'll be fine, wait and see," Ceil promised.

"Flight 23 is boarding," came the announcement.

I reached the entrance, where the stewardess was inspecting boarding passes.

My stomach started to swim; instant nausea made me double over. The attack hit with sudden, disabling force. I heard myself groan.

"I can't go on the flight," I said to Ceil.

"You've got to. Just try. Our luggage is already on."

I stepped aside and sat down. My hands were stretched out, as though to grab something, but there was nothing but space.

"Last call for Flight 23...."

I heard my father's voice, on our flight from Brooklyn to Los Angeles just before he died.

Rose. I have a pain in my chest, a terrible pain.

He's going to die. My husband's going to die. Oh, God, help me, my pressure, my pressure.

"Please try to get on," pleaded Ceil. "I'll be with you. You can listen to music through the earphones, or watch a movie, or just sleep. It'll be over in no time."

Why didn't she understand, I wondered, *that boarding Flight 23 was certain death?* I saw the bewildered faces of airline personnel, asking Ceil what they could do to help. I sensed Ceil's hopelessness when she shook her head and muttered, "Nothing."

Flight 23 arrived safely at JFK six hours later. Our luggage took the trip alone.

It was simpler, after a while, to stay in bed as long as possible. Joel had recently rented an office, with the hope of coaxing me from the house. I had agreed, not believing it would do any good. Morning after morning Joel called and said, "I'm here. When are you coming over?"

"I don't know if I can make it," was my standard response.

"You've got to get out of the house."

"I'll be there at ten-thirty."

Ten-thirty came and Joel would call again. "Do you want me to come and pick you up?"

"No, I...why don't we work here?"

"We have this office, and there'll be no distractions. We can get more done."

"Tomorrow, then."

Tomorrow repeated the same pattern. Joel hid his impatience. He realized I had a serious problem. But the cat-and-mouse game of will-you-or-won't-you-come-to-the-office eventually proved too much pressure for us. We surrendered the office to another tenant.

Pressure escalated. We were in the midst of building a new pool, and constant drilling noise scraped away at my eardrums. I wanted to scream: *Stop it. The noise is driving me crazy!* Instead I buried my head in a pillow, as my teeth ground into my lips and drew blood.

The noise stopped when our pool company went bankrupt. Ceil had to handle the nightmare of a lawsuit.

"I can't do this alone," she would cry. I was helpless to ease her burdens. The roles had reversed. I had always been the parent, taken care of every problem in my life. Now I felt unequal to the simplest responsibility.

Ceil kept after me until I took a tentative stop toward health. Friends recommended a licensed marriage, family, and child counselor named Maralyn Teare, a bright, sympathetic young woman who helped identify my inexplicable terrors. Maralyn, fortunately, was willing to come to my home. She understood how thoroughly agoraphobia could paralyze a patient's movements.

"There are agoraphobics," she told me, "who haven't left their areas of security for thirty or forty years."

I recalled the publisher Carl, in New York, and his wife. The woman everyone had laughed at—the phantom, the shadow—the poor soul who had been incapable of leaving her apartment.

"I thought only *women* had agoraphobia," I said.

"Just as many men have this problem as women," said Maralyn, "but men have a greater stake in concealing it. The fear makes them feel weak, unmasculine. The fact that so many men suffer from agoraphobia is often forgotten."

The forgotten agoraphobic, I thought.

"All I need," I told Maralyn, "is something to help me sleep."

"It's not as simple as that."

I plunged ahead. "Then, if I can get some rest, I can find the energy to *fight* this thing!"

"That's just what you shouldn't do," Maralyn said. "You don't fight agoraphobia; you don't conquer it with willpower. That's what you've been trying to do—beat it back with sheer will."

I stayed focused; I wanted a pill that would supply a miraculous answer. Pills, Maralyn felt, were a stop-gap solution, although there were anti-depressants that offered relief to agoraphobics.

The next time I saw Maralyn, I opened up more.

"I never used to be like this," I told her. "I jumped on a plane at a moment's notice. I was game for anything."

"Many agoraphobics lead normal lives—and then suddenly become paralyzed."

"What am I afraid of?"

"Well, for one thing, losing control." She went on to say that agoraphobics, being perfectionists, dread making fools of themselves. After a few humiliating episodes they develop a fear of revealing their panic and inadequacy before strangers. Ultimately they hide at home so their loss of composure won't occur publicly.

"Maybe," Maralyn suggested, "you put exaggerated importance on what people think. Approval matters too much. You're afraid...."

"I'm *not* afraid," I said automatically, though I had just used the word myself. I didn't like the sound of it from someone else's lips, even though my life was being ruled by fear. "And as far as what people think, I don't need them. If my work is going well, everything's fine."

"Really? It seems as though your work is going well now." After a pause, she added, "You've got to learn that everyone is afraid. And people, particularly phobics, feel isolated, as though their difficulties are happening only to them. You have to let your friends and

145

family know so they can help. You need positive reinforcement."

I took refuge in wordplay. "That's an analyst's phrase—'positive reinforcement.' "

She didn't let the jibe intimidate her. "There are relaxation exercises you should do."

I listened politely, unconvinced.

"Exercises where you visualize. Close your eyes and think of a calm blue ocean, a long stretch of desert, a sunset. If you have a pet you might concentrate on the pet. Many pet owners find their animals more soothing than any other image." That was the first suggestion that strongly registered with me. I had a cat, Snow, that I loved. Snow slept with Ceil and me, and his motionless white body, curled up on the edge of our bed, had always struck me as the essence of tranquillity.

"Once the body is relaxed," Maralyn continued, "the mind will follow suit. The trouble is, so many of us concentrate (what amounts to negative meditation) on all the things that can go *wrong*, the things that worry us. Positive imagery can counteract that."

Alone in my room, I did as she said. I found my mind resisting all efforts to be calm. My brain was like a piece of jerky, unedited film. As soon as a positive image flashed on, the film shook and blacked out and negative thoughts overran it. I became fidgety, or I began to itch. My toes wiggled. Or I would feel a need to clear my throat.

"It takes time," Maralyn said. "Of course your negative impulses will put up a fight. But concentration will win out."

Maybe I wasn't trying hard enough, or I just didn't fully accept her suggestions, much as I wanted to. I also tried to eat properly. Maralyn stressed proper nutrition, attempting to wean me from coffee and products containing caffeine, which caused excitability and lowered my blood sugar. She urged me to reduce my sugar intake too.

"I want to get better," I told her. "I want to move around freely again."

"You will. I promise."

Her influence was important, because it offered the first stirrings of insight. More insight followed when she brought up a na-tionally known program, TERRAP (Territorial Apprehension), which dealt exclusively with the symptoms of phobic illness. This highly effective program, which claimed a cure rate of 80 percent, was the creation of Dr. Arthur Hardy of Menlo Park, California. I saw Dr. Hardy on a "60 Minutes" interview and felt TERRAP might be the answer.

Like Maralyn, Dr. Hardy preferred a therapeutic approach to the steady use of anti-depressant drugs like Imipramine and Ami-triptyline, or anti-anxiety drugs like Valium.

The first night Ceil drove me to a TERRAP meeting, it took superhuman effort to leave the house. My fear was compounded by a reluctance to attend the meeting and risk possible exposure. I thought: *Industry people might see you. They'll think you're a weakling and say to themselves, "He's unreliable, an employment risk; look how far down he's gone."*

This particular group met in the cellar of a two-story house in Cheviot Hills. The descent down a narrow staircase to the base-ment aggravated my claustrophobia. There were fourteen people present that evening, twelve women and two men. The other man was heavyset, with gray hair and old-fashioned horn-rimmed glasses. His expression reflected the embarrassment I felt. I was also ashamed of being a minority male in a roomful of females.

How could I be suffering from such a feminine *disease,* I thought.

A woman named Elaine Garwood conducted the meeting, flanked by two assistants. All were former agoraphobics.

I looked around quickly, to make certain nobody I knew was in the room. I watched as Elaine scribbled "Agoraphobia" on a blackboard.

"How many of you have felt an attack spring out of nowhere?" she asked. There were nods and raised hands. Tentatively I raised mine.

All the physical symptoms Elaine described—the palpitations, fainting spells, drenched palms—were familiar to me. But she didn't shrug off the seriousness of a pounding heart.

"It's probably anxiety," she said. "Most of you will find there's nothing physically wrong; but just to be sure, go for a checkup.

147

Make *sure* you're physically okay, and after you've had a checkup, you can start on exercising. Exercise is one of the best ways of releasing tension and repressed hostility." She recommended visualization, like Maralyn, as well as relaxation tapes, and advised us to dictate our own suggestions into a machine. "Your own voice is often more effective than the voice of a stranger," she said. "Also, keep a journal. It will help you to unburden yourself and enable you to see how you're progressing."

Her advice made perfect sense, but I found myself wondering when the meeting would be over. I kept staring at my watch.

Elaine talked about sharing our problems, feeling a sense of community. None of her words pierced my loneliness.

"I can't *stand* it anymore!" A violent, male voice sheared through my self-preoccupation. "I'm a prisoner in my own home because of my wife. We never go on vacations, we never even go to a show. And what's worse, she resents it when I go out. What the hell am I supposed to do?"

His wife, a tiny, midfortyish blonde, exploded into tears.

"I do want to go on vacations," she sobbed.

"You don't, or you'd make more of an effort. You'd *try* harder."

"I am trying," she screamed. "I'm trying as hard as I can."

"That's right," I said to Ceil.

Elaine calmed the outraged husband down, reiterating what Maralyn had said to me: Phobic fears could not be banished by willpower alone.

After that the stories began flowing. An angry wife ridiculed her husband for his inability to sign his own credit card. "It's just plain stupid, to have a fear like that," she said. Her face was red; I could feel she was at the end of her rope. "Is the credit card going to bite him? It doesn't make sense."

"Maybe it makes sense if he had a bad experience in a bank when he was younger," Elaine pointed out.

The husband remained silent, resistant; his gaze shifted to the door.

Elaine waited, sensing his indecision.

"When I was a kid," the man said, without preparation, "my mom and I went to withdraw some money. She handed the teller her slip, filled it out and he..."

148

"Go on," Elaine said.

"He handed it back to her and said, 'There's no money here. Your husband withdrew it earlier today.' And my mother went crazy. She yelled at the teller and said it was impossible, they should check again and he shook his head. It was a terrible scene, and they had to drag her away. Everybody was *watching* us, staring, thinking, who's this crazy lady, the woman has lost her mind. She cried all the way home and the next day. But my dad had left town with the money." He cleared his throat. "He never came back."

"Oh, my God," said Ceil.

"That was twenty, thirty years ago," the man's wife said.

"Yes," said Elaine. "But certain memories...certain events that formed us...stay alive. They're as alive to us as the day they happened."

I studied Ceil. She loved me, and she had been supportive during my illness; but I knew she identified with the pain the man's wife was suffering. I knew agoraphobia was bewildering to her. It seemed so simple, from her point of view, to stand in line at a bank or ride an escalator, let alone step out of the house. At the next meeting we attended, she had the courage to admit before the group, "I love Al...but sometimes I just don't understand." Sympathetic murmurs followed her statement. It was cathartic for her to let her long-hidden feelings show. In a burst of emotion she pleaded, "Al's in such pain. Help him. Please help my husband!"

If I had ever thought I was alone in my agoraphobic world, I learned otherwise after statistics of the disease were revealed. According to the National Institute of Mental Health, one adult in every twenty suffers from it. Forty percent of phobics, Elaine said, had relatives with the same malady.

We learned further variations on visualization. Members were desensitized by exercises in which they imagined themselves trapped in frightening situations for increasing periods of time.

"Once you actually imagine yourself being in a plane or a supermarket or bank for fifteen minutes without fear, you can actually be in it," said a TERRAP counselor. "At first you'll experience every symptom of terror, because the brain literally

149

cannot distinguish between an image clearly visualized and a real event. But take comfort, your body can't sustain a high level of panic indefinitely, and if the phobic can be induced simply to endure the thing he feels *long* enough, his anxiety will wear off and he can often be cured at once."

Why can't I accept all this? I asked myself desperately. *It makes sense, but something in me keeps battling it.*

The family pool remained unfinished, and this seemingly insignificant difficulty mushroomed into a life-and-death issue. Ceil and I tried to avoid attacking each other directly by venting our rage on the progress of the lawsuit.

"You're not behind me," I would say accusingly. "You're not supportive."

"I've done everything I can do."

"I'm always there for people and no one is there for me," I ranted. "It's time somebody took care of me."

The charge was so unjust, so outrageous, in view of Ceil's loving efforts, that she wouldn't answer. She couldn't even cry. I watched her swallow, watched her face darken.

"You're just like my mother," I said. "It's Rose Kasha all over again."

Anger that had gone underground, anger crushed under the merciless weight of my mother's "Be nice," was gushing to the surface, threatening to tear apart the fabric of my life.

I chastised myself for being selfish. Why couldn't I appreciate what God had given me? So many blessings had come my way. I counted them daily. I observed other people less fortunate and gained increasing awareness of my good fortune.

Nothing lifted the depression.

Finally I couldn't cope with it anymore. Ceil and I were both exhausted from endless fighting. Our self-images were torn, bleeding. Neither of us could handle the sense of failure, the anger and disappointment flying in all directions. We could not possibly sort out our tangled emotions in a climate of twenty-four-hour togetherness.

"I want you to leave," Ceil said one night. "I can't stand this anymore."

She was crying as she packed my suitcase. "Not everything is my fault."

"I didn't say it was."

"I need some time alone. We both do. I can't see where I'm going. You've given up on the TERRAP meetings. You won't see a psychiatrist. You won't help yourself . . . so how can I help you?"

"Nobody can help me."

I spent that night, and the next three weeks, in a friend's apartment. Joel stopped by often and filled me in on our work developments. *If They Ask You, You Can Write a Song,* the book we'd written on composing, had come out and received good reviews. *Seven Brides* was scheduled to open at the Dorothy Chandler Pavilion in Los Angeles.

"Maybe you'll come to the opening," Joel said. "If you're feeling better."

"I'll see," I said, knowing I was emotionally incapable of mingling with crowds.

It was three in the morning. I couldn't sleep. I resisted the urge to take a Valium or a Melloril. I'd kick pills by myself, straighten out my life without the aid of a therapist. A week before, in a fit of self-reproach about my "weakness," I had stopped seeing Maralyn Teare.

Maralyn had warned me, "You can't do this with willpower. It's not that simple." I didn't believe her. Determination had always served me well before.

"Conscious fighting," she said, "only aggravates the tension."

The passivity she advocated was just too far removed from my natural inclinations. I had always thought I could control my fate by tightening my grip on it. As a result I had never trusted anyone to take responsibility. Unless I did it, it would never get done, or if done, it would be incorrectly executed. No matter how competently Ceil and Joel did a job, I worried every time a new challenge presented itself, unless it remained under my surveillance and supervision.

My palpitations were worse than ever. Despite Maralyn's assurance that they were harmless, I *knew* in my gut that they were

151

forerunners of a heart attack. How long, after all, could my body accept such constant punishment?

Despair filled me, despair so total that it exceeded grief. The despair stemmed from utter hopelessness. I heard myself moan, and the moaning built into a gasp, then a sob, then tears poured out. My body trembled, and the tears splashed from my eyes and down my face. I tasted those bitter drops on my tongue and the crying grew wilder, more desperate.

"God, if you're listening, help me," I said. As I said it, I couldn't help feeling I had made a mess of everything, I didn't deserve God's love. Nevertheless, I ached for it.

I stared at the ceiling, the floor, the window. Loneliness blocked me in every direction.

I reached for the television dial, as though it were a life preserver, and a fuzzy picture flashed on. I wiped away the tears and saw Reverend Robert Schuller.

It was a replay of an old Schuller broadcast on Trinity Broadcasting.

What was he saying? I struggled to hear it. It seemed vital to make out the words.

"Perfect love casts out all fear."

Big deal. How simplistic. I loved my wife and daughter. I loved my friends. I loved my work. What good did it do?

"Love casts out all fear."

And then, automatically, I reversed it.

"Fear casts out all love."

How much had I *really* loved anyone this past year? Wasn't the poison of bitterness my overriding emotion? Hadn't I become so fixated on resenting my parents and the old hurts of childhood that these hurts had finally taken precedence over any affection? Hadn't I, finally, failed to make the transition from my first family to my second, as Ceil had said?

"Fear casts out all love."

I had been afraid. Twenty-four hours a day, running in circles of fear, the fear growing every minute. Afraid of failing everybody—Ceil, Dana, Joel, my parents, the artists I worked with, the friends I had made. Until it became easier to imprison myself behind phobias, hide from the world.

152

I sensed, without quite knowing how to articulate it, that my only answer was getting off myself, tearing the focus from my own psyche and soul and transferring it. Self-analysis had been self-abuse.

"If you put your trust in Him, you'll find more peace than you've ever known."

I didn't have to take on all responsibility. I didn't have to strive for perfection; I only had to be real. Nor did I have to punish myself for what I perceived to be monumental failures. No human being was perfect; only God was. And all He asked of me, I suddenly realized, was to do my best. Through Reverend Schuller, He was telling me I could, at last, forgive myself.

"Jesus." I uttered the word hesitantly. Fear diminished and I kept saying the name, again and again, feeling my agony of spirit subside with every repetition.

And then, I had a sense that a blinding light was filling the room. It seemed to me a window had opened. Whether the window of my soul, or an actual window, I've never been quite sure. But there was an opening, a healing, a flowering inside that flooded my heart.

Tears had stopped, the end of a sudden summer shower. I had no urge to cry anymore. I left the television on. Reverend Schuller's voice gave me a childlike security, and I closed my eyes.

Without the crutch of Valium or any other pill, I fell asleep.

The next morning I drove home to see Dana and Ceil. I didn't have a need to call Ceil and ask her to pick me up. I got into my car, waiting for symptoms, shocked at their absence. Peace washed over me, a peace all the more powerful for its stillness. Unthinkingly I shouted with joy, and then began to laugh. The laughter became uncontrollable and I went with it, letting it sweep me up. The laughter was totally devoid of self-consciousness. It wouldn't have mattered if people looked through the window and wondered what madman was laughing all by himself. The old how-are-my-actions-affecting-people apparatus was, blessedly, failing to operate.

When I arrived home I hugged Ceil and Dana with pent-up feeling. I couldn't bear to let them go.

Ceil and I took a short walk, and she said casually, "Pat Hollis came by yesterday." Pat was a friend of ours, a performer who sang for a Christian record label. Ceil's casual tone changed. "She and I went to church."

I didn't answer, didn't breathe. I thought of Reverend Schuller, of my devastating, life-changing experience.

Pat called that afternoon, and suggested we all go to church the following morning. We did, and the visit was so inspiring and soothing that we went the next week, and the week after. I felt as though all demons had been put to rest—till tremors of anxiety rocked me during a service.

Hold on.

Don't fight.

Don't tense up.

Float with it.

"Are you all right?" Ceil asked, squeezing my hand.

"Yes."

A few minutes later I was. I looked up at the sunny stained glass ceiling of the church and offered thanks.

Ceil was thrilled by my change but guarded. "Do you want to go to a meeting?" she asked occasionally. We did, in fact, go to an occasional group session designed to help phobics, and I usually drove there. There were moments I longed to let Ceil take over, but I fought the feeling down. I had read an excerpt of a sermon by John MacCarthur, pastor of Grace Community Church in Sun Valley. MacCarthur had talked about the importance of man's role in marriage and in the home, the necessity for male strength and leadership. I kept reviewing those words as I drove, especially when assailed by that unexpected, out-of-nowhere dread that makes a phobic attack so frightening. In the beginning I drove slowly, less than twenty miles an hour. Ceil would lean over to help me steer till I gently pushed her hands away. I would park and pray; we both prayed.

The spiritual reinforcement steadied my quaking insides. Restarting the engine, I would manage to make it to our destination.

I viewed the meetings differently from before. The total self-involvement, typical of full-blown agoraphobia, had eased, and I gained greater awareness of the suffering experienced by others in a similar predicament. I was able, increasingly, to separate myself, to say "That poor man," rather than, "Poor me; that's how *I* feel."

I came to understand that the male was, both in press and public awareness, the forgotten agoraphobic. His uniquely painful isolation was all but ignored. The cliché about male strength made it difficult for men to step forward and admit they were being destroyed by phobic symptoms, and I felt it was my job to let them know they had someone to talk to.

16

Running a New Road

The influence of newfound faith helped me to step beyond my own insecurities, and I took to calling other phobics, persuading them to share their troubles with me over the phone.

The night before our thirteenth wedding anniversary, Ceil and I lay in bed, watching *Casablanca.*

"We came through, somehow," I said, just as Humphrey Bogart whispered, "We'll always have Paris."

"I know. I can't believe it." She touched my face. "It's our anniversary tomorrow, and I prayed things would be better by the time it came."

She felt small and defenseless in my arms. Ceil's body had been tense and rigid for so long that her frail, compliant embrace was a surprise.

"Can you ever forgive me?" I asked.

She clung tighter.

"You can lean on me," I said. "I promise I won't fall. Besides, we're not alone. We have a pretty impressive helper on our side."

"I didn't forget."

"We both have to remember—and keep remembering. How can you stumble when God's with you? And how can I stumble, ever again, if you're with me?"

Ceil turned away; compliments embarrassed her.

"Honey, you're everything to me. That's what God made me see most of all."

"You're so corny, do you know that?"

"Yes. When it comes to you I'm corny. Listen, I have an idea." I kissed her, then took her face in my hands. "Ceil, will you marry me?"

"Dear, I'm already married."

"I mean it. Let's get married again. Let's really start fresh."

"It's crazy, isn't it?"

"Maybe. So what? It's our chance to make a new—a new morning after for ourselves. What do you say?"

She clapped her hands together. "I love the idea. I love the thought of saying our vows again. Just the thought of it makes me feel like eighteen years old."

We held each other without another word, letting our unspoken joy and hope do the talking for us.

Two weeks later we were married in our living room, surrounded by friends. Gabriel Ferrer, son of Jose Ferrer and Rosemary Clooney, and a minister Ceil and I had become friendly with in church, performed the ceremony. Next to him was his soon-to-be-wife, Debby Boone.

Ceil and I kept looking at each other, savoring the miracle. We had never stopped caring for each other, but this was something different—a return to youthful feelings that had been buried under years of pressure.

I was falling in love with my wife all over again.

Discovery is exciting but difficult. Nothing worth gaining comes without effort, and Christianity is no exception. After the first, ardent weeks of any love affair, questioning begins.

I was Jewish. Did this mean I had to give up my heritage, my past, everything that had made me who I was?

No matter what path I followed, I knew I would feel a cultural love and connection to Judaism all my life.

Don't rush it, I told myself. A colt walks unsteadily at first, until he develops power in his legs.

My early spirituality was reinforced when Ceil and I attended a weekly Bible class. Gabriel Ferrer taught the classes in his mother's guest house.

I discussed agoraphobia at the class, and everyone was sympathetic and understanding. They prayed for me, for my permanent cure from the disease.

One young man in particular took a gratifyingly personal interest in my symptoms. His name was Clark Mathias, and he had come from Wheaton, Illinois, to manage a car dealership. Clark had a heart as big as his broad, 6'3" frame. Sandy brown hair and a beard completed the overall impression of a gentle giant.

His gentleness had a calming effect on me, and his knowledge of the Bible opened my eyes to its endless wisdom.

Clark was a symbol of everything I wanted to learn. Early in our relationship he placed a Bible, anonymously, on my doorstep. The Bible became a permanent companion; and months afterward, when Clark revealed himself as the secret donor, its value multiplied.

Our time together multiplied too, when he moved in with Ceil and me during a temporary work layoff. The live-in arrangement was my idea; I wanted Clark to share with us everything he knew about the Word of God. Our relationship was a series of emotionally stirring, stimulating discussions. But I resisted when Clark suggested we tackle flying.

"There's nothing to be afraid of," he promised.

"I can't."

Clark grinned. "What kind of a word is *can't*, if you have God on your side?"

"All right," I said. "I can't...now. But soon."

Flying seemed too great a hurdle, though my phobic attacks decreased. I was still uneasy away from home, still wary in restaurants, still apprehensive when driving. But I managed. I was defeating the fear, slowly.

The greatest enemy to overcome, I realized now, was my physical craving for pills. I didn't subject my body to massive shock by going cold turkey. But even gradual withdrawal forced up the anxiety level. Breathing would become labored at unexpected moments, and I had to cope with nervous tics and spasms, tightness around the neck, the shakes.

Then I would feel, with euphoria, that I had done it, that the

158

We found her an apartment; and she hated it, adding, "Why can't I live with you or Larry?" She found fault with the next place we suggested: "Too small." Other complaints: "Too expensive." "I don't like the neighbors." "The street is too noisy."

She viewed the new brotherly closeness between Larry and me with discomfort and tried to set us against each other.

My instinctive reactions weren't totally changed; the change was in how I handled them. When my mother said, "You're lucky Larry let you write the songs for *Seven Brides*," my first response was to snap back; "He hired me because I'm a good writer; luck had nothing to do with it." Then I saw she wanted to provoke me, so I merely replied, "Yes, I'm grateful to him."

It's hard to surrender lifelong games, and the temptation always returns to fall into old patterns again. My faith provided the strength to resist self-destructive impulses.

"I hope both my sons win Tonys," she said. Larry had already won his Tony for *Applause*.

That left only me.

I prayed for relief from physical tension, physical tension that kept my stomach in perpetual knots.

One morning, while driving past the Beverly Hills schoolyard, I noticed a solitary runner. It was six-thirty in the morning.

I parked and went through the open fence to watch him. He turned and smiled. "Come on."

I shook my head and watched him gracefully complete another quarter of a mile.

"Let's walk," the man said. He was in his mid fifties, tall and trim, with sparse white hair.

We fell in step.

"How come you're out so early?" I asked.

"Like to get on the track before the crowd," he said. We shook hands. "I'm Jack McKee."

"Al Kasha." I didn't explain why I was out so early. I couldn't tell a complete stranger that it was therapy—retraining myself to drive by choosing a time when noise was at a minimum and roads were empty.

161

"I'd like to get in shape," I told him.

"This is the way to do it."

Okay, Lord, I mumbled to myself. *If that's your plan, I'll be here tomorrow morning at six-thirty.*

And I was. My brain was a lot more eager to participate than my body. I became unpleasantly familiar with every neglected muscle. All of them screamed in unison, "Give me a break!"

My addiction started then—and I use that word deliberately. Addictive personalities will always be consumingly involved with *something.* The trick is to substitute constructive goals for the damaging ones. In place of uppers, I chose health foods. In place of Valium, I chose the relaxation of running.

At first, I hauled my rusty, flabby machine around the track, gasping for breath. And being still competitive, determined, and dedicated, I pushed too hard, ran too far, and nearly wound up in a hospital after the first week. Jack begged me to take it slow. But *slow* isn't a word workaholics understand.

It took a while to achieve what runners call "the pain-pleasure phenomenon." At the start it was all pain and no pleasure. When runners showed up, I automatically tried to match or surpass them. I saw myself entering marathons before I could comfortably complete two miles.

Gradually, though, my Nikes hooked onto those "wings of joy" runners talk about. I increased my goal from two miles to three, and I could feel my tension shedding like dead skin. My mind was clear, clear the way it had been under Ritalin, but bright and active without narcotics to jolt it.

From then on, I never missed a morning if I could help it. Ceil had to argue sense into me when I set off for the track with flu or fever. I felt closest to God on that track. We had the majority of our conversations while I raced along.

It was time to take on my next challenge—flying. I walked into Clark's room one Saturday morning and said simply, "I'm ready."

It wasn't Lindbergh and the Spirit of St. Louis, but I had the spirit of God to get me to Los Angeles International.

"Hope we don't crash," I said lightly.

Clark smiled and quoted a C. S. Lewis line: "Don't worry

about death...you never know when it's coming." He added: "Listen, I have news for you. If we crash I die too. And I'm not interested in dying."

I laughed. His logic was irrefutable, but I had to close my eyes and think of God's words.

Guard your heart and guard your mind. Think of beautiful things. Trust in God.

I can't control every situation.

Handle things moment to moment.

Manage rather than control.

Let go.

The Western Airlines 707 took off for San Diego. My palms began to sweat.

"Easy," whispered Clark.

The jet shivered in a sharp wind.

"Trust in God," Clark reminded me.

The flight took twenty-five minutes. I can't say I had no phobic reactions at all. Nor did I stop praying until we were back on the ground. My fist almost snapped the little red Bible in half.

Flying was easier from then on, however. I went to San Diego with Clark the following weekend, and after that, to San Francisco. The distances grew longer, the destinations further away. Each flight felt more natural, less dangerous. I watched with admiration when I saw Clark doze off or become immersed in a flight magazine. He never listened when the stewardess delivered her obligatory safety speech before takeoff.

A Sunday came when I woke up, actually looking forward to the sight of LAX, of boarding a plane. Flying changed from therapy to adventure, joy, and freedom.

I was no longer emotionally or physically grounded.

This was probably the happiest period of my life. There's a simplicity about identifying and meeting challenges. Like bowling pins, I selected them and knocked them down one by one.

When producers Mike Merrick and Don Gregory called me in 1979, though, I was afraid it would take more than a bowling pin or a Bible to knock down the hurdle they presented.

"Hi, babe," Mike's cheery, forceful voice boomed over the

phone. "Don and I talked it over and we're ready to move with *Copperfield*. We'd like to produce it on Broadway, open it early 1980. What do you say?"

Maybe this is the supreme test, I thought.

We gave the rights to Don and Mike. Their enthusiasm was contagious. They were also running a hot hand, with two hit touring companies of *My Fair Lady* and *Camelot*.

In March, 1980, two weeks before *Copperfield* was due to open, I lost my temper and clashed with Rob, our director.

There had always been something in his manner—a tendency to patronize—that broke through my "Be nice" defenses.

Our major disagreement arose over the show's big number, "Turn All the Lights on in London Tonight." Every line in the song referred to lights, lanterns, and candles, and we wanted a full-blown light extravaganza.

Rob disagreed with my concept. "Too obvious," he said. "Let's play *against* it." And when the number was staged, no emphasis was put on lighting.

Irwin tried to calm me down. "I've been through this a hundred times," he sighed. "You *will* survive it. But it's murder."

"Does it get easier?" Joel asked softly.

"Never."

I began to see Rob, unreasonably, as an undermining factor of my whole security base. I was anxious to be forgiving, and I had trouble forgiving him.

I didn't recognize the problem as an old enemy—achievement. I had always wanted to be ultra-successful as songwriter, producer, son. Now I wanted to be a perfect representative of faith, a walking example of God. For a while, coasting along on my euphoric cloud of discovery, I was positive I had reached that goal. The reappearance of clay feet—hostility, hurt, depression, as embodied by Rob—was threatening.

"Can we have a few weeks extra out of town?"

"Fellas, I'm sorry," said Mike Merrick. "In fact, I was gonna ask you something. Do you know anybody who can come up with an extra $150,000?"

"What happened?"

"Ahhh, this Greek shipping tycoon fell out. Happened last week. Don and I didn't want to worry you guys, but now we need the money."

"And if we don't get it?"

"Well, we can open," Mike said. "But there's nothing in the kitty for a run. Either we get raves or we close. We can't put up a fight."

Back in California, running had helped me to slam off tension. I turned to it again when we arrived in Manhattan, racing through the cold streets, as though the answers I needed were contained in the gusty March wind. If no other time was available I ran at night, ignoring Ceil's warnings that Manhattan at four in the morning was fraught with danger.

Joel and Jill were playing out the last destructive chapter of their control struggle. She was still pushing him to eat; he still resisted, then capitulated. As a result Joel was seriously overweight, Jill down to eighty-nine pounds. They were exhausted by the game, yet incapable of stopping it, addicted to patterns that were destroying them.

I wondered if they would bail out in time to save themselves.

We continued with our *Copperfield* rewrites, doing many of them at our old haunt, the Pink Cloud. It had brought good fortune before; maybe it would again. The omelets were just as underdone and tasteless, the juice flat. But there was comfort in a greasy spoon that represented youthful hope and optimism.

The conflict between Joel and Jill worsened. Nor was I in good shape. My mother, back in Los Angeles, had fainted on the street. A visit to her doctor disclosed inoperable cancer.

I felt guilty that I wasn't with her. Larry wasn't at her bedside either. He was touring with his own musical production, *Woman of the Year*, starring Lauren Bacall. At dinner, Larry informed me he was opening his show two days before *Copperfield*.

"I pray you both get Tonys," my mother said, attempting to stir up rivalry. Tired as she was, her focus remained relentless.

Though Joel and I were rewriting until opening night, I

165

jumped on a plane and flew to see her. I flew back that same night. A few days later, I returned to the hospital. After a while, I couldn't tell the difference between air and solid ground. The juxtaposition of writing and watching my mother slowly die turned the last weeks of the show into an unending nightmare.

My mother repeatedly asked, "Is Larry all right? He isn't working too hard, is he?"

"He's fine."

"I worry so much about him. You don't know the blood the theater takes from Larry."

"Yes I do. Believe me, Mom, I do."

On the night of the last preview I watched the show and fought to ignore all the mistakes I saw on the stage. Then I turned to Rob, who was hunched in his seat. He looked curiously young and old at the same time—the same red hair, same freckles, same youthful slenderness—but his eyes were tired, confused. I saw him differently in that moment; not as an enemy, but as a man who had become overwhelmed by the enormity of the *Copperfield* project and the handicap of having only ten days out of town. I saw Rob as someone who had tried to do the best possible job.

Understanding, without defensiveness, was a relief. I wasn't angry anymore. I had gotten past my own resentments, and I thanked God for teaching me how to do it.

Woman of the Year opened on a Sunday, *Copperfield* on a Tuesday. The reviews for *Woman* were generally good. Clive Barnes of the New York *Post* raved, and then Frank Rich of the *Times* published his all-important notice and determined the play's outcome. He felt, on the basis of Lauren Bacall's star quality, that the show worked.

"Always come to Broadway with a star," Larry had told me.

We had arrived with a cast of unknowns.

Copperfield was, and continued to be, an audience pleaser in previews. Jose Ferrer and Otto Preminger were among the celebrities who attended opening night and their praise gave us temporary hope.

The New York *Times* dashed that hope, however, conceding that the music was "tuneful," but objecting to liberties we had taken with Dickens.

"We'll have to post a closing notice," Mike Merrick told me at the opening night party. "Without the *Times* you don't have a shot."

Woman of the Year became a hit. *Copperfield* had a short run and closed.

17

Only with Love Can We Climb

But God, I was learning, always has a surprise up his sleeve, and when Tony nominations were announced, Larry and I were both among the nominees: he as producer, Joel and I for our *Copperfield* score.

"See," I told Joel. "There *was* a reason. This is God's way of telling us to try again."

He was also saying, I felt, that positive, upbeat shows could survive and triumph. In one form or another, they would gain recognition. I was grateful to the Tony committee for reinforcing that belief.

I was sensible enough to recognize that we had little chance to win. The gifted, clever Kander and Ebb, who had written *Chicago* and *Cabaret*, were front-runners for *Woman of the Year*.

Three weeks prior to the award ceremonies, my mother's condition took a sharp turn for the worse. Larry and I were planning to meet at the hospital. Ceil and I arrived first.

My mother looked terrible; her shrunken, sallow face brought back images of my father in his terminal days. She was smiling, however.

"Alfred, do you know who just called me? Dom DeLuise. He said he was a friend of yours, and he wanted me to get well in a hurry."

A gesture like that was typical of Dom. Dom wasn't just a superb comic, he was a solicitous human being—unquestionably the sweetest man in Hollywood.

"He said he might come by and see me."

"If he says it, he will."

"I'm so proud of you, Alfred."

"Thank you, Ma."

"I know you and Larry will both win."

"You'll know when we do, if you keep your TV on."

"Lean over, darling."

I did, and she kissed me.

"You know," she said, "if you had only let Larry direct *Copperfield*, you would have won a Tony for sure."

"Ma, don't try to talk."

"He would have done it so much better."

How do you know? You never even saw it!

"Lawrence is so talented." Then, "I have two wonderful boys. God bless you both."

She settled back on her pillow. "I'll pray you win. If I could, I'd go to temple. Maybe I still can...go to temple."

"Thank you, Ma."

Her mood changed. A streak of alarm crossed her pale face.

"Alfred, I just remembered something. I have to get up."

"You can't get up, Ma. You're tired. Relax."

"I have to get to the bank."

"The bank?"

Her mind was slipping away. She beckoned to the nurse.

"You've got to get me to the bank." Her tone turned shrill, frantic. "Please."

"Tomorrow, Ma, tomorrow."

She grabbed at my shirt. "Do you promise?"

"I promise."

"You're a good son, L'Alfred. And you too, Ceil darling. You've been a good daughter."

My mother died during the night. Three days later her will was read, and the contents of her jealously guarded blue bag were distributed. She left two thirds to my brother, one third to me.

Nothing to Dana.

"It's got to be a mistake," said Ceil, speaking words I was incapable of forming.

169

Larry put his hand on my shoulder. He was as totally unprepared as I was.

"You've got to get me to the bank."

Was that the reason for my mother's last-second agitation? A change of heart? Had she felt guilty in those final hours, guilty about slighting one son in favor of another? Guilty of overlooking her beautiful granddaughter, the granddaughter who had always been considerate and affectionate to her, who had listened to her grievances with love and sympathy?

I would never know.

On June 10, 1980, the Tony Committee announced its winners on TV. Ceil squeezed my hand until my knuckles burned. Joel sat with his sister Madeleine; his domestic situation was deteriorating, and Jill had chosen to remain in California.

Woman of the Year won for Best Score (among the four Tonys my brother collected). I reminded myself, *There's a reason.* I was too drained from my mother's death and from the trauma of the will to attach much importance to the award. Somehow I made it through the elaborate dinner afterward.

"I promise you one thing," Larry said, when we discussed *Seven Brides* and its proposed opening on Broadway the following year. "I'm going to put Mother's money behind the show, to give it a healthy budget and pay for the best people."

I was happy, but I couldn't help laughing at the irony. Because it was so against everything in her nature to take risks with money, to speculate. All her life, she had hoarded every cent, hidden all her assets from her husband and sons. One bed, roaches, broken furniture, deprivation on all levels—to gather up the backing for a Broadway musical.

Rose Kasha, the Broadway angel.

Rose Kasha, who would rather walk than take a bus, who bought all her clothes on sale on Delancey Street, who resisted giving birthday or Christmas presents to the end of her days—a posthumous Broadway investor.

The new touring company of *Seven Brides*, starring Debby

Boone, proved to be as commercially successful as the old one with Jane and Howard. Debby was outstanding in the part: a capable actress, a superb singer, a nimble dancer. Her faith was an intrinsic part of her, and it added an extra dimension to her work. I never saw a letdown of energy, honesty, or vocal perfection.

A year later Joel and I were nominated for another Tony. We didn't win, but the show became a permanent touring item, in the United States and abroad. *Seven Brides* broke records at London's Old Vic, and became a staple in Australia, New Zealand, Italy, and Spain. Its long life refueled our drive to continue in the theater and to do projects we believed in.

In 1982, unfortunately, our eighteen-year partnership fell apart. Joel and Jill decided to give their marriage one last chance, unencumbered by pressure, and spent most of their time in their Lake Arrowhead home.

The mountain calm and beauty of Arrowhead had come to symbolize, in Jill's mind, an escape from friction, from competing, from the world of show business. She had temporarily given up her own songwriting career to become a photojournalist. She encouraged Joel to write a novel, saying, "It's a quiet way of life, without all those producers and publishers breathing down your neck. You can work alone." Alone meant a "simple" life that included long walks, swimming, riding, and a minimum of entertaining.

Her own intense nature found the uncluttered calm of mountain living a relief. Joel, though, missed the buzzing activity of L. A. Bronx-born, a movie junkie, he had difficulty with the fact that Lake Arrowhead lacked *any* movie theaters. Joel had nursed a desire to be a film critic and commentator all his life, which he later fulfilled with his bestselling book *Rating the Movie Stars*.

Even so he insisted, "I have to try, give it my best shot. Jill and I love each other." He added, "It's not that we can't write."

"Of course we can write," I agreed. "You can drive to Hollywood, or I can come to the mountains."

But I knew better. It took energy to make a faltering marriage

171

work, and the geographical problems were a serious deterrent to regular creativity.

More crucially, I recognized that Joel's work would have to take a distinct second to his personal relationship. I know many relationships function that way. I've always felt, though—and still do—that a man's work is a basic part of him. I know how precious family and friends are, but I believe work is the fundamental outgrowth of what a man is.

In any case, I felt sad about the break, sad for all the lost dreams, the plans Joel and I had made. The movies, books, and shows that were never to be; the Rodgers and Hammerstein heirs we would never become. Ceil regretted the split as much as I did.

Joel and I met occasionally for lunch, and we would muse vaguely about "getting together to write." Once or twice we did actually start a song, but we rarely finished it; and when we did, it wasn't up to our old standard.

"Next time we'll get it," Joel would say, and both of us felt angry and depressed simultaneously. Gradually we stopped getting in touch, and I set about organizing a separate life.

I taught songwriting at churches and universities. I also launched a lecture tour, speaking about the influence of Christianity on modern music. It was exhilarating to move freely and accept engagements without paralyzing phobic symptoms.

During one of the tours I appeared on a small Philadelphia TV station. The guest immediately before me was a young woman who described her years of agoraphobia. Even though my topic on the show was songwriting, I mentioned to the announcer that I had been a victim of the same phobia.

Instead of rushing past my remark, he made it the basis for the entire interview. He wanted to know why an Oscar winner, a man who had succeeded in a difficult, competitive profession, would fall prey to incapacitating phobic illness. I answered gladly, seizing the chance to share my story with a broad audience. The station was deluged with calls, and I was invited back the following week to give a more detailed account of my recovery.

In every interview after that, I referred to my struggle with phobic illness. I received encouragement from a remarkable pastor

172

named Jess Moody. Jess was a tall, imposing man with a gloriously playful sense of humor and direct, engaging honesty. Although he grew up on a farm in Muleshoe, Texas, and I came from the streets of Brooklyn, we were of one mind and heart from our first meeting.

"You have an important story," Jess said, "and because you're a public figure you can have a strong effect. You're already helping people. Just keep on being real. Don't make speeches. Remember, more people tell their stories to bartenders than pastors, so be a *friend*."

That advice stayed with me when I guested on other TV shows. Some were secular: "Dinah Shore," "America," the "Mid-Day Show," the Michael Jackson radio show; others were Christian: "Robert Schuller's Hour of Power," "Pat Robertson's 700 Club," the "Paul and Jan Crouch Show" for Trinity Broadcasting. I became more and more determined to reach phobic sufferers on a national level.

I assured viewers that there was nothing to be ashamed of in having agoraphobia, and begged them to join any reputable group specializing in phobic treatment. I knew from experience that sharing anxieties would eliminate feelings of isolation, of hopelessness.

I continued to address many of my comments directly to the male agoraphobic. I knew, more than ever, that admitting this weakness clashed with their attempts to be strong, to convey a macho image. Powerful executives and businessmen hated to say they were beaten up by their fathers, hated to admit their lifelong fear of authoritative male peers. I reassured them that their fear, which I had always shared, was nothing to be ashamed of; that these terrors, developed in childhood, no longer had any validity.

Within weeks letters poured in from agoraphobics around the country—women and men. All of them had been through pressures I had described. Many were desperate.

"I don't feel self-respect anymore...."

"I'm too ashamed to even make love to my wife...."

"How could I be so *weak*? I want to be strong for her; I want her to feel she can lean on me."

173

"I'm afraid to tell my wife....She'll worry that I can't support her...."

"I'm afraid to tell my kids....They won't look up to me anymore."

"I'm afraid to tell my boss....He'll fire me."

Some men told me they had taken jobs, jobs beneath them both financially and creatively, to be close to home. One film editor described his terror when he was asked to go out of the office at lunch to bring back sandwiches for his co-workers. He had hidden in the bathroom, gathering up courage, feeling like a condemned man with every step toward a restaurant that was only across the street.

I answered all the letters, reminding each person to stand firm when symptoms recurred, stand firm and trust in God's help. "Remember," I wrote, "every minute you stay firm is more ammunition against panic."

It came to me, while writing to a phobic housewife who had spent the past five years indoors, that mail or even TV was too impersonal for totally meaningful contact. TERRAP proved beneficial to agoraphobics who could, with great difficulty, force themselves to leave home for short periods of time. But what of victims who *never* ventured from home base? They had to see an individual, up close, with the same affliction they had, see that he had beaten it, stepped out into the sunlight, made it through traffic, moved easily in crowded shopping malls.

I brought my own special phobic cure door to door. I became a salesman for serenity, for freedom.

"No, I *can't* go out there," was the statement that greeted me over and over again.

"I did it. So can you. Just take one step at a time. We'll try standing on the street, taking a short walk. Next week we'll walk a little farther. And I'll be with you."

I repeatedly emphasized that they didn't have to cover miles immediately, or drive to the other end of town. Half a block was a start. Sitting in a car was progress. Or parking near a supermarket without going inside.

Eventually, since I was in show business, I received calls from well-known people who were agoraphobics or their families. A world-famous director, for whom Joel and I had written a score, contacted me. His wife had not left their Beverly Hills home for three years.

"You weren't really an agoraphobic," she told me. Her blue eyes had a permanent squint, even in the safety of her living room, as though hiding from any trace of brightness outside. "Or else you'd be..."

"Nervous? Afraid? That's what I'm trying to show you. I *was* all of those things. I got over it. So can you."

She trembled. Just then we heard a garbage truck squealing to a stop. It made a deafening noise.

"It's only a truck," I said.

Her thoughts rang out as clearly as if they were blasting through a stereo speaker.

It's dangerous out there.

Unknown horrors are waiting.

I'll lose all control.

Humiliate myself.

Be a failure, a laughingstock.

Within the next three months, I persuaded her to walk with me. Often she fled back, slamming her door. I would call and she'd refuse to talk to me, or if I came to the house, she'd plead to be excused from our little expeditions.

I couldn't get her to any phobic center, but I spoke to her about God, about visualizing his image as positive reinforcement. I quoted a biblical passage: "Fear not, there is nothing to fear for I am with you."

We prayed together. My own attitudes about phobic treatment were crystallizing. The missing link, spirituality, had become obvious to me. Most of the programs and literature I had observed only zeroed in on psychological and medical aids, and these were fine—as far as they went. But the healing power of prayer was omitted.

I had discovered the force of that healing power, and I knew it could work wonders. Visualization, meditation, and proper nutrition were the foundation of treatment; prayer was the roof. Public speaker and pastor Tim Timmons, author of the bestselling *Hooked on Life*, said, "*Recovery without God* would be the title of the saddest book I could write." I understand, more than ever, what he meant.

A year later the director's wife drove to San Diego, her first substantial trip behind the wheel. She still has momentary setbacks, but I know her progress will be continuous from now on.

I worked with a rock star whose image was synonymous with sexuality. Millions of women responded to his virility and animal appeal. Twenty-four, 6'2", a dynamo on stage, Chet (a pseudonym) nearly fainted at the prospect of sitting in a crowded restaurant. I reassured him that although he felt like the forgotten agoraphobic, he wasn't. I hadn't forgotten him, and support groups and friends willing to help hadn't forgotten him either. Repeated attempts to confront his fear, along with visualization and prayer, finally gave him the courage to overcome the block.

I saw renowned producers, athletes, fashion designers, heads of corporations, break out in a cold, trembling sweat when they had to ride an elevator. I could no longer doubt that phobic illness was a national epidemic.

It was an epidemic that required armies of new recruits from every quarter. I spoke to the families of agoraphobics and stressed the importance of their constructive participation. It wasn't enough to tolerate phobic behavior and cover up for it. Nor could a phobic be pushed and criticized into a cure, as certain husbands and wives of phobic victims mistakenly tried to do. Relatives had to learn how to work with those in the grip of agoraphobia, to become, in effect, live-in phobia therapists. They had to be taught techniques most beneficial to their phobically imprisoned loved ones.

I supplied specific information for them through an organization I started, Faith Over Fear (FOF), which laid out known therapeutic methods along with the sayings and scriptures that had helped me toward recovery.

The ranks of door-to-door phobic recruits grew. I called for volunteers through every media channel available.

The words of Pastor Jack Hayford rang in my ears: "When a miracle happens to you, you must tell people about it and pass it on." Excitement filled me when I saw the stirring of hope on previously despairing faces. Sometimes I looked at their windows when leaving them. I caught them staring at me, waving, watching. I felt their burning gazes as I crossed the street and got into my car. I waved back and made gestures of victory.

I was gratified to learn that the insights God had given me were making an impact. One Arizona woman, who had been housebound for eighteen years, drove twenty-two blocks with her grandchild. Today she moves about freely, with total confidence. A forty-year-old man from Oregon called and said he had seen me on TV and had found the courage to walk ten blocks—seven more than he had ever gone. Now he travels with no fear.

When I read in *Variety* that *Seven Brides* was nominated for a Best Score Tony, I called Lake Arrowhead to share the exciting news with Joel. Jill answered and told me Joel was living in L. A. She didn't pursue the subject and I didn't either; but when I tracked Joel down, he admitted that he and Jill were separated and expected to get a divorce.

Over lunch at the Old World Restaurant in Beverly Hills, he furnished more details:

"They tell you that all you have to do is love each other and it'll work out all right. I guess that's why we kept hanging on. Because we did love each other. We still do. And yet, we couldn't agree on how to live." He laughed. "Anyway, I've got a big city mentality. I'm not a mountain climber or a hunter. I'd rather die on a movie lot with sheet music in my hand than on the ski slopes. I knew it was time to get back to civilization when I found three coyotes sitting in my backyard."

He turned thoughtful. "It all seemed to get out of hand. Funny, Jill's in therapy now. She's working at a hospital, helping alcoholics. She loves it. She's even planning to go back to school to get her license."

I watched him handle his pain—from humor to reflectiveness. But not a normal, natural spontaneity of feeling. Then it came.

"I *hate* all this. It's murder. You put so much into something for fifteen years...."

"I know."

177

"The thing is, it *hurts.*"

I resisted my old, typical tendency to say: Calm down, no reason to get upset, keep anger hidden, repress it, deny it.

"You have a right to all those feelings," I said. "You put your life into the relationship. You can't just brush aside fifteen years. You tried; Jill tried. And of course it hurts."

"What can I do with the pain?"

"You can pour it back into the Pink Cloud."

The name sounded ludicrous yet liberating. The heaviness of the moment was shattered, and we both broke out laughing.

"Think how it all began, and how much hope we had for the future. All the things we wanted to do."

He perked up, caught by my Pink Cloud energy, responding to it.

"You can't keep two guys from Brooklyn and the Bronx down."

All the obstacles—real and imagined—were clearing, leaving the road free for us to do what we loved above anything else.

Write.

"I still want us to be Rodgers and Hammerstein," I said.

"Great."

"No!" My throat went dry. "Let's change that. Let's not be Rodgers and Hammerstein."

"Huh?"

"That's right. We're *not*—I repeat, *not*—going to be Rodgers and Hammerstein."

I thought of all the press releases I had seen through the years: Another Streisand. Another Sinatra. Another Dylan.

I was suddenly swept up in an emotion I had never expected to feel: the intense, overpowering desire to be myself!

"Let's be Kasha and Hirschhorn," I announced. "We can stand for what they stood for, but let's be Kasha and Hirschhorn and be the best at that—the *very* best—that we can possibly be."

——— 18 ———

The Morning After

It was cloudy on the drive down to Hillside Memorial, but I noticed the sun breaking through by the time I passed the gate.

> ROSE KASHA
> MOTHER OF LAWRENCE AND ALFRED
> WIFE OF IRVING
> 1910–1980

"Hello, Ma," I said into the still air. "I'm sorry I haven't been here for a while."

I took a deep breath.

"You know, Mom, I believe in God now...like I never did before. It's such a relief when you have faith. I wish you could have known what it was like."

The sun grew hotter; I felt sweat on my forehead.

"I don't want to be angry anymore," I told her. "I don't want to hold on to things—like the will, and all those times when I brought victory home and you kept saying, 'Not enough, not enough.' What more could I have done?"

And the answer came to me: Nothing. Because constant dissatisfaction was my mother's way of holding on to me and to Larry. If she withheld her approval, we would always be tied to her by a compulsive desire to please.

"You could have trusted my love," I said, with belated understanding. "You could have said I did a good job, and I'd still have been there."

I hadn't expected to cry. The tears surprised me. So did my grief. I hadn't cried when she was dying, the way Larry had.

For a minute I surrendered to the tears, to my last, infantile yearning for a replay, a chance to start again and get it right.

"Shave me, Alfred. Shave me, son," I heard my father say. At least that moment had put a seal on our relationship, given it some kind of conclusion. I could come to terms with my father's violence, grasp the frustrations that had turned him into a child abuser. But the relationship between my mother and me had been left open-ended.

And that other question, always nagging at me, sprang out again, more insistently than ever.

Why didn't you ever leave my father? Why didn't you let me help you, support you? Rescue you?

"Save me, Alfred," I heard my mother say.

It was time to face the unfaceable, to answer my own question with a truth I could never bear to acknowledge.

She loved him.

If she had been serious about divorce, about the way out, she would have done it. "If I leave, what will happen to the business?" she had asked me. But of course, if they had broken up and she had managed the business alone, it would have gone on, even improved, without my father's drinking and hell-raising.

She would have let the policemen take him away when he beat us.

She would have found her own apartment, as soon as Larry and I had the means to support her.

Understanding brought an emotion I had never been able to feel for my mother before: pity. Because she had suffered. The suffering had been self-inflicted, the scars her own doing. But that didn't make them any less real.

"I forgive you, Ma," I said, to the sun-washed stone, "if you'll forgive me. I know you hear me. Let's start again. It's never too late."

I kneeled, touched the stone, and left.

180

I went to Larry's that night. He was alone, reading scripts.

He was startled; it wasn't my usual tendency to drop in without calling.

"Thought I'd see how you were doing."

"Anything happening in particular?"

"No. Do I need a reason to see my brother?" I knew the answer to that one too: yes. Our relationship wasn't the intimate let's-get-together-and-chat kind. Workaholics rarely spend time with anyone, even their families, without a reason, a plan; and Larry was a Rose Kasha-taught workaholic, like me.

"How about a drink?" Larry asked. "Oh, you're religious now. Well, how about coffee? Or grapefruit juice?"

I laughed and so did he; it broke the ice. "Grapefruit juice would be terrific."

"*Seven Brides* is opening in England. I'm flying over next week to see it."

"I went to Mother's gravesite today," I said, abruptly shifting the subject. "And I got to thinking. We're all we have."

"Boy, are *we* in trouble," Larry said. "Just kidding." He saw I was serious and adapted himself to my mood.

"We've been through the wars together. Don't you ever think what a miracle it is, Larry, that we're not on Avenue M anymore? It's all *over*: the fighting, the screaming, the drinking. It's over and we're in Hollywood, doing what we want to do."

"I guess you'd call it a miracle, yes."

"And who made it possible?"

"If you're going to tell me God, I'm afraid..."

"No, I'm not about to preach. Relax."

He nodded, signaling me to go on.

"Mother."

"*Mother?* I think there's a major rewrite in progress here. If my memory serves me correctly, she and Daddy were the obstacles we had to overcome."

"Sure she drove us crazy. She pitted us against each other. She was never satisfied. All that's true. But it's because of her we made it. She pushed us. By saying 'Never enough, never enough' she made us try harder."

181

"Like Avis."

"Okay, like Avis. But it's not so bad to be Avis, is it?"

"Well, if you can't be Hertz...."

"All kidding aside."

"I know what you're saying. And I agree. But there could have been an easier way."

"I agree. And I've spent the whole afternoon wishing it were different. I've spent my whole *life* wishing it were different. But then I thought...there's something in my life I can still make different."

"What's that?"

"Us."

A strange, embarrassed quiet filled the den.

"Us," I repeated, before we had time to evade the implications of the word. "You're my brother, Larry, and I want to say something. I want to thank you."

"Thank me, for what?"

"For standing between me and Daddy when he was hitting me. For helping me with my homework. For coming to school to get me in the first grade when I started throwing up and telling me not to be scared."

"Oh, that."

"Yes, that, and other things. For letting me stay with you when I left home. Sure, I know you hated it...."

"I didn't *hate* it."

"Yes, you did. It's honesty time. You'd just made your own escape and you wanted space and I can't blame you for that. But you took me in. You were there when my agoraphobia got bad, and you kept me busy on a show, helped distract me. When I think back on it, even though we haven't been as close as I wanted us to be, you were *there*, Larry. And I want to thank you. That's all."

"Well...you're welcome," he said awkwardly. My confession had stunned him. Even I was amazed by it.

"So..." I stood up. "Guess I ought to be going."

"I didn't mean to be flip," he said. "I just...I'm...I...I'm developing a speech problem. No, seriously, I'm happy you said

182

what you did about going through the wars. Because it's true. And now what you're saying is...the war's over."

"Yes, if you want it to be. Yes."

"I do."

"So do I. Larry, you're my brother. I love you."

We reached for each other, spontaneously, feeling the distance evaporate between us. I felt love and hope, and I felt relief. Pure, overpowering relief.

I had a brother.

More than that, I knew I had found a friend.

There's got to be a morning after
If we can hold on through the night.
We have a chance to find the sunshine;
Let's keep on looking for the light.

It was 1985, and I could look back over the past with a sense of unclouded joy. I had survived. Elvis Presley, Jimi Hendrix, Jackie Wilson, Janis Joplin, Mama Cass, Keith Moon, and scores of others were dead, but I had come through, and so had all the members of my Brill Building generation. Collectively, we had cut through the scarring underbrush and emerged intact. Burt Bacharach had won another Oscar. Carole King, after divorce from Gerry and a quiet spell in the early 1980s, was back writing for films and even acting in one of them. Mann and Weil were still turning out hits together. Jack Keller, in spite of a premature heart attack, was still prolific, still on the charts. Neil Sedaka, too, was active in personal appearances.

I was proud of my generation. They had changed with the times. All of us had been willing to keep pace with trends, not lock ourselves in. Our early training—that Don Kirshner insistence on writing for "the date" no matter what kind of artist— had given us the flexibility to switch gears on a moment's notice.

We had all chosen to live and grow, to keep trying, rather than be destroyed when the winds turned against us.

Joel got himself in physical shape again, slimming down to his proper weight. Shortly afterward he fell in love and remarried. His wife, Jennifer Carter, an Emmy-winning documentary producer, shares his interest in the world of film and music. But their strongest bond is a willingness to grant each other freedom. They know, from past experience, how harmful it can be when a relationship becomes a struggle for control. They are friends, teammates; and the laughter and warmth they radiate is wonderful to be around.

Life, I've discovered, can be as open and free, as packed with possibilities, as the shiny, heaven-lit road described in the Bible, or as dark and closed as the closet that once imprisoned me as a child. All of us have to choose. My mother and father, unlike my Brill Building friends, chose the darkness. I compromised, putting my head out of doors "looking for the light" while my feet remained firmly planted inside.

I couldn't stay behind or pull free, and the emotional split produced confusion and rage. Rage I couldn't deal with constructively because I couldn't admit I had it. My mother's "Be nice" kept the anger buried and permitted it to grow.

I've tried all my life to be gentle and soft-spoken, but everyone has natural anger. Things disturb and hurt us, and a certain amount of healthy hostility is needed to defend ourselves in a crisis. If someone tries to kill us, we're simply handing him the knife if we behave with inappropriate niceness.

My agoraphobia was repressed anger. Growing up I felt rage because my needs were never met. I resented being an adult from the cradle on, while my father stayed a child. I resented being a responsible working "man" when my friends were still concerned about baseball games and summer camp.

Later on, I resented the role of "parent" to everyone, even though I elected to take that role on. I wanted someone to say, "Don't worry, *I'll* take over"; but when Ceil tried to do just that, I fought against her help.

It's hard to ask for assistance; for a personality like mine, it was impossible. Asking for help meant: I'm weak, I can't handle things myself. I'm a failure. And there's always that fear—basic to a person who never had anyone to lean on—that the request for help, once finally made, will be denied, that people will turn their backs on you.

And they well might. This fundamental fear is not without a

certain amount of validity. By and large, human beings will extend a hand; but the risk of rejection is there.

Rejection—that terrifying word. All frightened people dread it, equate it with emotional death. A friend turns away. A lover wants to end a relationship. A parent is too preoccupied to listen to your problems.

As a person who has fought and survived the rejections of show business, I can say that rejection is largely a matter of what we perceive in advance. When someone—a publisher, a producer—says no, you swallow hard, stand up straight, and go on. The anticipation of it is what overwhelms you.

The word *rejection* is often the word of a victim. It implies "poor me, I'm unloved." But critics can strengthen character. If you don't fold up and become defensive, you can learn from them. If being loved and approved of isn't your only focus, you can gain knowledge on how to improve as artist and human being.

It's hard, though I try to do it more and more. Anger can erupt in the face of disapproval, and the anger can't be shoved under the rug and ignored. Emotion must be allowed to bubble to the surface; and when it does, it can be dealt with. Handled and resolved, by faith.

Faith, I've learned, calms a troubled spirit, helps people *hear* what's going on inside their minds and hearts. Prayer reduces the static. And prayer, contrary to the belief of those who must always be in control, doesn't imply weakness. It only indicates a willingness to trust in something higher than yourself, to admit there *is* something higher.

The miracle I experienced after discovering faith was a new ability to listen and truly hear a playback of myself. It's difficult to figure out what you want when you're totally outer-directed, when your only objective is satisfying others. You never stop to ask: "Is this what I need? Is it good for me? Is it constructive?" Only: "I'll show them. I'll prove myself."

But if you put yourself in the hands of a higher power, if you allow love to come in, the noises diminish and you truly begin to know yourself.

Wholehearted acceptance of God is a miracle cure that packs

more potency than any doctor's prescription. I had read so many self-help books, but I found that the Bible is the greatest self-help book of them all.

Loving and worshiping Jesus offers a wonderful, unexpected bonus: a deeply personal relationship with a *friend*—an unjudging, unwavering friend, not someone formidable and forbidding.

Having God in my life helped me think in positive terms. With practice it becomes easier to concentrate on beauty—the trusting hand of a child, the sweep of calm blue ocean—than to dwell on negative, self-defeating images.

I drifted naturally toward people who genuinely cared and wanted the best for me. I avoided those who criticized me "for my own good" or attempted to manipulate me for their own selfish gain.

My sense of wholeness was restored. I no longer had to play the convoluted phobic game, the game that said: people will feel sorry for me if I have agoraphobia, and then they'll take notice and forgive me for not living up to their expectations.

I surrendered all attempts at control, reminding myself, "We do the possible; God does the impossible."

I realize now that we're all like rats in a maze, chasing around the same corridors to resolve old wounds, never pausing to evaluate new alternatives. Jess Moody once said, "Insanity is doing the same thing over again, expecting different results." I was going to *make* my parents acknowledge what I was doing. If I'd taken the time to look at them, really look, I'd have understood that they were rats in a maze, unthinkingly reacting to unresolved conflicts of their own. They were children too.

I'd have understood, at last, that a child isn't capable of raising another child.

I intend to give my own child, Dana, the benefit of lessons I've learned. I'll do all I can to help and encourage her. If she wants to be an actress, a real estate broker, or an executive, that's fine with me. The choice has to be hers, to fulfill her own dreams, not mine.

I still work diligently; I always will. I'm simply less anxious about it now, because I have a rock-solid spirituality, an unbreakable rope beneath me. I have a role model and clearly marked guidelines I never found at home. Most of all, I have a faith that has helped me escape the darkness and reach my own morning after.

Recommended
Emergency Centers

ALABAMA
Parents Anonymous
P. O. Box 2638
Anniston, Alabama 36202
(800) 221-7127 (in State)
(205) 237-6097
30 chapters provide support for high-risk
or abusive adults

TERRAP programs (phobias)
Phoenix (602) 894-8292
Sally Schwartzenberger
Prescott (602) 778-3627
Charlotte Rudeau

ARIZONA
Phobia Society of Arizona
John A. Moran, Ph.D.
7530 E. Angus Drive
Scottsdale, Arizona 85251
(602) 947-5739

CALIFORNIA
NACOA (Children of Alcoholics)
Box 421691
San Francisco, California 94142
(415) 431-1366

Tim Timmons
1-800-4HOOKED

South Coast Community Church

5120 Bonita Canyon
Irvine, California 92715

FOF (Faith Over Fear)
Al Kasha
Psychology-spiritual program of recovery
for phobics
337 El Camino Dr.
Beverly Hills, California 90212

Maralyn Teare, M.S.
M.F.C.C.
383 Robertson Blvd.
Beverly Hills, California 90211
(213) 659-6440

G.I.V.E. (Incest)
P. O. Box 342
Elk Grove, Calif. 95624
Methodist Hospital Chapel
7500 Timberlake Way
Sacramento, California 95823

Parents United
Crisis Line: (714) 233-6739
Daughters and Sons United/Adults
Molested as Children United
6950 Levant St.
San Diego, Ca. 92111
(714) 560-3080
Treatment program for families

188

Family Services of Los Angeles
Emotional Counseling
(213) 484-2944 weekdays
(213) 829-7417 Saturdays

Children of the Night
1800 N. Highland Avenue
Hollywood, California 90028
(213) 550-7188—Dr. Lois Lee
Shelter for Teenage Runaways

Santa Clara Parents United
P.O. Box 952
San Jose, Ca. 95108
(408) 280-5055

California Self-Help Center
Referral Service
(800) 222-LINK (5465)

Child Sexual Abuse Treatment Program
   Parents United
P.O. Box 4013
San Rafael, Calif. 94903
(415) 499-7153 crisis
(415) 499-8490 office
Prevention, detection and treatment of
   sexual abuse
Paula Watkins, Cheryl Barnes

The Touch Program
(See above for address and phone)
Sherri Patterson

Victims Anonymous
(818) 993-1139
Northridge, California 91324

Alternatives to Violence
(213) 422-8585
For battered families and women

Survivor's Network
Christina Crawford
18653 Ventura Blvd. No. 143
Tarzana, California 91356

TERRAP programs (phobia treatment)
Oakland: (415) 376-5530
Joyce Kaplan
Menlo Park (415) 329-1233
Nancy Flaxman
San Francisco, San Jose, Monterey—
Call: Menlo Park

Sacramento: (916) 442-1902
Jack Leman
Fresno: (209) 435-8181
Marlene Bissell
Bakersfield: (805) 589-3788
Glendale: (818) 244-2465
Joanne Bruckner
W. Los Angeles: (213) 836-6445
Marlene Schenter
Orange County: (714) 891-4446
Harriet Gyor
Woodland Hills: (818) 702-0560
San Diego: (619) 565-8921

COLORADO
A.M.E.N.D. (Abusive men exploring
   new directions)
P.O. Box 61281
Denver, Colorado 80206
(303) 420-6759
A program to help men stop battering
   and establish healthier relationships
   with women and families
Michael Lindsay, therapist

CONNECTICUT
TERRAP program
(203) 481-6095
Jeffrey Rice

FLORIDA
TERRAP programs
Miami: (305) 823-8885 or
(305) 822-9143 Gerald Kurtz
Jacksonville: Alan Harris
(904) 739-3689 or 3688

GEORGIA
PSA—Columbus Chapter
Jean Bondurant
P.O. Box 5561
Columbus, Georgia 31906
(404) 324-3113

ILLINOIS
National Committee for Prevention of
   Child Abuse
Joy Byers
Bill Byers
332 S. Michigan Avenue
Suite 950

Chicago, Illinois 60604

Co-ordinated Youth Services
1524 Niedringhaus Avenue
Granite City, Illinois 62040
(618) 876-2383
Treatment Groups for victims, spouses,
    perpetrators of child abuse
Donna Daisy

C.A.U.S.E.S.
Dr. Nahman Greenberg
836 W. Wellington
Chicago, Illinois 60657
(312) 472-6924—Families and Incest

H.E.L.P.
Gabriella Cohen, Dir.
185 N. Wabash
Suite 1216
Chicago, Ill. 60610
(312) 332-2792
Works with sexual abuse and incest

Child Abuse Prevention Bureau
P.O. Box 265
Dolton, Illinois 60419
Diane Kreiman, Ex. Dir.
Speakers for adults and children in
    classrooms, also adult self-help
    groups

TERRAP
Chicago, Illinois
(312) 724-3450
Art Hyams/Larry Kroll

Voices in Action
P.O. Box 148309
Chicago, Illinois 60614
Free referral service. A network for
    survivors of incest and child sexual
    abuse
Lynne Lamb Bryant

Anna Bixby Women's Center
P.O. Box 354
Rosiclare, Illinois 62982
Anna Bixby, Wilma Gibbs
(618) 285-3139

INDIANA
TERRAP program

Indiana Counseling and Phobia Center
11994 Michigan Rd.
Zionsville, Indiana 46077
(317) 873-6452
Pat Foster

KANSAS
Great Plains Phobia Society
Connie Walters, OTR
Memorial Hospital
600 Madison
Topeka, Kansas 66607
(913) 354-5248

LOUISIANA
NCASA
1815 Robert St.
New Orleans, Louisiana 70115
Adult survivors of sexual assault

TERRAP programs
Lafayette: (318) 984-9809
Phyllis Chelette
New Orleans (504) 835-5819
Jane Stewart
W. Louisiana (318) 478-2663
Roberta Dowden

MASSACHUSETTS
TERRAP program
Boston (617) 369-5547
Randie Harmon Hendrick

Merrimack Valley Chapter PSA
Thomas W. C. MacLachlan
M.A.C.P.
166 N. Main St.
Andover, Massachusetts 01810
(617) 475-7249

South Shore Massachusetts
Chapter of PSA
Richard C. Raynard, Ph.D.
670 Washington St.
Braintree, Massachusetts 02184
(617) 843-7550

Greater Boston Phobia Society
Carol Goldman, LICSW
74 Reservoir Road
Cambridge, Massachusetts 02138
(617) 492-5163

190

Western Massachusetts
Chapter of PSA
63 Mulberry St.
Springfield, Massachusetts 01005
Walter A. Mitchell, Psy. D.
(413) 783-3042

MARYLAND
Phobia Society of Del-Mar-Va
Mary Jane Grovenor
Route 7, Box 216-A
Salisbury, Maryland 21801
(301) 543-9043

The Phobia Society of America
5820 Hubbard Drive
Rockville, Maryland 20852

MICHIGAN
TERRAP program
Detroit, Michigan
(313) 642-7764
Larry Cantow

Silent Voices, Inc.
4145 Kalamazoo, SE
Grand Rapids, Michigan 49508
(616) 455-5450
Ernestine M. Agnew, MSW, CSW A
  self help group for adult victim
  survivors of sexual assault

MINNESOTA
Sexual Abuse Anonymous
P.O. Box 405
St. Cloud, MN 56302
Meetings: 701 ½ Mall Germain
St. Cloud, Minnesota

MISSOURI
TERRAP Program
St. Louis (314) 576-7454
Ira Dubinsky/Y.M. Abramson
Phobia and Psychotherapy Center
14377 Woodlake Drive No. 212
Chesterfield, Missouri 63017

MONTANA
TERRAP program
P.O. Box 4862
Missoula, Montana 59807
Madgie Hunt (406) 721-6061

NEW HAMPSHIRE
S.A.R.A. (Self help group)
Sexual Assault recovery
Elmwood Center, Trahan St.
Manchester, New Hampshire 03103
Pat B. 432-7801 Lynn P. 432-8782
Mary C. 668-8138; Lauren B. 483-4431

NEW JERSEY
Reality House, Inc.
Gloucester County Health Ctr.
Woodbury, New Jersey 08096
(609) 848-0035 day 853-8184 eves
Outpatient facility for drug problems,
  sometimes stemming from child
  abuse
Victor Yorio, Director

TERRAP programs
North N. J. (201) 783-5588
Karen Levy
South N. J. (201) 574-9866
Rocio Day (Inc. Philadelphia)

Adele Paolino
Author-phobia counselor
50 Bedford Ave.
Breezy Point, New York 11697
(718) 634-5552
Agoraphobics newsletter, pen sessions
  for those unable to leave home

NORTH CAROLINA
Central Carolinas Chapter,
P.S.A.
Boice Triplett
2915 Providence Road
Charlotte, North Carolina 28211
(704) 365-0140

Triangle Phobia Society
Marjorie A. Howe
2321 Blue Ridge Road
Raleigh, North Carolina 27607
(919) 781-1707

NEW JERSEY
Central New Jersey Chapter PSA
Diana Leventhal
42A Apple Tree Lane
Old Bridge, New Jersey 08857

Westchester Chapter PSA

191

P.O. Box 1244
Riverdale, New York 10471-1244
Betsy Boruchoff (212) 548-8296

OKLAHOMA
Tulsa Chapter
Betty Smith
8418 So. 36th West Avenue
Tulsa, Oklahoma 74132
(918) 445-0581

PENNSYLVANIA
Central Pennsylvania PSA
Joseph A. La France, Jr.
P.O. Box 19
Hershey, Pennsylvania 17033
(717) 534-1451 or (717) 534-3652

TEXAS
Costal Bend Phobia Chapter, PSA
George H. Kramer, Jr., Ph.D.
6262 Weber Road, Suite 277
Corpus Christi, Texas 78413
(512) 855-6914 or (512) 855-2106

Dallas Phobia Society
Kirby Allsup
12860 Hillcrest Road,
Suite 119
Dallas, Texas 72530

(214) 386-6681 or (214) 386-6327

The Swiss Counseling Help Center
3611 Swiss Avenue
Dallas, Texas 75204
c/o Mike Smith
(214) 821-3680

San Antonio Phobia Society
Manijeh Nathan
7711 Louis Pasteur, Suite 814
San Antonio, Texas 78229
(512) 696-4041

VIRGINIA
Piedmont Phobia Association
Olga S. Pilson
239 Melrose Drive
Danville, Virginia 24540
(804) 792-1743

Dr. Jerilyn Ross
Roundhouse Square
1444 Duke St.
Alexandria, Virginia 22314
(703) 836-7130

Reaching the Morning After is an extraordinary book. It should be read over and over again. For Al Kasha has given us a truly inspiring story, his own life conveyed perfectly through vivid memories of early childhood—some sad enough to wrench your heart. And it moves forward with hope, courage, understanding....If ever you needed an uplifting experience, *Reaching the Morning After* is just that, and much more.

Herb Gluck
Best-selling author of
The Mick

Reaching the Morning After is a moving tale of a man's triumph over the horrors of an abused childhood.

[Al Kasha's] courage, will, and spiritual strength should serve as an inspiration to countless people who have suffered as he did.

Dodie Livingston
Commissioner
U. S. Dept. of Health and
Human Services, Washington, D.C.

Al Kasha is for real.

One only needs a brief encounter with this man of deep emotion and integrity to realize that Al is into living life on purpose.

The most incredible thing about Al is not where he is now, but how far he has come from where he began. *Reaching the Morning After* is a terrific example of hope that we can all move from "stuck" to "starting over."

Tim Timmons
Co-author of *Hooked on Life*
Senior Pastor
South Coast Community Church
Irvine, California